MEDIEVAL INTRIGUE

Medieval Intrigue

Decoding Royal Conspiracies

Ian Mortimer

continuum

Published by the Continuum International Publishing Group
Continuum UK, The Tower Building, 11 York Road, London SE1 7NX
Continuum US, 80 Maiden Lane, Suite 704, New York, NY 10038

www.continuumbooks.com

First published 2010

British Library Cataloguing-in-Publication Data
A catalogue record for this book is available from the British Library.

ISBN 978–1847–06589–6

Typeset by Pindar NZ, Auckland, New Zealand
Printed and bound by the MPG Books Group

Contents

This book is dedicated to my brother,
David Mortimer –
archaeologist, blacksmith,
and my most-loved critic.

Acknowledgements

I am very grateful to Ben Hayes at Continuum for commissioning and editing this book and to my agent, Jim Gill, who gave advice at the outset. Thanks are due too to the following specialists. To all those who commented on my first foray into historiography, 'What isn't history?', which was a catalyst to much of the thinking in 'Objectivity and information', namely Professor Mark Ormrod, Dr Margaret Pelling, Dr Simon Dixon, Dr Jonathan Barry, Professor Adrian Wilson and Dr Gary Gibbs. I would also like to thank Dr Barry and Professor Wilson who read and commented on drafts of 'Objectivity and information' itself, and Professor Pauline Stafford, who kindly allowed me to include an extended quotation from one of her essays.

With regard to the specific themed essays, I am very grateful to all those at the Edward II colloquium at the University of Nottingham in 2004, especially Dr Gwilym Dodd (who invited me) and Professor Ormrod (for his encouraging response to 'Sermons of sodomy', which I wrote in reply to his own piece at that event). In addition I would like to thank Dr Paul Dryburgh for commenting on drafts of 'The death of Edward II in Berkeley Castle', and also for his advice on my translation of the Melton Letter. My gratitude is due also to Elizabeth Danbury for giving me a photocopy of the Melton letter; to Kathryn Warner for advice on 'Twelve angry scholars' and the earl of Kent's plot; to Professor Chris Given-Wilson for details about the source material for John de Gales; to Christine Faunch and the Library of the University of Exeter for archiving the peer-review comments which are discussed in 'Twelve angry scholars'. Special thanks are due to John Earle, Susan Earle and Paul and Arabella Lizioli for advice on Sant'Alberto di Butrio, Oramala and the Oltrepo, as well as the Malaspina and the Val di Magra. Finally, I would like to record my gratitude to the anonymous referees who commented positively on 'The death of Edward II' and 'Richard II and the succession'.

I would like to make a special note of thanks to my wife, Sophie. Pursuing the lines of research in this volume has been very difficult, for a number of reasons.

No doubt she wishes as much as I do that Edward II really had been murdered in Berkeley Castle in 1327 – it would have saved me an awful lot of bother and many late nights. Instead I have had to work against a tide of negative and poorly thought-out criticism. Throughout everything she has supported me and been hugely encouraging, magisterially judicious in her advice, and loving.

Ian Mortimer
Moretonhampstead, 2010

Abbreviations

AEC	Adrian R. Bell, Chris Brooks and Tony K. Moore (eds), *Accounts of the English Crown with Italian Merchant Societies, 1272–1345*, List and Index Society 331 (2009)
'Afterlife'	R. M. Haines, 'Edwardus Redivivus: the "afterlife" of Edward of Carnarvon', *TBGAS*, 114 (1996), 65–86
Anonimalle	W. R. Childs, J. Taylor (eds), *Anonimalle Chronicle*, Yorkshire Archaeological Society, Record Series 147 (1991)
Battilana	Natale Battilana, *Genealogie delle famiglie nobili de Genova* (Genoa, 1825; repr., Bologna, 1971)
BCM	Berkeley Castle Muniments
BJRL	*Bulletin of the John Rylands Library*
BL	The British Library, London
Brut	F. W. D. Brie (ed.), *The Brut or the Chronicles of England*, Early English Text Society, Old Series 131 and 136 (1906–8)
'Captivity'	T. F. Tout, 'The captivity and death of Edward of Carnarvon', *Bulletin of the John Rylands Library*, 6 (1921), 69–114
Carr	E. H. Carr, *What is History?* (1961; Pelican Books edn, 1964)
CChR	*Calendar of the Charter Rolls Preserved in the Public Record Office, 1226–1516* (6 vols, 1903–27)
CCR	*Calendar of the Close Rolls Preserved in the Public Record Office, Henry III, Edward I, Edward II, Edward III, Richard II, Henry IV and Henry V* (51 vols, 1892–1938)
CCW	*Calendar of Chancery Warrants Preserved in the Public Record Office, 1244–1326* (1927)
CEPR	W. H. Bliss and C. Johnson (eds), *Calendar of Entries in the Papal Registers relating to Great Britain and Ireland*, vols 1–3 (1893–7)

CFR
Calendar of the Fine Rolls Preserved in the Public Record Office, Edward I, Edward II and Edward III 1327–1347 (5 vols, 1911–15)

Chronicles
William Stubbs (ed.), *Chronicles of the Reigns of Edward I and Edward II* (2 vols, 1882–3)

CMR
Calendar of Memoranda Rolls (Exchequer) Preserved in the Public Record Office, Michaelmas 1326–Michaelmas 1327 (1968)

CP
G. E. Cokayne, revised by V. Gibbs, H. A. Doubleday, D. Warrand, Lord Howard de Walden and Peter Hammond (eds), *The Complete Peerage of England, Scotland, Ireland, Great Britain and the United Kingdom Extant, Extinct or Dormant* (14 vols, 1910–98)

CPMR
A. H. Thomas (ed.), *Calendar of Plea and Memoranda Rolls 1323–1364* (Cambridge, 1926)

CPR
Calendar of the Patent Rolls Preserved in the Public Record Office, Henry III, Edward I, Edward II, Edward III, Richard II, Henry IV and Henry V (43 vols, 1893–1916)

Creton
J. Webb (ed.), 'Metrical history', *Archaeologia*, 20 (1824), 13–239

DBI
Dizonario biografico degli Italiani (72 vols, 1960–)

'DEII'
Ian Mortimer, 'The death of Edward II in Berkeley Castle', *EHR*, 120 (2005), 1175–214

'Documents'
Stuart Moore, 'Documents relating to the death and burial of King Edward II', *Archaeologia*, l (1887), 215–26

EHR
The English Historical Review

'Entail'
Michael Bennett, 'Edward III's entail and the succession to the Crown, 1376–1471', *EHR*, 113 (1998), 580–609

EUL
The University of Exeter Library, Exeter

Eulogium
F. S. Haydon (ed.), *Eulogium Historiarum sive Temporis* (3 vols, 1858–63)

Falconieri
Tommaso di Carpegna Falconieri, *The Man Who Believed He Was King of France: A True Medieval Tale* (Chicago, 2008)

Fayen
Arnold Fayen (ed.), *Lettres de Jean XXII* (2 vols, Rome, 1908–12)

Fears	Ian Mortimer, *The Fears of Henry IV* (2007)
Foedera (Rec. Comm.)	Adam Clarke, J. Caley, J. Bayley, F. Holbrooke and J. W. Clarke (eds), *Foedera, conventiones, litterae, etc.*, or *Rymer's Foedera 1066–1383* (6 vols, 1816–30)
Foedera (Rymer)	Thomas Rymer (ed.), *Foedera, conventiones, literae, et cujuscunque generis acta publica* (20 vols, 1704–35)
'Foundations'	Adrian Wilson, 'Foundations of an integrated historiography' in Wilson (ed.), *Rethinking Social History* (Manchester, 1993), 293–335
French Chronicle	C. J. Aungier, *The French Chronicle of London*, Camden OS 28 (1844)
Grandison	F. C. Hingeston-Randolph (ed.), *The Register of Bishop Grandison, Bishop of Exeter* (3 vols, 1894–9)
Gransden	Antonia Gransden, *Historical Writing in England: c1307 to the Early Sixteenth Century* (1982)
Greatest Traitor	Ian Mortimer, *The Greatest Traitor: The Life of Sir Roger Mortimer, 1st Earl of March, Ruler of England 1327–1330* (2003)
Hemingburgh	H. C. Hamilton (ed.), *Chronicon Domini Walteri de Hemingburgh*, English Historical Society (2 vols, 1848–9)
Historia Anglicana	H. T. Riley (ed.), *Thomae Walsingham Historia Anglicana* (2 vols, 1863–4)
HKW	R. Allen Brown, H. M. Colvin and A. J. Taylor, *The History of the King's Works: The Middle Ages* (2 vols, 1963)
Issues	Frederick Devon (ed.), *Issues of the Exchequer* (1837)
JMH	*The Journal of Medieval History*
Knighton	J. R. Lumby (ed.), *Chronicon Henrici Knighton* (2 vols, 1889–95)
Kuhn	Thomas Kuhn, *The Structure of Scientific Revolutions* (Chicago, 3rd edn, 1996)
Lanercost	Herbert Maxwell, *The Chronicle of Lanercost* (Glasgow, 1913)
Le Baker	E. M. Thompson (ed.), *Chronicon Galfridi le Baker de Swynebroke* (Oxford, 1889)
Lecuppre	Gilles Lecuppre, *L'imposture politique au Moyen Âge: la seconde vie des rois* (Paris, 2005)

Lunt	William E. Lunt, *Financial Relations of the Papacy 1327–1534* (Cambridge, Massachusetts, 1962)
Melsa	E. A. Bond, *Chronica Monasterii de Melsa* (3 vols, 1866–8)
Murimuth	E. M. Thompson (ed.), *Adae Murimuth Continuatio Chronicarum* (1889)
Northern Registers	J. Raine (ed.), *Historical Papers and Letters from the Northern Registers* (1873)
Norwell	Mary Lyon, Bryce Lyon and Henry S. Lucas (eds), *The Wardrobe Book of William Norwell* (Brussels, 1983)
ODNB	*Oxford Dictionary of National Biography* (online edn, 2004–)
Perfect King	Ian Mortimer, *The Perfect King: The Life of Edward III* (2006)
Polychronicon	J. R. Lumby (ed.), *Polychronicon Ranulphi Higden monachi Cestrensis*, vol. 8 (1882)
PROME	Chris Given-Wilson (ed.), *The Parliamentary Rolls of Medieval England* (CD edn, 2004)
Raccolta Praghese	Zdeňka Hledíková (ed.), *Raccolta Praghese di Scritti di Luca Fieschi* (Prague, 1985)
Rec. Comm.	Record Commission
Re-thinking History	Keith Jenkins, *Re-thinking History* (new edn, 2003)
Royal Wills	J. Nichols, *A Collection of All the Wills Now Known to be Extant of the Kings and Queens of England* (1780)
RP	J. Strachey *et al.* (eds), *Rotuli Parliamentorum* (6 vols, 1767–77)
Sapori	Armando Sapori, *I Libri dei Comercio dei Peruzzi* (Milan, 1934)
Scalachronica	Sir Herbert Maxwell (ed.), *Scalachronica: The Reigns of Edward I, Edward II and Edward III as Recorded by Sir Thomas Gray* (Glasgow, 1907, repr. 2000)
'Scam'	R. M. Haines, 'Roger Mortimer's scam', *TBGAS*, 126 (2008), 139–56
Sisto	Alessandra Sisto, *Genova nel Duecento: il Capitolo di San Lorenzo*, Collana Storica di Fonti e Studi 28 (Genoa, 1979)
St Albans	John Taylor, Wendy R. Childs and Leslie Watkiss (eds),

	The St Albans Chronicle: The Chronica Maiora of Thomas Walsingham. Volume 1: 1376–1394 (Oxford, 2003)
'Sumptuous apparel'	R. M. Haines, 'Sumptuous apparel for a royal prisoner: Archbishop Melton's Letter, 14 February 1330', *EHR*, 124 (2009), 885–94
Super-companies	Edwin Hunt, *Medieval Super-companies* (Cambridge, 1994)
Syllabus	T. D. Hardy, *Syllabus of Rymer's Foedera* (3 vols, 1869–85)
TBGAS	*The Bristol and Gloucestershire Archaeological Society*
THES	*Times Higher Education Supplement*
TNA	The National Archives, London
'Trouble'	Paul Strohm, 'The trouble with Richard: the reburial of Richard II and Lancastrian symbolic strategy', *Speculum*, 71 (1996), 87–111
'Uncertain death'	J. S. Hamilton, 'The uncertain death of Edward II?', *History Compass*, 6, 5 (2008), 1264–78
Usk	Chris Given-Wilson (ed.), *The Chronicle of Adam Usk* (Oxford, 1997)
Westminster	L. C. Hector and Barbara Harvey, *The Westminster Chronicle 1381–1394* (Oxford, 1982)
'Where is Edward II?'	G. P. Cuttino and T. W. Lyman, 'Where is Edward II?', *Speculum*, 53 (1978), 522–43
Wolff	Robert Lee Wolff, 'Baldwin of Flanders and Hainaut. First Latin Emperor of Constantinople: his life, death and resurrection, 1172–1225', *Speculum* 27 (1952), 281–322
Writing	David Bates, Julia Crick and Sarah Hamilton (eds), *Writing Medieval Biography 750–1250* (Woodbridge, 2006)

Introduction

This book has two purposes. One is to answer some difficult questions relating to some important events in the fourteenth century of a covert or conspiratorial nature, and to explore their implications. The other is to consider whether a philosophy of history that is sensitive to doubt and the theoretical work of postmodernists and critical theorists can, through a process of rigorous analysis, produce instances of historical certainty. In other words, can any of our answers to the 'difficult questions' ever be more than a matter of opinion?

As most readers will be aware, the background to the first of these themes is my sequence of biographies of medieval individuals. Four volumes have appeared to date, dealing with the lives of Sir Roger Mortimer, Edward III and Henry IV, and that of Henry V in the year 1415. When appraising key political leaders in a new way, it is inevitable that previously unasked questions will arise. In answering these it has sometimes been sufficient to supply an appendix in the relevant volume explaining the reason for discounting the traditional explanation. However, in a few cases, the radical nature of a piece of revisionism has required an article to be drawn up for the peer-reviewed press. Each of these articles in turn has provoked me to think about historical methodology and to consider whether the traditional approach to determining historical 'facts' is reliable. This has a particular relevance in the wake of postmodernism, for it may be said that many historians (especially medievalists) have failed to answer many of the criticisms of postmodernism and critical theory, and have continued writing history in spite of the intellectual developments of the rest of the world, increasingly addressing only a small peer group of scholarly colleagues. The end result is that history has begun to diverge from the intellectual mainstream of society, through refusing to answer its critics. As will be seen in this book, there is still a feeling among some historians that criticisms of their authority – that is to say, the historian's right to give an opinion on the past – must be answered by emphasizing that very authority and co-opting other professionals to reinforce it, not examining it to show the actual basis on which it is founded. Therefore the first theme of this book (the specific questions) have led naturally to the second (the theoretical stance).

The first scholarly essay that I published on a medieval theme was 'The death of Edward II', which appeared in *EHR* in December 2005. This pioneered an information-based approach to the past, which has subsequently proved invaluable in other contexts. It has the potential to answer fundamental questions about the nature of history that previously have proved difficult. Importantly, it works at both a theoretical and a practical level. Not only can we apply it to a large number of specific questions, it also leads to a broader philosophical question: if an information-based argument can be employed to show that Edward II was not killed in Berkeley Castle in 1327 and Richard II was certainly murdered in Pontefract Castle in 1400, can the same information-based methods be used to justify historical research in general? In short, through the process of achieving a point of certainty *historically*, can we achieve a point of certainty for history itself?

For many academics, this question is best ignored. Many people take the view that history has received its 'defence' in Richard J. Evans's thought-provoking book, *In Defence of History*, and the less historians inspect his arguments for cracks the better. However, I do not find any theoretical line in that book that allows a historian to prove aspects of the past, and especially not in a controversial context. Pro-history arguments still rely on emphasizing professional historians' expertise, judgement and authority, and the general reliability of the evidence. Such arguments work on the assumption that although a historian might be wrong in a few details here and there (because a tiny proportion of his or her source material was fraudulent, incomplete or inexact), most of the time, the evidence is reliable. But for the specialist in medieval intrigue, such generalizations are weak. We cannot simply work on the assumption that most of the evidence is correct – especially when it is patently obvious that most of it is no longer extant, and even more so when the traditional interpretation gives rise to many inconsistencies. Hence the need for the information-based approach that underpins much of this book.

Using information-based methods, it is possible to go much further than any earlier 'defence' of history allows: to determine how the composition of a text contained in a historical document related (and still relates) to past reality, and how one can, in certain limited circumstances, develop fixed points that limit the infinite set of possible re-descriptions of the past. This is the Holy

Grail of historical methodology – not least because it does away with the need for the historian's judgement and answers the critics of the historian's authority by *showing* the reasons for that authority, not just claiming it. Very simply, by treating information about the past in the same way that one treats information about contemporary society, information-science processes may be employed in both developing and testing a historical hypothesis.

As I wrote in the acknowledgements page in my book *1415*, being an experimental historian is never easy. History is perhaps the most conservative of all professions, and a radical historian is generally branded a maverick by the mainstream. Proposing new historical methods and coming to radical conclusions is almost guaranteed to make enemies, especially among those who have a vested interest in maintaining the orthodoxy of traditional interpretations of the past. However, it is to be hoped that innovation and new techniques can be accommodated within the profession as well as within society at large, and that the acceptability of original historical interpretations is dependent on the thoroughness of the research and logic of the arguments, not the traditions and vested interests which the researcher is deemed to be challenging. While the non-information-based arguments advanced in this book may be questioned, either to be absorbed within historical orthodoxy or disproved, the information-based ones should prove more durable. If I am wrong, the implication is that we cannot be certain about any specific aspect of the past – and the only accurate or provable history we can write is a general story of changing social conditions derived from a series of statistical averages that eliminate the individual and the isolated historical event altogether. However, if my confidence in the certainties made possible by this approach is well founded, there is no reason why historians should not put forward specific political narratives that defy theoretical criticism, resist historical contradiction and have lasting significance for society.

Objectivity and information:
a methodological introduction

To what extent can historians claim to know any aspect of the past with certainty? The question is important for two main reasons. First and most obviously, it is fundamental to the intellectual standing of the profession as a whole, and historians' ability to speak about the past individually. Secondly, the professional awareness that historical certainty is deeply problematic has itself conditioned the way that history has developed and is currently taught. Long before postmodernism and critical theory codified various means to criticize the authority of the historian, historians were themselves pulling apart each other's work at a practical level. The nineteenth and twentieth centuries saw some bitter intellectual feuds.[1] Even those who were not criticized by their contemporaries wrote with a growing awareness that much of their work would be discarded by future generations, and might one day even be scorned as founded in ignorance and naivety.[2] We might say that, over the course of the twentieth century, historians came to accept the idea that the future is not only the greatest undermining epistemological force in history writing but that *it always will be*, and that consequently its power to revise any historical understanding is absolute. It follows that no historical interpretation has actual substance, or inherent correctness, but rather is the same as a physical theory in that it is, in the words of Stephen Hawking,

> always provisional, in the sense that it is only a hypothesis: you can never prove it. No matter how many times the results of experiments agree with some theory you can never be sure that the next time the result will not contradict the theory. On the other hand you can disprove a theory by finding even a single observation that disagrees with the predictions of the theory.[3]

If that is so, then the study of history has no permanent epistemological value, and very little research into remote periods of time has any real meaning, except in relation to us ourselves, our contemporaries and our careers.

Given this long heritage of criticizing and denigrating historical knowledge on a practical as well as a theoretical level, it is ironic that it was postmodernism that caused history to retreat intellectually. The postmodern position was above all a theoretical stance, held for the most part by non-historians and directed mainly at the straw man of 'the historian', not practising writers' actual work. It might have been expected that historians' own considerations of the actual limitations of historical practice would have been given greater weight. It was not difficult to see the limited epistemological trust one could have in postmodernism; its principal strength was its ability to criticize.[4] But many historians ran scared of the extra-mural challenge, and ignored or avoided postmodernism altogether. Those who did not tended to argue against it from an unreflexive position, refusing to moderate their views and allowing the agenda to be set by history's critics. Defences of history ironically served to undermine the discipline further by drawing public attention to the criticisms of postmodernists and responding to the specific criticisms, as if somehow the entire critical stance could be undermined by a tit-for-tat discussion in which the initiative lay wholly with the critics. Most of all, the epistemological basis of the profession was not supported by an authoritative voice at a theoretical level. What history needed in the 1990s was not a 'defence' in the form of a critique of postmodernism but a coherent programme of explanation and elucidation which re-grounded history in the study of the past: a philosophical counter-movement supporting history which was not confined to the pages of *History and Theory* but embraced the majority of practising historians and the public.[5] Needless to say, it did not get one.

There were significant reasons why many historians ignored postmodernism – not the least of them being that the university systems of the Western world paid many of them to do so. The philosophers and critical theorists could afford to question and undermine 'the historian'; it was part of their job. Historians themselves were employed to continue as before, to research, write and above all else, teach history in line with their job descriptions. Defending their profession was not part of their remit. It could be said that the postmodern challenge revealed how remarkably inflexible institutional history is; the laissez-faire character of history as an academic discipline (in contrast to, say, the medical or legal professions) meant that senior scholars could not coordinate a robust and lasting response. It thus became easy for critics to declare that history within academic institutions was an arcane ritual, in which academics 'fetishised documents' and created 'fictive' accounts of the past 'at the pleasure of the historian'.[6]

Looking back from the vantage point of 2010, the elevation of postmodernism to a special height of critical authority seems disproportionate. There is no doubt that history suffered a huge intellectual battering in the 1980s and 1990s, and many criticisms of supposed historical practices were justifiable (regardless of whether historians actually followed them or not). But with respect to the larger and more important question of whether we can say anything with *certainty* about the past, postmodernism may be seen as just one subset of a large number of critiques of historical methodologies, most of them devised by historians themselves. They all were – and still are – methodological challenges, not insurmountable barriers. Epistemological progress remains possible and desirable.

There is thus a double importance to what we might call 'the certainty question'. First, there is the 'supply-side' of history – the need to re-establish history's reputation as an authoritative intellectual discipline. As Justin Champion has said, 'anxieties about the epistemological foundations of our discipline . . . have meant we have retreated into the increasingly dark corners of the academic community, publishing research in exclusive, recondite and expensive journals and monographs'.[7] One cannot help but feel that scholarly historians should try to do better, to overcome such anxieties and meet such challenges in the open, even if academic structures make it very difficult for them retrospectively to develop epistemological underpinnings of value systems which they take for granted.

Secondly, there is the 'demand-side' of the problem. Members of the public want to know about the human race in the past and about the historical objects which surround them, and historians have a social mandate to tell them as accurately and as truthfully as possible.[8] If historians cannot do so with a satisfactory measure of confidence, they are not fulfilling this aspect of their social mandate. There is of course a profound educational benefit in the study of historical ambiguity and doubt, but it is of limited importance for history outside education. If a historian faces a significant question in the life of a medieval individual – say, whether he murdered his cousin or not – and refuses to come to a decision, then that refusal is tantamount to a social failure, even if such doubt is both reasonable and understandable in professional terms. One may compare it to an engineer's failure to build a bridge over a chasm: his view that it is impossible to span the chasm may well be professionally correct; but the result is still the lack of a bridge. An unresolved historical doubt is both an intellectual cul-de-sac in its own right and a failure to provide a hypothesis which others may criticize or build on. For even an erroneous conclusion allows further experimentation, as the error can be subjected to further analysis, just as physical theories can be put to the test. But most of all, a failure to define the limits of certainty, and to explore the extremes of what may be considered 'certain', equates to a failure to determine the limits of one's own confidence, which in turn does nothing to inspire confidence in a reader. If we have only doubts about the historical past, how then can we fulfil our roles as historians? Why should any critical reader trust a historian who does not know the limits of his or her own material, and by implication, has a limited grasp of how to make the most of it? Conversely, why should anyone trust a historian who expresses doubts for the sake of academic caution, or who blithely states that he or she is 'unconvinced' by an argument? Such a response might be shorthand for knowing an argument is wrong on the basis of specialist knowledge and superior insight, but equally it could be an excuse for personal bias or inferior insight, prejudice, idleness or even a simple failure of understanding.

For all these reasons it is incumbent upon the professional historian to demonstrate how one might distinguish the certain from the uncertain. The matter was of burning importance in the decades of R. G. Collingwood, E. H. Carr and Geoffrey Elton, and it remains so today. This chapter examines the question by means of the twin aspects of historical objectivity and information from the past, the correlations of which limit the possible re-descriptions of past events, things and people. In linking the viewpoint of the historian ('objectivity') and the evidence ('information'), it follows in the tradition of history being a 'dialogue', established by Collingwood and followed by Carr, E. P. Thompson and Adrian Wilson, among others.[9] As a whole, it amounts to an argument that history is akin to the physical sciences in that certainty is not only desirable but actually attainable in some cases, and its determination thus sets limits on the extent to which the past can be 'infinitely re-described' – much as scientific definitions limit the ways in which the world can be understood.[10]

THE IDEA OF AN INTEGRATED HISTORIOGRAPHY

In discussing Collingwood's seminal 1946 study, *The Idea of History*, E. H. Carr paraphrased Collingwood's philosophy of history as 'concerned "neither with the past by itself" nor with "the historian's thought about it by itself", but with "the two things in their mutual relations".[11] Carr's line is interesting, for through it we can see how he developed Collingwood's idea to come out with his own, more succinct version. History, as he saw it, 'is a continuous process of interaction between the historian and his facts, an unending dialogue between the past and the present'.[12] This theme of dialogue across the ages was in turn lifted by E. P. Thompson in presenting his notion of the 'dialogue between concept and evidence' in his essay 'The poverty of theory'. The dialogue across the ages is thus a common theme running through twentieth-century writing on the means to achieve knowledge about the past.

Thompson's 'dialogue of concept and evidence' was the starting point for Adrian Wilson's often-overlooked essay, 'Foundations of an integrated historiography', published in 1993.[13] The exact question which Wilson sought to address was 'can the discipline of history – whether social or otherwise – lay any claim to generating a reliable knowledge?' Wilson sought to explain what Thompson might have meant by his otherwise unexplored notion of 'the dialogue between concept and evidence'. On the concept side of the 'dialogue', Wilson highlighted the importance of 'concept criticism', this being the constant correction of what we think about the past as we undertake research. Through adjusting our ideas, reflecting on the genealogy of our ideas, and examining ourselves to see whether our ideas are sound, concept criticism causes us to re-evaluate our position. At the same time we assume what Wilson describes as one of three 'hermeneutic stances' or methods of interpreting the evidence.

1. The first hermeneutic stance is the oldest, 'scissors-and-paste' history (as Collingwood and Carr describe it), in which a historian selects the evidence and uses it as he or she sees fit. In this method, the documents are treated as authorities. The drawback is obvious: they only allow us to see what the primary-source authors wanted us to see.

2. The second hermeneutic stance is 'source criticism' or 'critical history', in which a historian seeks to evaluate the sources on the strength of criteria such as aegis, proximity and authority. This is a superior approach for it allows us to extract facts carefully, as opposed to simply 'cutting and pasting'

them. For many years it seemed to Collingwood to permit scientific history. The drawback, as Collingwood later realized, is that it tends to collapse into the first hermeneutic stance. The process of trying to extract the truth from the evidence presupposes that the truth is within the documents in the first place. Both stances amount to 'winnowing out the false residue' and using the remainder.

3.   Wilson's third hermeneutic stance is to regard the documents as effects. In order to understand them, we must investigate their genesis, how they came to be created. As Wilson states, 'the move from source-criticism to the study of document genesis is only practised with difficulty, has seldom been advocated explicitly, and has proved deeply resistant to theorisation.'[14] However, it is this third hermeneutic stance which is the key in determining certainty, and which will be developed further in this chapter.

Unfortunately Wilson's work attracted little attention outside the academic circle which read his book, *Rethinking Social History*. It offers a platform on which writers may build their own theoretical constructs justifying their own methodologies. For as Wilson observed, critics of history have tended to presume that 'the historian' adopts only the first and second hermeneutic stances.[15] It is only in moving *away* from these, towards the third – understanding document genesis – that historians ascend the 'gradient of rigour' and pass beyond the form of history that is prone to criticism.[16] From any historical point of view, understanding how a document was made is hugely significant, for 'the society we are studying generated the documents we are using. In investigating the genesis of the documents we are thus investigating that society.'[17] The implications are that every enquiry into the meaning of a text entails an examination of the creation of the text, its bias, its representativeness, its role, why it was created and by whom, the agency which initiated the process and other aspects of its creation. What otherwise is simply a text becomes a multi-layered descriptive process, an encoded event in itself, full of metadata. This in turn affects the historian's concept criticism, forcing the historian to refine it, so Thompson's 'dialogue of concept and evidence' can be seen to produce historical readings which are both socially aware with regard to the past and reflexive with regard to the present.

To explain this more simply, the following is an adaptation of an example Wilson himself uses. If we were to set about investigating disputes between neighbours in early modern England, we might reasonably turn to the records of the ecclesiastical courts. There we would find plenty of evidence. However, as Wilson points out,

> a neighbourly quarrel could only get into the court through some process of co-operation or collusion, or coincidence between the quarrel itself and the activities and interests of the mediating authorities . . . Should we overlook this, and seek to use diocesan court records as transparent windows upon 'the occasions of neighbourly quarrel', our research procedure would consist simply of extracting the chosen cases from the documents.[18]

To avoid this weakness, Wilson suggests that, in order to consider instances of neighbourly quarrels properly, 'the historian has to take account of the ways cases came into court and the procedures by which they were recorded'. Thus all the ecclesiastical officers must also be considered, as with the minister and churchwardens and any other mediating authorities who might have helped bring the case to court. The roles performed by these officers become part of the object under study, thereby widening the objective scope of the enquiry. In this way we can say certain things about neighbourly quarrels as before, and we can also describe the filters and conditions placed upon the quarrels which resulted in some giving rise to the texts.

Unfortunately, Wilson's method is not the complete answer to the problem. It cannot determine falsehoods. It cannot in itself be used to determine a document created in good faith from one created in bad faith. When used in a socio-historical or cultural context, this does not matter greatly, for it is only important that we understand the production of a text and its mediators, regardless of their intrigues. In court, even falsehoods had to be believable, and thus have cultural value. Similarly, when using statistically significant numbers of documents, the occasional mendacious document or falsely reported entry in an account cannot affect the overall measure of change based on several thousand records. The rise in the frequency with which Kentish probate accounts record medicine being bought for the terminally ill and dying between 1570 and 1720, for example, could not have been falsified by a single agency.[19] However, when applied to political events, particularly those which entail bias and propaganda, document genesis is of more limited value. It *can* be of help: understanding how the Parliament Rolls were created allows us to understand how and why the 'Record and Process of the Renunciation of King Richard' was included in the roll for 1399 and yet is a greatly sanitized and probably inaccurate version of Richard II's abdication.[20] But it is of limited use in determining the veracity of a specific event. No degree of studying the circumstances and creation of Walsingham's chronicle can determine whether Sir John Arundel and his men actually raped eighty nuns in the autumn of 1379, abducted them from their convent, and threw them overboard during a storm off the coast of Ireland.[21] The story is highly unlikely but that in itself does not mean it is false. Walsingham clearly believed it, and, although no nunnery near Southampton had so many nuns, there is circumstantial evidence for some form of atrocity committed by Arundel's men in the area at the time.[22] The point is that, when it comes to specific events, and especially medieval intrigue, the third hermeneutic stance, or 'document genesis', is not enough.

The foregoing passages suggest that, while it is possible to say some things which are 'certain' with regard to social and cultural history – e.g. there was a massive rise in the purchase of medicine on behalf of the terminally ill in Kent between 1570 and 1720 – the certainty of 'the event' in narrative history remains problematic. We are methodologically hardly any nearer ascertaining the truth of an event than our Victorian forebears were. Indeed, we are probably further from it, for we have more sophisticated means of criticizing those who attempt to assert something is a 'historical fact'. This is not always due to postmodernism; sometimes it is simply advanced historical methodology. And even the most reliable, propaganda-free documents may succumb to this form of criticism. As Chris Given-Wilson has shown, the appearance of the name of a magnate as a witness in the Charter Rolls does not prove that he was present on the given day, as normally supposed.[23] A study of document genesis only reveals *why* we cannot rely on the Charter Rolls as irrefutable evidence of a man's attendance at court on the said day. The student who wishes to know whether the magnate was actually there or not has a more difficult path to tread.

BIOGRAPHY AND OBJECTIVITY

If we are interested in an individual event, be it political or routine, then we are concerned with the individual (or individuals) who took part in that event, and that ultimately means we are engaged in a biographical enquiry. When we study an individual biographically, we adopt a deliberately narrow or sympathetic view, in order to try and understand why he or she did something from his or her own point of view.[24] As John Tosh states, 'biography is indispensable to the understanding of motive and intention'.[25] Only through biography can we determine why something happened and why something else did *not* happen, and so why the event took place as it did.

In the twentieth century biography was widely seen as an intellectually weak discipline. K. B. McFarlane declared that medieval biography was 'an impossibility'. As he saw it, a biography should describe the inner life of the individual as well as the outer life. 'The historian cannot honestly write biographical history; his province is rather the growth of social organisations, of civilisation, of ideas'.[26] J. H. Plumb lamented this view in 1956, but as late as 1987 a contributor to the *THES* could still declare that biography 'is despised by the hard and practised by the soft in one discipline after another'.[27] Only at the end of the twentieth century did the value of biography come to be widely recognized as an important tool in determining what happened in the past, and moreover, *why* it happened.[28]

The change in biography's fortunes was most clearly brought to light in a conference at the University of Exeter in July 2003, entitled 'The Limits of Medieval Biography'. At this conference, a large number of leading medievalists professed their faith in the biographical approach and later published their reasons in *Writing Medieval Biography* (2006). As the editors stated in the introduction, biography 'offers insights which no other genre, no other analytical tool, can do'.[29] In Janet Nelson's words,

> I take life-writing to involve trying as hard as possible, even if that means sailing close to the imaginative wind, and certainly into the eye of the speculative storm, to make the acquaintance of my subject as a person, to guess plausibly, if no more, at what made him tick – as Frank Barlow did with Becket . . .[30]

Similarly the keynote speaker, Pauline Stafford, put forward a trenchant vindication of biography as a methodological tool, especially where it involved breaking down the life into a study of structures and roles.

> Such a practice provides many benefits. It supplies ways of reading the limited sources available to the early medieval biographer . . . An approach through roles and structures but also through their acting out in complex situations may be a liberation from the alleged limitations of medieval sources for the biographer, since it is not dependent on the sort of personal sources often felt to be essential to biography. It may be felt that this approach destroys individuals, breaking people down into a series of overlapping and accumulating roles . . . But ironically that breaking down provides the great vindication

of studying the individual: because it is only in an individual life that all these roles and structures are lived out. Structures and roles in that sense do not determine and write the individual, they become effective through the individual, and through the uniqueness of each life. And it is in that uniqueness that their possibilities, ambiguities and contradictions become apparent. Biography may not only be desirable, the human face of the past, but one of the most important historical genres, making clear the room for choice, however limited, that is also a motor of historical change.[31]

By deliberately attempting to understand an individual, especially in respect to the 'structures and roles' in which he or she operated, we can aspire to a new objective position from which to describe historical events.

For a practical example of how the biographical approach can lead to a better historical understanding, consider the relationship between Henry of Lancaster and Richard II in the 1390s. Most scholars to date have either taken an impartial view of the relationship or have sought to emphasize the legitimacy of Richard II's point of view (he being the king and thus assumed to have been, legally, always 'in the right'). Within this framework, Richard's gift of a breastplate to Henry in 1389, and his conferring on him of a dukedom in 1397, have led scholars to see a neutrality – even a friendship – between the two men until at least 1397.[32] Analytically speaking, there is nothing wrong with this interpretation: there is no evidence of a lasting rift before this time. But if we take Henry's point of view, and seek to understand his situation in the light of his reasonable expectations (based on those people around him), not only is there a context for a rift, there is considerable evidence of confrontation too. With regard to the context: in 1385 Richard II sought to murder Henry's father.[33] In 1386 he sought to establish that the Mortimers were heirs to the throne, not Henry's family, in defiance of Edward III's entail of the Crown (see Chapter 8). In 1387 Henry took arms against the king's favourite and the following year joined with the four other Lords Appellant in destroying the king's friends in the Merciless Parliament. In 1394, when the question of the succession was again raised, Richard again refused to acknowledge Henry as his heir. In 1396 Richard declared his intention of joining the king of France in a campaign against Henry's friend and ally, the duke of Milan. Over and over again Henry's aspirations and associations appear threatened or thwarted by Richard. Despite all these points, it would still be wrong to infer that Richard and Henry were enemies before 1397. Not only is there the evidence of the 1397 dukedom to be considered, there is no evidence that Richard undertook any unfriendly act towards Henry, or vice versa (except perhaps stopping him from travelling on the crusade). It is only when we view things from Henry's point of view that we get the full picture. Richard had failed to act positively in a manner respectful of his cousin's status. The evidence for the rift lies in the *absence* of references to gifts from Richard to Henry, and this does not emerge from a critical view of the texts themselves but only from seeing those texts from a biographical standpoint. Richard showered substantial gifts on his friends but he never gave Henry anything of real value – he never gave him the keepership of a castle or a forest, for example, or a wardship – and he never entrusted him with any diplomatic position, even though he was a fellow Knight of the Garter, and, according to Edward III's entail, second-in-line to the throne.[34] The two men spent very little time together as grown men, and almost all the time they did spend together was in the pacifying company of Henry's father, John of Gaunt (who had sworn an oath in 1376 to protect Richard II as king). In this light, the evidence for friendship – the gifts of the breastplate and the dukedom – may be reconsidered. When we realize that the breastplate had formerly belonged to one of Richard's closest friends, Lord Beauchamp of Kidderminster, executed at Henry's instigation (he being one of the Lords Appellant), the gift of the dead man's breastplate to the killer assumes the nature of a threat, not a sign of reconciliation.[35] As for the dukedom, according to Henry's own testimony in January 1398, there had been a plot by several of Richard's friends to murder him immediately after his creation.[36] Whether we read the dukedom as a reward to Henry for standing by and letting his fellow Lords Appellant be arrested, or as bait to lure him to his death, we cannot regard this as evidence of friendship. In this way it can be seen that, by focusing sympathetically on one man in order to understand his motives and actions, we encounter a different set of questions and meanings from those raised by the pursuit of a single statement of 'objective truth' about the two men in the traditional manner.

As postmodern critics and most scholarly historians now agree, 'objective truth' in its traditional guise is an impossibility.[37] It is widely recognized that it is impossible for a single historian to achieve an impersonal and balanced view of all the 'facts' (however they are defined) which allows one to state what actually happened from every contemporary's point of view. As in the traditional readings of the relationship between Richard II and Henry IV, the philosophical point at which we might achieve such 'objective truth' is static, absolute and universal. It is a sort of 'god's-eye view' of the past as it unfolded. If such god-like objectivity were possible, then everyone who achieved it, and who consulted the same evidence, would come to the same conclusions about the past.[38] However, given the same evidence, historians invariably come to different conclusions, depending on their respective characters, intelligence, learning and experiences. In his *Defence of History*, Richard J. Evans admitted as much, concluding that 'through the sources we use, and the methods with which we handle them, we can, if we are very careful and thorough, approach a reconstruction of past reality that may be partial and provisional, *and certainly will not be objective*, but is nevertheless true'.[39] Historians simply cannot escape their own cultural values, education, prejudices, language and temperament in order to view and express something with complete impartiality or total objectivity.

Despite this, the idea of 'objective truth' continues to exercise a potent force.[40] Even if we admit that we cannot achieve the whole truth, it is still necessary to pursue objectivity, for only by so doing can the historian demonstrate that he/she is deliberately eschewing subjectivity, and minimizing the problem that his own personality and preferences inevitably condition his/her reading of the evidence. But this view stems from the idea that, in history as well as philosophy, objectivity and subjectivity are opposites, the former an external point of view and the latter an internal one. This is questionable for two reasons. First, and most obviously, there are varying forms of objectivity. We can shift our view on any aspect of the past – for example, from the purely biographical to the general. The second reason is no less important. In history, objectivity is not the opposite of subjectivity. History is not about the past; it is about the *human* past. The history of a hitherto-unknown, uninhabited desert island is not within the orbit of the historian but is the subject of the natural historian, the geologist and the botanist. History as studied by historians is about people, and is only about inanimate objects and animals so far as they relate to people. Therefore the opposite of traditional historical objectivity – the 'god's-eye view' of the past – is not subjectivity but sympathy.[41]

Let us say that you are trying to describe a history book on a shelf. What you are describing is wholly outside you, and yet a measure of subjectivity enters your description. For a start there is the language you choose to use to describe it. Then there is your experience, which may or may not inform you that the symbol on the spine indicates it was published by a particular university press, and that the name on the dust jacket is that of a particularly eminent scholar writing about the fourteenth century in a London college in the late 1950s. That name might mean you give the book some value-related description, e.g. 'reliable' or 'outdated'. Overall, the objective description is informed by your experiences, your subjective knowledge. As Wilson and Ashplant put it, 'what any human observer "sees" is a function not simply of the object(s) that observer is observing, but also of the observer's own categories, assumptions, values, expectations, hypotheses, preconceptions, purposes, intents, attitudes.'[42] Now replace the book with a man. You might describe him equally objectively, his facial features, stature and height. Your own subjective experiences will again inform the description, probably causing you to use the same language and to interpret the expressions on the man's face as happy or sad, threatening or welcoming. There will still be an appropriate mixture of objective perception and subjective experience in the description. But if you try to describe what the man himself sees and feels, you are moving towards a position of sympathy. Imagine that he has just been hurt in some way. Through describing his grimace of pain, and the way he is holding his bleeding leg, you are likely to describe *your* perception of how *he* feels. This is still not subjectivity; you are not describing the way that *you* feel. Nor are you describing the way that people feel in general. You have simply shifted to a more interpretative form of objectivity (your perception of a man's appearance and then his discomfort). In so doing you have moved from the impersonal to the personal, but the personal element does not directly relate to you, it relates to the man.

Obviously, in describing the Middle Ages, which are by definition outside the self, objectivity is unavoidable. Contrary to the implication in Evans's statement above, objectivity is not rendered 'unattainable' by the existence of subjective factors – no more than subjectivity is rendered unattainable by the existence of the exterior world. The historian exists in relation to the world at large, and thus his or her objectivity co-exists with his or her subjectivity. But this does not render them mutually dependent. Subjective knowledge is necessary to achieve an objective understanding of why a human acts the way he does; for instance, that a crying man is not happy; or that with only one seeing eye he cannot judge distance so well. We might say that objectivity may be considered a spectrum ranging from the personal (or sympathetic), through the impartial, to the impersonal. Obviously each band of the spectrum shades into the others somewhat, but they may roughly be characterized as follows.

1.   At the least-personal extreme, there is the objectivity of environmental

historians measuring changes in the general landscape, for example changes in the sea level over the last five hundred years. It should be noted that even this most impersonal form of objectivity is not devoid of investigative and authorial subjectivity, which includes choice of dates and regions under examination, the language of expression, accuracy, skills of analysis and above all else, awareness of an audience for the final written conclusions.

2.   Next we might identify the quantitative analysis of individuals, for instance changes in longevity in a given parish. This is more sympathetic, and less impersonal, because we cannot undertake the study without recognizing the subjects as people. Similar subjective considerations apply as above. For instance, researchers coming across evidence of a one-hundred-and-ten-year-old man would be inclined to discount his longevity on account of their preconceptions about extreme age.

3.   More sympathetic (but still on the impersonal side of the spectrum) is the historian writing an overview of a large number of people over a certain period of time: a text which involves individuals and explains the movements of the society in which they live but which does not directly seek to sympathize with any one of them (for example, *The New Oxford History of England*). Again, a degree of sympathy is inevitable.

4.   More sympathetic is the study of a group of people who all have something in common, studied collectively in an attempt to understand that common feature – women in fourteenth-century England, for example, or the dying.

5.   A more sympathetic band still is the traditional historical study of an individual, for example a study of a medieval magnate. Such books – history books about individuals – are bound to be more sympathetic than history books about a nation, being defined in relation to an individual life and thus requiring the author to address changes and stages in that subject's life by reference to his or her own experience and the experiences of acquaintances.

6.   The second-to-last band is the sympathetic biography. This seeks to understand the individual: as Janet Nelson put it, 'to make the acquaintance of my subject as a person, to guess plausibly, if no more, at what made him tick'. With regard to an individual, this position may be contrasted with the preceding one in the following way. A history book about an individual is one in which the subject is seen in relation to his contemporaries; but in a sympathetic biography, his contemporaries are seen in relation to him.

7. Pseudo-autobiography, in which the historian deliberately plays the role of 'being' a historical person, in order to try and understand his or her actions as fully as possible.

As we move through the spectrum, different forms of subjectivity become more or less relevant. It does not automatically follow that the greater the sympathetic input, the greater the subjective element. One can write sympathetic history without it being laden with subjective inferences. How Henry IV may reasonably have expected his cousin Richard II to have treated him in the 1390s is a good example. If Richard was rewarding all his other cousins with lavish presents, for Henry to be the only one who received nothing at all singles him out in a distinctive way, especially given the context of their relationship. The sympathetic reading of the evidence here does not depend on a subjective stance on the part of the historian, it is evident from a direct comparison of the way Richard treated Henry in relation to the way he treated his other royal kin.

To recapitulate, there are three key postulations here which need to be borne in mind. First, as widely accepted, objective description devoid of subjectivity is impossible: the two are as interwoven as sight and recognition. Secondly, histobjectivity is not a static point – a 'god's eye view' – but a spectrum of objective bands, ranging from the sympathetic through to the impersonal. Thirdly, as subjective factors are present in all of these objective bands, there is no intrinsic reason to prefer an impartial objectivity over a sympathetic one (or vice versa) in reading events. We cannot say that one is right and another wrong. In different contexts, each may be more revealing than all the others. Collectively these bands constitute a range of historical tools.

OBJECTIVE INCONSISTENCIES

The reason for outlining these different bands is not only to demonstrate the nature of historical objectivity; it is also to provide a framework for demonstrating that the ways in which historians use source material vary according to the degree of sympathy with which they view a historical subject. Consider the range of approaches in the above example of Richard II and Henry IV. We might view the evidence for the crisis of 1397–9 as impersonally as possible, with a wide-focus perspective, maintaining an equal distance from all parties. Alternatively we could adopt a narrow-focus perspective, attending mainly to one man's actions and outlook as perceived by his contemporaries. The third option is to take a deliberately sympathetic view of one of them, maintaining a consistent partiality in order to try to understand his actions and outlook from his own point of view. If we choose the wide-angled perspective, a payment in a 1398 account for a bezoar stone is simply evidence of a belief in the power of bezoar stones in that year (a bezoar stone being a supposedly magical object which, when dipped in a goblet of wine, neutralizes any poison). Employing the narrow-focus perspective, the fact that the payment for this bezoar stone was made by Henry of Lancaster suggests that he believed in the power of such stones. Employing the sympathetic perspective, the payment may be used as evidence that the crisis of 1397–9 caused Henry of Lancaster to fear he might be poisoned. The ways in which we use any piece of evidence vary according to the position we assume within the objectivity spectrum.

While the example of the bezoar stone is simple and without great consequences (in that it is not historically problematic), other examples are more significant. If we consider the events of 1330 as impartially as possible, with a wide-focus perspective, there is nothing intrinsically wrong with the fact that the earl of Kent was executed for trying to rescue his half-brother, Edward II, from Corfe Castle. It might appear that he was gullible to believe the man was alive but only if he himself had good reason to believe that the man was dead. However, if we narrow our focus on the earl, we find that he did indeed have good reason to believe Edward II was dead: he had attended his funeral at Gloucester in December 1327. It follows that either he discovered that the man was not dead – or he was 'gullible' in the extreme. This gullibility is a striking contrast to the responsible character and judgement of a man who was placed in sole command of military operations in Gascony during the War of Saint-Sardos, and was entrusted (in preference to his elder brother) to negotiate the marriage of the king's eldest son, and was supported in his attempt to rescue Edward II by Archbishop Melton of York and others. An explanation which works easily in the impersonal, wide-angled view of history ceases to work close up. It is revealed as an objective inconsistency.

In this way it may be seen how unhelpful it was for twentieth-century historians to deny validity to biography and to insist on there being a single, static point of objectivity from which to view the past. It denies the very possibility of variable objectivity. Such a position may be likened to a man standing in front of a pyramid, and insisting that what he sees before him is only a triangle, and that there is no other way of describing the shape, because he refuses to shift from what he believes is the only point from which he may appreciate the 'objective truth' of the object he sees. It needs to be said that a few leading historians had begun to embrace multi-dimensional views of the past before the end of the last century but they were mostly social historians, and their multi-dimensional approaches were based on a series of cultural viewpoints. When political historians presented multiple viewpoints on the past they did so through describing the positions of contemporary commentators – separate chroniclers, for instance – thereby assuming one of Wilson's first two hermeneutic stances. The value of variable objectivity – achievable through correlations of biography, multiple biography, prosopography, political microstudy and general political history – is that it shows how historians can themselves obtain a multi-dimensional view of the past for individual events, as well as cultural roles.

Before going further it needs to be stressed that objective inconsistencies are not the same as conflicts of evidence. Conflicts of evidence can be dealt with by prioritizing one piece of evidence over the other (as in source criticism). Historians do this all the time; every medievalist is familiar with texts containing details that could not possibly be true, and thus are certainly mistakes made by their compilers. In many cases it is possible to identify and eliminate the mistakes: the result is that the 'bad evidence' or mistake is laid aside. With objective inconsistencies it is not possible to discard evidence in this way, for it is not necessarily 'a mistake' on the part of the compiler or copyist. In such cases laying aside a single piece of evidence is to fall into the trap of *selecting* the evidence (a point regarded as bad practice by followers of Elton as much as their postmodern critics). But more importantly, discarding evidence does not resolve the inconsistency. A conflict of evidence is simply a disjuncture between two or more pieces of evidence; an objective inconsistency is two irreconcilable but well-founded interpretations, each based on considerable evidence.

This last point embodies the most important principle arising from the concept of objective inconsistencies. An objective inconsistency, by definition, indicates that an existing understanding is flawed (even if it is not possible to see why). It might be a slight misunderstanding easily resolved or it might be an intractable problem, but, either way, if an objective inconsistency is perceived, then that perception implies that at least one of the two compared objective explanations of an event is flawed.

The principle of objective inconsistencies carries with it an important methodological spin-off. It demands that circumstantial evidence be considered and explained, in addition to the direct evidence. Traditionally, it is not bad practice to regard circumstantial evidence as less important, as it cannot contribute to certainty or 'proof'. Be that as it may, the point of variable objectivity is to see how various objectivities can be used to test the integrity of a complete description of an event. Hence the details arising from that event acquire a new significance: they cannot be simply discarded because they too need to be correlated with each of the alternatives. Indeed, in terms of testing for objective consistency it becomes almost impossible to distinguish between direct and circumstantial evidence. For example, in investigating whether Richard II declared that the Mortimers were the heirs to the throne in the parliament of 1385, it is a circumstantial detail that John of Gaunt and Richard dined together at the end of that parliament. That the Lancastrian heir remained on good terms with the king suggests Richard had not just insulted him publicly by denigrating his claim to the throne and elevating the earl of March to the position of heir apparent. Conversely there is circumstantial evidence that the earl of March was elevated in this way in the story that Roger Mortimer pressed his claim to the throne personally in 1394, during a parliament. Traditionally, one would make a decision and prioritize one view over the other, discarding the alternative as 'without foundation' (precisely as R. R. Davies did in his article on Roger Mortimer for the *Oxford Dictionary of National Biography*). However, when presented as an objective inconsistency, in which each possibility must be considered, all the evidence (circumstantial and direct) needs to be considered in relation to the actual event, not just a historical explanation of it. Circumstantial evidence might not amount to proof but it still demands explanation, especially if it seems to clash with other evidence, creating its own inconsistency.

The problem is that biography only identifies objective inconsistencies; it cannot normally rationalize them. Objective inconsistencies cannot be solved with any degree of certainty by attempting to understand the men involved, nor by any recourse to motive. Such processes cannot lead to certainty. Any reading of character – as with any emotional description of a person – is bound to be heavily subjective, and it is impossible to divorce the subjective element from the objective in trying to determine past motives. Attempting to do so does not necessarily amount to bad history – in fact, quite the opposite is true – but it does preclude certainty, for the subjective element will always be open to question. Returning to the problem of the earl of Kent in 1330, we cannot presume that the man was 'gullible' or 'stupid' (as T. F. Tout stated) or in any other way misled. To do so is to read the evidence having already made up our minds as to how to resolve the objective inconsistency at the heart of the problem. Conversely we cannot simply assume that, because the earl of Kent believed his half-brother was still alive in 1330, that he was correct. This is tantamount to setting all the evidence for the king's death aside without explanation. Readings of character and motive do not amount to evidence. In such cases, a more sophisticated methodology is necessary.

RETURNING TO FIRST PRINCIPLES

One of the most significant problems with controversial debates is that the evidence is no longer easily readable. This is not just due to linguistic, archival or palaeographical complexities; it is because what the key evidence actually says has all but disappeared under layers of earlier readings and accretions of widely accepted meanings. This goes for 'bad evidence' as well as 'good'; it applies to pieces of political propaganda as well as conscientiously recorded entries in chronicles. Of course it need not apply only to documents: objects too have their accretions of stories and meanings. Whatever form it takes, in order to read the primary evidence of past events in a primary way we have to suspend all hitherto accepted conclusions and interpretations. It is necessary to eschew all pre-existing arguments, all pre-existing selections of evidence, all pre-existing narratives, and all previous linkages of facts. We must 'shed all prejudices and preconceptions and approach the documents with a completely open mind.'[43] We must set aside the exhortation to 'err on the side of caution' for this is still an exhortation to 'err', to be cautious (and thus, occasionally, biased) in questioning past interpretations of evidence. We must accept Janet Nelson's exhortation to sail 'close to the imaginative wind, and certainly into the eye of the speculative storm'. This is not easy, not least because, in order to expose all the relevant evidence concerning an event so that it may be fairly re-evaluated, we must set aside the historical assertions of our peers. As Thomas Kuhn observed in *The Structure of*

Scientific Revolutions, established figures within any knowledge-based profession sometimes defend their old paradigms against revisions – and even against proof – for personal reasons.[44] To enter into a scholarly debate with the approach that, in order to assess the evidence with an open mind we must first set aside our colleagues' findings, is to invite accusations of disrespect.

If we do manage to set aside accretions of meanings and interpretation, we are left with a pile of contemporary and near-contemporary evidence, and cultural and geographic frameworks within which the events are supposed to have occurred. Even these things are open to criticism. With regard to evidence, why choose some documents and not others? Why trust any textual meaning? With regard to geography, how do we know how the terrain has changed? Similarly, a cultural framework to the past implies historical preconceptions which themselves might be wrongly applied in a particular instance. The concept that common law inheritance was the legal method of passing on an estate might lead the historian to believe that this was the legally correct way of passing on the Crown in 1399. But as Chapter 9 shows, the common law did not apply.

To return to first principles is thus not an easy task. For a start we have to acknowledge that the past is not just 'the practical past'; we cannot limit it simply to 'what historians do'.[45] It is the unrecoverable past as well as the recoverable – and that includes 'the impractical past'. However, having acknowledged this general broadening of the historical framework, progress becomes possible. As the age of almost anything organic may be determined by some means (including the use of scientific methods), we are able to develop a series of archaeological certainties about the past. Everything which has lived can, in theory, be dated to a series of unique days, months and years. Sometimes the dates will be approximate, but most pieces of evidence can be related to the central axis of time – central as it runs through all human history and, in terms of solar days, is universally comprehensible. This includes documents, and thus the texts which we have available are not free-floating discourses but temporally located discourses. Although we have no way of assessing their veracity on first inspection, we can say that such-and-such a text was known or in circulation at a certain time. These texts thus may be regarded as archival certainties in the same way that the sixteenth-century timbers of the *Mary Rose* are archaeological certainties. For example, it is an archival certainty that the roll of the first parliament of Henry IV contains a text which is described as the 'Record and

Process of the Renunciation of King Richard', and that this roll dates to 1399 (a date which could be scientifically checked). Regardless of how sanitized it is as an account of Richard II's deposition, it is an archival certainty that it is a text of that antiquity.

The ideas in the previous passage are adumbrated in various responses to postmodernism. In the words of the authors of *Telling the Truth about History*,

> history is never independent of the potsherds and written edicts that remain from past reality, for their very existence demands explanation. The past cannot impose its truths upon the historian, but because the past is constantly generating its own material remains, it can and does constrain those who seek to find out what once took place.[46]

These 'potsherds and written edicts' are not just moral 'constraints' they are also archaeological and archival certainties. As such they are, in some respects, absolute, for all archaeological and archival certainties imply historical certainties by their very creation. These may be only the most basic antiquarian certainties – e.g. that the Bayeux Tapestry depicts an eleventh-century battle, that the *Mary Rose* contained cannon as well as bows and arrows, that the 'Record and Process' tells a story about Richard II – but they are nonetheless important. We cannot ignore them; they are not selections applied to the past but survivals from it, and as such they are immovable markers on the central axis of time. As such, they go some way to reverse the theoretical contention that 'we are free to conceive history as we please'.[47] As I have expressed it elsewhere,

> The central axis of time provides a chronometric framework for representing the past not as a pure theoretical discourse but as a series of archaeological and archival certainties, all of which imply a range of historical certainties, on which we may build a theoretical discourse. We may question when Queen Victoria actually died, but one cannot do so without reference to the historical certainty that her death was publicly reported on the 23 January 1901 as having occurred the previous day, and the lack of evidence for any alternative date is equally certain. No amount of theory can obviate the need to account for both aspects of these complementary arguments. Thus the principle of archaeological certainties may be used to refute Jenkins's dictum that 'the gap between the past and history . . . is such that no amount of epistemological effort can bridge it'. Quite simply, Jenkins's view is too absolute, and prone to the same objections which apply to claims that a history book is comprehensive or definitive.[48]

This is what is meant by a return to first principles. It is to strip all the possibly relevant archaeological and historical certainties of their layers of meaning and cultural interpretation, and to relate them only to the central axis of time and the spatial layout within which they were created. It is to eradicate potential conceptual weaknesses by eradicating the conceptual element altogether and focusing on what exists, as if all historical items were solely antiquarian relics. It is only when we have reduced our knowledge of the past to this level, and reduced our subjective input to the level of reading and translating the relics (documents), that we may start to rebuild our concept of history by evaluating their veracity.

EMPIRICAL PROBLEMS

Two empirical problems arise from the previous passages. The first is that even preserved items change their form over time, as David Lowenthal pointed out in *The Past is a Foreign Country*. We cannot arrest change, the most we can do is try to divert it. A castle might be crumbling, and a heritage organization might step in to stop its decay, but in so doing they shore it up, and introduce barriers and alter its appearance. Rather than being covered in ivy it becomes covered in signs saying 'Do not climb on the walls'. This is no nearer its original form than the decaying pile. It is the same with historical texts. We might argue that the archival certainty of a medieval chronicle – say a French *Brut* – is impervious to the sort of changes mentioned above. However, as theorists working in the wake of Ferdinand de Saussure's *Course in General Linguistics* (1916) pointed out, we can break up the representations of historical reality contained in that chronicle into the atoms of 'signified' and 'signifiers' and the relationship between the two changes over time. Words come to mean different things; phrases come to have different connotations. When we read of the Prophecy of the Six Kings, for example, it is very difficult for us to know what the chronicler meant by these things, whether they were intended to convey dynastic challenges, warnings to those in political authority, or moral guidance.

The second problem is the fundamental one of 'falsehoods' – misinformation and disinformation. This includes aspects of the first problem, namely the limitations of text (including plain errors and ambiguities). As Paul Strohm has observed, 'the unreliability of the chronicles is due in part to the properties of narrative itself, with its propensities for selective treatment, imputation of motive, and implicit moralization'.[49] Nor do routinely created records (as opposed to chronicles and literary texts) guarantee a more reliable account of the past. Even though we might be certain that a medieval inquisition post mortem was issued on a specific date, and its enrolment means that we have a contemporary copy of the text, it still does not follow *for certain* that the named subject was dead (as the case of Thomas of Woodstock reveals, discussed in Chapter 10). Even medieval kings told lies. Hence the 'constraints' posed by the 'potsherds and written edicts' described by the authors of *Telling the Truth about History* do not necessarily lead us to historical certainty, for the archival certainties represented by the 'edicts' allow us to conclude only that they were issued, not that they were issued in good faith.

The first problem mentioned above is one of understanding how descriptions of reality change over time. This is of limited relevance. Original texts do not change except in terms of being damaged, so the key issue is that of understanding shifting norms, altered meanings and changing concepts. In answering this problem with regard to the issue of historical certainty, a distinction needs to be made between matters of information – temporally located statements which are not relatively defined, such as 'King Edward III died today, 21 June 1377' – and relative statements, such as 'Edward II loved Piers Gaveston like David loved Jonathan'. It is arguable that we can only achieve positions of certainty with regard to the former: non-relatively defined statements. Life and death have the same physical meaning today as in the past – so have the events of a man sending a message, striking his enemy, or having sexual intercourse with another person – and we may test the historical certainty of such reports of events. It is not possible to be certain as to the meaning of relatively defined statements; these are more open to interpretation. However, it is worth noting that a lack of certainty with regard to these subjects does not amount to the freedom 'to conceive history as we please . . .' As Mark Ormrod's analysis of descriptions of Edward II's sexuality and Paul Strohm's work on a range of matters such as 'the rebel voice' have shown, we can use cultural historical techniques to contextualize contemporary stories, including Edward II's ditch-digging and the deeds of those involved in the Peasants' Revolt.[50] Such analyses allow readers in the modern world to sympathize with the way or ways in which a text would have been read by the medieval reader. This sensitivity to medieval readings of texts hugely restricts the possible interpretations that may be applied to some non-relatively defined subjects.

This leaves us with the second empirical problem, misinformation and disinformation. Given the statements in the previous paragraph, this particularly applies to those archival certainties that are not relatively defined, and which we might wish to argue are 'absolutely certain', such as the reports of specific actions by identifiable people on particular days. Such actions lie at the very core of narrative history. If we cannot be 'certain' about non-relatively defined aspects of the past, as recorded in contemporary documents, then we cannot be 'certain' about anything, and ultimately narrative history is entirely a matter of trust and is not grounded in past reality but only in the writings of those who wished to preserve one view of it. Hence this is the key area for discussion in the rest of this chapter.

THE PARADOX OF PRIMARY SOURCES

In assessing the veracity of archival certainties, it is essential to understand that it is not 'the evidence' that we need to verify – all evidence is 'true' in the sense that it proceeds from the past – it is the veracity of the information contained within that evidence. Thus, when considering a contemporary chronicle which states that Richard II starved himself to death in Pontefract Castle, we need to be aware that the single question 'is this evidence reliable?' implies several questions relating to information.[51] Did Richard II die in Pontefract? Did he die of starvation? Did he himself instigate that process of starvation? Did he maintain it to the end? Was the death directly attributable to malnutrition and dehydration? Who is the author of this chronicle, when was he writing, why was he writing, and did he have a personal reason not to repeat the information about this event exactly as he heard it? And most important of all, from whom did the chronicler obtain his information?

In this light, Wilson's exhortation to ascertain a correct view of the past by examining the genesis of the document appears a tall order. For a start we need to establish how 'the document' (which might not be the chronicler's original but an amended copy) came to include these pieces of information. Even if we refer to another chronicle and establish whether these views are corroborated, we would be simply undertaking a form of source criticism and, as we have seen, that does not necessarily reveal truth (because the two chroniclers may have had the same original source). For this reason there is a widespread understanding that we cannot 'get closer' to a historical event than the sum of the evidence at our disposal. Or, to put it another way, there is a widespread acceptance that the 'mists of time' obscure the linkages of event, event-description and event-documentation, so it is permissible to make a number of presumptions about these linkages precisely because they are obscured by these timely fogs.

As a result of this inability to see the linkages through the fog, historians tend to view any single fact contained in a piece of evidence as a static piece of information, to be verified by either (1) its internal credibility or (2) its external relationship with some other data (both of these being aspects of source criticism). When we take any particular fact and use it in a narrative, we might present it as reliable, or questionable, or perhaps doubtful, or even wrong, but we refer to it as a fact and describe it in relation to the evidence (e.g. 'As Adam Usk states . . .'). It is immutable: if a source for the Battle of Shrewsbury says that Hotspur's supporters cried 'Henry Percy King!' at the moment they saw a knight struck down wearing Henry IV's armour, we may trust the evidence or we may doubt it, or we may use it with a caveat, but we cannot change the wording of the exclamation (except as a bona fide translation). As a result, even if historians consider absolutely *all* the evidence at their disposal, they have to discard evidence that conflicts with their chosen narrative even if they have no better reason for doing so than simply the inability to make it fit. In Figure 1.1, a historian who believes story C will discard the evidence for story A and story B.

Event	Information	Evidence	History
	–	– Document, story A	
	–	└ Chronicle, story A	
	–	– Chronicle, story B	
Past reality	–	└ Chronicle, story B	
(various	*[fog, or the*	– Document, story B	Historian's work
perspectives)	*mists of time]*	– Chronicle, story B	
	–	– Chronicle, story C	
	–	└ Chronicle, story C	
		– Document, story C	
		└ Chronicle, story C	

Past .... *Time* ....Present

Figure 1.1 Traditional reliance on evidence as a 'primary' source

This may or may not be justifiable on historical grounds; either way the process depends on the historian's judgement, and that is prone to error.

This highlights a paradox in the way historians handle evidence and present it to readers. In the above model, relevant facts are selected from the evidence, and treated as immutable. This is paradoxical because, in history, the facts may have already been changed – before they were written down. Evidence is not normally the start of a process of information dissemination; it is created at a later point in the life cycle of the information (to paraphrase the archival concept of 'the life cycle of the document'). Information has an existence before the creation of the evidence in which it will eventually find its immutable form. But, in some cases, much of the 'fog' which allows us to take evidence at face value can be swept away, and we can start to reconstruct how information passed from the 'event' to the writer of the evidence.

In Figure 1.2, the benefit of studying information linkages is shown. Unable to find a good information stream for story C, it is considered merely as a possibility and held in abeyance while the others are tested. The inconsistency of story A and story B is resolved by finding two independent information streams for story B which correlate, showing that the apparently reliable story A was probably created in bad faith, despite the traceable source of the information.

Just as Wilson's third hermeneutic stance encourages historians to study documents in the context of their creation, so too we may study information in

Event	Information	Evidence	History
	– ————	– Document, story A └ Chronicle, story A	┐
Past reality – (various – perspectives)–	———┐ ———┘ ———┐ ———┘	– Chronicle, story B └ Chronicle, story B – Document, story B – Chronicle, story B	├ Historian's work
– – – 	[fog]	– Chronicle, story C └ Chronicle, story C – Document, story C └ Chronicle, story C	——?—— ——?—— ——?—— ——?——
Past .... Time ....Present

Figure 1.2 Information-based approach to evidence

the context of *its* genesis and genealogy – its prehistory before its embodiment in a document. In some cases we can penetrate the fog. We can use the knowledge that any possibly correct information underlying a primary source is the end-product of an information network or stream extending back to the creation of the information, and, through its originator, back to the event itself. In order to understand how archival certainties relate to past events – how they reflect events in space-time – we must overcome the paradoxical element inherent in the use of primary sources and examine the relationship between a primary source and the event. We must regard evidence not as a primary source with some unchallengeable 'primary' status but simply as a container in which pre-existing information was stored and transmitted to us in the present.

THE INFORMATION-BASED APPROACH

Physicists using special relativity refer to objects in space-time using a series of four coordinates: three dimensions and time. For historical purposes we might add additional time elements, relating to the dates when something was created and when it ceased to exist, or when creation started and terminated. We might describe the creation of a document, say the final volumes of Domesday Book, at a series of coordinates between the date when writing commenced and the series of coordinates of the place and time it was completed. This followed on from the creation of preliminary drafts of the work (such as Exon Domesday) at different coordinates in space-time at an earlier date. This process of document genesis may be conjectured all the way back to the tours around the country undertaken by those who actually gathered the information. These tours too have unique coordinates in space-time. Moreover those coordinates are *real* – in theory we could define them precisely, if we had sufficient data. Thus Domesday Book represents a network of information links in space-time connecting a preliminary stage of events (questioning, informing, writing, travelling), with a more concentrated second stage (drafting) and a third stage (writing the finished volumes). After that, the network of information links contracts to a single path through space-time, dependent on the physical location of the volumes over the centuries, until they are copied, edited, corrected and published, and the network of information links begins to expand again.

With this in mind, the life cycle of information might be modelled in a more sophisticated way than in Figures 1.1 and 1.2 in the previous section:

1. In the initial stage – in the witnessing of an event or the hearing of a pronouncement, for example – there were witnesses. Each witness forms a view on what he or she has seen or heard, and commits it to memory, and articulates it to one or more person(s) in the next stage.

2. There may be some intermediaries in the process of circulating the information, who have been informed as to what has been said or done, and who memorize what they have heard and repeat it, or a version of it, to those in the next stage.

3. The writer may be informed by the witness (from stage 1) directly, or he might be informed indirectly by an intermediary (from stage 2). Either way, the writer will also need to recall what he has heard, in order to write it down.

4. The writer's words may be copied, with or without changes (including translation), in later copyists' work.

5. The historian reads the final text incorporating the information.

The above model may be varied in many ways. A witness might be both a writer and a copyist himself. There may be many hundreds of intermediaries, and the writer might speak to just one or many of them. The whole process may be a written one, from witness to eventual writer. Many years and large distances may pass between stages, memory performing the important (albeit problematic) function of data storage. The important thing to remember is that, as information is disseminated, time passes. One cannot write down what happened before it has happened, not without breaking the integrity of the flow of information. Stage 1 must occur before stage 2 can take place, and so on. If a clerk writes about an event before it has happened, he is not recording the event itself but the anticipation of that event. Just as archaeological and archival certainties derive their 'certainty' from their fixed positions on the axis of time, so the stages of the above model depend on chronological consistency. As all existence is moving forward through time, we could say it is a physical law that information dissemination must take place in a sequence of chronological stages.

This brings us to what might be described as a 'fourth hermeneutic stance', following Wilson's terminology, or an information-based method of assessing the linkages between documentary evidence and the events it supposedly describes. The existence of a document, when temporally located, amounts to an archival certainty, and this in turn implies a historical certainty – that all the intrinsic information (regardless of whether it was true or not) was incorporated in a text written at a specific date or over a specific period of time, and so was known to the writer at or before that time. Underlying each piece of information is at least one – and probably many – networks of information in space-time, each consisting of articulations, reports, viewpoints and impressions, collectively linking witnesses of the event and the author of the documentary evidence. These networks may thus be said to embody both *information genesis* (the original articulation of reports) and *information genealogy* (the transfer of such reports). Finally, we must consider *information integrity* (whether the information contained within a document is resistant to mutation and alteration).

Obviously the problem of information mutation means that the theory is most useful in discussing the accuracy of a single detail which is not relatively defined, so its integrity may be verified. The theory is, for example, far more useful for assessing whether reports of a man's death are trustworthy than reports of his emotional affairs. Reports of a death permit a series of hypotheses, all of which may be tested and either found true or false. Whichever we are trying to test, 'death = true' or 'life = true', can be reconfigured in terms of the other, 'death = false' and 'life = false'. If we may disprove something on information grounds, it follows that we may prove its opposite true. For anyone involved in the task of making definite pronouncements about specific events in the past, this provides a means by which we can be more accurate about subjects which have hitherto been left to historians' personal impressions or statements of fact based simply on the grounds of perceived motive (a subjective inference).

To recapitulate: this information-based method incorporates key areas in which specific enquiry might be pursued in order to ascertain the veracity of a piece of information.

1. *Information Genesis*: one may question whether the original report was articulated in good faith;
2. *Information Genealogy*: one may question the connectedness or integrity of the entire chain or network of reports, linking the event and the evidence, including whether the initial articulators of a report were actually witnesses of the event;
3. *Information Integrity*: one may question the integrity of the information itself – the accuracy of the reports at each and every stage in the dissemination of the information, including the writing of the evidence.

This three-part test can be conducted for both of two conflicting narratives, for instance, the possible survival of Richard II can be formulated as a series of four questions:

a. 'Richard II alive after 1400 = true' b. 'Richard II alive after 1400 = false'.
c. 'Richard II dead in 1400 = false'. d. 'Richard II dead in 1400 = true'

With regard to the first of these, (a), it is impossible to discern an information stream rooted in past reality that attests to his living. With regard to the second, (b), there is the check by Jean Creton on the identity of the pretender in Scotland, which turned out to be a definite denial that the man was alive. With regard to the third, (c), it is possible to find statements in contemporary evidence that the man was still alive but the only information streams that can be discerned suggest the participation of William Serle in issuing letters in the ex-king's name with his seal. As for the fourth, (d), several information streams can be identified that correlate with his being killed: for example, those originating in news delivered from Pontefract in February 1400, and the public exhibition of the corpse in London and Westminster, and perhaps the evidence of Hotspur and his father in the Percy Manifesto, given their closeness to Henry IV at the time. The point is that, when necessary, the historian can move beyond all three of Wilson's hermeneutic stances – 'scissors-and-paste history', 'source criticism' and 'the genesis of the document' – and go beyond the need for disputable 'facts' contained in or deduced from that evidence. Rather he or she can look for information streams that relate to false as well as true reports of past reality.

INFORMATION STREAMS VS. FACTS

As that last passage suggests, the information-based approach has clear implications for general historical methodology because it touches on the question of what constitutes a 'fact'. For Sir Geoffrey Elton, a historical fact was:

> something that happened in the past, which had left traces in documents which could be used by the historian to reconstruct it in the present. In order to perform this operation successfully, the historian had in the first place to shed all prejudices and preconceptions and approach the documents with a completely open mind.[52]

These are Elton's words succinctly paraphrased by Richard J. Evans. As Evans went on to point out, Elton's definition was written in response to that of E. H. Carr, whose view was that a fact only became a historical fact when it was selected by the historian and treated as one; in his words 'a mere fact about the past is transformed into a fact of history'.[53] His example was the murder of a gingerbread salesman killed at Stalybridge Wakes in 1850, which only became a 'historical fact' when a historian selected it for his argument. Carr's distinction between 'fact' and 'historical fact' might be described as a matter of semantics; but, far more philosophically, Hayden White took the distinction much further and demonstrated that a historical event and a 'fact' are not the same thing. An event is an actual happening in the past; a 'fact' is something that is known to the historian in the present. Traditional historians have tended to see this distinction as something to be resisted for it prevents there being any historical facts at all. It consequently inhibits their ability to say anything with certainty about the past based purely on evidence. Richard J. Evans in his *Defence* labels such thinking a 'misunderstanding', stating that 'a fact does not have to be an event: for example it could be a building, now long since disappeared, in a certain place'.[54] However, Evans himself seems to suffer from a 'misunderstanding' in this respect. Obviously a building's existence *can* be seen as an 'event' (albeit one that takes place over a long period of time) but that is not the point. The point is that, by declaring that a vanished building's existence could be regarded as a 'fact', he is resisting the distinction between past reality and the evidence for the past, and trying to conflate both in one 'factual' entity. This flat denial of Hayden White's sound observation is unhelpful. As this book shows, it is not possible to regard Edward II's death in Berkeley Castle as a 'fact' – nor is it possible to regard his death anywhere else as a 'fact'. Nor is this a unique, isolated case; it is common to all historical events. Consider Evans's proverbial 'building, now long since disappeared, in a certain place': if the building in question was one of the friaries in thirteenth-century Dunwich – long since lost to the sea – then the 'fact' of its location would be open to endless dispute. It would be as unrecoverable as the names of the individuals who built Stonehenge. So too would be everything else about it. The only 'facts' available to us are that it is recorded to have existed, perhaps founded by a certain individual at a certain date. If the foundation charter turns out to be a fake, then very little is factual at all. Maybe the word 'Dunwich' was a copyist's error for another place, and the building never existed at all. In this way it can be seen that the past reality of the building's physical existence is quite distinct from the evidence that it existed, and the very use of the word 'fact' to describe its existence is presumptuous and may be misleading. Going back to Carr's example of the 'fact' of the death at Stalybridge Wakes: the memoir could be part wrong or even completely imaginary, so the event cannot be regarded as a 'fact' – let alone a 'historical fact'. All we can have confidence in, and all we can claim as 'factual', is the wording in the extant memoir describing the death. The very concept that 'facts' may be deduced from the evidence with any degree of *certainty* prevents the historian approaching that evidence with an open mind – which was one of Elton's prerequisites for the historian successfully performing the operation of reconstructing what happened in the past.

Hayden White's position – that one must distinguish between 'events' and 'facts' which are constructed by historians out of evidence and the remains of the past – would appear thereby to be vindicated.[55] A 'fact' that appears in a piece of evidence does not imply a 'fact' in past reality because it is not necessarily rooted in past reality. However, as Figure 1.2 showed, it is wrong to regard past reality and evidence as unconnected, or to suppose, like Keith Jenkins, that 'the gap between the past and history . . . is such that no amount of epistemological effort can bridge it'. The information-based approach outlined above indicates how past reality and evidence may be connected. The 'past reality' in question might have been described by an author in good faith, or it might have been described in bad faith (the result of the author's bias), or it might have been created as a result of a mistake or an outright lie (in which case the term 'past reality' is hardly applicable). Nevertheless, in many cases the connections between the evidence and the past reality it describes will be good. Sometimes we can test these linkages. Sometimes we can demonstrate that we have multiple eye-witness accounts of a historical event. Sometimes we can find archaeological remains that are a direct consequence of an event (arrowheads and cannonballs on a battlefield, or the charred remains of a burnt house, for example). In such cases the words used in the fourteenth century to describe the use of cannon at a battle or a house being burnt may come down to us with as much integrity as the physical remains of the cannonball or house. Hence, if we are going to postulate a form of historical certainty that is capable of withstanding criticism, it needs to be based not on the traditional conflation of event and documentary evidence (as Evans suggests) but on the information linking the past reality and the present.

As soon as one starts to use information in this way, the approach starts to become constructive and not just an epistemology of disproving things. That Richard II announced the death of his uncle before it happened places him in a position of culpability: there are at least three information streams attesting to the duke's survival in Calais after the announcement of his death in England (see Chapter 10). In this way, a few key certainties allow us to say something positive about the past. Information in an extant text of a certain date can be correlated with information in other texts of a similar date, and the information genesis, genealogy and integrity compared to reconstruct information streams relating to an event, described and recorded by a certain date. These information streams, based on archaeological and archival certainties, are like multi-dimensional 'facts' for they incorporate data about possible past reality and the metadata of how that data came to be passed on and written down. Thus to refer to them as plain 'facts' is a superficial description. Indeed, when confronting the problem of historical certainty, the word 'fact' is best discarded altogether. What is important are information streams, for only these can give us data with sufficient metadata to ascertain the correctness of reports of past reality. If a fact cannot be understood as the consequence of an information stream, its 'factual' status is in doubt and it is a historical prejudgement to call it a fact.

ARCHIVAL INTEGRITY

It needs to be remembered that, with regard to the deaths of Edward II, Thomas of Woodstock and Richard II, we can only shift to a position of information-based certainty because life and death are polar opposites: they are not relative concepts. Certainty in each case is achieved through undermining the opposite point of view. As Karl Popper argued with regard to scientific discoveries, it is falsification of the antithesis which leads to certainty.[56] Just as mathematicians may prove one theorem by proving the alternative false, so historians may proceed to certainty by discrediting the information underlying one of two opposing narratives.

This general principle of disproving alternatives has an important spin-off in respect to historical certainty. Indeed, historians use it regularly without realizing, for, like document genesis, it too has 'proved deeply resistant to theorisation'. It concerns the *lack* of evidence for a contrary narrative. Consider once more the example of the relationship between Richard II and Henry of Lancaster in the 1390s. It was remarked above that the evidence for the rift between the two men lies in the *absence* of evidence for the substantial gifts and appointments which Henry could normally have expected to receive, if he was on good terms with the king. Because the sequences of the Patent Rolls, Close Rolls, Fine Rolls and Charter Rolls for this period are archivally intact and retain their original order (stitched together, chancery-style), we may use document genesis to demonstrate a negative. Although we are actually studying an absence of evidence, that very absence amounts to positive information. It also has absolute integrity. Hence we may say that it is an archival certainty that no substantial gifts or appointments to positions of trust and authority to Henry of Lancaster were made, prior to his dukedom in 1397.

This is not open to question or doubt. The only possible error lies in the idea that the record of a grant has been cut from the rolls prior to the texts being stitched and numbered, or omitted in the compilation of the roll. But if a grant or appointment *had* been made, and cut or omitted from the rolls, we would expect the nature of the grant still to be reflected in Henry's title in later documents. As these complementary archival series also retain their integrity, the theoretical possibility that the evidence is only partial is ruled out. Although we cannot describe with certainty the nature or extent of the rivalry between Richard II and Henry IV, we can *prove* that Henry was not the beneficiary of any substantial grants from the king which compare with those to other members of the royal family and Richard's friends (with the highly dubious exception of his ducal title, which was soon confiscated). Finally, it is worth observing that such historical certainties, once discovered, are likely to have permanent epistemological value. Only by the destruction of the records in whole or in part, and thus the creation of new epistemological doubts through the destruction of the integrity of the series, could this certainty be undermined.

The above is obvious to all practising historians. What is less obvious is the intellectual defence it offers against some of the charges of postmodernism. Postmodernists concentrated on criticizing historians for the *positive* statements they made about the past, not the negative ones. If one considers negative evidence, then Hayden White's statement that 'the number of details identifiable in any singular event is potentially infinite' should be balanced with the statement that the number of details *absent* in any singular event is also potentially infinite.[57] If archival integrity is seen as the bounds of these 'potentially infinite' details, then the negative evidence it presents historians may allow them to say many things *for certain*.

OBJECTIVITY AND INFORMATION

As Collingwood, Carr, Thompson and Wilson all agree, the writing of history is a product of the relationship between historians and their sources. Whether this is described as a 'dialogue between the past and the present' (as Carr would have it) or a 'dialogue between concept and reality' (Thompson), it amounts to a dialogue or relationship of some sort. On one side are present-day historians, with their concepts, learning, experiences and subjective impulses and insights, which include the desire to find out something about the human past. On the other are the vestiges of that human past: archaeological, archival and bibliographical certainties. Common to both, and linking them, is space-time: the geographic or spatial layout in which events took place, and the central axis of time itself, with its implicit chronological integrity.

Both sides of this relationship afford a limited measure of certainty. With regard to present-day historians, reflexivity and 'concept criticism' allow the form of certainty which is simply the realization that we have been wrong about something. The principle of objective inconsistencies – the implication that one of two or more conflicting understandings of an aspect of the past must be flawed in some respect – embodies a similar realization of the incorrectness of a concept. With regard to the evidence side of the 'dialogue', the existence of so many archaeological and archival certainties allows the historian at a social and cultural level to make general statements which are grounded in the reality of the past, through the process of describing the archaeological certainties themselves or describing the process whereby a document came to be created. In addition, and most significantly with regard to narrative history, it is sometimes possible to determine whether there is a reliable information basis for an event or not. Where this relates to a non-relatively defined event, certainty might be possible by proving a false opposite. Finally, one may be certain about some things which did not happen by demonstrating the lack of evidence in a series of documents which retain their archival integrity.

In narrative history, the perception of an objective inconsistency encourages the scrupulous historian to return to first principles, to throw off all preconceptions of interpretation, and to test all the evidence which might have led to that inconsistency. If it is found to be based on false or dubious information, and if its antithesis is found to be based on a first-hand account, then he or she has no option but to re-investigate previous understandings to see whether the objective inconsistency can be resolved. If it can be, then revisionism is bound to result. The discredited status quo is not an option.

The implications of this stance are many and far-reaching. With regard to narrative history, the opportunities to be certain about highly complicated questions are limited only by historians' ability to recover and test the information linkages between the witnesses of an event, those witnesses' biases, and the creation of archival certainties. In some cases this can be done at a purely theoretical level. One such case is the supposed rape of the countess of Salisbury by Edward III. Traditionally historians have regarded the story as propaganda and inherently improbable. Using the information-based method outlined above, we can go much further towards disproving it, observing that the elements which make up the story cannot have been assimilated by any one witness.[58] Therefore we may be certain that it is a concoction of stories which have either been artificially threaded together at a later date to form a single narrative (if they have any basis in reality) or fabricated, in part at least, by non-witnesses.

Even more far-reaching, however, are the theoretical implications with relation to the postmodern criticism that the past can be 'infinitely re-described'. As I have written elsewhere,

> To understand this, one needs to understand something about what 'infinitely re-described' actually means. As Georg Cantor pointed out in the nineteenth century, there is no one 'infinity' as such. There are big 'infinite' sets and small ones. A big infinite set is one on an axis stretching away from zero. Between the numbers one and two in that set there is a smaller infinite set of numbers, all the possible fractions. Similarly between 1.1 and 1.2 there is a yet smaller infinite set of numbers. There is an infinite set between 3.1415926 and 3.1415927; the number π lies in this range. If all we knew about π was that it lay between these two numbers, it would be true to say that it may be 'infinitely re-described' as a number in this range, but the actual room for variation is relatively small. The implications for readings of history are obvious. If there are some things which are archaeologically and archivally certain, and by implication some things which are historically certain, these certainties impose limitations on how big each set of infinite re-descriptions can be. The potential for re-describing them is 'infinite' only if the variations themselves are infinitesimally small. What Hayden White and his followers have done in suggesting the potential for an infinite set of re-descriptions of the past is to confuse an infinite set of infinitesimally small variations with an infinite set of substantial variations. To put it another way: if the past can be 'infinitely re-described', it is only in that sense in which Beethoven's Ninth Symphony can be infinitely re-interpreted: no two professional performances are identical but they are all recognisably similar, for the score remains essentially the same.[59]

The implication is that any single certainty in history – no matter how small – limits the possible re-descriptions of the past. As the mere existence of temporally located objects, documents and books can be regarded as archaeological, archival and bibliographical certainties, every single datable object limits the significance of each 'infinite' set of possible re-descriptions, forcing the variations to become smaller and smaller.

The above is only half of the argument against the 'infinite re-descriptions' theory. It is only the 'can say' half; there is also the 'cannot say'. Just as every single archival and historical certainty constrains the 'infinite' set of re-descriptions, and each additional certainty diminishes the significance of each possible re-description, so too each additional certainty enlarges the range of negatives we can say about the past. For example, if we know that Edward III was at York on a Wednesday, then demonstrating that he was at Doncaster on the Friday limits the number of places where he was on Thursday. At the same time it massively *increases* the number of places where we can say he was not present – he could not have been in London, for example, or anywhere more than one day's ride from York or Doncaster.[60] In this way we expand the infinite sets of things which we can be certain did not take place, which, due to the nature of human activity, is always going to be far larger than the infinite set of things which possibly did.

This duality of 'infinite' sets – neither of which is conceptually valid without the other – means that the more certain we are about the past, the more we can shrink the significance of possible alternative narratives and the more we can be certain of what did *not* happen, and by implication, what did. The whole process theoretically tends to the point at which differences in accounts of the past are of a non-empirical nature, arising from the particular interests, ideology, character, prejudices, language, literary skill, social environment and perceived readership of each individual historian.

CONCLUSION

Historical methodology has undergone a series of Kuhnian paradigm shifts over the last two hundred years. It has gone from 'scissors-and-paste' history (in which 'facts' can supposedly be selected from evidence) to source criticism (in which 'facts' can be deduced from evidence) to the more advanced thinking of Collingwood's final years, which in turn led to Wilson's 'document genesis' (in which 'facts' can be deduced through studying the creation of the evidence). Finally we have come to this new suggested paradigm, in which the 'facts' themselves are seen as two-dimensional and artificial; and in instances of doubt they need to be set aside in favour of information streams that take account of the genesis, genealogy and integrity of the information underlying the evidence. Over more or less the same period, the conceptual side of the 'dialogue' has seen moral and social ideology replaced by objectivity. It has seen objectivity forced to compromise with historical subjectivity, ultimately leading to the principle of objective inconsistencies (as laid out above), or the positive benefits of identifying conceptual error. The whole amounts to a double revolution: on the evidence side we may prove or disprove details of historical information on information-based grounds (where before we simply had to trust the evidence, or not, as we chose). And on the concept side we have shifted equally radically, from the view that unsatisfactory and problematic sources can simply be laid aside, to the opposite position, wherein unsatisfactory and problematic sources must be accounted for, as they otherwise might lead to objective inconsistencies and a demonstrably flawed view of the past.

Given that this in itself represents a change of epistemological stances, how can we be sure that the philosophy of history that this chapter represents will lead to any lasting empirical certainty? The answer is straightforward: tools may become outdated but that does not mean the workmanship becomes worthless. Indeed, very many 'facts' determined by scissors-and-paste techniques are still both theoretically acceptable and widely accepted, as are many conclusions of source criticism and document genesis. As Wilson has remarked in describing his three 'hermeneutic stances', each successive hermeneutic stance embodies the others.[61] The same is true of this fourth 'hermeneutic stance', or information-based approach: it embodies document generation. It is simply a more rigorous approach than the earlier methods. Moreover we can be sure that this information-based method is the end of the line, for it permits the history of the information to be conceptualized and traced all the way back to the genesis of the information, and thus to the event itself. It is the theoretical final link between the present-day historical question and the reality of the past.

It would be nice to end on that positive note but reality must intervene. The first and most obvious problem is that certainty is not achievable with respect to all the specific questions we might want to ask. For instance, it is not possible to say Edward II did not commit an act of sodomy. All we can do is demonstrate that the sodomitical reputation he acquired was not directly related to him. Likewise we cannot describe with certainty the nature or extent of the rivalry between Richard II and Henry IV; we can be certain only of the fact that Henry was not the beneficiary of any substantial grants from the king which compare with those to other members of the royal family. The key point is that it is not the event itself (in these cases, the sodomy or the rivalry) which we are testing but the information relating to it and its outcomes. With regard to the 'death' of Edward II, what is *certain* is the correlation of several information streams consistent with the survival, and the unreliability of the sole information stream consistent with the death, not the survival itself. Likewise, with regard to the murder of Thomas of Woodstock: it is the correlation of several information streams consistent with the murder that is *certain*, not the murder itself. Having said that, it is worth remarking that the possibility that these certainties do not amount to proof is only theoretical: the identifiable information streams to the contrary have been shown to be weak and unreliable in both cases.

There is a second, more subtle reason why the quest for certainty remains problematic. Advanced historical methods allow historians to see the path which leads to the top of the mountain but ironically they make it harder for them to reach the top. Not only is the path often incomplete, requiring difficult leaps which not all can (or will) make, the higher one ascends, the more one is starved of the oxygen of public support. This is not just a matter of the intellectual capacity of the general reader. There is a natural inclination to be suspicious of the motives of anyone who tackles a particularly difficult question for the sake of a single fact. Readers suspect that the quest for the truth is actually a cover for a desire for publicity – whether the true object of desire be book sales or an ideological pursuit. Accordingly they may refuse to follow 'the path' or argument because they are suspicious as to why the historian is seeking certainty in the first place. It is hugely ironic that the very reasons why historians might want to reach positions of certainty are not resolved by actually reaching those positions, for the very fact of success raises questions over their ideology and motives. History therefore has its own 'Uncertainty Principle' (*pace* Heisenberg) in that the more a historian tries to prove something, the more unlikely it is that that proof will be widely accepted.

Fortunately not all positions of certainty are difficult to achieve. Many straightforward archival and bibliographical certainties can be taken at face value. All have an impact upon the limits of re-description: the ever-expanding infinite sets of what we can demonstrate did *not* happen and the ever-shrinking infinite sets of possible variations on what we might suggest did. Thus one can have no doubt that empirical history has its place, and that the vast bulk of factual analysis has lasting epistemological value (for it never will be revised, being grounded in reality, even if it is theoretically doubtful). Furthermore, if any of these 'straightforward archival and bibliographical certainties' turn out to be not-so-straightforward, and give rise to an objective inconsistency, then their veracity can be subjected to the full-blown process of a return to first principles, followed by a series of checks on the genesis, genealogy and integrity of every relevant piece of information. The endeavour only fails when there are insufficient archaeological and archival certainties to permit the historian to distinguish between legend and fact.

History may be 'doubtful' in many respects, but it is also 'certainty-full' too. If the questions which reveal doubt about the past are valid, then so too are those which reveal certainty. As will be discussed below (in Chapter 4), this is not a return to nineteenth-century Positivism but a limited positivism which exposes the dreaminess of the misleading statement that the past may be 'infinitely re-described'. What has been discussed here are simply the foundations of historical narrative, the things which (as Carr put it) 'the historian must not get wrong'.[62] Historians will continue to redefine and re-describe the human past for as long as there are people, and their subjective experiences, language, ideologies, delights, fears, moral outlook, curiosity and audiences will all continue to affect their interpretations and explanations of the past in much the same way that our experiences affect our interpretations and explanations. What we create cannot help but be an art, if we seek to go beyond the limits of scientifically deduced facts. If it is great art, it will have lasting value, on account of its human understanding and its inspirational and literary qualities. But if we wish to ground such a historical art in the reality of the past, then the information basis of our work must also be open to scientific examination and testing. This is also achievable. Through the systematic application of the principle of objective inconsistencies on the one hand and the application of information-based methods on the other, we can advance on existing methodologies and make historical pronouncements which are certain and which defy 'the greatest undermining epistemological force in history writing' – namely, the future.

Notes

1 For example, the feuds between Froude and Freeman, and Acton and Creighton, and many others in Kenyon, *The History Men*, esp. 122–4, 138–40.

2 See the contrast drawn by Carr between Acton's faith in 'ultimate history' in 1907 and George Clark's view in 1957, that 'historians of a later generation do not look forward to any such prospect. They expect their work to be superseded again and again.' Carr, *What is History?*, 7–8.

3 Hawking, *A Brief History of Time*, 11.

4 See for example, Stephen Haber, 'Anything goes'.

5 With regard to the lack of consideration of the public in the postmodern debate, see Mortimer, 'What isn't history?'.

6 Jenkins, *Postmodern History Reader*, 158. The term 'fetishises documents' appears in *Re-thinking History*, 58. It echoes Carr's reference to Victorians' 'fetishism' of facts and documents (*What is History?*, 16).

7 Champion, 'What are historians for?', 182.

8 Mortimer, 'What isn't history?', 472.

9 Carr, 21–2; Wilson, 'Foundations', 294 (referring to Thompson, *The Poverty of Theory*, 231, 236).

10 *Re-thinking History*, 77.

11 Carr, *What is History?*, 21.

12 Carr, *What is History?*, 30

13 'Foundations'.

14 'Foundations', 305.

15 'Foundations', 303–4; Wilson, 'Collingwood's forgotten historiographic revolution', 55–6.

16 Wilson, 'Foundations', 305.

17 Wilson, 'Foundations', 315.

18 Wilson, 'Foundations', 314.

19 See Mortimer, *The Dying and the Doctors*.

20 *PROME*, Henry IV, 1399 October, quoting the National Archives C 65/62.

21 *Historia Anglicana*, i, 419–24.

22 There is a commission suggesting that an outrage of some kind took place. See Richard Barber, 'Arundel, Sir John (*c.* 1348–79), *ODNB* (2004).

23 Given-Wilson, 'Royal Charter Witness Lists', 35–93.

24 *Fears*, 8–12.

25 Tosh, *The Pursuit of History*, 79.

26 Bates, Crick and Hamilton (eds), *Writing Medieval Biography 750–1250*, 8; Harriss, *Cardinal Beaufort*, v.

27 J. H. Plumb, 'History and biography', quoted in Tosh, *Pursuit*, 81; Eric Homberger, *THES* (9 October 1987), 11, quoted in Harriss, *Cardinal Beaufort*, v.

28 I am thinking here predominantly of the 2003 conference leading to *Writing Medieval Biography*; and Blanning and Cannadine (eds), *History and Biography: Essays in Honour of Derek Beales*, following Beales's own *History and Biography*.

29 *Writing Medieval Biography*, 11.

30 *Writing Medieval Biography*, 16.

31 Stafford, 'Writing the biography of eleventh century queens', 109.

32 For example, Goodman, *Loyal Conspiracy*, 52, states that at this time Richard was 'cultivating' Henry. Saul, *Richard II*, 203, states that the gift of the breastplate 'marked the growth of a warmer and more intimate relationship between them'.

33 *Fears*, 56.

34 The only exception is an instance when Henry was appointed to an embassy led by his father in 1384, when he was still only eighteen. It needs to be remembered that this appointment was the council's decision.

35 *Fears*, 82–3.

36 *PROME*, 1399 October, section 53 ('The bill of the duke of Hereford against the duke of Norfolk').

37 Carr, What is History?, 8, quoting Clark; Evans, *In Defence of History*, 3; Appleby, Hunt and Jacob, *Telling the Truth about History*, 254.

38 For example, W. H. Walsh stated that 'we might attempt to maintain not only that historians are influenced by subjective factors, but that they must be'. Walsh, *An Introduction to Philosophy of History*, 20.

39 Evans, *Defence*, 249. The italics are mine.

40 Evans states 'for my own part I remain optimistic that objective historical knowledge is both desirable and attainable'. See Evans, *Defence*, 252.

41 Carr, who disregarded objective truth (which Elton later held to), declined to use the word sympathy on account of his belief that it implied agreement with those studied. He preferred 'imaginative understanding'. See Carr, *What is History?*, 24.

42 Wilson and Ashplant, 'Whig history', 15.

43 Elton, paraphrased in Evans, *Defence*, 75.

44 Kuhn, *The Structure of Scientific Revolutions*, chapter 12, esp. 151.

45 For the concept of the practical past, see Oakeshott, *On History and Other Essays*, 1–44; White, 'Public relevance', 334. For history as 'the work of historians', see Mortimer, 'What isn't history?', 457–60.

46 Appleby, Hunt and Jacob, *Telling the Truth*, 255.

47 White, *Metahistory*, 433.

48 Mortimer, 'What isn't history?', 468.

49 Strohm, *Hochon's Arrow*, 33.

50 Ormrod, 'The sexualities of Edward II'; Strohm, *Hochon's Arrow*, 33–56.

51 White argues in *Figural Realism*, 71, that 'any attempt to provide an objective account of the event, either by breaking it up into a mass of its details, or by setting it within its context, must conjure with two circumstances: one is that the number of details identifiable in any singular event is potentially infinite; and the other is that the context of any singular event is infinitely extensive or at least is not objectively determinable'. In this particular instance we may note that this is to mistake the complexity of describing some events (e.g. why the Peasants' Revolt 'failed') with the relative simplicity of others, e.g. when and where a man died and what was the physical cause. A second criticism of this stance appears later in the text.

52 Evans, *Defence*, 75.

53 Carr, *What is History?*, 12.

54 Evans, *Defence*, 79.

55 Hence Evans is mistaken when he declares that '[Hayden] White is wrong to imply that historiographical consensus about any event in the past is difficult to achieve and is always open to revision from another perspective, if he means that future historians will start to say that the Stalybridge Wakes did not take place in 1850, or that there were no gingerbread salesmen there . . . or make some other factual assertion of this kind. Only if new evidence is found to amend or cast doubt on the historian's account of a fact – as in the case of the gingerbread seller's death at the Stalybridge Wakes – does the revision at this level take place.' See Evans, *Defence*, 79.

56 Kuhn, *Struture*, 146, quoting Karl R. Popper, *The Logic of Scientific Discovery* (1959), chapters 1–4.

57 White, *Figural Realism*, 71.

58 Mortimer, *Perfect King*, 91–8.

59 Mortimer, 'What isn't history?', 468–9.

60 To be exact, at twilight on Thursday he had to be within one day's ride of Doncaster, which in Spring (for example) is a maximum of about 30 miles for a king. However, he cannot have been on the far side of Doncaster from York, as he did not leave there (33 miles away) until the previous day. Presuming he could have travelled all 33 miles in one day, but that this was his maximum, and that we are actually describing a potential of three whole days of daylight (Wednesday, Thursday and Friday), we may be sure that he was within approximately a day's travel of a point on a line between York and Doncaster. This is a total area of $2r^2 + \pi r^2$ where r = the maximum of one day's travel, in this case 33 miles. The result, 5,600 square miles, is considerably smaller than the 30,791 square miles of space he could have travelled to or through (excluding rivers and other physical barriers), had we not been able to place him at Doncaster. And of course the far larger area in which he

could *not* have visited (the rest of the world) is made even larger by this one piece of information.

61 Wilson, 'Foundations', 307–9; Wilson, 'Collingwood's forgotten historiographical revolution', 56.

62 Carr, *What is History?*, 10.

2

Sermons of sodomy:
a reconsideration of Edward II's sodomitical reputation[*]

Those who have dealt with the reputation of Edward II's sexuality constitute a whole spectrum of historical commentators. Arguably the least-informed element of that spectrum is composed of those who presume Edward II may be taken as a gay icon, representing the king as a homosexual in order to reinforce arguments about homosexuality in society. Another band consists of those who objectively classify the king as a homosexual in an attempt historically to understand fourteenth-century homosexual identities, presuming that such identities existed. Another consists of those who present Edward II's sexual inclinations in a genuine attempt to understand the personality politics of the fourteenth century. And at the highest end of the spectrum we find a narrow band of writers who are careful about making presumptions about Edward II's personal sexual inclinations but who nevertheless realize that contemporary perceptions of Edward's relationships are of crucial importance to an understanding of the reign, and that the possible homosexual connotations of his acts cannot be ignored. Without any doubt, Mark Ormrod's essay, 'The sexualities of Edward II', takes pride of place among such analyses.[1]

As Ormrod shows, there are many methodological parameters to the debate. If one strips out the extraneous arguments concerning the modern politicized understandings of homosexuality, similarly setting aside the presumptions

---

[*] This essay was first published in Gwilym Dodd and Anthony Musson (eds), *The Reign of Edward II: New Perspectives* (York Medieval Press, 2006), 48–60. In that volume it immediately followed Mark Ormrod's essay, 'The sexualities of Edward II', to which it makes several references. It has only been altered in so much as it may now be read as a stand-alone piece and its conventions and layout conform with the rest of this volume.

about a repressed homosexual identity in medieval society, one may return to the core evidence and interpret it in the light of what we know about medieval approaches to sexuality generally. This permits a deconstruction of the evidence for Edward II's 'sexuality', the whole complex question being broken down into its constituent elements: his emotional dependence on his favourites, his reputation as a sodomite, immorality and the perceived 'degeneracy' of his behaviour. In this way we may distinguish a number of behavioural aspects which, although they may not have endangered a politically unimportant man, certainly compromised the standing of a man whose political importance was absolute.

In adopting a gendered approach to the evidence for Edward II's supposed sodomy, however, Ormrod presents a cultural context to the accusations of sodomy as opposed to the more usual political one. This raises some important questions, most obvious of which is the implication of the last point in the preceeding passage: to what extent were references to Edward's degeneracy a symptom of inadequacy as a king as opposed to inadequacy as a man? Had Edward been a middling sort, say a knight, would any chronicler have focused on his manly shortcomings? In all probablity his 'degenerate' behaviour would not have been cause for attention unless he had become politically important. Hence, when Ormrod writes that 'a failure to conform to "kind" was sometimes observed or articulated as a decline from the masculine to the feminine' it is very important to bear in mind that in Edward II's case 'conforming to "kind" meant conforming to expectations of kingship, not just expectations of manliness.[2] This is important, for if we may distinguish between behaviour which is universally 'degenerate' and behaviour which is simply a sign of 'degeneracy' in a king, we may well ask whether the accusations of degeneracy are indicative of political dissent alone or truly indicative of behaviour which would universally be recognized as degenerate.

In trying to answer this question we need to consider the evidence in its precise political context as well as the cultural framework of fourteenth-century society. In particular we must investigate the information sources for the chroniclers' statements. At first sight this seems impossible, and indeed is a process rarely embarked upon for the simple reason that there is normally insufficient data for there to be any confidence in the conclusions. However, in certain circumstances, when dealing with a specific research question relating to a particular event or individual, it is worth pursuing an information-based approach if only because of the possibility that what was once thought to be a general rumour has a limited and specific – if not unique – source. If that source has an identifiable political motive, then through information-related techniques we may gradually broaden our understanding of how certain stories might have originated. Therefore the following suggestions are made not with a view to their undermining Ormrod's conclusions and stamping another set of views on his but for the purpose of identifying a possible alternative origin for the accusation of sodomy, which would permit different conclusions to be reached about the origins and circulation of the story that Edward was a sodomite.

As Ormrod makes clear, the accusation of 'sodomy' is not one without its complications. Scholars have tended to tiptoe around the difficult subject of its literal male-male-intercourse implications, preferring a non-sexual understanding. Ormrod is bolder, and justifies his boldness through correlating the accusations of sodomy with the supposed 'anal rape' form of murder of the king in 1327. In his words:

> If the disturbing eroticism of the murder story is acknowledged, and if the narrative is taken in itself as the principal articulation of a contemporary discourse about Edward II's sexuality, then it is no longer necessary or valid to hide behind the suggestion that the general charge of sodomy made against Edward II at and after his deposition did not include or imply his participation in male-male penetrative sex.[3]

Therefore, in applying the methodology outlined in the previous paragraph, we need to investigate the evidence underpinning the two narratives which Ormrod suggests correlate: the accusation of sodomy and the 'anal rape' narrative.

THE ACCUSATION OF SODOMY

There are many allusions to Edward's abnormal behaviour dating from before 1326, and several important expressions of disquiet at the personal aspects of his rule, from as early as 1312 (in the case of the *Vita Edwardi Secundi*); but the earliest specific accusation that Edward was a sodomite appears in a sermon preached by Adam of Orleton, Bishop of Hereford, at Oxford in October 1326. To be precise, in 1334 Orleton was accused by John Prickehare, a Winchester cleric, of a number of crimes connected with the fall of Edward II, including that at Oxford he had preached that Edward was a 'tyrant and a sodomite' (*tyrannus et sodomita*), his motive being 'to subvert the status of Edward II'.[4] The same source states that he repeated this accusation at Wallingford in December 1326.

This evidence is interesting for a number of reasons. The most obvious is that the first accusation of Edward being a sodomite dates from before his capture, and therefore before Mortimer, Isabella and their fellow invaders knew whether they would be in a position to depose him. This removes the political accusation from the deposition process of 1327 and firmly places it, as R. M. Haines has said, in the context of publicizing the case that it was 'lawful to rebel' against the king.[5] But more importantly we may observe that in April 1334 – seven and a half years after after the Oxford sermon – Orleton was still specifically associated with the 'tyranny and sodomy' accusation against Edward. Nor, in his defence, did he deny that he had said these things; rather, he claimed that he was innocent of defaming Edward III's father on the grounds that he had meant Despenser (not the king) was a tyrant and a sodomite (in which light we have to note that John de Shordich, one of Edward III's most trusted enforcers, was present and a witness to all that was said).[6] In addition the sermon was preached as the word of God to 'copious multitudes' on each occasion, including 'knights and other vassals of the king'. As a result we can see that a key agent – if not the sole one – in overtly publicizing the idea that Edward was a sodomite, or confirming public speculation on the matter, was Bishop Orleton, and his means of publicizing this information was a sermon.

The foregoing postulation – that Orleton was the original source for the public idea that Edward was a sodomite – is important. In the second of these sermons, preached in December 1326, at Wallingford, Orleton also preached that the reason Isabella would not go near her husband was because he was prepared to kill her if she came near him, and that he carried in his shoe a knife specially for this purpose; and if he did not have his knife with him he would strangle her.[7] This story also appears in the passage preceding the 'anal rape' account of the death in the longer continuations of the French *Brut* chronicle.[8] As Orleton's defence on this point was that he had first heard this in the presence of the archbishop of Canterbury, and so believed it at the time, it would appear that Orleton's sermon was the original source of the public story that Isabella feared to go near her husband. Further support for this lies in the fact that this story too was specifically associated with Orleton in 1334, seven years later. This shows that the author of the longer continuation of the *Brut* was the direct or indirect recipient of information from the second sermon at Wallingford in 1326, and thus also the recipient of the news of the accusation that Edward was a tyrant and a sodomite. As the longer continuation of the *Brut* is the earliest reference to the 'anal rape' form of murder, the latter cannot be said to be independent evidence of the sexual nature of the previous accusation of sodomy. It does not clarify what Orleton meant in 1326, and may have been pure conjecture imagined by someone in the wake of hearing the accusation of sodomy. In connection with this, it is important to remember that the actual narrative of the 'anal rape' murder has not one but several precedents in the various thirteenth-century chronicle accounts of the death of Edmund Ironside.[9]

The origin of the story that Edward II was a sodomite is only one aspect which we need to consider. We also need to examine the impact of such accusations, and the cultural framework within which accusations of sodomy had previously been made. Although there were many similar accusations in the fourteenth century with political overtones, few compare with those brought against a king. However, if we focus on Orleton as the key mover or principal instigator of the accusation of sodomy, two are immediately important. The first is the accusation of sodomy brought against Pope Boniface VIII in 1303 and the second the charges brought against the Templars in 1308. As is well known, the prime mover behind both of these accusations was Guillaume de Nogaret, chief minister of Philip the Fair. As with the accusations against Edward II, they were highly political accusations brought at key points in the moral destruction of their subjects. They were both, like the accusations against Edward II, anonymous, in that they were accusations of 'sodomy' or being a 'sodomite'; they were not accusations of sodomy with someone in particular. They were thus accusations of a subversive or immoral tendency as opposed to a specific illegal event. Obviously de Nogaret's authorship allows us to connect the two earlier accusations, but the later of these also may be connected with Orleton. Orleton travelled five times to Avignon between 1307 and 1317, spending six years out of the kingdom in that period.[10] He would thus have been at Avignon around the time that de Nogaret formulated his accusations against the Templars. He was constantly at Avignon from March 1314 to May 1317, and so very familiar by the end of this period with the politics of the papal court. In particular, in 1311 he was responsible for making arrangements for the English delegation to the Council of Vienne, at which the sodomy accusations against the Templars were again aired. It is perhaps in the cultural context of these political accusations of sodomy, brought against politically powerful men with religious or divine as well as secular responsibilities, that we should understand the accusations brought against Edward II in 1326. Lastly, it is not without significance that de Nogaret's accusation against Pope Boniface was brought with the specific intention of deposing him. The pope was seized by de Nogaret and Cardinal Colonna, and probably would have been deposed had he not died first.

Summing up this appreciation of the 1326 accusation of sodomy, we may say that there are precedents of which Orleton was undoubtedly aware for the political accusation of sodomy in connection with the moral destruction and deposition of those in positions of political and religious authority. He would appear to have used these precedents to undermine the moral integrity of the king in two sermons in 1326. The impact of his sermons seems to have been profound and widespread. Elements were repeated in a chronicle seven years later, and the year after that Orleton was still specifically associated with spreading the accusation that Edward II was a sodomite. After the sermons of 1326 it would appear probable that Edward II's sexual 'offence' become a subject for discussion and elaboration, and may have contributed to the association of his supposed death in Berkeley Castle with the anal rape story told earlier in connection with Edmund Ironside. By the time of the writing of the Meaux chronicle (1390s),[11] the story had become accepted in some recollections of Edward II's reign, giving rise to the idea that Edward had given himself over 'too much to the vice of sodomy'.[12] It is therefore possible that the popular idea that Edward II engaged in sodomitical acts was entirely and exclusively due to the sermons which Adam of Orleton preached in 1326.

THE ANAL RAPE NARRATIVE

The only evidence we have which suggests that the above is an under-estimate of the strength of popular belief in the period 1326–34 that Edward engaged in sodomitical acts is the story of Edward's murder in an overtly sexual manner: through a metal item inserted into his rectum. Ormrod argues that this should also be considered evidence of a popular understanding that Edward indulged in sodomy. Although the anal rape death was not exclusively associated with Edward, its archetypal character dating from the thirteenth century does not undermine Ormrod's case, for its sexualized nature (if we accept it as such) may be considered a commentary on Edward II at the time of the announcement of his death (less than a year after Orleton's first sermon on his sodomy). Therefore we must turn our attention to the anal rape narrative, to see whether it was indeed common, and whether it could have developed within the information stream initiated by Orleton's sermon or whether it displays characteristics independent of Orleton's propaganda statements.

Original contributions to the chronicle tradition which deal with the death of Edward II begin with accounts written very soon after the event. The principal texts to mention the death are summarized in the appendix to this chapter. Nine of the twenty-one descriptions either express doubt about the murder or simply state that Edward II 'died' in Berkeley Castle. Taken at face value, this would not strongly support the idea that Edward II's anal rape death was a widespread rumour. However, this is a simplistic appreciation of the evidence. Some of the above chronicles are very rare, and express only a single viewpoint, while others are known from dozens of manuscripts and express a wide variety of viewpoints. The latter tend also to be dispersed, in that they reflect views of different times and places. Lastly, the various chronicles represented here are spread across seventy years, and therefore do not all have the same connection in time to the rumours of c.1327–40. A more particular appreciation is necessary.

The shorter *Brut* continuation is probably the earliest unofficial record of the death, being 'composed close to the events it describes'.[13] The editors of the version which has become known as the *Anonimalle Chronicle* suggest that the original continuation text was started in London and came to York as a result of the removal of the government offices there, probably in 1332.[14] This would be consistent with the *Anonimalle Chronicle* giving the correct but rare date of burial (20 December), also noted by the annalist of St Paul's. In addition, since the cause of death is given as illness, it is probable that this passage was composed in its original form before the trial of Roger Mortimer in late 1330, whose crimes were said to have included the murder of the ex-king, and which every Londoner and royal clerk at York in 1332 would have known. Thus it almost certainly predates the information 'threshold' of November 1330, when the official cause of Edward II's death (as circulated by the king) was altered from natural causes to murder.

The importance of the shorter *Brut* continuation in the present context is that it is a lay chronicle, written in French. It is very interesting that the copyist of the version known as the *Anonimalle*, who was very probably based at York and possibly involved with royal administration, was not disposed in 1333 to follow Edward III's pronouncements of 1330 and to revise the cause of death from one of illness to one of murder. This is even more important when one realizes the extent to which he revised and greatly added to other portions of the text; in other words, the integrity of the original was not a sufficient reason *not* to revise the text. As a result, the *Anonimalle* might be said to reflect a belief that the king died of natural causes which was current in London before 1330 and current – or at least not sufficiently doubted to warrant a major revision – at York in or not long after 1333.[15] The same may be said for the copyists of several other British Library manuscripts, which stick to the story that Edward died of natural causes, while bearing other variations.[16] Some copyists of the shorter *Brut* did update their manuscripts, but the majority did not.[17] Therefore, wherever they were around the country, and whenever they were writing, the majority were not confident that they knew the circumstances of Edward II's death better than that he died of an illness. None repeat Archbishop Melton's pronouncement in 1327 that he had died of a 'fall' (which perhaps is odd, considering this was also information circulating around York).[18] In this light it is worth noting that some other authors who used manuscripts of the shorter *Brut* – for example Thomas Gray, the Lanercost author and the Bridlington author – express doubts about the nature of his death. Clearly the Bridlington author saw a shorter *Brut* continuation or similar chronicle – perhaps a longer *Brut* continuation – with a violent and explicit death narrative and refused to believe it. On the strength of these accounts it would appear that the 'anal rape' narrative of Edward II's death would appear not to have been in circulation much before the completion of the longer *Brut* continuation in the mid-1330s, and was treated with scepticism in those places where it was received after that, at least until the circulation of the popular second redaction of Higden's *Polychronicon* in the 1340s.

The circulation of those accounts which became most popular in the fourteenth century – the longer *Brut* continuation and Higden's *Polychronicon* – would thus appear to be important media through which the story of the anal rape took hold. Both of these are known from hundreds of manuscripts, about 160–170 of each being known. Being specific as to the cause of death, they had much influence on other versions. Coupled with the chronicle of Murimuth (whose account has much by way of detail on the king's captivity), they account for almost every statement regarding the death by every later chronicler. In addition, the *Polychronicon* has no detail which can be said to be 'original', rather it is its wording which is most 'original', being very brief and mentioning an iron implement, like the *Historia Aurea*, rather than a copper one, like the longer *Brut*. It appears that most later anal rape narratives are literary quotations from one or both of these two influential chronicles (the *Brut* and the *Polychronicon*), sometimes used in conjunction with the suffocation element drawn from Murimuth's account. Finally, although Murimuth records that it was 'popularly' (*vulgariter*) said that Maltravers and Gurney killed the king – supporting the notion that the longer *Brut* continuation supports a general rumour – he himself ascribes their method to suffocation, thereby questioning how widespread was the anal rape narrative in 1337 (the date of the first redaction of his chronicle).

As a result of the foregoing discussion, it seems that the rumour of the anal rape narrative of Edward II's death was slow to form and late to become widely accepted, and only became established through the popularity of two very influential chronicles, both written after 1333. Many of those writing or copying texts in the 1330s did not accept the version of events in the longer *Brut*; many did not even accept that the king had been murdered. Only the gradual demise of this generation left the way clear for the anal rape story to become established as the most widely accepted narrative concerning the death.

CONCLUSIONS

Drawing together the strands of the argument which have been separately examined, it emerges that both information streams for the sodomitical reputation of Edward II were very narrowly based in the years before 1340. The accusation that Edward II was a sodomite was sufficiently narrowly-based in 1326–34 for it to be closely if not uniquely associated with Orleton and his two sermons, during which time we may safely presume that this information was not common knowledge (except in connection with Orleton's sermons). The rumour that Edward II had died from an anal rape torture was sufficiently narrowly based in the period 1332–9 for every author and copyist except those working on the longer *Brut* to assign the death to natural causes or some other form of murder. Furthermore, the second narrowly based tradition almost certainly arises within the context of the first, as shown by the longer *Brut* continuator's repetition of Orleton's statements about Queen Isabella's reluctance to see her husband in

1326. All this together suggests a propaganda origin for the accusation, based on de Nogaret's charges against Pope Boniface VIII and the Templars, repeated by Orleton and then adapted by the informant of the continuator of the longer *Brut*, perhaps to accentuate the duplicity of Isabella and to accentuate the victimization and suffering of Edward II. Obviously the link between the accusation and the method of murder remains a loose one, but one thing is certain: the sexual nature of the popular story of the death cannot be assumed to be independent corroboration of the supposed sodomitical reputation of Edward II.

In this light it perhaps is worth returning to the political battleground which has so confused popular approaches to Edward II's sexuality. It is perhaps inevitable that some will seize upon these findings to suggest that Edward II was not homosexual. It has to be strongly emphasized that the foregoing passages say nothing about Edward II's sexual inclinations or his affections. Indeed, although this note builds on Ormrod's theoretical approach as to Edward's sodomitical behaviour, it does not go anywhere near as far as Ormrod's piece on the matter of degeneracy as a man (his ditch-digging, for example). Therefore the above arguments that the contemporary evidence for Edward II's association with sodomy is highly (if not entirely) political in origin should not be used to comment on his sexuality per se. It may be argued that the very choice of political accusation – sodomy – was selected by Orleton not only because it had been proved to work in 1303 and 1308–14 but also because of his perception that Edward II was vulnerable on this precise issue, due to gossip about his affection for various favourites. It would therefore appear most reasonable to conclude that, although the evidence for Edward's engagement in sodomitical practices appears to be more closely related to political propaganda than widespread rumours of his personal behaviour, its very selection as a means of attacking the king is consistent with the degeneracy of the king, as a man as well as a ruler.

APPENDIX 2.1

CHRONICLES WHICH MENTION THE DEATH OF EDWARD II, 1327–1400

Chronicle	Approx date of composition	Date of death of Edward II	Date of burial of Edward II	Cause of death	Murderers?
Anonimalle, 135	A shorter *Brut* continuation, copied after 1333. Relevant section probably drafted in annals form before 1330	21 (St Matt.)	20 (vigil St Thomas)	Illness	n/a
Other shorter *Brut* continuations, e.g. BL Cotton Cleopatra D vii (fo. 174v); BL Cotton Domitian A x (fo. 87r); BL Harley 6359 (fo. 83r)	Copied after 1333. Relevant section probably drafted in annals form before 1330	21 (St Matt.)	21 (jour de St Thomas)	Various, mostly grief-induced illness. MS Dom. A x has 'fust mordre'.	n/a (None mentioned in MS Dom. A x)
Alan de Assheborne, 'Lichfield Chronicle', BL Cotton Cleopatra D ix (fo. 63r)	c.1333, probably drafted in contemp. annals form	21 (die Lune in festo sancti Matt.)	Not stated	Murdered, possibly strangled ('iugulatus')	None mentioned

(continued)

Chronicle	Approx date of composition	Date of death of Edward II	Date of burial of Edward II	Cause of death	Murderers?
'Annales Paulini' in Chronicles, i, 333, 337	1330s, probably drafted in contemp. annals form	20 (vigil St Matt.)	20 (xiii Kal. Jan.)	'died'	n/a
Murimuth, 52–4	1332x1337, notes drafted at the time	22 (x Kal. Oct.)	Not stated	Suffocation	Maltravers and Gurney
Brut, i, 248–9, 253; and other longer Brut continuations, e.g. BL Royal 20 A xviii (15th cent.) and BL Royal 20 A iii (14th cent.)	After 1333 (translated late 14th cent.)	21 (St Matt.)	Not stated	Red-hot copper rod	Maltravers and Gurney
Chronicles, ii, 97 (Bridlington Chronicle)	Before 1339? It is not clear whether the entry dates from a later 14th-century revision	21 (St Matt.)	20 (vigil St Thomas)	Writer does not believe 'what is now being written'. Used a shorter Brut	n/a
'Woburn chronicle', BL Cotton Vespasian E ix (fo. 80r-v)	After 1335, probably drafted in contemp. annals form	21 (xi Kal. Oct.)	Not stated	'died'	n/a

Polychronicon, 324	2nd redaction, extended to 1340 (1327 redaction ended just before the death of Edward II)	21 (c. fest. St Matt.)	Not stated	Red-hot iron	None mentioned
French Chronicle, 58	1343 or later	Not stated	Not stated	'vilement murdriz'	Maltravers and Gurney
Tait (ed.), Cronica Johannis de Reading, 78	1346?	Follows Murimuth	Follows Murimuth	Suffocation and red-hot iron. Based on Murimuth and a Brut.	None mentioned.
Lanercost, 258–9	1340s	Not stated	21 (St Thomas)	'either by a natural death or the violence of others'	n/a
'Historia Aurea' in Hemingburgh, ii, 297–8	1346x7?	21 (St Matt.)	Not stated	Red-hot iron. Based on a Brut?	None mentioned
'Chroniculum' in Le Baker, 172	1347	20 (xx Sept.)	21 (xxi Dec.)	'died'	n/a
Eulogium, iii, 199	c.1354–64	20 (xx Sept.)	21 (xxi Dec.)	'died' (as 'Chroniculum')	n/a
'Chronicon' in Le Baker, 27–34	c.1356	22 (x Kal. Oct.)	Not stated	Suffocation and red-hot iron. Based on Murimuth and a Brut	Maltravers and Gurney (following Murimuth and longer Brut)
Robert de Avesbury, 'Gestis Edward III' in Murimuth, 283	1360s?	Not stated	Not stated	'died'	n/a

(continued)

Chronicle	Approx date of composition	Date of death of Edward II	Date of burial of Edward II	Cause of death	Murderers?
Scalachronica, 74	1363	Not stated	Not stated	'died, in what manner was not known'	n/a
Historia Anglicana, i, 189	1370s	21? (c. fest. St Matt.)	Not stated	Murder based on Brut and Murimuth, also quoting Higden	Maltravers and Gurney (following Murimuth)
Melsa, ii, 354–5	1390s	21 (xi Kal. Oct.)	Not stated	Murder quoted from Higden	Thomas Gurney (following Murimuth)
Knighton, i, 448	c.1400	22 (x Kal. Oct.)	20 (xiii Kal. Jan.)	killed ('occisus')	Not mentioned

Notes

1 W. M. Ormrod, 'The sexualities of Edward II'.
2 Ormrod, 'Sexualities', 30.
3 Ormrod, 'Sexualities', 39.
4 *Grandison*, iii, 1542.
5 Haines, *King Edward II*, 42.
6 *Grandison*, iii, 1543.
7 *Grandison*, iii, 1542.
8 For example, BL Royal 20 A iii, fo. 224r–v; BL Royal 20 A xviii, fo. 331v. The English translation appears in *Brut*, i, 252–3.
9 Chaplais, *Piers Gaveston*, 112.
10 Usher, 'Adam de Orleton', 33–47 (at 33–4).
11 Gransden, *Historical Writing in England II*, 356–7.
12 Meaux chronicle quoted in Haines, *Edward II*, 42.
13 *Anonimalle*, 22.
14 *Anonimalle*, 20.
15 Against this one might say that copying was a drudge's function, or a routine activity, perhaps often assigned to junior members of a community, or professional copyists, and thus not requiring revisions. However, in this case there are very significant counter-arguments. The *Brut* in its French form was a lay chronicle, not exclusively copied by monks but much more frequently copied by and for laymen and secular clerks, and thus one cannot presume that the task was delegated to junior members of a community. Second, no event would have rendered the chronicle out of date so much as a failure to record the alternative death of the ex-king, i.e. that he was murdered. In this respect it is important that many of the *Brut* texts would have been purchased to read aloud to an aristocratic audience (Gransden, *Historical Writing*, 62) so the outdated element mentioned in the previous point would not have passed unnoticed. But most importantly there is the simple fact that many later *Brut* continuations were considerably altered, the *Anonimalle* itself being a prime example. Also, where texts were not altered, they did not often receive a gloss like the manuscript of the Peterborough chronicle, which, where it records a nondescript death, has in the margin 'That Edward was healthy in the evening and dead in the morning, is a fabrication' ('*Edwardus vespere sanus in crastino mortuus est inventus*'). BL MS Claudius A v, quoted in R. M. Haines, '*Edwardus Redivivus*', 72.
16 For instance, BL Cotton Cleopatra D vii, fo. 174v ('*le roi eu maladist illueqes et murust*'); BL Harley 200 fo. 77v ('*en maladie al chastel de Kenilworth grevousement de graunt dolour & murust*'); BL Harley 6359, fo. 83r ('*es maledy grevousement de graunt dolour el dist chastiel de Berkelegh et tout apres murust*').
17 Two examples of shorter *Brut* continuations which were changed include the

French Chronicle of London (see Appendix 2.1) and BL Cotton Domitian A x fo. 87v ('*malveisement fust mordre en le chastel de Berkeleye par ces enemys*').

18 *Northern Registers*, 355. This is wrongly dated to 1328 by the editor: correctly, 1327. See Hill (ed.), *Register of William Melton*, vol. 3, 77 (no. 148).

3

The death of Edward II in Berkeley Castle[1*]

When in the 1870s a French archivist found the text of the Fieschi Letter, which purports to account for the movements of Edward II between 1326 and about 1335, he started a contentious – but extraordinarily slow-moving – debate.[1] Although some early twentieth-century Italian writers enthusiastically pursued the idea that Edward II died in Italy, no serious scholarly contribution was made from a revisionist perspective until Cuttino and Lyman published an article in 1978.[2] In this they pointed to a number of features of the Fieschi narrative which can be verified, and several aspects of the traditional account which are doubtful, and implied that they believed that the document was written in good faith. R. M. Haines responded to this work in the mid-1990s, using a wider range of sources, and suggested that the Fieschi Letter was a contemporary forgery designed in order to appeal to those who would pity the late king.[3] However, neither of these pieces was comprehensive in its consideration of the evidence, and neither reading has convinced many scholars. The revisionist camp has failed to answer the all-important question of how and why so much evidence for the death was created if Edward II escaped from Berkeley Castle, and the traditionalists have failed convincingly to answer the question of how and why the Fieschi Letter (which is surprisingly detailed) came to be written, or forged, and why Lord Berkeley claimed in 1330 not to have heard of the ex-king's death in his custody. Historians generally have not changed their opinion, maintaining that 'it is

---

* This essay was first published in *EHR* in December 2005 (vol. cxx, 1175–214). It is reproduced here in its original form except for the stylistic changes necessary for consistency in this volume and the correction of minor typographical errors. The name 'de Bayonne' has been standardized on 'de Bayouse'. Two errors in the original have also been corrected. In Note 44 the earl of Lancaster in question died in 1361 (as the first duke of Lancaster), not 1345 as originally stated. The date of the arrest of the earl of Kent has been corrected from '14 March' to '13 March', in line with *CP*, vii, 146, and *Anonimalle*, 143.

almost certain that Edward II was murdered in Berkeley Castle in September 1327', and that the order to kill him was issued by Roger Mortimer, later 1st earl of March.[4]

In 2003 a new dimension to this argument appeared in this writer's biography of Roger Mortimer.[5] As no one had previously considered the matter from his perspective, a number of significant questions were raised for the first time. Two findings in particular need mention here. First, early fourteenth-century embalming practices obscured the facial features of the corpse, thus explaining the widespread doubt in 1329–30 that Edward II was dead. Second, there are substantial inconsistencies in the proceedings of Berkeley's trial in 1330 indicating that both the accuser and the accused were uncertain whether the ex-king was dead or alive. As a result of these and a number of other points, it was suggested that Roger Mortimer's relationship with the young Edward III was one of power, holding the underage king's father secretly in prison, not merely one of association through the affections of Queen Isabella, as traditionally thought.

It is fair to say that the consensus of scholarly opinion is that definite statements along these lines are probably unsustainable, with the implication that the evidence for the death should not be questioned. Scholars have been noticeably reluctant to adopt a similarly cautious approach to the opposite view, and to express scepticism of statements regarding the death.[6] Only the possibility that the Fieschi Letter might have been written in good faith has attracted a more detailed and critical response.[7] These two reactions – general scepticism of revisionism and particular doubts about the Fieschi Letter – tend to obscure the important point that Edward II's survival is not synonymous with the veracity of the Fieschi Letter. Indeed, even a completely fraudulent origin for this document would not imply that Edward II died in 1327. Similarly, even if the original of the Fieschi Letter were to be found, still with the author's seal attached, it would not prove that Edward II was alive in 1330–5, for Manuele Fieschi could have been deceived by a clever imposter. In determining whether Edward died in 1327 or not, the Fieschi Letter is a distraction. We can significantly further the debate only through a rigorous examination of the sources for the death of Edward II, and the information structures underpinning them. Hence this chapter was prepared, to determine which evidence may be relied upon as certain, and which may be suspected or discounted. This includes evidence relating to a number of other events contingent on the death, such as the earl of Kent's plot and the burial of Edward II at Gloucester. The entire process of information dissemination has been outlined systematically in order to clarify a number of widespread misunderstandings. Attention has also been paid to the propaganda advantages of the various statements regarding the death and non-death narratives.

The background to the Berkeley Castle plot has been examined in depth many times and needs only a short introduction here. In January 1327 parliament was persuaded by a consortium of rebels, including Roger Mortimer and various prelates, to depose Edward II.[8] A subsequent deputation to Kenilworth Castle, where the king was being held by Henry of Lancaster, used this decision to force the king to abdicate in favour of his son, then aged fourteen. Edward III's reign accordingly began on 25 January 1327. Edward II remained at Kenilworth until 3 April, when his custody was officially transferred to Lord Berkeley, son-in-law of Roger Mortimer, and Sir John Maltravers, a long-standing Mortimer adherent and Berkeley's brother-in-law. The ex-king was taken to Berkeley Castle via the abbey of Llantony-next-Gloucester, where he spent the night of 5 April.[9] In late June a conspiracy led by Thomas and Stephen Dunheved was temporarily successful in rescuing him, but Edward was back in custody in August 1327.[10] At the beginning of September, Mortimer left court and, if we accept the evidence of a 1331 legal case involving William Shalford, his agent in North Wales, Mortimer was at Abergavenny on 14 September 1327.[11] There he purportedly received a letter from Shalford informing him of a new plot in North and South Wales and suggesting that he find a suitable remedy to the risk of the king falling into Welsh hands. The Shalford case goes on to state that Mortimer handed the letter to William Ockley or Ogle, once a Mortimer family retainer, now an esquire in the royal household,[12] who took it to Berkeley Castle with Mortimer's unwritten instructions to Maltravers and Berkeley to effect this 'suitable remedy'.

Our understanding of what happened next has traditionally depended on the evidence of the chronicles and the accusation at Mortimer's trial in November 1330 that he was responsible for the murder of the ex-king. Most contemporary monastic annalists state simply that Edward died at Berkeley and was buried at Gloucester, although the Lichfield Chronicle adds that Edward was 'iugulatus', suggesting strangulation.[13] The earliest account which gives a specific cause of death is the shorter continuation of the French *Brut*, whose relevant section was very probably composed in London before the arrest of Mortimer. This states in the majority of its surviving manuscripts that he died of a grief-induced illness.[14]

As this was a lay chronicle copied frequently after 1333, it is possible through an examination of the many variations to demonstrate that doubts about the manner of his death remained widespread for many years, well into the 1330s and 1340s.

There are only two chronicles which contribute originally and significantly to the standardized version of the death which came to be repeated regularly in the later fourteenth and fifteenth centuries.[15] The first is the *Continuatio Chronicarum* of Adam Murimuth, who was very probably at Exeter at the time of Edward II's supposed death.[16] Murimuth states that Edward was moved from Berkeley to Corfe and elsewhere, but was eventually returned to Berkeley where he died.[17] He adds that it was commonly rumoured that the king had been murdered by Thomas Gurney and John Maltravers as a precaution. In a later entry relating to Mortimer's execution, he specifically states that he was smothered.[18] The second chronicle contribution is the longer continuation of the *Brut*, written around 1333, probably at York.[19] This has much in common with Murimuth's account, including references to the supposed murderers being Gurney and Maltravers, and to the king's removal from Corfe and (in some manuscripts) back to Berkeley.[20] After this section, there is a seemingly distinct passage which includes the notorious red-hot metal torture (originally the implement was said to be copper, not iron). This is specified as being carried out at Mortimer's personal command.[21] In addition to these two accounts, a word must be said about the most famous of all contributions to the traditional narrative: Geoffrey le Baker's chronicle. This includes the detail that Edward was thrown into a deep pit of rotting carcases at Berkeley. However, this is the only original element in the whole of his long account of the death. Dating inconsistencies show Murimuth's narrative to have been unfamiliar to le Baker at the time of composing his *Chroniculum* in 1347.[22] Since Murimuth's narrative forms a major part of le Baker's later work, we may assume that le Baker's sourcing of his material dates from after 1347. The reference to the pit came from another of his sources for this post-1347 work, the testimony of one William Bishop, whom he says he consulted after the plague. Bishop claimed to have transported the ex-king to Berkeley, and thus he would have seen the garderobe pit beside the cell usually said to be the place where the king was thrown. However, Bishop did not claim to have had anything to do with, or to have known about, the actual killing of the ex-king; le Baker's account of the death is drawn entirely from Murimuth and the longer *Brut*.

The important question to be discussed here is how close were Murimuth and the author of the longer *Brut* to describing events rather than rumours? Although Murimuth was probably in the West Country at the time, and has a number of references to the imprisonment which are verifiable, including the removal of the ex-king from Berkeley to Corfe and other places, he did not pretend to know what had happened to Edward.[23] Indeed, he deliberately distances himself from the story of the murder, stating that it was merely what was 'commonly said'. In so doing he is drawing attention to the fact that he had no reliable source for this story.

The longer *Brut*, written at York in the mid-1330s, also does not have a reliable aegis. Instead it is drawn from a number of sources, some of which predate the death. In particular, its narrative concerning the king's threat to kill Isabella – and hence her reluctance to see him in his captivity – was first aired publicly in the bishop of Hereford's sermon at Wallingford in December 1326.[24] The references in common with the chronicle of Adam Murimuth may have been derived by the *Brut* author from Murimuth himself, or vice versa, as the *Brut* was probably written at York, when the Exchequer was based there, and Murimuth's idiosyncratic dating scheme (beginning the year at Michaelmas) is an Exchequer accounting year.[25] The form of murder in the *Brut* – a piece of metal inserted through the rectum – was closely based on the form of murder assigned to an earlier king, Edmund Ironside, and repeated in thirteenth-century chronicles.[26] Therefore it seems probable that the death narrative in the *Brut* has been concocted from a number of sources and rumours, not a single reliable witness. In support of this we may add that the political bias of the author – heavily pro-Lancastrian – is very unlikely to have allowed him or his lordly superiors to win the confidence of those intimate with the event, especially after it began to be described as murder. Lastly, the most significant reason to doubt the veracity of the chronicle narratives is that both Murimuth and the longer *Brut* state specifically that John Maltravers was one of the men responsible for the actual killing. This conflicts with the parliamentary prosecutions in November 1330 (which do not even accuse him of the crime) and with independent record evidence that he was probably in the vicinity of Corfe (discussed later in this chapter). We may conclude that no chronicler had access to a first-hand account of the king's death, and it seems each reflects a local or partisan rumour current at the time of composing their texts, arising in the wake of the two official pronouncements: that the ex-king had died of natural causes (September 1327), and that he had been murdered (November 1330). Maltravers's culpability in the chroniclers' accounts probably stems from his responsibility for the ex-king's safe-keeping and his exile at the time of the two chronicles being written (albeit for another crime).

THE DISSEMINATION OF THE NEWS OF THE DEATH

In the night following Wednesday 23 September, Edward III, who was then at Lincoln, received a letter from Lord Berkeley stating that Edward II had died on 21 September at Berkeley Castle.[27] This letter and another for his mother had been carried by Thomas Gurney, a Berkeley family retainer.[28] The Berkeley family historian, John Smyth of Nibley, adds that Gurney returned from Lincoln with orders from Mortimer to keep the news secret locally until All Saints.[29] The accounts rendered by the clerk of the king's official keepers, Berkeley and Maltravers, agree that Edward died on 21 September. They claimed £5 per day for their expenses in guarding Edward from 3 April (the date they received him) to 21 September, and after that they claimed the same rate for custody of the dead king's body until 21 October, when the corpse was handed over to Abbot John Thoky of St Peter's, Gloucester.[30]

The supposed date of death is significant, for on that same day one William Beaukaire started his period of watching the corpse.[31] Beaukaire's presence at Berkeley from the very day of the death is explained by the fact that he was at Berkeley already, for he appears on Lord Berkeley's receiver's account roll for the period.[32] This in itself makes him a suspect witness. His disappearance from the list of royal sergeants-at-arms after Mortimer's fall casts further doubt on his independence.[33] Considering the likelihood that he had been despatched to Berkeley by Mortimer, it would be foolish to regard him as an independent witness of events within the castle on and after 21 September as he was almost certainly acting on the instructions of the instigator of the plot. No other independent watchers attended the corpse until 20 October, when the formal attendants assembled at Berkeley in preparation for the removal of the corpse to Gloucester.

The exposure of the corpse has prompted much speculation.[34] The facts are that it was watched day and night by a number of men from 20 October, was carried on Abbot Thoky's carriage to Gloucester in procession, and then laid in state on a great hearse in the abbey for two months. Eight hundred gold leaves were purchased for gilding a leopard onto the cover placed over the body.[35] Knightly robes and tunics were commissioned for the attendants.[36] Four great lions were made by John de Estwyk, the king's painter, who gilded them and covered them with mantelets adorned with the royal arms, and these were placed at the four corners of the late king's hearse. De Estwyk also constructed four images of the Evangelists to sit on top of the said hearse, and eight incense-burners in the form of angels with towers of gold, and two rampant leopards for the exterior of the hearse.[37] A certain master was paid for cutting and carving 'quondam ymaginem de ligno ad similitudinem dicti domini Regis E. defuncti' and making and gilding a copper crown for this effigy.[38] Oak beams were supplied to keep the crowds away from the masses of candles which were placed on and around the hearse. Armour, including two helmets, was purchased, for the deceased's tomb.[39] It has been said that the funeral could not have been falsified on the strength of this display.[40] However, such a statement does not take into consideration the most important physical aspect of early fourteenth-century royal embalming. This is that the face and whole body were covered with cerecloth and obscured from view.[41]

This point requires amplification, for it suggests not only a means whereby the state of the body could have been concealed but also the means by which the identity of the body could have been falsified. The key issue is whether the body – the face in particular – was viewed by anyone outside Mortimer's circle before it was covered in cerecloth. There are two questions here, one relating to the covering of the face and the second being the date at which it was covered. With regard to the first, we may be sure that the process of embalming obscured the face by referring to the body of Edward I, whose face still bore traces of cerecloth when his tomb was opened in 1774.[42] Evidence that it was necessary to remove the cerecloth to recognize an embalmed man may be found in the case of Richard II, from whose face cerecloth was removed so that he could be identified on his way south from Pontefract in 1400.[43] Further evidence that the face had to be exposed to be recognized lies in the fact that, after Edward II's funeral, royal burials were habitually carried out with the face exposed.[44] As a result, it is possible that the corpse buried in 1327 was not that of Edward II but another man, perhaps a tenant or a stranger who had died within Lord Berkeley's demesne or within the castle, who was embalmed in place of the king.[45]

In turning to the date at which the face was covered, the embalming process would have been expected to be performed very soon after the death, if only to stop the corruption of the body: Edward III is said to have been embalmed 'immediately' after his death in 1377.[46] It is likely that the body buried in Gloucester Abbey was covered in cerecloth before 29 September, for a payment for one hundred pounds of wax appears on the receiver's account of Berkeley Castle (which terminates on 28 September).[47] This would suggest that there was a very narrow window for examining the unembalmed face of the corpse. Since the public announcement of the death of Edward II was not made until 24 September at the very earliest, and since it would normally have taken at least three days for a magnate, knight or prelate to cover the 110 miles from Lincoln to Berkeley,[48] it is very unlikely indeed that any independent high-status witness saw the body within six days of the death, by which time the woman who embalmed the corpse would have started – and probably had completed – her work. This likelihood is greatly increased if one accepts Smyth's statement that Gurney returned from court with orders to keep the death secret locally until 1 November.[49] Even if a swift rider sent by Edward III on 24 September had arrived at Berkeley on the 26th – in time to return to Lincoln before the court left for Nottingham – he could have gained access to the body only with Lord Berkeley's permission, as Lord Berkeley was at the castle until 28 September.[50]

The implications of this are important. Edward III's letter of 24 September to the earl of Hereford – DL 10/253 in the National Archives – explicitly states he heard the news in the night of the 23rd. This proves that Edward III began disseminating news about his father's death without any check upon the identity of the corpse. If there was any subsequent check prior to the more general announcement at Lincoln, then it could only have been undertaken on the 26th and with Lord Berkeley's permission, in other words, under the same aegis as the letters had been sent. Any question of the later exposure of the face is gravely undermined by the evidence of the sole chronicler to mention the exposure of the corpse, Adam Murimuth, who states that many knights, abbots and townsmen of Gloucester and Bristol attended the corpse by 'invitation', but that they were only able to see it 'superficially'.[51] Some West Country knights – John Pecche, John Gymmynges and Ingelram de Berengar – who certainly would have known those West Country knights whom Murimuth mentions, believed Edward II was alive at the time of Kent's plot, in March 1330. Certainly once the body was at Gloucester there was no exposure of the face: a cover decorated with a golden leopard lay 'over the corpse of the late king at Gloucester'.[52] Nor was the face exposed on the day of the funeral itself: the earl of Kent was also sure that Edward II was still alive in 1330, despite his having attended the funeral.[53]

As a result of the foregoing analysis, there is no doubt that the process of disseminating the news began on no authority other than the letters of Lord Berkeley carried by Thomas Gurney. It is very unlikely that an independent check on the identity of the unembalmed corpse subsequently took place, and no evidence that it did so. On this basis we can reconstruct the process by which the news of the death of Edward II was disseminated.

1. The first stage of dissemination was the letter sent by Lord Berkeley via Thomas Gurney to the king and Isabella, 'advising' them of Edward II's death.

2. The agents of the second stage of dissemination were the recipients of the letters carried by Gurney – Edward III and Isabella and, we may suppose, Mortimer – who told certain people, such as the earl of Hereford, that the ex-king was dead very shortly after receipt of the information, from 24 September.

3. The third stage of dissemination was the publication of the news, by way of announcement to those who were with the court at Lincoln (before 29 September), and by messengers to receivers of royal writs around the country.

4. In a very short while the third stage of dissemination was supplemented by a fourth: uncontrolled rumour and speculation. In one important aspect, however, the rumours were comparable to official dissemination: they were triggered by the official announcement of the death. The crucial point is that each stage of dissemination relied upon the previous one. If Lord Berkeley's initial report on 21 September was made in good faith, then Edward II did indeed die in Berkeley Castle. If not, the whole subsequent chain of events – and the whole edifice of chronicle and record evidence that Edward II died – was founded on a deception. It is thus the veracity of this single report which is integral to the whole narrative of the death.

THE VERACITY OF THE SOURCE:
THE SENDER'S TESTIMONY

Our only first-hand evidence of whether Lord Berkeley's message in September 1327 was sent in good faith lies in his trial statements in parliament in November 1330. When questioned as to how he wished to acquit himself of responsibility for the death and murder of the king, he answered '*quod ipse nunquam fuit consentiens, auxilians, seu procurans, ad mortem suam, nec unquam scivit de morte sua usque in presenti parliamento isto*' ('that he was never an accomplice, a helper or a procurer in his death nor did he ever know of his death until this present parliament').[54] These words have worried historians for decades. Generally they have been disregarded, or rather regarded as an inexplicable anomaly because it is obvious that their literal meaning cannot be squared with the widely accepted narrative of the death. But the failure of a piece of evidence to comply with a traditional narrative is not a good reason to disregard it: quite the reverse. In the light of the above argument, and conscious of its implications, it is necessary to subject Berkeley's statement to much closer scrutiny than it has previously received.

First we must acknowledge that this is a parliamentary clerk's summary of Berkeley's statement. They are not necessarily his actual words. However, the nature of the statement as a whole, ending with Berkeley's request to put his case before the king's court, on the grounds of his lack of knowledge of the death, is a logical enough progression of phrases, albeit remarkable in its content. The response, which was to reaffirm to Berkeley that Edward II had died in his and Maltravers's custody, is entirely consistent with such a denial of knowledge of the king's death. Thus, although these phrases are probably a clerk's version of the dialogue, there is no reason to suppose there is anything significant missing here, and no obvious reason to set aside this evidence reflecting Berkeley's testimony.

If we take the most obvious meaning of '*nec unquam scivit de morte sua*' ('nor did he ever know of his death'), this was plainly an indirect but public confession to parliament that he had lied about Edward II's death in September 1327, as Berkeley was widely known to have been the king's custodian and to have led the funeral procession into Gloucester. However, the phrase is not entirely unambiguous. We might argue that Lord Berkeley could have meant that he had never heard about the death, i.e. he was ignorant of the circumstances. Such a meaning would have to relate to feigned ignorance, as genuine ignorance would imply that he had not enquired into the circumstances of the king's father's death in his custody despite the passage of more than three years and despite his legal liability for the man's safety. It is also inconsistent with the entry in Berkeley's own account roll that Thomas Gurney was sent 'pro mortu patris Regis Regi et Regine notificandum cum litteris domini' ('with the lord's letters for the king and queen to be notified of the death of the king's father'). A third possibility is that, in the context of Edward II being 'murdratus et interfectus' ('murdered and killed') in his keeping, he could have meant that he had not previously heard this 'about the death', in the sense that he had not been aware of the suspicion of murder until November 1330.[55]

It is important here to remember that Edward III consciously allowed Berkeley to lie his way out of trouble. Berkeley claimed that 'at the time it was said that the Lord King was murdered and killed, he himself was ill at Bradley outside the castle and he could remember nothing'. Berkeley was indeed ill – the Berkeley Castle accounts include payments for pomegranates (most frequently used for gastroenterological complaints) obtained from Hereford and Winchester and alms offered 'in his sickness' at about this time – but he was at Berkeley, not at Bradley.[56] Therefore what Lord Berkeley was saying was untrue, and Edward III knew it was untrue, for the letters which he and his mother had received about the death had come from Lord Berkeley himself, via Thomas Gurney. That Edward III was prepared to accept what he knew to be a lie proves that in November 1330 he believed he knew the truth about his father's fate, and that he was not interrogating Lord Berkeley with a view to finding out what happened but in order to find a way publicly to acquit him of murder. In this context it is very unlikely that 'nec unquam scivit de morte sua' relates to Lord Berkeley's feigned ignorance about the murder of Edward II. Since Edward III knew that Berkeley had been at the castle at the time of the murder, it is very difficult to explain why the king knowingly allowed him to lie about his whereabouts if he was actually involved in the killing. If he was not involved, as seems far more likely, it is difficult to see why he claimed not to know 'about' the death rather than explain why he was innocent.

It is similarly very unlikely that 'nec unquam scivit de morte sua' relates to Berkeley not hearing 'about' the specific accusation of murder until November 1330. Such an interpretation implies that he was maintaining that his September 1327 message was sent in good faith. Edward III's assertion was to the contrary:

that his father had been murdered (an accusation probably first made by Henry of Lancaster in late 1328).[57] If Berkeley had lied in September 1327 about the cause of death, it is difficult to explain why Edward III knowingly allowed him in 1330 to pretend he had not been at the castle, and, by implication, had concealed the cause of death being murder.

The above is not a conclusive argument that by '*nec unquam scivit de morte sua*' Berkeley was declaring that his September 1327 message had been fraudulent, but it does nothing to reassure us of the veracity or reliability of that message. The literal interpretation implies that Edward was not dead in November 1330. The second interpretation requires us to believe that Edward II was killed in Berkeley Castle, while Lord Berkeley was there, without his complicity, and that Edward III in 1330 knew how this was possible but Lord Berkeley was reluctant to say, even though on trial for his life. The third interpretation represents Berkeley's attempt to stand by the truth of his September 1327 message and claim that Edward II had died of natural causes, only for Edward III to state that the message had been wrong with regard to the cause of death, and then to take no action against Berkeley for lying to him, instead protecting him from the implications of that lie. As a result, it is clearly possible that Berkeley's often-dismissed statement – '*nec unquam scivit de morte sua*' – was exactly what it appears to be: a claim that his initial letter announcing the death had been a lie.

THE VERACITY OF THE SOURCE: THE RECIPIENT'S TESTIMONY

A claim by Lord Berkeley in 1330 that he had lied in 1327 may or may not amount to an admission: he was not necessarily telling the truth. Indeed, his switching of his story from not knowing that the man was dead to a demonstrable untruth suggests we should treat his evidence with scepticism. We must therefore search for evidence which might corroborate or disprove the above finding. In particular we need to focus on Edward III, the key recipient of the September 1327 message.

Initially Edward took the news of his father's death at face value, as shown by his letter of 24 September to his cousin. In addition, the news was publicly announced at Lincoln within a few days, in the knowledge that this information would quickly spread around the country. He, his mother, his uncle and many other notables attended the funeral. Masses were sung for the dead king on his anniversary. However, Edward was just fifteen years old at the time of the funeral, and firmly under Mortimer's and Isabella's control. Even if he had doubted what had happened to his father, he would have had little or no opportunity to do anything about it. Hence the saying of masses for his father's soul in the period 1327–30 cannot be held as evidence that he believed his father died on 21 September 1327, as the anniversary was widely recorded while Mortimer and Isabella were still in power. As early as 6 October 1327 the abbot of Crokesden was given permission to hold an anniversary on St Matthew's Day for the dead king.[58] In addition, the king revisited Gloucester in October 1328, December 1328, August/September 1329 and June 1330, and no doubt attended masses on these occasions for his father.[59] But Mortimer was always in the party, including 20 December 1328, the first anniversary of the burial.[60] Whether Edward II was dead or not, Mortimer and Isabella certainly wanted the country to believe he was buried in Gloucester, and thus they encouraged men like the prior of Canterbury and the abbot of Crokesden to hold the anniversary of the death. Hence the establishment of his father's anniversary on 21 September was a matter beyond Edward's control. Similarly, although no official accusations of murder were levelled against Mortimer or his accomplices until November 1330, we cannot say Edward's actions before this time were those of an independent king, able to act on his own beliefs and judgement. We need to assess his actions after this date, when we may be more confident that he was in possession of the facts.

One thing we can say with respect to the period of Mortimer's ascendancy is that Edward almost certainly learnt further details about his father's fate during this time. All he knew on 24 September 1327 was what Berkeley had told him in his letters and via Gurney; but in November 1330 he believed that he knew as well as, or better than, Lord Berkeley what had happened to his father. This is shown by his conscious acceptance of Berkeley's lie. We may reasonably assume that he was able to obtain some information from the woman who embalmed the corpse, as she was sent to the queen on the orders of the king when the royal family was at Worcester, a few days after the funeral.[61] Since the queen was with the king at this time, and Mortimer too was in attendance, we may hypothesize that the purpose of bringing this woman to the royal presence was precisely so the queen had an independent witness to convince the young king that his father had not been buried in Gloucester, but someone else had been, and that his father was actually being kept alive, and safe, away from plotters such as the Dunheved brothers, who would have set his father back on the throne at the risk of both kings' safety and the stability of the kingdom. We may certainly believe that Edward's relationship with Berkeley remained strong, for Berkeley did not flee prior to his trial, and his knight, Thomas de Bradeston, and his brother, Maurice Berkeley, were two of the twenty knights with Montagu at Mortimer's arrest.[62] Edward never actually punished him for involvement in the supposed death of Edward II. It is thus probable that Edward learned from either the embalming woman or Lord Berkeley, or both, exact details regarding his father's fate prior to November 1330.

Edward III's actions as de facto as well as de jure king are not wholly consistent with his publicly professed belief that his father was murdered in September 1327. The parliamentary rolls show that Edward fully understood that both Maltravers and Berkeley were jointly and equally liable for the safe-keeping of the ex-king.[63] This was repeated several times at Berkeley's trial: that Edward II was killed while in their joint safe-keeping. But Maltravers was not charged with murder, or failing to prevent the murder, whereas Berkeley was. Here we may consider an argument previously advanced elsewhere: 'as only one of the two men equally liable was charged, either the charge which ought to have been brought against both of them lacked substance or the king was trying to protect one man, Maltravers'.[64] We can be sure that Edward III was not protecting Maltravers as he was sentenced in his absence to the full traitor's death for his part in the plot against Kent. It would follow that the charges of murder and of failing to prevent the king's death, brought successively against Lord Berkeley, were groundless.

If correct, this argument would have important implications. It would be proof that Edward III did not believe in November 1330 that his father had been murdered in Lord Berkeley's and John Maltravers's joint custody. So it is vitally important to look for potential flaws in the reasoning. Any objection regarding the accuracy of the parliamentary clerks is not sustainable, as no charges relating to the ex-king's death were mentioned on the two later occasions when Maltravers received permission to return to England to face trial for the earl of Kent's death in 1345 and 1347, or when he was back in England, being acquitted of that charge in 1352. Edward simply never pressed charges against him for the murder of his father, or even for failing to keep him safely. The only weakness in the logical argument laid out above which this writer has been able to find is suggested by a line in Murimuth's chronicle. Murimuth recorded that Lord Berkeley had custody of the ex-king one month and John Maltravers had custody of the man the next.[65] Consequently we might argue that Edward III took action only against Berkeley because the ex-king died at Berkeley Castle, and John Maltravers was not at the castle at the time of the death.

In investigating this possibility we may note that there are two payments in Lord Berkeley's receiver's roll for carrying letters from Lord Berkeley to John Maltravers in Dorset and 'at Corfe' before 29 September 1327.[66] The same source notes that Maltravers was paid no less than £258 8s 2d for service 'on behalf of the king's father in Dorset' in this period.[67] This last entry is the second to last in the account. The payment for sending Berkeley's letters to Maltravers 'at Corfe' is the last mentioned in the section of the account dealing with letters sent out, after a payment to Sir Roger Mortimer in North Wales which must postdate his departure from court (then at Nottingham) at the beginning of September, and probably postdates his likely presence at Abergavenny on 14 September.[68] So it is likely that the last of these payments for taking letters to Maltravers may be dated to mid-to-late September. If so, it follows that Maltravers was away from Berkeley – at Corfe or in the vicinity – at the time of the supposed death.[69]

THE VERACITY OF THE SOURCE:
COMPARATIVE CONSISTENCY

We have come to a point at which a broader analysis of the implications of the foregoing passages is necessary. There are four possibilities. Either Berkeley was telling the truth in his initial announcement of the death – that the king died of natural causes – or he was lying in one of three ways: that the king was murdered and Berkeley knew it; that he was murdered and Berkeley did not know it at the time but discovered it, as he said, 'at that parliament' in 1330; or that he did not die in Berkeley Castle.

Let us begin by considering the possibility that Edward II died of natural causes. Laying aside the obvious point – that Edward was only forty-three – there are grounds for objecting to this. If Berkeley sent his September 1327 message in good faith, and then was falsely accused of the murder, this would mean that Berkeley – to whom Edward III was otherwise very respectful – was falsely charged with murdering the king's father. Also his was not the only groundless accusation of murder: his co-defendants also stood accused. The only explanation for such a course of action is that Edward III fabricated the charges against Berkeley, Ockley, Gurney and Bereford in order to make or strengthen his case against his real enemy, Mortimer. This argument falls down on several grounds. First, there is evidence that Edward III wanted Mortimer killed at Leicester on the day after his arrest, and thus was prepared to take action against him without the legal case of murdering Edward II to justify his actions.[70] Second, the writs to arrest Thomas Gurney and William Ockley as the murderers were not issued until 3 December, several days after the parliamentary trials of the conspirators began. Indeed, why were they charged at all? If the message was sent in good faith, Gurney was guilty of nothing more than reporting to Edward III in September 1327 that Edward II had died. Lastly, one might add that the case against Mortimer was very strong without a false murder charge. If the charge of involvement in the plot to trap the earl of Kent was enough to secure a traitor's death for Maltravers, it should have been ample excuse to eliminate Mortimer, when combined with the other twelve crimes of which he stood accused in November 1330 (besides the murder of Edward II). As a result, it is beyond belief that Edward III fabricated the charges of murder in 1330 in the wake of a genuine and truthful report of the ex-king's death from natural causes in 1327.

If Berkeley sent the message consciously knowing that Edward had been murdered, thus lying about the cause of death, then it is difficult to explain why he was not punished, retaining his life, lands and lordship. This is especially the case as Edward III knew that Berkeley had been at the castle at the time of the murder. In order to accept this narrative we must presume that, for some reason (perhaps friendship with Maurice Berkeley), the king wanted to absolve Thomas of any part in the murder, and believed he had not willingly participated. We must also presume that his failure to accuse Maltravers of complicity in the crime was due to his knowledge that he was in Dorset at the time of the murder, and could not have known what had happened to the ex-king.

The third possibility is that Berkeley sent the message that Edward II had died of natural causes not knowing at the time that he had been murdered. This requires us to believe that Ockley and Gurney or other men within the castle deceived Berkeley into thinking that the prisoner had died of natural causes and, despite this, were later found out by the king. It is by no means impossible that Ockley and Gurney were acting on Mortimer's orders, without Berkeley's consent or knowledge. They might have strangled the man or smothered him, and then reported a natural or accidental death to Berkeley, who disseminated the news. Maybe they represented the cause of death as a fall, as circulated by Archbishop Melton. However, it is hard to believe that following such a murder, Edward III discovered the truth and yet Lord Berkeley was incapable of providing an explanation at his trial: so incapable that he had to pretend he was elsewhere at the time. It also does not explain why Edward charged Berkeley with murder, if he knew him to be innocent. He did not feel the need to charge Maltravers similarly with his father's death.

The last possibility is that Berkeley lied in reporting in 1327 that the king had died. This would mean that the first interpretation of '*nec unquam scivit de morte sua*' is correct: Berkeley had not yet heard that the man was dead. This requires us to question all the evidence that Edward II died in Berkeley Castle. This includes not only the official announcement but the organization of the funeral, popular rumours about the king's death, the regime's policy of publicly maintaining that he was dead and Edward III's very public but (in this context) undeniably false accusations of murder in November 1330. Moreover, it implies that there were two separate public fabrications of the death. The first fabrication was the 'natural death' at Berkeley, controlled and publicized by Lord Berkeley, almost certainly on Mortimer's orders. The second fabrication was the 'murder' at Berkeley, controlled and publicized by Edward III and Sir William Montagu at the time of the palace revolution in October 1330. Such a series of events begs the question 'why?'. So too does the only other possible interpretation of the evidence: that the deposed king was murdered by Ockley and Gurney without Berkeley's knowledge or consent. We must therefore turn next to examining both of these narratives in respect of motive.

THE VERACITY OF THE SOURCE: MOTIVES FOR MURDER AND FABRICATED DEATH

Before proceeding with a discussion of motives, first we need to deal with a basic assumption: was Edward II even in custody in September 1327? Given that we know that a rescue attempt led by William Aylmer and Thomas Dunheved was at least temporarily successful in July 1327, it is possible that Lord Berkeley made a false announcement in order to conceal the loss of the ex-king to rogue elements of the community. Paul Doherty has suggested that if Edward escaped from Berkeley Castle, then 'Dunheved was probably the one who freed him'.[71] This would appear to be based on the events of June and July 1327 and an assumption that Edward II escaped, based on the Fieschi Letter. However, a number of objections can be raised to this suggestion. Doherty himself mentions one: 'We can assume that the king had been recaptured [by 20 August 1327] because Isabella told the sheriff [of Oxford] that [William Aylmer] was to be indicted for trying to free Edward of Carnarvon'.[72] We may add that the earl of Kent would probably not have made such strenuous efforts to free Edward II from his incarceration in a royal castle (Corfe) if Edward was at liberty in the period 1328–30. It is thus extremely unlikely that lack of custody of Edward II was a motive for falsely declaring the man dead in September 1327.

Assuming that Edward II was in custody at the time of his supposed murder, and that the custodian was someone answering to Mortimer, we may consider the advantages that such custody may have imparted. Let us begin with the traditional motive assigned to the murderers: that Edward was killed as a precaution, to destroy any chance of his release and restoration. Such a motive would have been of limited benefit to Mortimer and Isabella. Its sole advantage would have been to prevent attempts to rescue and restore the ex-king (which, considering the earl of Kent's later actions, it failed to do). More importantly, it presumes that keeping Edward II alive imparted no political advantages, although it had been the cause of conflict between Mortimer and Lancaster from as early as spring 1327. It also presumes that Mortimer was safe from Edward III's judgement on his father's murderer. In fact Mortimer's position at court in 1327 was precarious. He held no official position in government, and his adultery with Isabella was an insecure basis for controlling the young king. As can be seen from the charges brought against Mortimer in 1330, Edward III bore a great number of personal grudges against him, some dating from the Scottish campaign of the summer of 1327. In September 1327 what Mortimer needed most was a way to control the young king's antipathy towards him. As Edward II had been forced to abdicate against his will, he remained a potent threat to the young Edward III, who had no wish to see his father return to the throne. It also must be remembered that Edward III was still under age. Thus it would have suited Mortimer to fabricate the ex-king's death: it would have removed the liability of the man as a public prisoner while at the same time allowing Mortimer to maintain an influence over Edward III. If Mortimer were to be arrested, for example, and Edward II released, then Edward III would probably have had to contest with his father as to his right to be king. Edward III might have reasonably feared that a civil war might have broken out if his parents had not managed to agree on a mutually secure basis of power-sharing. In such circumstances he would not have wanted his father released, especially if there was a risk that he could have fallen into the hands of his enemies. To this we can add the motive of reduced risk for Mortimer. If he actually ordered the killing, he ran the risk of being accused of the murder. Not killing the ex-king and feigning the death allowed him a perfect alibi: if accused, he could have produced the living Edward II.

If the announcement of the death in 1327 was false, and Edward II was still alive in 1330, Edward III and Montagu may have realized that they could reduce or even eliminate the advantage to Mortimer of his secret custody of Edward II by declaring that the man had been murdered on Mortimer's orders. It is possible that we have supporting evidence for just such a strategy in Edward III's references to a 'secret design' underlying the plot to seize Mortimer in 1330.[73] Edward stated that Sir William Montagu 'had worked nobly' in pursuit of this 'secret design' although the actual seizure was contrived at probably only a day's notice.[74] We might add that declaring Mortimer guilty of murder carried the added benefit of strengthening public feeling against him. Finally we may add an important motive for the second fabrication: rumours that Edward II was still alive were beginning to incite rebellion. Such rumours were widespread several months before the Kent plot, they persisted after his execution and the arrest of his co-conspirators, and were still current at Avignon in August 1330.[75] Reinforcing the story that Edward II was dead with official accusations of murder reduced the risk of pro-Edward II factions finding and releasing the ex-king to the detriment of Edward III, his friends and his mother.

The above reconsideration suggests that we should not assume that there were strong motives for Mortimer to kill the king. Given the advantages to him of keeping the man alive, and permanently in his custody, we may suspect that the motives ascribed to him are retrospective explanations based on the assumption that Edward II was murdered. They are little more than the simplistic motive of precaution against escape assigned to his murderers by the sole contemporary chronicler to suggest a motive for the murder, Adam Murimuth. However, in this case motives are a matter of conjecture, and it would be foolhardy to base any firm statements about the death on the strength of perceived motives alone.

THE VERACITY OF THE SOURCE: CONCLUSIONS

Hitherto the presumption has been that, unless it can be proved that Edward II was still alive after 1327, then it is safest to presume that he died in Berkeley Castle, probably murdered on Mortimer's orders. There is a strong information-based argument why this presumption is not 'safe':

1. There was no credible exposure or identification of the corpse prior to burial, and therefore no certainty that it was Edward II buried in Gloucester on 20 December 1327.
2. The evidence that it was Edward II buried in Gloucester depends directly or indirectly on the flow of news about the death from the court from 24 September 1327, and this information depends on the letters sent by Lord Berkeley to the king and Isabella, which arrived on the night of the 23rd.
3. These letters were accepted at face value by Edward III on receipt, without any check on the identity of the body, as shown by his revelation of the news to his cousin on 24 September.
4. Any check on the identity of the body after 24 September would have had to have taken place with Lord Berkeley's permission, and this is unlikely to have been given as Lord Berkeley's message was fraudulent in one of two ways: either Edward II had not died a natural death or he was still alive.
5. The most probable meaning of Berkeley's statement '*nec unquam scivit de morte sua*' is that in 1330 he had certain knowledge that Edward II had not died in 1327.

The importance of this argument is that, while it does not amount to proof, it demonstrates logically how a large body of seemingly unambiguous evidence for the death could be misleading. In so doing it nullifies any argument based on the evidence relating to the death created in the period 1327–30, however overwhelming or conclusive it appears. It also casts doubt on the post-1330 evidence, which can be explained as propaganda designed by Edward III and his advisers to encourage widespread belief in the death during his minority.

After attaining the age of twenty-one (November 1333), he might well have been reluctant to admit that he had been an accessory to such a deception for the last six years. He certainly would have been reluctant to admit that his father was still alive if he had by then ascertained that he was in the custody of an overseas power. The key point is that if all the evidence relating to the death could have been created in good faith and yet still be flawed, then clearly we have a much bigger problem than scholars to date have been prepared to admit.

RUMOURS AND NARRATIVES OF EDWARD II'S SURVIVAL, 1328–30

It is an important but rarely mentioned fact that the evidence for Edward II's survival predates the evidence for his murder. The earliest official accusation of murder was the charge brought against Mortimer in November 1330. Kent's attempt to secure the release of Edward II from Corfe was made eight months before this. Thus we must address the question: who was spreading these rumours in 1329 and early 1330, and why were they believed?

At the outset it is necessary to comment on the recent upsurge in historical generalization which has resulted from cultural interpretations of the deaths of kings. Historians have noticed that a number of monarchs are rumoured to have outlived their supposed deaths, and have started commenting on a tradition. While such studies are generally informative, the danger is that the general is used to inform the particular. Indeed, one recently published study went so far as to say that Edward II's survival should be discounted because 'it fits too neatly into the folklore tradition'.[76] This is reductionism. It also ignores the fact that in England there was no such 'folklore tradition' at this time. One has to look back to 1066 to find the previous story of an English king 'living on', in the form of Harold II, publicly killed at Hastings. To assume that Saxon affection for a Saxon hero who fell resisting invasion is part of a tradition which remained dormant for one hundred and sixty years, until revived in favour of a widely distrusted king whose deposition was agreed in parliament, is too far-fetched. In addition, to invent such a 'tradition' is to discount the chronological context of such survivals. For example, Richard II's 'survival' could have been dreamed up in the 'tradition' of Edward II's 'survival', but not vice versa.

Another problem we have to contend with is that Mortimer's reputation has been distorted, firstly by contemporary propaganda, including actions and statements made by Edward III, and subsequently by six centuries of historical prejudice. Scholars looking at the post-1330 evidence find it difficult to know what is fact about Mortimer and what is propaganda. For example, it has been widely accepted for centuries that Mortimer was responsible for spreading the rumours that Edward II did not die in Berkeley Castle. This directly contradicts the equally widely accepted argument that it was in Mortimer's interest to have Edward II murdered, 'as a precaution'. Mortimer's low status as a historical figure has meant that scholars have not felt obliged to put him at the centre of a study and ask why the accusations levelled at him are inconsistent. For the same reason, no one has examined the possibility that Edward III's accusations against Mortimer with respect to the earl of Kent's plot were merely propaganda designed to explain why he (Edward) had allowed the execution of his own uncle for the crime of trying to release a supposedly dead man from prison. Once arrested, Mortimer was the obvious scapegoat, and the chroniclers were keen to believe the propaganda.

With very few and slight exceptions, the Kent plot has been examined only in the context of Edward II having died in Berkeley Castle. The basic outline is that Kent was arrested at Winchester on 13 March 1330 for planning to force the release of Edward II from Corfe Castle. His guilt, which he did not deny, was proved by a letter written by his wife (Mortimer's cousin) promising the supposedly incarcerated ex-king that he (Kent) had the support of most of the great men of the realm and much treasure and many arms ready to effect his restoration. This letter was given to an agent of Mortimer's at Corfe, John Deveril, who promptly betrayed Kent, handing the letter to Mortimer, who read it out at Kent's trial in parliament. These facts are described in great detail in the longer version of the French *Brut*.[77] In his confession a few days later, Kent claimed that he had been informed about his half-brother's survival by a friar who had summoned up the devil. He went on to implicate many important men, including the archbishop of York, the bishop of London, the pope (whom he had been to see about the matter) and many other pro-Edward II supporters.[78] As a result of this, he was beheaded on 19 March. Those he had implicated in his confession were arrested, if they had not already fled. Some, like the archbishop of York, faced trial and were acquitted; only Kent suffered the death penalty. Most of those implicated were enemies of Mortimer, and several (including the archbishop of

York) were restored to favour by Edward III.[79] Soon after Mortimer's arrest, Kent's estates were restored to his widow and heir.[80]

There are two particularly difficult questions arising from this series of events which no one to date has adequately managed to explain. These are: why did Kent believe his half-brother was still alive? And why did so many important and intelligent men believe him, including several who were later trusted by Edward III? Explanations in the past have tended to concentrate on Kent alone, ignoring his many collaborators, and thus ignoring the second question. With regard to the first, it is normally said that Kent was foolish, and historians have pointed to his mismanagement of the Saint-Sardos campaign as evidence of his gullibility. His swings from one political camp to another have been quoted as evidence of his instability.[81] We might add that his belief that his half-brother the ex-king was still alive on the strength of a friar conjuring up a devil is evidence of a gullible mind. But these are tenuous explanations, arising from a general tendency to follow T. F. Tout, who declared that Kent was 'stupid'.[82] Tout, like most scholars, assumed that Edward II was murdered, and therefore sought to make the details about Kent and his plot correspond with this fact. He thus ignored the obvious inconsistency in his argument: if Kent was a fool, and Edward II dead, why was it so important for Kent to be executed that the king reluctantly permitted it? Tout was also guilty of stretching his evidence dangerously far. An error of judgement by a young commander in his first campaign is not evidence of stupidity and certainly does not indicate the level of gullibility required in this particular case. Nor are Kent's changes of allegiance inexplicable; indeed, they are rational, and show considerable political versatility in his being able to shift allegiance without suffering long-term losses.[83] To at least one pro-Lancastrian contemporary, Edmund of Woodstock was 'the good earl of Kent'.[84] As for the devil, Kent was covering the identity of his informant, whose safety might otherwise have been jeopardized. His ecclesiastical co-conspirators are unlikely to have supported him on the evidence of a devil-worshipping friar alone, especially Pope John XXII and the archbishop of York. Strong evidence that he was not considered gullible by his contemporaries lies in his very selection as the leader of the English force on the Saint-Sardos expedition and his appointment by Edward II to negotiate marriage agreements on behalf of his children before the Saint-Sardos campaign (on both occasions being chosen in preference to his older brother, Thomas of Brotherton). We may also note that he was appointed by Mortimer as a member of the tribunal that judged the Despensers, and that he alone was chosen by Isabella to add his name to hers and Prince Edward's in her open letter or proclamation against Edward II of 15 October 1326. His name was clearly an asset rather than a liability in this latter instance. Then we must consider the powerful persuasiveness he must have had to organize his plot. If his contemporaries had considered him a fool, especially the archbishop of York and the pope, they would not have offered him huge sums (£5,000 from the archbishop; unlimited funds from the pope) to effect the release of Edward II. Nor would Kent have managed to convince so many other lords and knights that his half-brother was alive. Mere foolishness or gullibility is therefore not a satisfactory explanation of why the earl believed his half-brother was alive in 1330.

If Kent was not irrational or gullible, logically his faith in his half-brother's survival must have been due to the persuasiveness of a third party. At his trial Mortimer was accused of luring him into a treasonable plot, and his prominent role in Kent's arrest would appear to support this accusation. However, other evidence suggests that Mortimer merely reacted to Kent's prior knowledge. Rumours that Edward II was alive were widespread throughout the country in late 1329,[85] and Mortimer would hardly have tried to convince the whole country that the ex-king was still alive just for the sake of fabricating such a charge against his cousin's husband; there were many less dangerous ways of disposing of the man. In addition, Mortimer permitted Kent to liaise with the pope and a large number of his (Mortimer's) opponents for at least twelve months between Kent becoming convinced that his half-brother was alive and being arrested.[86] We may therefore dispense with the idea that Mortimer told Kent that Edward II was at Corfe in order to lure him to his death, and we may assume that this narrative was a piece of propaganda put forward by Edward III at his trial, believed by Geoffrey le Baker, and the author of the longer *Brut*, and subsequently followed by Tout.

The foregoing argument relates to Mortimer luring Kent into believing that Edward II was alive; it does not in itself demonstrate that Mortimer did not start the more general rumours. For this we must re-examine the events of 1327–30. The 'conspiracy' to free Edward revealed by Shalford to Mortimer when the latter was at Abergavenny on 14 September 1327 was completely halted by the announcement of the ex-king's death; it therefore suited Mortimer entirely to insist that the man was dead. The two or three attempts to retrieve Edward from captivity in 1327 were followed by none in 1328 and none (that we know about) in 1329. Indeed, the rumours that Edward II was still alive were not widely circulated in 1328. The earl of Lancaster, having lately heard a secret – probably relating to the king's possible survival – from Kent in autumn 1328, did not even dare to put it into writing when informing the mayor of London.[87] In late 1329, when the rumour of Edward's survival became common (according to the *Brut* and the *Annales Paulini*),[88] Mortimer and Isabella acted very quickly to quash the rumour-mongers. On 7 December 1329 (three months before Kent's arrest) they ordered a widespread inquiry into the then-current rumours threatening the government, which probably related to Kent's plot, and the imprisonment of anyone found to be spreading them.[89] In March 1330, they insisted that Kent should have believed that Edward II was dead as he had attended the funeral, and even one month after Kent's execution, in April 1330, they were prosecuting people for repeating that Edward II was alive.[90] It was at their instigation that an embassy went to the pope to stop such rumours in Avignon in August 1330.[91]

If the Mortimer regime was not responsible for the rumours of Edward II's survival, who was? Given that the rumours were widespread in December 1329, we must search for Kent's source at some point before that date. As the *Brut* records, and as Kent himself confessed in 1330, he went to see Pope John XXII to seek support for his half-brother's rescue. This may have been in 1328 or 1329, as Kent went overseas in both years. On 21 May 1329 he appointed attorneys during his stay overseas.[92] However, his plans obviously predated this by some time as one of the men later arrested for involvement in the plot, John de Asphale, had appointed attorneys while he went overseas 'in the company of the earl of Kent' on 23 April 1329.[93] If we accept that the secret information which Lancaster had heard from Kent in November 1328 was news of the survival of Edward II, we may push Kent's faith in his half-brother's survival back into 1328.

There is evidence which suggests that Kent's relationship with Mortimer broke down in early 1328. Kent and Mortimer had been close during their period in exile on the continent. Kent had married Mortimer's cousin, Margaret Wake, while abroad.[94] In addition, on 22 November 1327, it was at Kent's insistence that Mortimer was granted the manor of Church Stretton for life, for services abroad to Isabella and the king.[95] At Christmas 1326, men of Kent's company were rewarded with gifts from Mortimer and Isabella, and his countess likewise received a partly enamelled and gilded silver cup.[96] On 1 March 1328 Kent received a large grant of Despenser lands, the disposal of which was largely controlled by Mortimer.[97] But thereafter there is no evidence of closeness between the two men, and after the 1328 Salisbury parliament, at which Mortimer was created earl of March, Kent switched sides to support Lancaster in open hostility to Mortimer. The Charter Rolls' witness lists demonstrate that, although Kent was regularly at court until 3 March 1328, after that date he appears only infrequently.[98] Therefore there are grounds to suspect a split between the two men early in 1328, and, in view of his later actions, it is possible that this was due to Kent believing that Mortimer was keeping his half-brother alive.

Kent's confession in 1330 involved a large number of people in his plot; nearly fifty were ordered to be seized in the two weeks after his arrest.[99] He pointed an accusatory finger at an unnamed Dominican friar for discovering that Edward II was still alive by conjuring up the devil. As mentioned above, we may suspect that this story was a ruse to cover up his actual information source. However, his confession does name one man who would certainly have been in a position to know whether Edward II was at Corfe Castle in January 1328: Sir John Pecche.

No one has previously drawn attention to the role of Sir John Pecche. After the death of the earl of Warwick in 1315, he was in charge of the town of Warwick, the future inheritance of Thomas Beauchamp, whose right of marriage was purchased by Roger Mortimer, a kinsman of the Beauchamps.[100] Pecche sided with Mortimer during the initial stages of the Despenser War, but later was reconciled to the king. On 16 December 1325 he was appointed custodian of Corfe Castle.[101] In September 1326, he transferred his allegiance back to Mortimer and retained favour, gaining new grants and retaining his position as constable of Corfe until replaced by John Maltravers in 1329.[102] He was a resident custodian at Corfe, at least before the 1326 invasion.[103] Whether or not there in person (he was given letters of protection for two years overseas in February 1327), he was nominally in charge at Corfe when John Maltravers was there in the autumn of 1327.[104] He was back in England by February 1328.[105] If the ex-king had been led to the castle during his period of custody, as Kent planning his trip to the pope before April 1329 implies, it is difficult to believe that Pecche was unaware of the fact.

Pecche's specific role in the Kent plot of 1330 was not one of action but information dissemination. As Kent's confession showed, Pecche's role was that of informing the Somerset knight Ingelram de Berenger that Edward II was alive, and then sending de Berenger to the earl of Kent to help him procure the man's rescue.[106] Logically, as both Pecche and Kent had similar information about Edward's survival and custody, either one informed the other at an earlier date, or they were both informed by someone else. But if anyone else (including Kent) had falsely informed Pecche that the ex-king was at Corfe, he could have checked the truth of the matter. It is incredible that he would have risked his life and lands in 1330 on the strength of a mere rumour when it was within his power to check whether Edward II was at Corfe or not. He made arrangements to go abroad in February 1328, at almost the same time as Kent.[107] Thus we have good reason to suspect Pecche as the original source of Kent's belief that Edward II was at Corfe Castle. He might also have encouraged the Dunheved brothers' continued stirring of the Dominican order in Edward II's favour: Pecche had links in Warwickshire with John Dunheved.[108]

If Pecche was Kent's source, could he have been acting as an agent provocateur for Mortimer? This is extremely doubtful. The idea that Mortimer spread rumours about the king being at Corfe is not sustainable, as shown above. In addition, Mortimer took immediate action against Pecche and his son Nicholas following Kent's plot, with the result that Pecche lost his lands and was out of favour until August 1330.[109] And, thirdly, he was not included among those charged by Edward III for spreading the rumour which led to the death of Kent: Maltravers, John Deveril and Bogo de Bayouse were the only men so accused in November 1330. As a result of this, we are left with the high probability that Pecche was in a position to find out whether Edward II was at Corfe or not in January and February 1328, and in good faith told Berengar – and probably Kent – that Edward II was alive.

Another hitherto overlooked aspect of the events of March 1330 is that Kent was not the only one to speak of Edward II's imprisonment at Corfe. The widespread rumour across the country has already been mentioned. The large number of nobles and prelates who believed him is evident in the transcript of his confession and in the writs issued after his execution.[110] Even parliament itself seems publicly to have acknowledged that Edward II was still alive. The detailed accounts of Kent's trial which appear in the longer *Brut* are unambiguous.[111] The fullness of the entries suggests that this section is nearly contemporary with the events of March 1330. Unlike Murimuth's chronicle (written up in 1337), it does not state that Kent tried to rescue 'the king who is now dead'; rather it claims Kent sought 'to make privily deliverance of Sir Edward, sometime King of England ... who was put down out of his royalty by common assent of all the lords of England'.[112] These words are meant to have been spoken by Mortimer. Kent's incriminating letter to Edward II (given to John Deveril at Corfe), was received at Winchester not with laughter or derision but with a cold death sentence. In his judgement, Robert Howel declared that Kent had been 'on the point of delivering the body of that worshipful knight Sir Edward, sometime King of England ... to help him become king again, and to govern his people as he was wont to do beforehand', again suggesting that men at that parliament spoke as if the ex-king was indeed alive.[113] The earliest entry in the parliamentary rolls concerning the attempted restoration of Edward II in 1330 similarly makes no reference to the ex-king being dead.[114] Finally we have the testimony of Edward III himself from the *Brut*. If we may trust this detailed account, Kent was sentenced to death 'save the grace of our lord the king'. Edward did not save his uncle, although he wanted to.[115] But if his father was dead, Edward III could have repeated the actual circumstances of the death, and saved his uncle's life. That he upheld the death sentence suggests that the charge was valid: Kent and his allies were on the point of delivering Edward II from prison, as the prosecution claimed, to the detriment of Edward III.

Edward III's sympathies for his uncle's predicament are mirrored in his later support as de facto king for Kent's adherents. Pecche was restored to favour. Even more striking was Melton's promotion. As Kent's confession shows, Melton was one of the leading protagonists in the Kent plot. A recently discovered letter shows that Melton acted independently of Kent in arranging the attempted rescue of the ex-king, in conjunction with William de Clyf and the London merchant Simon de Swanland, to whom he communicated 'certain news' of the ex-king's survival.[116] Yet only days after Mortimer was executed, Melton was reappointed to his old position of Treasurer.[117] Edward certainly knew that Melton had believed in his father's survival, as Kent made his confession in parliament, and implicated Melton on numerous occasions.[118] Giles of Spain was another Kent adherent entrusted by Edward III with important business shortly after Mortimer's fall.[119] He was sent to hunt down Thomas Gurney in Spain. It is interesting that Edward III should have sent a man who believed Edward II was still alive to arrest the man who had first informed him of his death.

In drawing together the various strands of the Kent plot we may observe that it is impossible to explain the sequence of events in the traditional context of Edward II's death in Berkeley Castle. Even if we resort to the demonstrably spurious argument that Kent was mad and a significant proportion of the English secular and ecclesiastical nobility, as well as Pope John XXII, were led astray by him, we cannot explain why Sir John Pecche was punished by Mortimer as a Kent adherent in March 1330 if he was acting as an agent provocateur in disseminating news about the survival of Edward II. In addition it is difficult to explain why Edward III upheld the death sentence on his uncle, against his own will, if the charges against him were false and the man was simply misled. It is impossible to understand why Melton, who was a firm believer in Edward II's survival, was so quickly appointed Treasurer after Mortimer's downfall if Edward's reason for acting as he did against Kent was due to a fear that the plotters wanted to remove him from the throne and replace him with someone other than his father. The Kent plot conflicts with the traditional narrative of Edward II's death in almost every detail.

OTHER EVIDENCE

The Kent plot is not the only sequence of events which tallies with the narrative of Edward II's survival better than with that of his murder. The survival of Edward II in custody would explain Mortimer's powerful influence on Edward III, and what Edward III meant in his repeated accusations that Mortimer had 'accroached royal power'.[120] It would explain why Isabella was not prosecuted for any part in her husband's death, why the judgement against Roger Mortimer was declared wholly erroneous in 1354, why Edward III so completely forgave the Mortimer family that he eventually restored the contentious title of earl of March to them and married his first granddaughter to the great-grandson and heir of Roger Mortimer, and why Westminster Abbey was refused the honour of receiving the supposed ex-king's body in 1327.[121] It would explain why Berkeley and Maltravers were never punished for their failure to keep Edward II safely, and why both remained peers and held on to their titles, and why Berkeley's estates were not confiscated and Maltravers's were fully restored to him, albeit after a long sojourn overseas which seems to have been at least partly voluntary.[122] It would explain why Edward came to trust Maltravers so completely with his overseas business, despite his widespread reputation as Edward II's murderer.[123] It would explain why Maltravers was able to come back to England with impunity for a meeting with Lord Berkeley, Maurice Berkeley, William Montagu, John Molyns, Edmund Bereford and others in 1335, and with no negative repercussions for him or those who entertained him, all of whom were the king's close friends.[124] All these are obvious analogues of the survival narrative.

On the other hand, there are some details which, if the traditional narrative is to be questioned, become problematic. The principal objections are those emanating from the royal household. Why did Edward not mention Mortimer's custody of the king in his charges against him? Why was such a magnificent tomb erected in such a prominent position within the abbey if the body beneath was not genuine? Why did Isabella have the heart of 'Edward II' buried with her if it was false? Why did Edward III continue after 1330 to celebrate his father's anniversary on or about 21 September? Why was the long period of three months allowed to elapse between the death and burial of the body, if it was not Edward II? And why did the men accused of complicity in Edward II's murder flee in 1330 if they had not killed the king?

All of these questions may be answered and explained within the context of Edward II's survival by logically extending the propaganda arguments outlined above. Let us assume for the sake of argument that Edward II was alive in 1330. Edward III would have had no wish to publicize his father's survival because Edward II had been forced to abdicate, and if news that the ex-king was still alive leaked out, and became widespread, it is possible that Edward III (being still under age) would have come under pressure to recognize him. As Mark Ormrod has succinctly put it: 'medieval kings had the power to annul actions forced upon them against their will'.[125] Edward II had done so with regard to the Ordinances in 1322, and it may well have been precisely this reversal of his father's abdication that Edward III feared. He might even have run the risk of being accused of treason himself, having a poor track record of filial loyalty. Also we may dispute the premise of the first question in the previous paragraph – it is possible that such a crime was tacitly mentioned in the charges against Mortimer – for the parliamentary rolls state that the fourteen specific charges did not include many others which were 'not shown at that time'.[126]

The second question – why such a magnificent tomb was erected in such a prominent position if the body beneath was false – might be countered with the suggestion that it was erected in good faith by the abbey itself, to whom the glory of being seen to hold a king's corpse meant a stream of visitors, pilgrims, noble benefactors and wealth.[127] However, it is far more likely that it was commissioned by the royal family (despite the absence of an extant record of payment for the work) as the Crown not only paid for Edward II's funeral and burial but also habitually paid for the tombs of members of the royal family, whether at Westminster or elsewhere. Therefore we should prefer the explanation that the tomb was part of Edward III's propaganda programme, commissioned to encourage the widespread belief that his father was dead.[128] To this we may add the crucial point that the tomb may have been constructed in the 1330s with the intention that it would eventually contain the real king. Indeed, Edward II's bones – if not his whole body – could have been interred in the grave at a later date, during the extensive building works at the abbey during the 1330s and 1340s.[129] We may even postulate how such a restoration of the body was effected. In 1337 the abbey began to rebuild the choir not far from the tomb.[130] The man who was probably in charge was the Surveyor of the King's Works, William Ramsey, as the architecture was the new London or 'Perpendicular' style, known only in two earlier structures, both of which had been supervised by Ramsey.[131] Ramsey may have been partly responsible for the tomb at Gloucester as well, as he was the architect of the canopy if not the whole of John of Eltham's tomb at Westminster (dating from the period 1337–9), which is very similar to Edward II's tomb in many respects.[132] Apart from overseeing £4 of work at St Stephens in 1337, and John of Eltham's tomb, he is not known to have been working on any royal project in the period 1337–9.[133] Therefore it seems likely that Edward II's tomb was still unfinished in 1336 (when Ramsey was appointed surveyor), and that he contributed both to the tomb and to the fabric of the church. With the choir enclosed as a building site, it would have been relatively easy for Ramsey or one of his subordinates to place the body of Edward II in his nearly finished or recently completed tomb. So there is a double explanation as to why Edward II's tomb would have been commissioned on a grand scale in the wake of a false death: to reinforce the idea that he was dead in the short term and to provide a suitable royal tomb to hold the ex-king's corpse after he eventually died. In this context it is worth noticing that Edward III visited the tomb he commissioned for his father only once in the twelve years between Mortimer's fall and March 1343, and that that one occasion corresponds with the beginning of the reconstruction work in the choir, in September 1337.[134] After 1343, Edward III and his family were to pay Edward II's grave much more attention.[135]

As for the burial of the heart of Edward II in Isabella's tomb, Haines sees this as conclusive evidence that Edward II died in 1327.[136] However, his argument is based on the assumption that the heart was ordered to be removed from the body in 1327 by Isabella herself, knowing her husband to be dead. He ignores the possibility that it was requested by Edward III, in good faith, or that it was simply removed as a matter of ritual. This would not have been considered unusual; one could say that the heart of a king had to be removed in order to conform with the idea of a royal burial. The heart of Richard I was buried at Rouen, that of John at Croxton Abbey, that of Henry III remained at Westminster for nineteen years before being taken to Fontévrault, and that of Edward I was ordered to be sent to the Holy Land. The same heart-removal applied to other members of the royal family too: Eleanor of Castile's heart was given to the Dominicans, Richard of Cornwall's heart was given to the Franciscans and that of his son, Henry of Almain (who died in Italy) remained in its silver vase on an altar at Westminster Abbey for many years. The other crucial point which Haines overlooks is that the heart buried with Isabella in 1358 was not necessarily the same organ as was handed over to her in 1327. If Edward II had not died in 1327, the heart handed over to her as part of the burial rites would have been kept on an altar somewhere until it could have been replaced by the genuine heart, brought to her in a silver vase (probably together with his embalmed body) from wherever he had passed the end of his life. If the postulation in the preceding paragraph that the genuine body of Edward II was interred at Gloucester under the supervision of William Ramsey is correct, we might expect him also to have taken receipt of the heart. It is perhaps significant that the person who apparently placed Edward II's heart in Isabella's tomb in 1359, in accordance with her own instructions, was William Ramsey's daughter.[137] The issue of the anniversary of the death of Edward II may also be explained within the context of propaganda. Edward III almost certainly attended a mass every year in memory of his father. Frequently in the wardrobe accounts one encounters payments of 2s or 2s 6d for such a purpose.[138] He habitually issued a pittance of a penny each to one thousand paupers to mark the anniversary, a gift of £4 3s 4d.[139] Having started this custom under Mortimer and Isabella, Edward III could hardly have discontinued it without encouraging rumours of his father's survival. In addition, it is noticeable that the sum of a penny per day is singularly the lowest amount doled out: on all other feast days paupers received a penny and a half, including Edward's own birthday, and two pence at Easter and Christmas. It was therefore a low-status anniversary. It could be argued that this was due to Edward III's low esteem of his father, but other evidence – for example the giving of costly gifts in 1343 and 1353 to Gloucester Abbey – suggest that this is not a good explanation.[140] In addition, it seems that Edward might not have been consistent on the matter of whether he marked his father's death on 21 or 22 September.[141]

It has been remarked that when the supposed corpse of Edward II was laid to rest in Gloucester Abbey, three months had elapsed since the first report of the death. It is reasonable to ask why, if this was a charade.[142] Using the propaganda argument outlined above, it is logical that a sustained period of viewing the embalmed and cloth-covered corpse and the wooden effigy in the hearse was a way of maximizing the number of viewers, thus reinforcing the official line. In addition we must consider what was thought appropriate for a royal corpse, and to do this we must reflect on the death and burial of Edward I, the previous king, and the only dead king whom Mortimer would have seen. Edward I died at Burgh on Sands on 7 July 1307, but did not arrive at Waltham Abbey until 4 August. He then lay there for almost three months before being taken to London, finally being buried in Westminster on 28 October.[143] Isabella similarly lay in the chapel at Hertford for almost three months, from 25 August to 23 November in 1358, attended day and night like the supposed body of Edward II.[144] Philippa of Hainault's body lay even longer above ground in 1369. It is therefore arguable that a prolonged period of lying in state was not only a way to maximize publicity but also commensurate with royal status, like separate heart burial.

The last problem – the flight of the men involved in the murder – is a particularly interesting question. As many historians have wondered over the centuries, if Edward II was not killed, why did his supposed murderers flee? The short answer to this is that they did not. The men who were accused of the murder were Mortimer, Bereford, Berkeley, Ockley and Gurney. Mortimer and Bereford were executed. Berkeley did not flee, but stood trial, as discussed above. Ockley and Gurney were charged in November 1330 with the murder of Edward II, and found guilty in their absence, but Gurney at least was being sheltered by Lord Berkeley at the time.[145] Several days then passed before the order to arrest them was made, on 3 December.[146] Therefore Gurney – and probably Ockley – fled not because they had committed a crime and felt guilty but because they had already been sentenced to death. And there were other people involved in the supposed murder who did not flee. In 1332, Edward's agent Giles of Spain, who initially pursued Gurney, found William de Kingsclere at Rochester and Richard de Well near Northampton, both of whom he stated were connected with the Berkeley Castle plot.[147] Some men who were involved, like Beaukaire and Shalford, were never accused or arrested. Shalford in fact was rewarded for long loyal service in 1337 at the request of the earl of Arundel and William Montagu.[148] John Maltravers, who fled with Gurney after his death sentence in 1330, went to Flanders. He briefly returned to England with impunity in 1335, and was back in royal service in Flanders by 1339.[149]

FINAL ANALYSIS AND CONCLUSION

The discovery of the Fieschi Letter has led to a fundamental misconception among historians. Modern analysts have tended to contrast the plethora of evidence created under the aegis of the English Crown and the Church with a single letter created under the aegis of a papal notary. If they have considered a greater degree of complexity than this, it has been to compare other groups who doubted the death narrative (e.g. the earl of Kent and his supporters) with Fieschi and to dismiss them as dissidents from, or opponents of, the regime in power. This is an inaccurate framework within which to consider the evidence. The real debate about Edward II's death is how Lord Berkeley's statement that Edward II died of natural causes on 21 September 1327 reflected the strategy of his political masters, Mortimer and Isabella. Was he covering up the ex-king's murder or facilitating his continued custody in secret? The evidence must therefore be considered in the context of the regimes which generated it.

As we have seen, Lord Berkeley's message was accepted at face value at Lincoln on 24 September 1327. This should not surprise us, as there is no doubt that Lord Berkeley was acting on the orders of Mortimer and Isabella, and therefore they had no reason to query his news. But we should be surprised that there was no credible public identification of the corpse. All we have is Murimuth's oblique statement that many people saw it 'superficially'. It was without any doubt an unconvincing show. The very high profile of the burial stands in marked contrast to the concealment of the corpse's identity, and we have to ask why this was, if the body was genuinely that of the ex-king.

The first significant set of anomalies in the information pattern established by Berkeley's announcement in 1327 relates to the ex-king being alive. As the traditional explanation that Kent and his associates were all deluded has been found severely lacking in credibility, Kent's death sentence for trying to rescue Edward II is a strong piece of evidence that Edward II was alive in March 1330, especially given that Robert Howel contextualized his crime in parliament in terms of the ex-king's restoration. In addition, Sir John Pecche had an exceptionally good claim to know whether Edward II was at Corfe Castle or not in 1328–9, and his role in disseminating such information cannot be dismissed as the work of a Mortimer adherent. Nor can it be dismissed as an element of Mortimer's and Isabella's propaganda. These facts – Kent's confession, Robert Howel's judgement against him and Pecche's role in information dissemination – support the idea that Mortimer and Isabella did not reveal Edward's face because he was not the man buried in Gloucester.

The second set of anomalies in the information pattern established by Berkeley's announcement in 1327 arises in conjunction with the events in and after November 1330: that Edward was murdered. This idea is supported by Edward III's accusations in parliament, his continued insistence on commemorating the anniversary of his father's death in masses and pittances, and the building of the tomb. Since we cannot assume the veracity of Berkeley's initial message, the post-October 1330 material is the first independent evidence that Edward II died in 1327, for it was not generated by the same political authority which had announced the death. The independence of this body of evidence, however, does not guarantee its accuracy, for Edward III also had an interest in maintaining that his father was dead. It is possible that all these factors were part of a propaganda exercise designed to deal with the legacy of his father's survival and to discredit Mortimer's and Isabella's regime.

Edward III's prosecutions in November 1330 are riddled with inconsistencies. Six in particular may be mentioned. First, the accusation that Mortimer intentionally lured Kent into believing that his half-brother was alive and at Corfe Castle is not sustainable: it was probably introduced to explain why Edward III had agreed to his uncle's execution for trying to rescue the ex-king. Second, no charges were brought against Sir John Pecche, a man certainly involved in Kent's plot, and probably Kent's informant. If he had wrongly lured Kent to Corfe, he should have been charged along with Mortimer, Maltravers, Deveril and de Bayouse. Third, in insisting that his father was murdered in Berkeley Castle, Edward III consciously allowed Lord Berkeley to pretend he was elsewhere at the time, thereby alleviating him of the charge of failing to keep the king safely, of which he would have been guilty if Edward II had died. Fourth, however one translates 'nec unquam scivit de morte sua' it amounts to a denial of knowledge of or about the death, despite Lord Berkeley having been the one who originally wrote to Edward III informing him of the event. Fifth, Berkeley was not punished but allowed to retain his lordship and titles, even though he appointed the supposed murderers, Ockley and Gurney. Sixth, the failure to order the arrests of Ockley and Gurney until several days after they were accused is inconsistent with Edward III allowing Berkeley to lie regarding his whereabouts on the basis that they had committed the murder without his knowledge. As the only meanings of 'nec unquam scivit de morte sua' which are consistent with the death imply that Berkeley was unaware that they had killed the ex-king, it is extraordinary that the order to arrest them was not issued sooner. It seems Edward III was deliberately giving them a chance to flee.

To sum up: there are substantial grounds for believing that the initial letter announcing the ex-king's death from natural causes and the subsequent ostentatious funeral were elements of a deliberate attempt to mislead people into thinking that Edward II was dead. Despite the widespread acceptance of the news, several reliable sources later emerged attesting to Edward II's survival which independently corroborate each other and which cannot be explained within the paradigm of the propaganda war between Mortimer and Isabella on the one hand and Edward III on the other. Probably the most important two are Robert Howel's judgement against Kent in parliament and Sir John Pecche's position as custodian of Corfe at the time of the initiation of the Kent plot. These are independently supported by the literal and most likely reading of Berkeley's own testimony in November 1330 and a great mass of circumstantial evidence, from sequences of events (such as the concealment of the corpse's identity and the failure to punish those responsible for maintaining the king safely) to documents which overtly state that the king was alive (such as Kent's own confession and Archbishop Melton's letter to Simon de Swanland). Finally it is possible to answer all the major objections which have so far been raised by traditionalist historians through a close examination of the developing political situation at the start of Edward III's reign and an understanding of that king's very considerable abilities in manipulating public opinion.[150] When Edward III inherited Mortimer's and Isabella's propaganda programme, it was falling apart, as belief in his father's survival had spread far and proved lasting. In November 1330, in order to reassert his juvenile kingship against those at home and abroad who might have supported his father's restoration, he was forced to strengthen the official line that his father was dead. His new statements regarding the murder created a second series of anomalies and inconsistencies in the written record but helped to establish a new political equilibrium. In 1330, that was all that mattered.

As a result, we cannot say that Edward II 'almost certainly' died in Berkeley Castle, rather that the reverse is true: it is almost certain that he did not. In stating this the author is not unaware of the professional taboos connected with the historical revision of the death of a medieval English king, but on a thorough examination of the evidence it seems considerably more likely that Edward II was still alive in March 1330, that Kent's plot was a genuine one to rescue and restore him, and that Lord Berkeley was telling the truth when he said in November of that year that he had not heard of his death.

Finally it may be noted that the foregoing conclusions are independently supported by the Fieschi Letter. Although there is insufficient space here properly to explore that document – and it has to be emphasized that this analysis does not imply that the Fieschi Letter is accurate or even that it was written in good faith – there are clear parallels between the Fieschi narrative and the above conclusions. First, the letter provides independent corroboration of the central findings of this article: that Edward II was still alive in 1330, and that he was maintained secretly, and that Edward III was unaware of his precise whereabouts. It would appear from the above passages that at some point before September 1329 (Pecche's removal as custodian of Corfe) – and very probably before February 1328 (Pecche's and Kent's protection documents for overseas travel) – Edward II was taken to Corfe Castle. The Fieschi Letter supports this in that it claims that the ex-king was removed from Berkeley and taken to Corfe before the funeral at Gloucester (December 1327). The Fieschi Letter also supports the idea that it was under Mortimer's authority that Edward II was kept alive. It states that the keeper who had accompanied the ex-king from Berkeley to Corfe remained with him at Corfe, and, at the time of Kent's plot, took him to Ireland: a country very well known to the Mortimer faction (including Sir John Maltravers).[151] Nine months later the ex-king's keeper disappears from the Fieschi narrative, and Edward II was set free. This coincides with the date at which news of Mortimer's execution would have reached Ireland: early to mid-December 1330. It seems that, with the exception of one previously identified chronological error, the Fieschi Letter broadly agrees with the probable facts of Edward's life in the period 1327–30, so far as they may be determined from the sources and information structures examined in this chapter.[152]

Notes

1 This letter, which is in the Archives départementales d'Hérault in Montpelier (G 1123), has been discussed by the following, among others mentioned in subsequent notes: *Chronicles*, ii, cvi–cviii; 'Captivity', 69–113; Fryde, *Tyranny*, 202–3; Harding, 'Regime of Isabella and Mortimer', 140–9.

2 'Where is Edward II?', 522–43. The first part of the article only is relevant to the matter under debate here; the second part deals with a specific question about a Romanesque piece of sculpture and its relationship to the Edward II story, which was disproved.

3 'Afterlife', 65–86. A revised version appears in Haines, *Edward II*, 219–38.

4 Ormrod, *Reign of Edward III*, 49.

5 Bibliographical details under *Greatest Traitor*.

6 For a broader look at the problem of historical revisionism and scholarship see Mortimer, 'Revisionism revisited'.

7 Phillips, 'Edward II in Italy', 209–26. Phillips refers to arguments that Edward II survived only in the context of the Fieschi Letter; he does not comment on these but 'assumes' (p. 211) for the purposes of his own argument that they are wrong.

8 Valente, 'Deposition', 852–81.

9 'Captivity', 83.

10 Doherty, 'Isabella' (DPhil thesis), 207–10, 225–6; Harding, 'Regime', 130–40; *Greatest Traitor*, 289, n. 29.

11 Mortimer was still with the court at Nottingham on 3 September and back at Nottingham on 4 October. *CPR 1327–30*, 166; TNA C53/114 (no. 15). For the Shalford case see 'Captivity', 109–10. Being a legal case between Englishmen and Welshmen, this document, Tout suggests, may contain other biases underlying the claims.

12 Ockley was one of the two men-at-arms with Mortimer's wife during her imprisonment in 1322. *CPR 1321–4*, 77. See *CCR 1327–30*, 484, for his tenure of Ellesmere manor in July 1329. His name appears in the list of household retainers

in 1328, among the esquires. *See CMR 1326–7*, 371.

13 The Lichfield Chronicle of Alan de Assheborne states that Edward '*apud Berkeley in custodiam machinamento iugulatus occubuit*'. This is not found elsewhere. See BL Cotton Cleopatra D ix, fo. 63r.

14 For example: BL Harley 200, fo. 77v; BL Harley 6359 fo. 83r. Both BL Cotton Domitian A x, fo. 87 r and BL Cotton Cleopatra D vii, fo. 174v have just 'illness', as does the *Anonimalle* chronicle. See *Anonimalle*, 22.

15 This total excludes William Melton's letter of 23 October 1328, offering an indulgence for those who prayed for the soul of Edward II, which claims he died of a '*fatalis casus*', although whether a literal or metaphorical fall is not made clear. See *Northern Registers*, 355. It also excludes the work most frequently cited in this respect, *Polychronicon*, which simply states that Edward '*cum veru ignito inter celanda confossus ignominiose peremptus est*', which appears in the earlier longer *Brut*. See *Polychronicon*, 324.

16 Murimuth, a Canon of Exeter, was appointed on 18 October 1326 to deal with the administration of the diocese after the death of Bishop Walter Stapeldon and prior to papal confirmation of the appointment of James Berkeley on 27 April 1327. Bishop Berkeley died just two months later, on 24 June 1327. Grandison was consecrated at Avignon on 18 October 1327. In the intervening period Murimuth was once again the *sede vacante* administrator. See *Grandison*, i, i–xiii, 1–14.

17 *Murimuth*, 52–4.

18 *Murimuth*, 63–4.

19 Taylor, *English Historical Literature*. Taylor suggests that up to this point it may have been kept on an annual basis.

20 For an example of a longer French *Brut* manuscript which preserves the reference to his being returned to Berkeley, see BL Royal 20 A xviii, fo. 331v. BL Royal 20 A iii, usually said to be more complete, omits the reference to the ex-king being returned to Berkeley. The original copy which omitted this detail is probably the source for the error in some later chronicles that Edward died at Corfe.

21 BL Royal 20 A xviii, fo. 331v: '*Al iour seint matheu en septembr[e] lan de grace mill cccxxvii que sir le Mortimer maunda pour lettre la manner de la mort*'.

22 In the *Chroniculum* the death was noted simply in the style of a monastic annalist and assigned to 20 September; in the *Chronicon* the details were drawn from Murimuth. See *Le Baker*, 31–4 (*Chronicon*), 172 (*Chroniculum*).

23 BCM Select Roll 39 (available on microfilm no. 1278 in Gloucestershire Record Office). The last entry in particular refers to Henry Pecche's expenses for the king's 'hospic' [household? or accommodation?] at Berkeley and elsewhere. There are in addition payments to Maltravers for his services keeping on behalf of the ex-king in Dorset.

24 *Grandison*, iii, 1542, 1546.

25 Cheney (ed.), *Handbook of Dates*, 12, 32.

26 Chaplais, *Piers Gaveston*, 112–13. The same narrative of a horrific murder was to be employed in the fifteenth century in relation to Humphrey, duke of Gloucester.

27 Harding, 'Regime', 145; Doherty, *Isabella and the Strange Death*, 134; 'Afterlife', 85, n. 98, all quoting TNA DL 10/253, which is dated 24 September but specifically mentions hearing the news in the night of the 23rd. The accounts of Lord Berkeley mention Gurney being despatched with letters for the king and the queen mother before 28 September (BCM Select Roll 39). See also Smyth, *Lives*, i, 296–7. For the date, see *Anonimalle*, 135.

28 BCM Select Roll 39.

29 Smyth, *Lives*, i, 297. Gurney had returned by 29 September, but the source for Smyth's statement is now unclear. Some shorter French *Brut* manuscripts state that the announcement of the death was not made until All Saints. For example: BL Cotton Domitian x, fo. 873 and BL Harley 6359, fo. 83r. However, as noted below, the abbot of Crokesden was given permission on 6 October 1327 to hold the anniversary on St Matthew's Day.

30 'Documents', 217. Although Doherty in his thesis states that the corpse was moved sometime after 10 November, the account states that Maltravers and Berkeley on 21 October '*liberaverunt corpus dicti defuncti Abbati Sancti Petri Gloucestrie apud Gloucestriam per breve Regis . . .*'. See Doherty, 'Isabella' (DPhil thesis), 231; 'Documents', 223.

31 'Documents', 226. The text of the account specifies his watching from the day of the death, '*videlicet xxj Septembris quo die Rex obijt usque xx diem Decembris proximum sequentem*'.

32 BCM Select Roll 39 includes a payment of 20s. from Lord Berkeley's household to William 'Beuquere'.

33 See *CMR 1326–7*, 375, where he appears as a sergeant-at-arms in 1328; he no longer enjoyed this status in 1330, after Mortimer's arrest, as shown by the respective list of royal sergeants-at-arms for that year (ibid., 380).

34 See in particular 'Documents'; 'Where is Edward II?', 525–6; 'Afterlife', 73.

35 TNA E101/383/3 m. 1.

36 TNA E101/383/3 m. 3.

37 TNA E101/383/3 m. 3.

38 TNA E101/383/3 m. 6.

39 TNA E101/624/14.

40 For example, 'Afterlife', 73.

41 St John Hope, 'Funeral effigies'. Elizabeth Hallam, writing more recently but less specifically, states that in fourteenth-century England, in contrast to thirteenth-century practice, 'a funeral effigy occupied the place of the royal corpse on the bier', adding that the first time this happened was 'probably at Edward II's funeral'. See Hallam, 'Royal burial', 366–7. In view of the cerecloth over the face, and the cover over the whole corpse, there is no reason to suppose the innovation of the effigy

was directly connected to concealing the identity of the corpse buried at Gloucester in 1327.

42 St John Hope, 'Funeral effigies', 529; Ayloffe, 'Account', 380–1.

43 St John Hope, 'Funeral effigies', 533, quoting T. Hearne (ed.), *Thomae Otterbourne Chronica* (Oxford, 1732), i, 229; and *Historia Anglicana*, ii, 245–6.

44 Henry of Lancaster (d. 1361) willed that his body should not be embalmed for three weeks after his death. John of Gaunt willed that he should be left unembalmed for no less than forty days. See *Royal Wills*, 83, 146. Edward III was led to his grave with his face uncovered: Johnes (ed.), *Froissart*, i, 511. The practice appears regularized in '*de exequiis regalibus*'. See Ayloffe, 'Account', 387–8.

45 If Edward II was being kept alive for a political purpose, the gravity of the matter would not necessarily require the surrogate to have died of natural causes. It is perhaps worth remarking on this point that the Fieschi Letter states that the body buried as that of Edward II was a porter killed by Edward and his custodian during their departure from Berkeley Castle. Obviously, if the Fieschi Letter was based on a genuine confession of Edward II, this would simply be his interpretation of his own funeral made in hindsight.

46 St John Hope, 'Funeral effigies', 532.

47 BCM Select Roll 39. It is unlikely that this quantity of wax relates to candles, as it was obtained from Winchester, about 60 miles away. Wax candles would have been available in bulk in Gloucester or Bristol, each of which is 40 miles nearer to Berkeley than Winchester. In addition the same account includes payments for two palls and other cloth, red dyes (alkanet and madder) and some spices, including galingale (3s 8d) and saffron (12d), but there are no payments for 'balsams and other oils' comparable to those purchased 'to prevent decay' in the case of Edward III's corpse (costing £21; see TNA E101/398/9 fo. 23v). This is perhaps surprising, since Edward II's funeral took place three months after his supposed death, and Edward III was buried just two weeks after his. However, it is possible that payments for preservatives were accounted for separately by another office of Lord Berkeley's household, whose accounts have disappeared.

48 Rarely did magnates or prelates travel faster than 30 miles per day. However, specific 'express' messengers could travel up to 80 or more. Edward I died in the mid-afternoon of 7 July 1307 and his son in London heard by express messengers by the 11th. See Chaplais, *Piers Gaveston*, 23. For an example of sustained long-distance travel at this speed: news of the seizure of Roger Mortimer at Nottingham in the night of 19 October 1330 reached the pope at Avignon on 3 November; a merchant with more up-to-date news passed through Avignon four days later. See *CEPR*, ii, 498. Several fifteenth-century examples of messengers – not important individuals themselves – covering in excess of 80 miles per day are included and discussed in Armstrong, 'Distribution and speed of news'.

49 Smyth, *Lives*, i, 297. Gurney must have returned before 29 September as his

expenses are entered on BCM Select Roll 39.

50 Smyth, *Lives*, i, 296. The court left Lincoln on 29 September, according to the TS itinerary in the TNA Map Room.

51 *Murimuth*, 52–3, 63–4. The text reads: '*Et licet multi abbates, priores, milites, burgenses de Bristollia et Gloucestria ad videndum corpus suum integrum fuissent vocati, et tale superficialiter conspexissent . . .*'. There is no evidence supporting Haines's assertion that this viewing 'must have taken place at Berkeley prior to embalming'. See 'Afterlife', 72. Nor is there any context to support Fryde's interpretation of the word '*superficialiter*' as 'from a distance'. See Fryde, *Tyranny*, 203.

52 TNA E101/383/3 m. 2.

53 *CCR 1327–30*, 132; Doherty, 'Isabella' (DPhil thesis), 293.

54 *RP*, ii, 57. This was in response to the question '*Qualiter se velit de morte ipsius Regis acquietare?*'.

55 I am grateful to David Smith, the archivist at Berkeley Castle, for suggesting this further interpretation.

56 BCM Select Roll 39; 'Captivity', 91–2; Smyth, *Lives*, 296.

57 *Brut*, i, 259.

58 'Where is Edward II?', 539, quoting *Foedera* (Rec. Comm.), ii, 2, 718.

59 TNA TS itinerary for 1–7 Edward III (Map Room).

60 TNA C53/115, no. 33 (4 Oct. 1328); C53/115 no. 10 (20 Dec. 1328: the first anniversary of the burial); C53/116, nos 24–30, 32 (18–30 Aug. 1329).

61 'Documents', 226.

62 Shenton, 'Edward III and the coup of 1330', 24–6.

63 *RP*, ii, 57.

64 *Greatest Traitor*, 250.

65 *Murimuth*, 52.

66 BCM Select Roll 39.

67 This sum may have been an allowance for recapturing Edward after the temporarily successful freeing of him in the summer of 1327. Alternatively it may have been due for a more routine removal of the king from Berkeley to Corfe, as suggested by Murimuth. It is unlikely that this sum relates to the king's stay at Corfe after 21 September and before the 29th. However, it is possible that the ex-king had been taken to Corfe before that date. It would be wise to see this entry as evidence merely that at some point in his captivity he was in Maltravers's custody in Dorset.

68 *Greatest Traitor*, 312.

69 The chronological arrangement of these entries is not certain, but is likely given the arrangement of the section dealing with 'expenses of the lord', which is chronological.

70 *Scalachronica*, 87.

71 Doherty, *Isabella and the Strange Death*, 217.

72 Doherty, *Isabella and the Strange Death*, 123.

73 *RP*, ii, 56.

74 Doherty, 'Isabella' (DPhil thesis), 313–14.

75 The earliest action to counter the rumours was probably on 7 December 1329, when a writ was issued. The rumour itself is not specified. See *Foedera* (Rec. Comm.), ii, 2, 775. For later actions against rumour mongers, see *CCR 1330–3*, 132. *CEPR*, ii, 499.

76 Evans, *Death of Kings*, 156.

77 *Brut*, i, 263–7. The details about the letter, and Kent being unable to deny it was his, with his seal attached, and his belief in his half-brother's survival, are supported by Edward III's letter to the pope explaining his actions against Kent, dated 24 March. See *Foedera* (Rec. Comm), ii, 2, 783. There are errors in the *Brut* account: John Deveril was not the constable of Corfe in 1330, John Maltravers was.

78 *Murimuth*, 255–7, quoting BL Cotton Claudius E viii, fo. 224.

79 The Kent plot is described by most chroniclers, for example, *Murimuth*, 59–60; *Melsa*, ii, 359; *Le Baker*, 43–4; *Historia Anglicana*, i, 192–3 (where the reluctance of all present to execute the earl is noted). The confession is described independently in *Lanercost*, 264–5.

80 *CP*, vii, 147.

81 For example, Doherty, 'Isabella' (DPhil thesis), 294.

82 'Captivity', 97.

83 His allegiance to Edward during 1322 was natural, the king being his brother. His switch to the rebel side in 1325 was partly a reaction to the failure to support his campaign in Gascony, reinforced by his newly acquired family link with Mortimer, through his wife, Margaret Wake, and partly because he distrusted the Despensers. He did not anticipate his brother's destruction. The latter alienated him from the regime, and forced him towards Lancaster, whom he supported until it came to taking up arms. Since by this time he seems to have believed that his brother was alive at Corfe, the joint departure of both him and his brother Norfolk from Lancaster's camp can be explained by Lancaster's refusal to countenance the release of Edward II, as well as a reluctance to fight the king. The final change of allegiance, to opposition, needs no justification further than Mortimer's objectionable presence at court.

84 BL Harley 200, fo. 78v. This is the version of the shorter *Brut* to 1332 which is continued by Avesbury.

85 *Brut*, ii, 262, which states 'all the commons almost of England were in sorrow and dread whether it were so or not'. See also a similar phrase in the *Annales Paulini* in *Chronicles*, i, 349.

86 Doherty suggests more than fourteen months. See Doherty, 'Isabella' (DPhil thesis), 294.

87 *CPMR*, 72; Doherty, 'Isabella' (DPhil thesis), 263.

88 *Brut*, i, 263; *Chronicles*, i, 349.

89 *Foedera* (Rec. Comm.), ii, 2, 775. The invasion from the north would have been headed by Kent's adherent, the earl of Mar.

90 *CCR 1330–3*, 132.

91 *CEPR*, ii, 499.

92 *CPR 1327–30*, 391.

93 *CPR 1327–30*, 385.

94 *Greatest Traitor*, 273, n.13, 340; *CP*, xiv, 623.

95 *CPR 1327–30*, 192.

96 TNA E101/383/3, fos 24r–24v.

97 *CPR 1327–30*, 246.

98 Charters witnessed by Kent are as follows: TNA C53/115, nos 69 (21 April 1328), 68 (3 May), 63 (6 May), 52 (11 May), 47 (18 May), and 28, 27 and 21–3 (parliament at Salisbury, Oct.–Nov. 1328); C53/116, nos 3 and 49–51 (15 Feb. 1329), 52 (1 March), 12a and 7 (3 Dec.) and 1 (7 Jan. 1330).

99 *CFR 1319–37*, 169.

100 *Greatest Traitor*, 94; *CP*, x, 342.

101 *CPR 1324–7*, 202.

102 Pecche was appointed keeper of the king's parks of Freemantel and Crokham on 27 December 1326. *CPR 1324–7*, 339. For his continued keepership of Corfe, see *CP*, x, 343. No changes of keepership 1326–29 are noted in the pages of *CFR* or *CPR*, where such changes are otherwise consistently recorded for the period.

103 *CP*, x, 343, note b.

104 Simple protection for two years for John Pecche, going overseas, 14 February 1327 (*CPR 1327–30*, 11).

105 Letters nominating attorneys 13 February 1328, he going overseas with his wife Eleanor (*CPR 1327–30*, 234). Also complaint dated 18 February 1328 against John Pecche and Thomas de Rous for removing eight horses and £28 in money at Warwick (*CPR 1327–30*, 280).

106 *Murimuth*, 253–6.

107 John Pecche and Eleanor his wife, going overseas, nominated attorneys for one year on 13 February 1328; Kent obtained letters of protection for one year on 24 February 1328 (*CPR 1327–30*, 234, 237). The Charter Rolls (see Note 98 above) suggest that Kent did not actually depart until after 18 May.

108 On 16 May 1329 John Dunheved (who also had lands in Gloucestershire) acknowledged a debt of £100 to Pecche. See *CCR 1327–30*, 543. This despite a violent dispute between the two men before 1327 in which Pecche attempted to kill Dunheved. See TNA SC8/18/863. The Dominicans Stephen and Thomas Dunheved of Warwickshire (where Pecche also had lands) were notorious in their attempts to free Edward.

109 TNA E199/15/11, E199/39/10; *CFR 1327–40*, 168–9; *CP*, x, 343.

110 *Murimuth*, 253–6; *CFR 1319–37*, 169.

111 *Greatest Traitor*, 229–31.

112 *Brut*, ii, 267.

113 *Greatest Traitor*, 231.

114 *RP*, ii, 31.

115 *Brut*, i, 267. His reluctance to kill his uncle is demonstrated by his reversal of the sentence and restoration of the earl's heir's estates.

116 Warwickshire County Record Office: CR 136/C/2027. I am indebted to Elizabeth Danbury for drawing my attention to this document, a translation of which appears in Chapter 5.

117 Melton was appointed Treasurer on 1 December 1330. He had previously served 3 July 1325–13 November 1326.

118 *Murimuth*, 256.

119 *CFR 1319–37*, 169.

120 *RP*, ii, 52–3.

121 Haines, *Edward II*, 228–9.

122 Maltravers did not return to England until thirteen years after his first known post-1330 employment by Edward III, and seven years after his first safe-conduct to come to England was granted.

123 TNA E101/391/8, m. 2 includes a writ dated Westminster, 7 October 1351, to the steward of the lands and tenements reserved to the king's chamber, informing him that 'whereas considering the loyalty and goodwill which John Maltravers, who was indicted for the death of Edmund, late earl of Kent, for which reason he sued many times in divers parliaments and councils to have such judgment annulled, as he claimed that it was less than righteous, and because the king thereafter employed him as his lieutenant in Flanders elsewhere, the king, wishing to do something grandiose for him, with the assent of the dukes, earls, barons and other magnates and peers of the realm, restored him to his former estate and reversed the judgment against him by his letters patent on 20 June last past'.

124 *CPR 1334–7*, 88, 89, 111, 112. This may have been in response to Maltravers's letter of March 1334 stating that he had information concerning 'the honour, estate and well-being of the realm', in response to which Montagu was sent to see him. See Harding, 'Regime', 332.

125 Ormrod, 'Edward III', 20–6.

126 *RP*, ii, 53.

127 Cuttino and Lyman quote H. M. Colvin to the effect that the king did not pay for the tomb, with the implication that it was presumably commissioned by the abbey. See 'Where is Edward II?', 525. More recent work casts doubt on this notion.

128 Assertions that the Gloucester effigy dates from soon after 1330 seem to be based on the assumption that the tomb should have been constructed not long after his death. Attention has been drawn to the similarity to the effigy of John of Eltham in

Westminster Abbey, the de Lucy family effigy, originally from the Lady Chapel at Lesnes Abbey, Kent, now in the Victoria and Albert Museum (V&A), London, the effigy of Sir John Iffield (d. 1343) at Ifield, Sussex, and Robert FitzElys (d. 1346) at Waterperry, Oxon, and another at Spilsby, Lincs. The V&A attributes the de Lucy effigy to 'School of London' and dates it to c.1340–50. See Welander, *Gloucester Cathedral*, 141–63, esp. 148, 155; Lindley, 'Ritual, regicide'; Duffy, *Royal Tombs*, 127.

129 For the building works at Gloucester see Welander, *Gloucester Cathedral*, 141–63. See *Greatest Traitor*, 263, for a suggestion of when the body may have been placed there.

130 Welander, *Gloucester Cathedral*, 164; Wilson, 'Excellent, new and uniforme', 99, 119, n. 6.

131 These two earlier perpendicular buildings were St Stephen's Chapel, Westminster, and the Chapter House of St Paul's Cathedral (both now destroyed). The Perpendicular style also appears in one window (the south) of the south transept at Gloucester, supposedly rebuilt 1331–6, but not the other windows of this transept. It may be that the Perpendicular style was taken to Gloucester in around 1336. See Wilson, 'Excellent, new and uniforme', 98–9; Harvey, *English Cathedrals*, 88–9.

132 The Gloucester tomb canopy is very similar to (although somewhat more elaborate than) the engravings of that of John of Eltham (d. 1336). The angels bearing the heads are almost identical. They are the two earliest extant alabaster effigies and thus we might suspect that they were commissioned together. Both tombs use different stone for the arcade around the base of the chest. See Note 128 above with regard to the effigy in the V&A. Ramsey was also responsible for at least one other royal tomb at this time: the first tomb of Blanche (d. 1343), daughter of Edward III. See Duffy, *Royal Tombs*, 124, 128, 131.

133 *HKW*, i, 177, 182, 515–17. Unfortunately the fabric accounts for the building of the abbey church at this time are no longer extant.

134 TNA E101/388/5 m. 4. Edward processed into the town on the 15th and remained there for the next day. I can find no source for Welander's claim that Edward visited in 1334 (Welander, *Gloucester Cathedral*, 164). Edward's last previous visits to Gloucester were in May and June 1330, before Mortimer's fall (*CCR 1330–3*, 32, 42, 43, 144, 146).

135 Edward III himself made a pilgrimage to Gloucester in March of that year. Later he gave expensive gifts to the abbey in gratitude for his late father's intercession during a near-death experience at sea. (See *Murimuth*, 135. Also see the Gloucester chronicler, Walter of Frocester, translated in Welander, *Gloucester Cathedral*, 630, which gives details of Edward's lavish gifts.) On the strength of this evidence there can be little doubt that in 1343 Edward III knew his father to be buried at Gloucester. Ormrod agrees, although he points out that the ship gift was one of a series of five, given at the high altar at Gloucester and three other places: London,

Walsingham and Canterbury (which received two ships). Murimuth notes all these recipients of a golden ship as places to which Edward made his pilgrimage in March 1343. See Ormrod, 'Personal religion', 860. Ten years later Edward III's eldest three sons attended the anniversary of Edward II's death at Gloucester. TNA E101/392/12 fos 33r, 35r. Walter of Frocester remarks on other royal gifts after 1343.

136 'Afterlife', 74.

137 Agnes Ramsey was paid £96 18s 11d in connection with the construction of the tomb 'as a result of an agreement made with the queen's council made during her life'. TNA E101/393/7 m. 13. No female master masons are known, and the likelihood is that there were none, so Agnes was not carrying out the work herself but supervising it. This begs the question why she in particular had been chosen by Isabella in her lifetime to carry out this part of the work. The argument that Agnes received this money for work her father did does not hold water as he died in 1349, nine years before Isabella.

138 For example, 2s 6d for a mass in the Tower chapel on 22 September 1337, TNA E101/388/5 m. 4.

139 The payment for 1337 is noted in TNA E101/388/5 m. 14; those for 1338 and 1339 in E36/203 (see *Norwell*, 211); those for 1342–3 in E36/204 fo. 76r.

140 For example, the cloths of gold laid across his father's tomb in September 1353, TNA E101/392/12 fo. 35r, and the golden ship mentioned in n. 135.

141 TNA E101/388/5 m. 4 has a mass being celebrated on 22 September 1337 in the king's presence for the soul of his father at the Tower. E101/389/8 m2 refers to alms given at a mass held in the king's chapel for the soul of Edward, the king's father, 'on his anniversary' 22 September 1340 [2s 10d]. E101/392/12 fo. 33r has the king's sons celebrating a mass at the tomb in Gloucester for Edward II's soul on 22 September 1353, but on fo. 35v a pittance given to one thousand paupers on St Matthew's Day (21 September), which is described as the anniversary. In most years – for example 1337 and 1342–3 – the anniversary was held on St Matthew's Day. TNA E101/388/5 m. 14; E36/204 fo. 76r. In connection with this, it may be noted that Murimuth – a royal clerk – believed the king had died on 22 September. See Thompson, *Murimuth*, 53.

142 This point emerged in the refereeing of the paper this chapter reproduces. I am grateful for the opportunity to address this issue.

143 St John Hope, 'Funeral effigies', 528.

144 Blackley, 'Isabella of France', 26.

145 Ockley was never heard of again. Gurney was protected by Lord Berkeley until the trial. After Berkeley's line of defence had been refused, and Gurney had been sentenced to death, he was given money by Berkeley in order to escape. He fled from Mousehole with Maltravers, and went to Spain, being captured at Burgos in 1331. He evaded his captor but died in 1333 in custody at Bayonne, despite the efforts of two physicians to save him. See 'Afterlife', 77; Smyth, *Lives*, 297; Hunter,

'Measures taken', 274–97.

146 *Syllabus*, i, 258.

147 Hunter, 'Measures taken', 282–3.

148 *CPR 1334–8*, 399.

149 *CPR 1338–40*, 378; *CPR 1343–5*, 535. For his service in Ireland see *CPR 1343–5*, 244, 245, 334.

150 See for example McHardy, 'Some reflections', 171–92; *Perfect King*.

151 Mortimer was one of the most important English landowners in Ireland and had spent several years there, including periods as King's Lieutenant and Justiciar. Maltravers had initially travelled to Ireland with Mortimer in 1317. See *Greatest Traitor*, 82.

152 The one chronological slip is that of stating that Edward was at Corfe for only one and a half years, whereas if he left Berkeley before the funeral at Gloucester, as implied by the Fieschi Letter, more than two years and three months must have elapsed before the execution of the earl of Kent. It is possible that the copyist has made an error, writing one and a half instead of two and a half. See *Greatest Traitor*, 254.

4.

Twelve angry scholars: reactions to 'The death of Edward II'

In one of Hayden White's earliest critiques of history, published in *History and Theory* in 1966, there is the following passage.

> Everywhere there is resentment over what appears to be the historian's bad faith in claiming the privileges of both the artist and the scientist while refusing to submit to critical standards currently obtaining in either art or science.[1]

These words sum up many of the issues arising from the previous chapter, which was originally published as 'The death of Edward II in Berkeley Castle' in *The English Historical Review* (hereafter: 'DEII'). Like most difficult historical problems, the question is generally construed as one of interpretation or impressions of probability. Therefore most historians are used to answering it in terms of how plausible they find a certain element of narrative. In such contexts, responses like 'it is not convincing' or 'it is more probable that . . .' are given weight because, in the absence of any perceived chance of certainty, the authority of the experienced historian is the best means whereby one may arrive at a conclusion. However, 'DEII' advances an argument that is not based on impressions but on information; therefore it requires an information-based answer, not an impressionistic one.

As will be shown in this chapter, the few commentators on the article have continued to judge the argument as a matter of personal opinion. In so doing they have strayed into the area of dubious integrity that Hayden White identified more than forty years ago. To be specific, they have disregarded the information-based argument and assumed that their professional opinions are a meaningful form of discourse. However, all historical opinion is only relatively meaningful (in that some opinions are better informed, more carefully nuanced or less prone to prejudgement than others); by themselves they do not constitute an argument, let alone proof. If a professional opinion is based on the superficial appearance of a piece of evidence, and ignores the process by which that evidence came to be created, then it is liable to the same error as the opinion that the Sun orbits the Earth.

Partly because of this propensity to judge 'DEII' as a matter of personal opinion, and partly because its conceptual framework seems to have escaped most commentators, the fundamental principle will be outlined here as simply as possible, as a reference point for the rest of this chapter.

'DEII' evaluates several separate information streams. One of these gave rise to the evidence for Edward II's death. The others gave rise to the evidence for his survival. With regard to the first information stream, we can be certain that the sole source was Lord Berkeley, who sent the news about the death to Edward III. We can be confident that the news was created in bad faith in one respect or other, as Edward II's 'death' (real or imagined) was not natural, as Lord Berkeley stated, but resulted from Lord Mortimer's instructions to Berkeley via William Ockley. Confirmation of the bad faith of Lord Berkeley's original report is to be found in the parliamentary record, where the sender himself later cast doubt upon its integrity. All this is summarized in the section subtitled 'The veracity of the source' (see p. 70–81). Therefore it is not logical to say that the traditional account of the death is a safe default position and should continue to be accepted unless it can be proved otherwise. The very opposite is true: without us even having to examine the evidence for his survival, the traditional account is demonstrably flawed. It depends on a single message sent in bad faith and contradicted by the sender. In the absence of any evidence for a verification of the identity of the corpse buried as that of Edward II in 1327, the 'default position', has to be that there is no reliable information indicating what happened to Edward II in Berkeley Castle in September 1327, and certainly none that should lead us to conclude that he died.

The other information streams are those arising from the ex-king's putative survival. These are based on eight texts contained in six documents, the eight texts being (in approximate chronological order of composition):

1. Archbishop Melton's letter to Simon Swanland, dated 14 January [1330], in which he declared he had received 'certain news' that Edward II was still alive (a translation of which appears in the next chapter).

2. The letter from the earl of Kent to his brother, Edward II, whom he believed to be in captivity at Corfe Castle, assuring him he was about to help him escape (a translation appears in the next chapter).

3. The confession of the earl of Kent, March 1330 (repeated in the next chapter). This notes that the information that Edward II was at Corfe Castle was corroborated by Sir John Pecche, who had been constable of Corfe until 1329.

4. The records of the parliamentary trial and judgement of the earl of Kent in March 1330, overseen by Robert Howel, coroner of the king's household, for the crime of being 'about to have delivered the person of that worshipful knight Sir Edward, sometime king of England, your brother, and to help him that he should have been king again and govern his people as he was wont [to do] before'.[2]

5. The inconsistent charges on the parliamentary roll against Lord Berkeley and John Maltravers, both of whom were responsible for keeping the king safely, neither of whom were punished in this regard (listed in the previous chapter).

6. The testimony of Lord Berkeley on the parliamentary roll, who declared in the parliament of November 1330 that he had not heard about the death of Edward II until that parliament (discussed in the previous chapter).

7. The Fieschi Letter (a translation of which appears in Chapter 6).

8. The official royal wardrobe account of William Norwell, which notes that a man claiming to be the king's father was brought to Edward III in October 1338 and subsequently maintained for three weeks at royal expense in December that year (given in Chapter 6).

The integrity of the last two texts is in dispute, as it can be argued that they were both created in the context of an unidentified royal pretender in Italy, so these will be discounted for the time being. We are left with six texts, all of which were created in 1330, under the authority of: the archbishop of York (no. 1); the earl of Kent (nos 2, 3); Edward III's government, under the influence of Lord Mortimer (no. 4); Edward III's government without Mortimer's influence (no. 5); and Lord Berkeley (no. 6). Dealing with these in order, we can identify the following four information streams, all independently attesting to the ex-king's survival:

1. Sir John Pecche's information. There were probably several informants who led the earl of Kent, the archbishop of York, the bishop of London and many

other men to commit themselves to rescuing Edward II from Corfe Castle in 1330. One William de Kingsclere was accused of informing the archbishop (as noted in the next chapter). There were also the various friars who worked hard to secure Edward II's freedom and collaborated with the earl of Kent (as he stated in his confession); we cannot be sure of the source of their information. However, we can be sure how one undoubted informant, Sir John Pecche, had access to the castle, as he was the constable there until replaced by Lord Maltravers in 1329.

2.   Lord Mortimer's information. Mortimer was the instigator of the situation that Kent was trying to remedy in 1330 and the catalyst of whatever happened to the ex-king in 1327. The traditional account of the death, which explains Kent's faith in his brother's survival as the result of Mortimer's agents provocateurs, implies that both Kent and Mortimer had the same information source for the king's survival, namely Mortimer's lies. But as 'DEII' demonstrates, that does not hold water with regard to Mortimer himself (see pp. 84–5), nor does it hold water with regard to Kent, who had at least one good information source in John Pecche. So Mortimer's own information is significant. Had he known that Edward II was dead, then the receipt of intelligence in 1330 that Kent was attempting to rescue him from Corfe would have been unimportant: he could have given the earl of Kent free access to the castle without risk. That he had the earl arrested, tried in parliament and sentenced to death by the royal coroner for the 'crime' of trying to rescue the ex-king from Corfe implies that he saw Kent's plot as a real threat.

3.   Edward III's information. This arose with the woman who did the embalming of the body of his supposed father. Edward III consulted her in late December 1327. His confirmation of the death penalty on his uncle in 1330 for the 'crime' of trying to rescue his father indicates that he was in agreement with Mortimer in respect of the seriousness of his uncle's plot. Lest it be said that Edward III was manipulated by Mortimer in this matter, Edward's view that his father had not died in Berkeley Castle is also implicit in his failure to punish either Lord Berkeley or Lord Maltravers for allowing his father to come to harm (see pp. 74, 96).

4.   Finally, there is Lord Berkeley's information, contained in his own testimony that he had not heard of or about the ex-king's death in November 1330, despite it supposedly happening in his castle while he was there.

As a result, the balance swings decidedly in favour of the survival narrative. Against the single unreliable source for the death we have four information streams for the survival, two arising from the custodians of the very castles in which the ex-king was held. As the 'default position' is a lack of any reliable information about the king's death, one would have thought that these four information streams would have put the matter of the survival beyond doubt – especially given that the Fieschi Letter and William Norwell's account potentially constitute two further eye-witness information streams for the ex-king's survival. Indeed, one would have thought that historians would have seen sense in exploring the implications of this new narrative as it resolves a number of hitherto insurmountable objective inconsistencies – for example, the plot of the earl of Kent, and Edward III's leniency towards Berkeley and Maltravers – which are problematic within the conceptual framework of a murder.

And yet this is where the historiography becomes interesting – for about a dozen scholars have tried to maintain that the traditional account of the death is completely reliable, whether in publications or in a series of anonymous peer reviews. In so doing they have presented an array of stances and judgements which collectively show how historical narratives are formed and how the 'sharp-end' of the history profession works. As this in itself is a very revealing subject, essential to the theme of historical certainty (not to mention the validity of an information-based approach), the rest of this chapter will deal with these reactionary arguments in detail.

REACTIONS TO *THE PERFECT KING*

The first notice that most people had of the publication of 'DEII' was the publication in March 2006 of my biography of Edward III, *The Perfect King*. This carried an appendix devoted to a shortened account of 'DEII' and gave bibliographical details of that article's publication in *EHR*, in December 2005. Therefore a few historians had an early opportunity to respond to the article in print, in their reviews of the book. However, only two reviews published in 2006 even alluded to the fact that I had taken my work on the death of Edward II a stage further, and neither of them mentioned 'DEII'.[3] There was a sudden and complete failure to exercise scholarly methods in judging the basis for the survival narrative, and an increasingly urgent desire to dismiss the whole question.

The first review by a specialist medievalist, published in *The Literary Review* in February 2006, declared that the death of Edward II is 'one of the great mysteries of English history'. The author mentioned the Fieschi Letter and went on to criticize me for treating the survival 'as an established fact'. No reference was made to 'DEII' or the information-based nature of my argument, or that it has nothing to do with the Fieschi Letter. Much the same could be said of the second medievalist to comment on the book, in *The Spectator*, who stated that

> the author is already well known for his advocacy of the theory that Edward II was not murdered at Berkeley Castle in 1327 but lived on as a wandering hermit a dozen years or more into his son's reign. This is stated here as fact, and pursued with all the ingenuity that enthusiasts commonly devote to impossible propositions.[4]

Neither expert seemed to have looked at the peer-reviewed article – certainly neither referred to it. *The Spectator* reviewer even suggested that the 'ingenuity' of the argument counted against it: a strange comment indeed.[5]

The Literary Review and *The Spectator* were not the only periodicals to carry reviews of *The Perfect King* which paid no attention to the article on which much of its most contentious narrative elements were based. *The Sunday Telegraph* reviewer wrote

> These formative years of Edward [III]'s reign are overshadowed by the author's conviction – set out in his earlier biography of his fourteenth-century namesake – that Edward II survived his supposed murder in Berkeley Castle and lived on until the early 1340s, latterly as a hermit in Italy. As Mortimer knows, it is a thesis which cannot be definitively proved – but he is clearly irked that it has not yet been more widely accepted . . .[6]

And, similarly, the *Times Higher Education Supplement*, stated that

> The story that the king's father, Edward II, escaped the threat of a red-hot poker and lived into the 1340s may seem to be a bid for headlines and a descent into conspiracy theory. It is even suggested that Edward III met his father in 1338 in Germany, where they discussed Edward I. This is guesswork, piled on hypothesis, yet there are arguments in favour of this story. Mortimer is convinced of its veracity; there is no ultimate proof.[7]

None of the four expert reviewers quoted here even mentioned 'DEII', let alone engaged with its argument, even though it was laid out in the appendix of the book that they were reviewing. Instead they avoided it. Their methods of avoidance were (1) to misrepresent my argument, stating that it was based on the Fieschi Letter; (2) to dismiss it as 'impossible' with no further argument; (3) to presume that the matter cannot be 'proved' or 'definitively proved' and therefore should be discounted; (4) to describe it using disparaging language, such as 'a bid for headlines', 'conspiracy theory' and 'guesswork'.

How does one explain this widespread avoidance strategy? My book was praised in general terms by these same reviewers, so it was not a matter of rivalry. Moreover, my publishing record showed that this was not a one-off, unfocused or misguided step into scholarly publication: it was clear that I was not an amateur conspiracy theorist or unqualified sensation-seeker. Nor could the integrity of *EHR* be disregarded: it is one of the most prestigious scholarly historical journals in the world. There had to be some other reason why the profession was so hostile to this one area of research.

Prejudice comes in many shapes and forms; and it arises for many reasons. In professional contexts it is normally a symptom, not the cause, of a problem. Protection of personal achievements is one possible form of prejudice – in its specific form, the prejudgement of an issue. One might hypothesize that some historians did not want my research findings to undermine their life's work. Just such a hope – that people should cease 'speculating' as to whether Edward II survived – was overtly expressed in 2005 by the editors of *Thirteenth Century England X*.[8] But personalizing these issues is less interesting than understanding the way that social groups (including historians and history-readers) form collective views over and above individual prejudices and prejudgements.

First and foremost, there is a widespread prejudice against revisionism in the history-conscious English-speaking world and, one suspects, further afield. On 16 June 2003 President George W. Bush gave a speech in which he defended his decision to take military action against Iraq. As I put it in an article, 'Revisionism revisited', published in 2004,

> The description he [Bush] gave of those who had suggested that there had never been a real threat from Saddam Hussein's regime was startling: "Now there are some who would like to rewrite history – revisionist historians is what I like to call them . . ."[9]

Immediately this public speech connected revisionism with those who wanted to change the past to suit *their own* ends, and it confirmed the very negative position in the public mind which the president understood revisionist history occupied. President Bush was wrong on many things, but in presuming revisionist history is generally derided, he was not wrong. It is destabilizing. It is normally subversive. As the *THES* review above suggests, it is close to 'conspiracy theory' in the popular consciousness and thus easily disparaged. The public see it in terms of sensationalism without substance and professionals hesitate to correct them, being themselves reluctant to embrace revisionist ideas. This professional reluctance is understandable: what if those ideas turn out to be wrong? But it is also extremely defensive: scholars do not want their work to be outdated and they will resist revisionism that threatens to eclipse the significance of their research.

In 'Revisionism revisited' I expanded on this general prejudice against revisionist history to draw attention to identify two further reasons why revisionism has a low reputation. These are (1) the cultural value of certain heritage stories – that Alfred burnt the cakes, that King Harold was struck by an arrow in the eye, that the first heavier-than-air flight was performed by the Wright brothers, that Edward II died with a red-poker up his colon – and the social importance of maintaining them; and (2) the role of the professional as the debunker of myths. With regard to the second, we have become used to professional historians challenging and ultimately refuting extraordinary stories which are based on little evidence. Scholarly historians burst bubbles, and they make rational and reasonable what at first seems amazing. They do not create amazing stories. So for a historian to suggest that an amazing story is true goes against the professional grain. It is almost 'unprofessional'. Moreover to do this without finding any new piece of evidence, which automatically forces the adoption of a new reading of the past, is doubly dubious, for it begs the question why other historians working in the same field did not think of this new narrative for themselves. The end result of all this is not just a general social prejudice against revisionism and not just an assumption that revisionism is a bid for headlines: it amounts to a consensus that anyone who tries to rethink a professional interpretation or paradigm must be motivated by unprofessional or non-professional reasons. A sort of 'group-think' operates, in which scholars reassure themselves that the person breaking ranks and challenging orthodoxy is wrong, subversive and disloyal.

A similar 'group-think' situation was to be observed in the run-up to the war in Iraq in 2003, in which experts around the world convinced themselves and reassured each other that Saddam Hussein had weapons of mass destruction. Their evidence for continuing to believe this had little to do with the Iraqi leader and his regime and everything to do with their own professional caution, political affinities and mutually reassuring discourse. Those who questioned the consensus were excluded from the group and lost power and influence. It was a classic case of professionalization limiting the scope and vision of the professionals, leading to 'a considerable resistance to paradigm change'.[10]

That is, I believe, why so many expert reviewers were able to dismiss the peer-reviewed argument that Edward II did not die in Berkeley Castle without even bothering to read it. It was a case of an awareness of the public prejudice against revisionism, and the constriction upon historians' views imposed by the profession and the public alike. One or two reviewers may have prejudged the article, to preserve the validity of their own past writing for selfish reasons; but the majority probably acted to maintain the integrity of a professional consensus. This position is succinctly outlined by Kuhn in *The Structure of Scientific Revolutions*,

> Normal science, the activity in which most scientists inevitably spend almost all their time, is predicated on the assumption that the scientific community knows what the world is like. Much of the success of the enterprise derives from the community's willingness to defend that assumption, if necessary at considerable cost. Normal science, for example, often suppresses fundamental novelties because they are necessarily subversive of its basic commitments.[11]

Replace 'science' and 'scientists' with 'history' and 'historians' and you have a clear picture of why historians saw fit to defend the status quo and tried to quash 'DEII'. It was a subversive 'novelty'.

There was a second reason for reviewers to ignore 'DEII', although none of those mentioned above articulated it. The revolutionary conclusion of Edward II's survival was not just a 'novelty' (in that historians would henceforth have to consider the possible implications of Edward's survival in their own work), it was a new methodological paradigm. The information-based approach threatens many other research findings. As Chapter 2 shows, it can be used to identify information streams which indicate Edward II's sodomitical reputation was the product of a programme of sodomy-related political propaganda going back to 1303, not a consequence of the king's personal behaviour. In *The Fears of Henry IV* the approach was used to demonstrate that Richard II was certainly murdered on the orders of Henry IV. Information-based methods threaten to overturn a traditional reliance on evidence and to create new certainties that might be very difficult or impossible to accommodate within traditional accounts. The approach makes possible proofs where historians have previously presumed proof was not possible – for example, the *proof* that Richard II did not make any kindly grants of lands or titles towards his cousin Henry, earl of Derby between 1390 and 1397 (mentioned in Chapter 1). In this respect it is a new, limited form of Positivism – a philosophy with which historians have had a love-hate relationship for considerably more than a century. This neo-positivism only allows for comparatively few things to be regarded as certain, and in that respect it differs enormously from nineteenth-century Positivism, which had a far more optimistic view that everything would eventually be rendered certain; but nevertheless it contains the power to prove things in certain instances, and demonstrates that some evidence which historians had previously unanimously dismissed might be correct and essential to the proper understanding of the past.

As Chapter 1 makes clear, the information-based method is probably the strongest defence against the postmodernist denial that historians can know anything about the past with certainty. It is hugely ironic, therefore, that it also threatens the existing norms and paradigms of the history profession. But that is certainly the case. We can establish certainties which limit the possible re-descriptions of the past – but some of the eliminated re-descriptions might be widely accepted interpretations. Similarly, we can establish as indisputable that the announcement of Edward II's death was accepted at face value by Edward III, and that the originator of the news was among those who later cast doubt on its veracity. This is the genuinely subversive element in 'DEII': it answers both the theoretical criticisms of postmodernism and the weakness of professional historical opinion with specific logic. It is just unfortunate for some that the conclusions are not those with which historians, reviewers and readers are familiar and comfortable.

THE PEER-REVIEW PROCESS

While these reviews were appearing in the mainstream press, a second article, entitled 'English kings and papal friends: Edward III, his father and the Fieschi', was under consideration by the *Journal of Medieval History* (*JMH*). This article – a revised form of which appears as Chapter 6 in this book – deals with the question of what happened to Edward II after 1330. The anonymous reviewers' reports collectively say much about how historical articles are accepted or are rejected for publication in the scholarly press.[12]

The editor of *JMH* sent copies of the article to two reviewers. As the only professional writer at that time maintaining that Edward II did not die in 1327, it was inevitable that my identity could not be concealed from any expert in the field. However, as is usually the case with peer review, the reviewers' names and identities were unknown to me. (In describing them below, I refer to them all as 'he' for the sake of space and fluency; I do not know whether they were all men or not.)

The responses were poles apart. One stated that

> I find this to be a scholarly and entirely plausible argument about the fate of Edward II. I am particularly impressed by the author's ability to link the specific argument about the king's fate to the broader issues influencing Edward III's foreign policy in the 1330s. I certainly think the piece merits publication.[13]

The second began:

> Although I found the article interesting, I could not recommend it for publication . . . There is too much emphasis on the supposed survival of Edward II. The author argues that Edward's survival is now beyond doubt. I am not personally convinced of this, by this article or the body of work by Ian Mortimer, to which this work clearly follows throughout. It also argues that the hermit brought to Edward III is the same man as the Edward II figure described in the Fieschi letter. The evidence for this is circumstantial and again not convincing. In fact, much of the evidence presented is circumstantial. Surely, the argument regarding the survival of Edward II has been made elsewhere and it does not need to be made again in such detail as it is in this article.[14]

The second reviewer patently considered the piece as an argument that Edward II survived, even though that was not the subject under debate: the article was rather an exploration of the implications of Edward II's survival *after* 1330, not whether he died in 1327. He was therefore admitting his prejudice against the piece on the grounds that he was 'not personally convinced' by 'DEII' or 'the body of work by Ian Mortimer'. It was thus doubly personal – in respect of his personal reaction to this piece and to everything else written by me personally. As for the point about circumstantial evidence; I made no claims to certainty in arguing for Edward II's existence in Italy. That country just happens to be the only place for which there is any evidence of Edward II after 1330; and one has to work with the evidence available.

The above contrast of a positive endorsement of the scholarly standards of this essay and a deeply negative view of my work is itself interesting. Even though these two experts had been selected by the same editor, their processes of appraisal were different. It might be considered strange that experts in so rarefied a field as medieval English history should use different processes in judging a scholarly essay, but it happens surprisingly often. In fact the very same thing had happened in connection with 'DEII'. In that case, one reviewer had recommended publication, stating 'I am impressed by the thoroughness of his research. He has examined each point in more detail than any of his predecessors . . .'. But the second had objected on the grounds that (1) demonstrating a king was not murdered was 'too narrow in character' for an article in *EHR* (!); (2) disproving a long-held 'fact' was 'entirely negative'; and (3) the reviewer did not want my work to appear 'in the near future'.[15] Quite why he wanted to delay the article one can only guess; but it is difficult to see any reason for temporarily suppressing research findings other than personal interest. Thus it was not surprising that the journal's then editor went back to the other, more positive reviewer and asked for detailed comment on his colleague's opinion. The first reviewer echoed my own thoughts: 'I don't feel that the referee engages very closely with the author's arguments; his tone is briskly dismissive . . .'. And so the article was accepted for publication.[16]

With regard to the article submitted to *JMH*, in that case the editor chose to seek further advice from two other scholars. The third reviewer expressed doubt as to whether the piece should be published because (as he himself admitted) he was still of the opinion that Edward II died in 1327. He or she stated that my article 'is based on substantial research', 'is scholarly in its presentation' and 'contains much interesting material' but on the negative side he stated that 'there is simply too much in this article which is hypothesis. It is not possible to disprove the suggestions, but they are simply implausible.' The fourth review did not bother engaging in the article's arguments at all but stated that my article

> tends towards the Dan Brown variety of history in which a surprising or shocking event for which there is no definitive evidence or proof is kept secret by conspirators because its revelation could change the course of history.[17]

With all due respect to Dan Brown, to compare my scholarly research to his fiction was insulting. To both of us. The same reviewer's last paragraph was no less astonishing and just as derogatory.

> The paper (and the recent *EHR* article as well) raise intriguing issues about pretenders,

such as when and why they flourished at different times. If the author were more skeptical of the idea of Edward's non-death, he might have speculated more on the role of pretenders. After all, Edward personally confronted at least one pretender in his lifetime, who claimed to be the real son of Edward I. Following the author's methodology, we should begin by presuming that the pretender was correct and proving that Edward II was an imposter. Or maybe it was himself he confronted.

One has to have some sympathy for an editor in such a situation: it is embarrassing to have to accept flippant advice and yet she could hardly go ahead and publish my article; all she could do was pass on to me these comments.

Shortly afterwards I revised the piece in line with what little positive advice had been forthcoming, re-titled it 'The Fieschi Letter reconsidered' and submitted it to *EHR*. According to the new editor of that journal, one reviewer recommended rejection while the other declined to offer a firm recommendation either way. The reasons given by the negative reviewer were familiar: 'it assumes what is as yet unproven' he said, going on to outline at great length what he thought had happened in 1327. This lacked references and contained a large number of assumptions and much unfounded and misleading rhetoric. One comment was that 'it requires an act of faith to accept these *soi disant* former kings were whom they claimed to be', thereby damning Edward II's case by association with other instances of royal pretenders. As noted in 'DEII', this is reductionism – one cannot simply presume that, just because most royal pretenders were not whom they claimed to be, that every single one was a fraud. What each reviewer actually said of my work was not made clear to me by the editor, who withheld the original advice; but enough was communicated for me to realize that the negative reviewer was not prepared to consider my earlier work with an open mind, let alone any extension or continuation of it.[18]

The whole process was extremely revealing. Even if an article is deemed 'scholarly' and 'impressive' by some members of the professional group, there is scope for others to dismiss it as 'impossible', 'unconvincing' and unsuitable for publication 'in the near future' without having to articulate why they think these things. Their peer-review comments do not have to be referenced, polite, open-minded, or even rational. The very split in opinion of the 'plausibility' of my work – the first *JMH* reviewer saying my work 'scholarly and entirely plausible' and the second rejecting my conclusions as 'implausible' – makes it clear that no universal test of plausibility was applied: these 'plausibility' comments were personal reactions. But although the methods of judging the article varied, close examination reveals that all of the negative comments were based on a refusal *in principle* to accept a revision to the common belief that Edward II died in 1327. Not one of the six reviewers said the article *nearly* met the standard for publication. The reviewers who recommended rejection did not do so because the work failed to meet scholarly standards. They did so because they did not agree with the hypothesis – the reason for doing the research in the first place – or the conclusions. Like the editors of *Thirteenth Century England X*, mentioned above, they wanted to 'put an end to speculation that the king survived.' In such circumstances, the correct place for these reviewers to express their disagreement with my work would have been in their own books and articles, not in anonymous reviews to which I could not respond.

Can we still have faith in the double-blind peer-review system? Yes, of course: my own experience in having peer-reviewed articles published for a wide variety of subjects from the fourteenth century through to the twentieth, and having acted as a peer reviewer myself, allows me to speak in its favour. But it is evident that, in contentious areas of debate, the system is open to abuse, especially when a researcher comes up with conclusions that challenge the professional consensus. As Kuhn observed in a passage quoted above, the academic community 'suppresses fundamental novelties because they are necessarily subversive of its basic commitments'. But, in suppressing contentious arguments on personal grounds, scholars are acting against their own interests because they are prioritizing descriptions of the past which are based on inclination rather than information. Furthermore, they are inviting their own work to be appraised on personal grounds, and in the wake of postmodern critiques of history, that is tantamount to admitting that the discipline of history has no authority at all.

PUBLISHED RESPONSES (2007–10)

A few scholars have expressed their disagreement with my research publicly, insisting that the traditional account of the death is reliable. This first to appear was a short note in an article by Roy Martin Haines on 'The Stamford Council of April 1327', published in February 2007. Although it was presented as a 'Notes and Documents' piece, and although the document being edited was on a separate subject, the author introduced a footnote drawing attention to 'DEII' and stating that

Ian Mortimer . . . argues that Edward of Caernarvon did not die in Berkeley on the night of 21/22 Sept. 1327 but was deliberately kept alive by Roger Mortimer and subsequently by his own son, Edward III. I do not find his argument convincing, and in my view it lacks adequate supporting evidence. The death of Edward II could only have been of assistance to Mortimer. The former king's life, even his simulated life, provided a focus of rebellion, as the earl himself demonstrated with his *agents provocateurs*. When faced with death, he admitted the deception that led to the earl of Kent's wrongful condemnation and asked for mercy.[19]

Once again we have the word 'unconvincing' wielded like a banner on the battlefield of Edward II studies. The brief, three-sentence justification is flawed in several respects. The assumption that 'the death of Edward II could only have been of assistance to Mortimer' reveals a limited understanding of the characters involved. If Edward II had died and Edward III blamed Mortimer for his death, what hope was there for Mortimer at court in the future? He would have been vulnerable to the accusation of being a royal murderer. Isabella too, who gave presents to her husband in his captivity, may well have been less than pleased if Mortimer had allowed her husband to be murdered. In addition, Mortimer stood to benefit from keeping Edward II alive: in terms of influencing the king. So in this statement Haines is making a wild assumption which is disputable on at least three grounds. The subsequent line, that 'the former king's life, even his simulated life, provided a focus of rebellion . . .' is true enough; but the risk was manageable, especially after 24 September 1327, when he was widely believed to be dead. As 'DEII' states, 'The two or three attempts to retrieve Edward from captivity in 1327 were followed by none in 1328 and none that we know about in 1329' (see pp. 84–5). So the fake death quelled rebellion for over two years, and would probably have done so for longer, if it had not been for John Pecche, the archbishop of York and the earl of Kent. As for Haines's third sentence, that 'when faced with death, he [Mortimer] admitted the deception that led to the earl of Kent's wrongful condemnation and asked for mercy', this is incorrect. Mortimer was reported by the earl's widow to have confessed publicly at his execution that Kent had been killed *tourcenousement* (wrongfully), 'for which he prayed mercy'.[20] No mention was made of Mortimer admitting any deception or plot – that only came later, in the government's reply to the earl of Kent's petition and that of his widow. Kent was indeed 'wrongfully' killed because his execution was for the 'crime' of trying to free an innocent man, his half-brother, from unlawful detention (which amounted to imprisonment contrary to the terms of Magna Carta).

In June 2007, David Carpenter (a professor of history at King's College London, best known for his work on the thirteenth century) published a book review of the paperback copy of *The Perfect King*.[21] This was a lengthy review, largely devoted to a discussion of my work on Edward II's death rather than the book itself. Professor Carpenter thereby became the first person actually to try to advance an argument against 'DEII'. Unfortunately, because of his attempt to deal with the article in a review of a separate book, he repeatedly shifts from commenting on the book to commenting on the article, often leaving it unclear as to which he is criticizing. Nevertheless, for the sake of comprehensiveness, his comments must be considered here.

Carpenter begins his argument by talking about motives. Roger Mortimer, he states, 'had every motive for wanting Edward dead'. This has been dealt with already – Mortimer had good reasons *not* to kill the king and Isabella did too. As regards Isabella's motives for not wanting her husband killed, Carpenter states that he is 'sceptical about this' – as if his scepticism in itself constitutes a historical argument. Regarding Mortimer's motives for not killing the king, he mentions only one: that Mortimer could have used his position to manipulate Edward III. Having raised a few rhetorical questions about this, he concludes that the advantages were nil because 'Edward [III] had nothing like as much to fear as Mortimer were the plot uncovered and his father known to have survived'. This flies in the face of the fact that Edward II had been forced to abdicate and, had he been widely known to be alive, *he* would have been the natural opposition to Mortimer, not the fifteen-year-old king (see pp. 79, 90). But all these questions of motive are a distraction. Motive is internal to character: it is only useful for the explanation of why something happens; it cannot be used to determine past reality. As I put it in 'DEII', 'motives are a matter of conjecture, and it would be foolhardy to base any firm statements about the death on the strength of perceived motives alone' (see p. 80).

With regard to the identity of the person buried as the supposed king, Carpenter admits that an image was shown in its place for the laying in state but declares 'many people would have certainly seen the body before that'. There is no evidence for this, as shown in 'DEII'; rather the evidence is to the contrary (see pp. 66–9). Carpenter notes only Murimuth's comments about the knights and burgesses seeing the corpse 'superficially'; he states 'this probably means that they couldn't see how the king died, not that they couldn't see his face'. This is a personal interpretation of the evidence: an explanation of what Carpenter wants the evidence to say, not a translation of what it actually says. No part of the word *superficialiter* relates to judging a cause of death. All it means is that the view of the corpse was inadequate in some visual way.

What Carpenter misses throughout this piece is the information basis of the argument. Only on the third and final page of the review does he touch on the question of information. There he asserts that there is no 'convincing' evidence for Edward's survival and then states that

> Ian Mortimer sets great store by a statement made by Lord Berkeley in 1330 when accused of Edward II's murder . . . "*quod ipse nunquam fuit consentiens, auxilians, seu procurans, ad mortem suam, nec unquam sciuit de morte sua usque in presenti parliamento isto*". When taken with the sentence as a whole, by far the most natural meaning of *scivit de morte sua* is that Berkeley did not know anything about the alleged circumstances of Edward's death: that is he didn't know anything about the murder, not that he did not know Edward was dead. If, on the contrary, Berkeley's defence was that the king was still alive, why didn't he say so explicitly?

Laying aside Carpenter's assumption here that Edward was murdered, there are a number of fundamental problems with this passage. First, he is imposing his own meaning on a Latin passage (*nec unquam . . . isto*) to make it signify what he wants it to signify – just as he did with Murimuth's use of the word *superficialiter*. Let us be absolutely clear on this issue, because an over-elaborate translation of this passage appears in every criticism of 'DEII'. The word *nec* means 'nor'; *unquam* means 'ever' or 'once'; *scivit means* 'he did know' or 'did he know'; *de* means 'of' or 'about;' *morte sua* means 'his death'; *usque* means 'until'; *in presenti parliament isto* means 'in this present parliament'. In *The Parliamentary Rolls of Medieval England*, J. R. S. Phillips translates this passage as 'nor did he ever know of his death until this present parliament'. That is all that is written. Nothing about 'the alleged circumstances', nothing about 'not knowing about the murder'. Besides, if my literal reading of this sentence were so far from the mark that it can be dismissed, then I would be alone in translating it thus. But I am not alone in observing that the literal meaning of that passage is incompatible with the death narrative. In 1979 Natalie Fryde pointed out that

> in the course of his interrogation, Berkeley claimed that he did not know until the present parliament that the king was dead. This is at first a most surprising statement until one considers another piece of evidence, the mysterious confession of 'Edward II' [The Fieschi Letter].[22]

It is therefore entirely sensible for me to translate the phrase literally (on the grounds of good practice). The only reason for not doing so is a prejudgement that Edward II was dead. Tellingly, this public explanation of Lord Berkeley's innocence was not allowed to stand. He was forced to come up with another alibi: that he had been elsewhere. As for why Berkeley did not say the king was still alive, as Carpenter asks in a rhetorical question, the most likely answer is that he simply did not know if he was alive or not in 1330. As Berkeley himself said, he had not heard of the king's death at that time. He had probably not heard of the ex-king at all since Edward II left Berkeley Castle in September 1327.

The most significant problem with Carpenter's treatment of this piece of evidence, however, is his misunderstanding of my use of it in 'DEII'. I investigated the death carefully in relation to a series of information streams. The first was the source of the information that the ex-king died of natural causes in Berkeley Castle: the message sent in bad faith by Lord Berkeley in 1327. Whatever he said about that message at a later date is a separate matter, for he could not retrospectively make his original message truer than it was. His comment in November 1330 that he had not heard of or about the ex-king's death thus not only casts further doubt on the veracity of his earlier message, it also creates a separate information stream: that he had not subsequently heard of the ex-king's death either. Even if Carpenter's translation of *nec unquam scivit de morte sua* is correct, it means that Berkeley had never 'known about the death' that he had reported to Edward III in 1327. The only way one can square this with the traditional story is to assume 'that Edward II was killed in Berkeley Castle, while Lord Berkeley was there, without his complicity, and that Edward III knew in November 1330 how this was possible but Lord Berkeley was reluctant to say, even though on trial for his life'. All this was dealt with in 'DEII' (see pp. 70–2).

As for the other information streams for the survival, Carpenter ignores Mortimer's information and Edward III's and mentions only that of John Pecche. He admits that Pecche was in a good position to know whether Edward II was at Corfe Castle or not between 1327 and 1329 but he simply assumes that Pecche's information was false, giving only a motive in support of his assumption: that Pecche wanted to damage Mortimer and Isabella. He presents no evidence to justify this, just a question: 'what better way to undermine the regime than by spreading the rumour that Edward II was alive?' This is easy to answer. For a start, a false or rumoured 'Edward II' could do nothing to remove Mortimer from power, for when the time came for the rumoured ex-king to assert himself, his falseness would have been discovered. Second, Pecche would have incurred the anger of the young king, who would have been threatened by any attempt to put a pretender on the throne. Third, claiming Edward II was still alive would have also undermined one of the main charges against the unpopular Mortimer – that he had had the ex-king murdered.

The postscript to Carpenter's piece was an exchange of letters in the *LRB*. My letter appeared on 5 July 2007, observing that the review 'suffers from methodological flaws and an underlying assumption that the evidence for the ex-king's death has a reliable foundation'. I pointed out that I had 'resorted to information science . . . to identify who knew what and when they knew it . . . No one has yet demonstrated a fault in my argument, yet Carpenter does not believe it', and tried to encapsulate in two short paragraphs the outline of my argument. One week later Carpenter's reply appeared. He showed no awareness that his review was a series of personal and mostly speculative readings of texts. Nor did he seem to understand that the dissemination of information was crucial to the very existence of the evidence he was using. Clearly there was no point carrying on this discussion in the letters pages of a magazine. I wrote the first chapter of this book, 'Objectivity and information', in order to explain to him and others like him the theoretical basis of my work.[23]

J. S. HAMILTON, 'THE UNCERTAIN DEATH OF EDWARD II?' (2008)

In September 2008 the first peer-reviewed argument that the traditional narrative of Edward II's death appeared in an online journal, *History Compass*.[24] This was by J. S. Hamilton, a professor of history at Baylor University.[25] The essay promised much because its author showed that he was aware that in 'DEII' I had 'attempted to shift the burden of proof onto supporters of the traditional account of Edward II's death.'

The article contains ten pages of text, pages 1264–73 of the journal. The first six pages are a survey of the literature prior to 'DEII'. On page 1269 he starts to discuss my article. In recapitulating my principal arguments he makes a number of minor or contrived criticisms – such as I am 'somewhat misleading' in downplaying the reliability of the chronicler Adam Murimuth because I claim he 'had no reliable source for this story' (see p. 65). Hamilton's argument here is that, because Murimuth gave the accepted date for the death as 21 September, he must have had reliable information concerning what went on in the cell in Berkeley Castle. Murimuth obviously had news of the date publicly announced; but this is not what I was driving at. He himself expressed doubt as to what happened in the castle on that date, stating the story of the king's suffocation was the 'common rumour' at the time. So the matter is not in doubt: he had no reliable information as to what actually happened in Berkeley Castle.

Hamilton's determination to criticize 'DEII' causes him to overstate his case in the next paragraph. He refuses to accept that there was no check on the identity of the corpse. He states that 'nowhere in the chronicles or documentary evidence regarding the embalming process is this the case'. Quite so, and this is why I specifically used the best alternative evidence concerning what was normal practice for English kings, taking the archaeological and documentary evidence available for other fourteenth-century royal figures (see p. 67). These showed that the royal face was concealed in Edward I's case and only exposed in funerals *after* Edward II's (very probably because the earlier practice of obscuring the features had led to such doubt in the minds of magnates and prelates in 1327–30). Without some evidence that refutes this, one can hardly accept Hamilton's assertion the body *was* viewed at Berkeley prior to embalming.

Hamilton continues in this same vein: 'We have no record to indicate that he [the fifteen year-old Edward III] did indeed remove the cerecloth from his father's face and gaze upon it. Equally we have no record that he did not.' This is obtuse: medieval chroniclers recorded things that *did* happen, not things that did not; and compilers of official documents (accounts and official letters) certainly had no medium for recording things which did not take place away from the court. Moreover it counters what evidence we do have – Edward III's own actions are in line with his father's false death, reflected in his confirmation of the death sentence on his uncle for trying to free the man in 1330 and in his failure to punish Berkeley and Maltravers for failing to keep Edward II safely. Like Carpenter, Hamilton regularly uses rhetorical questions as argument, especially with regard to the failure to expose the corpse. In this same long passage we read: 'If indeed the corpse of an imposter was immediately embalmed, sealed in cerecloth and never viewed by any independent witness, what was the point of burying this fake with the coronation robes of the former king in addition to the outward display of the regalia with the effigy?'[26] Hamilton neglects the fact that the evidence for the royal regalia being 'buried' with the king is in the royal account of it being *sent* from London for the purpose, and my argument states that those in London who provided all this material for the funeral did so in good faith, believing they were satisfying the requirements for a genuine royal funeral.[27]

Next, Hamilton starts to attack what he calls my 'other central argument', namely Lord Berkeley's testimony to parliament that he had not heard of or about the death of the ex-king (pp. 1270–71). Like Carpenter before him, Hamilton chooses to apply his own translation to *nec unquam scivit de morte sua* rather than literal one: 'Berkeley appears to be arguing that he had not known the circumstances (i.e. murder) of Edward's death, not that the death had occurred'. What 'appears' to Hamilton is not the same as what is written: his is a reading contrived to accord with the traditional narrative. The problem in this and the subsequent passages is that he assumes that Edward II was murdered, so he is only intent on exploring the possible weaknesses in texts that contradict that version of events. He does not employ a neutral reading of the evidence. Like Carpenter he argues that Lord Berkeley was claiming that the murder took place in his castle without his knowledge, even though he was there at the time. In support of this reading, Hamilton asks another rhetorical question: 'is it too much to imagine that Berkeley received Gurney and Ogle [Ockley], agents of his father-in-law, along with a verbal commission to ask no questions of them?' Yes, this is indeed 'too much to imagine'. It is plainly unreasonable to start 'imagining' such an explanation when it is based on no evidence, runs directly contrary to the information streams at our disposal, and when it begs us to believe that Lord Berkeley set aside his legal responsibility for the ex-king's safe-keeping and yet was sufficiently aware of the details to announce the death himself. In addition, if Hamilton were correct and this explanation was a genuine case of Berkeley being ignorant of the circumstances of the death, Edward III should have accepted it in line with what he knew about the death from the embalming woman. He did not: instead he demanded that Berkeley put forward an alternative alibi.

Hamilton protests in the next line: 'whether Edward III knew that any part of Berkeley's testimony was a lie is incapable of proof' (p. 1271). In saying this Hamilton is attempting to portray my argument in 'DEII' (see p. 71) as speculation. But his explanation, hidden in an endnote, reveals a very weak justification: 'The fact that Berkeley sent the letter informing Edward and Isabella of Edward II's death did not in and of itself place him at Berkeley.' Hamilton is obviously assuming that the letter was undated and its bearer, Gurney, did not mention his lord's presence at Berkeley to the king. He is also suggesting we should believe that Edward III did not know where the news came from, even though he knew it had been sent by Lord Berkeley, who was then at Berkeley Castle, stating that his father had recently died in that same castle. Hamilton's postulation is extraordinarily unlikely; yet on this basis he rushes to judgement, stating baldly that 'Mortimer is not correct.' If someone writes something which is not proven but highly probable, it does not mean he is incorrect. Edward III certainly had every reason to think Berkeley's actual lie about his whereabouts *was* a lie, and would have known it was so if the letter he had received in 1327 had been dated and sealed at Berkeley, or if Thomas Gurney had given any further information about the 'death'.

To list all the misrepresentations of my argument, the unwarranted aspersions, the exaggerations of doubt and the plain mistakes contained in Hamilton's piece is impossible within the scope of this chapter.[28] But one has to note that the last page and a half is truly astonishing for its catalogue of misleading analysis and unarticulated dismissive rhetorical flourishes. He begins page 1272 by dismissing my explanation of how the heart buried with Isabella in 1358 could have been her husband's if he had not died in 1327 with the words 'far-fetched to say the least'. That is not an argument. Three lines later readers are told that the connection I make between Agnes Ramsay and the tomb at Gloucester (on which her father almost certainly worked) 'is tenuous at best'. Three lines later my explanations of the advantages to Lord Mortimer in keeping Edward alive are dismissed as 'unconvincing'. Although here Hamilton does attempt an explanation of why he is unconvinced. He states: 'It is hard to see how any subsequent charge of murder could have been countered by the production of the "real Edward II", who would inevitably be seen as an imposter at this point.' None of the high prelates or magnates (many of whom had served Edward II and supported him) would have *seen* the man as an imposter. Had Mortimer, Berkeley or Maltravers walked with the living Edward II into parliament in 1330, he most certainly would not have been seen as fake, especially as so many by then believed him to be alive. Hamilton states that 'Mortimer and his supporters failed to produce the real Edward II between the time of his arrest in Nottingham on October 30 and his trial at Westminster a month later.' As Roger Mortimer was walled up (literally) in a chamber in the Tower and guarded by six guards around the clock, this is not surprising.

When Hamilton comes to pass judgement on the conclusions of 'DEII', he declares that, of the five points listed under 'The veracity of the source: conclusions' (see p. 80), 'only the second and third points are established facts, the other three being speculative'. However, the basis of his own judgements in each case is his own speculation. As regards the first, the failure to expose the corpse, his reason for doubting this is nothing more than his speculation that exposure must have taken place (even though there is no evidence that it did and a mass of circumstantial evidence that it did not). As regards the fourth, that no royal check on the corpse would have been possible without Lord Berkeley's permission, Hamilton ignores the fact that there is no evidence for such a check, and that some of those at the funeral later believed Edward II was still alive. With regard to the fifth point, *nec unquam de morte sua*, it is not 'speculation' to say this means 'he had not heard of the death'. That is what it says. It is a straight translation unadorned by Hamilton's suggestions as to how it might be made to conform to the traditional narrative.

Towards the end of the piece, Hamilton's tone of frustration becomes even more acute and, with it, his statements become totally wayward (and this, remember, is a peer-reviewed piece of work). Drawing to the end of page 1272, Hamilton declares that my 'assertions that Kent was supported by the pope . . . are drawn from thin air' even though the earl's own confession in March 1330 states that

> the pope charged him upon his benison that he should use his pains and diligence to deliver Edward, his brother, sometime king of England, and that thereto he would find his costs.[29]

The very next line states reads: 'the argument that John Pecche could have verified the presence of Edward II at Corfe in January and February 1328 is speculative at best'. No explanation is given at all for this dismissal, which flies in the face of all logic. As Pecche had the means to find out whether Edward II was really in his castle, he is unlikely to have risked his life and estates in the ex-king's cause without checking. The lowest point of Hamilton's argument appears on page 1273, where he addresses my observation that the frequently repeated statement that those accused of complicity in the supposed murder of Edward II all fled was misleading. As I point out in 'DEII', only two men possibly fled and the reason one of them did so was because he had already been sentenced to death (see pp. 93–4). Hamilton states: 'to claim that those accused in the death of Edward II did not flee is disingenuous. Two fled this life: Mortimer and Bereford.' Being killed is not synonymous with 'flight'. Hamilton adds that Gurney fled (failing to note that he did not flee until *after* he had been sentenced to death), he does not mention Lord Berkeley (who did not flee) and he admits there is no evidence as to what happened to Ockley. Given that he cannot fault my observation in any respect, the 'disingenuous' label is hardly merited.

Hamilton's article shows very clearly how a historian who is deeply committed to a traditional paradigm, and feels threatened by a refutation of it, will forget many aspects of good practice in his rush to defend his position. To be exact, he misrepresents the opposing arguments, misreads evidence, claims events happened despite a lack of evidence, and casts a number of aspersions at the professional integrity of the author of the threatening piece. But even more interesting is the fact that this piece passed peer review for *History Compass*. It suggests that peer reviewers will similarly overlook a large number of very obvious failings when the defensive piece accords with their own views. Hamilton's final conclusion was that it was 'safest to presume' that he [Edward II] died in Berkeley Castle, probably murdered on [Roger] Mortimer's orders'. In that you have his argument: a recommendation 'to presume' that everything I have written on the subject of Edward II's death is wrong and the discredited death narrative is somehow correct. One can only assume that the editors, expert adviser (named) and the anonymous peer reviewers are all in agreement with this recommendation – to base their account of a crucial historical event on a presumption.

R. M. HAINES, 'ROGER MORTIMER'S SCAM' (2008)

Also in 2008 an article by Roy Martin Haines, entitled 'Roger Mortimer's scam', was published in the *Transactions of the Bristol and Gloucestershire Archaeological Society*. Haines was briefly mentioned above but a more detailed note on him is required here, for the substance of his article is not without precedent and comes at the end of a very long and prolific career, in which he has asserted on numerous occasions that Edward II died in Berkeley Castle. In this case,

E. H. Carr's exhortation to 'study the historian before you begin to study the facts' is particularly apposite: a review of Haines's publications is most instructive in understanding his arguments.[30]

Haines submitted his Durham MA thesis in 1948 and his MLitt thesis on Wolstan de Bransford, Bishop of Worcester 1339–49, in 1954. From then on, until he retired from his post as a professor of history at a Canadian university, medieval English ecclesiastical history was his main professional interest.[31] With retirement his publications shifted in emphasis towards Edward II himself. By the time 'DEII' appeared in December 2005, he had published three pieces that dealt explicitly with the death. The first of these was an article, also in the *Transactions of the Bristol and Gloucestershire Archaeological Society*, which appeared in 1996.[32] This article formed the basis of his account of the ex-king's demise in his *King Edward II: His Life, His Reign and its Aftermath, 1284–1330*, published in 2003.[33] Between those two dates he had also published *Death of a King: An Account of the Supposed Escape and Afterlife of Edward of Caernarvon, Formerly Edward II* . . . in 2002.[34] In all three works he followed the traditional account of the death. He also mentioned the death in several other articles, for example: in an article on an appeal against Pope John XXII's translation of Bishop Adam Orleton to Winchester, published in 2001; an article entitled 'Sir Thomas Gurney of Englishcombe, regicide', published in 2004; an article on bishops during the reign of Edward II and the regency of Mortimer and Isabella, published in 2005.[35] Finally there was his note on the Council of April 1327, mentioned above, containing the footnote dismissing 'DEII' in three lines, published in February 2007. Thus it can be seen that most of his sixty-year-long career has been spent describing the reign of Edward II, and never has he wavered from the traditional death narrative in any of his works.

'Roger Mortimer's scam' starts out with a review of Hugh Glanvill's account of the preparations for the funeral of the corpse buried as that of Edward II, first published in 1886.[36] This is a strange beginning. Glanvill was an Exchequer clerk and not present at Berkeley in September 1327, so any information conveyed to him would have come through the machinery of the royal household and, as shown in 'DEII', this was dependent on Berkeley's announcement of the death. Haines notes that the period of attendance for those watching the embalmed corpse did not start until 20 October – in the cases of Bernard de Burgh and Richard de Potesgrave – or the following day in the case of the bishop of Landaff.

According to Glanvill, only one person was in attendance before that: William Beaukaire, who had been guarding the corpse since the day of the supposed death, 21 September. As noted in 'DEII', Beaukaire was probably already at Berkeley (see p. 66). If not, his presence on the 21st indicates he acted in response to Mortimer's order to William Ockley to go to Berkeley and bring about a 'suitable remedy'. Whether sent by Mortimer or one of Berkeley's entourage, he was certainly not appointed by Edward III or one of his household officers (then more than 100 miles away, at Lincoln). Haines's starting point therefore only underlines the fact that there is no evidence that there was any independent verification of the body buried as that of the supposed ex-king – a point contrary to his subsequent argument.[37]

Haines's tendency to trust the chroniclers' narratives raises difficulties. Although he has checked the date of the break-up of the parliament and found it to be the 23rd, he follows the chronicler William Dene in stating that the king's death was announced 'in parliament' on that day.[38] However, as the announcement of the death was addressed to the king, and we know from the king's own letter (written the following day) that he received the news during the night of the 23rd, Dene's testimony is suspect. It was written later and further away geographically, and so must be regarded as less reliable than the king's own testimony on this matter. Whatever the reason for Dene's confusion (perhaps there was a short gathering after parliament had broken up on the morning of the 24th to tell the news to those who were still at Lincoln), it cannot resolve satisfactorily in his favour.[39]

Next Haines turns to more weighty subjects: the veracity of the message carried from Berkeley to Lincoln.

> The suggestion that it was untrue, thus concealing the fact that the former king remained alive, cannot be substantiated, nor can the response of Thomas Berkeley when indicted [in the presence of the king in full parliament] – the assembly of November 1330 at Westminster – be reliably interpreted to fit this model.[40]

The first of these two assertions is astonishing. If Professor Haines genuinely believes that the message sent by Lord Berkeley was not 'untrue' then he is suggesting that the ex-king died of natural causes at precisely the same time as Lord Mortimer sent the message about finding a 'suitable remedy' to Berkeley via William Ockley. There can be no two ways about this: the message was untrue in some respect or other – and thus issued in bad faith – as I pointed out in

'DEII' (see pp. 75–6). As for the response, although Haines states it 'cannot be substantiated', he goes on to attribute a definite meaning in bold italics in the next sentence: 'his claim was that he knew nothing *about* or *concerning* the death'. We have already gone over this in regard to Professors Carpenter and Hamilton: to assign a definite meaning of this nature to Berkeley's words, with the implication that the literal meaning may be discounted, is to mislead the reader. Moreover, if Berkeley was claiming (in 1330) that he 'knew nothing about or concerning' the death, then he could not have conveyed a 'true' message (as Haines would have it) in 1327. Despite this inconsistency in his own argument, Haines states that my own literal reading of this evidence 'is unsound'.

Haines attempts to refute my claim that there was no display of the unembalmed corpse. In reply to my statement that 'there was no credible exposure or identification of the corpse prior to burial' he argues that 'this is not strictly accurate'. Like Hamilton, he does this by 'explaining' the meaning of the words that run contrary to his interpretation, in this case Murimuth's *superficialiter*. Haines acknowledges that the body must have been embalmed prior to its delivery to Gloucester on 20 October, but states that *superficialiter* means 'they could not inspect it very closely'. This is incorrect: it means 'superficially'. Haines adds that Murimuth 'did not suggest that those who came could not recognise the corpse as that of the king, nor did any other chronicler . . .'. As mentioned above, chroniclers do not normally say what did *not* happen, so this is a spurious line of argument. As for any other chroniclers – there were none. No other chronicler mentions any exposure of the corpse at all. It turns out that Haines's basis for stating that my statement 'is not strictly accurate' is that he imagines some check on the identity of the corpse took place, even though there is no evidence that it did.

Haines agrees with me that there was 'a very narrow window for examining the unembalmed face of the corpse' in 1327 but then states baldly that 'what was feared was the manner of the death', without any evidence why that was particularly 'feared' at this juncture, or who by, or why anything was 'feared' at all in the days after the 21st in Berkeley Castle.[41] There is no evidence that anyone except those with Lord Berkeley's permission saw the face of the corpse at this time. Haines failure to grasp this point is exposed in the very next line: 'one cannot assume that Pecche or Berenger really *knew* that the king was alive'. Haines fails to realize that Pecche's knowledge did not come from seeing the embalmed and concealed face of the supposed ex-king but from gaining access to Corfe Castle in the wake of the concealment of the face of the ex-king in December 1327.

Given this misunderstanding, Haines's article is particularly weak on the Kent plot. He does little but recite the traditional narrative as if it is gospel truth: 'no one could have been more gullible, it would seem, than Kent', he declares on page 149, ignoring my points about Kent's gullibility being a modern conceit contradicted by contemporary evidence (see pp. 83–4). Haines then explains the unambiguous statements that Kent had tried to release the ex-king from Corfe and make him king again by stating that 'it was Kent's intention that was on trial rather than the veracity of his belief'. As the Melton Letter and as Kent's own confession both reveal, both the archbishop and the earl wholeheartedly believed that Edward II was alive in 1330 and sought to rescue him. They were not stupid men. If Archbishop Melton could believe that Edward II was still alive in 1330, then clearly it was entirely plausible that he was. In this sense, it is misleading to distinguish between 'intention' and practice. This explanation is particularly hollow when it is the inference of a modern historian who has no evidence that his subjects made such a distinction themselves.

As we near the end of the article, Haines's reliance on the chroniclers becomes more overt. On the question of the information underpinning Kent's plot, he ignores everything in 'DEII' about Pecche having access to Corfe Castle and resorts to the age-old story in the chronicle of Geoffrey le Baker, written more than twenty years later, about Lord Mortimer's agents provocateurs luring Kent into a treasonable plot. He ignores the arguments in 'DEII' against Kent's belief in his brother's survival being due to Lord Mortimer. Instead he states that 'it was Mortimer who had an interest in furthering the idea that the king was alive'.[42] This is stated as fact despite being both an assumption and questionable on at least three grounds, as stated in the comment on his note on the Stamford Council in *EHR* in 2007 (see above). On this same page he repeats the other mistake he made in that note: that Mortimer 'admitted before the people the deceit he had practised on the earl of Kent who had been put to death wrongfully'. As stated above, Mortimer only admitted that the earl was put to death 'wrongfully'. He did not admit deceiving the earl. Finally, Haines tries to discredit each of the six inconsistencies that I point out in the proceedings of the parliament of November 1327. Some of his remarks were anticipated and dealt with in 'DEII'. Others are repetitions of the traditional explanation for the inconsistencies in the death narrative.[43]

There is no new evidence here, nor any example of old evidence being used in a new, reliable and meaningful way. There is no engagement with the information-based argument, which requires the evidence for the death and the evidence for the survival to be seen together, in balance. There is no sensitivity to the fact that the historian who wishes to maintain that Edward II died in Berkeley Castle has to put some new argument together: he or she cannot simply presume it happened on the basis of the chronicles, official record entries and various commemorative events in abbeys and priories – the information basis for all that evidence has been questioned and shown to be a single message sent in bad faith, which was later contradicted by the sender. Like Hamilton's article, Haines's argument is based on criticizing my points one by one and hoping thereby to discredit my entire argument, leaving the traditional narrative untarnished. Laying aside the fact that that does not answer my argument, his piece solves none of the objective inconsistencies in the events following on from the death. Haines admits that 'many difficult questions defy elucidation' – ignoring the fact that my argument solves most of them, if not all. Sadly, he then goes on to cast aspersions on my work, coming up with lines such as 'the entire scheme has an air of unreality' (p. 151), and that my work is 'no more than a theory' (p. 153). Earlier he had stated that 'Agatha Christie would have revelled in a plot of such complexity' (p. 143). After being compared to Dan Brown, a reference to Agatha Christie comes as no surprise. But Haines's piece, like Hamilton's and Carpenter's, is a protest, not a coherent historical argument that accounts for all the evidence.

One last point arises from this article. Many of the arguments it contains appeared in the peer reviewer's comments on my second submission to *EHR*. Indeed, so strongly were those comments reminiscent of Haines's previous publications that I wrote to the editor to point this out, and expressing my sincere hope that he had not sought a review from a man who had repeatedly shown himself to be an ardent supporter of the veracity of the death narrative. The editor's reply sought to clarify the decision-making process without naming names. However, certain similarities in the text reveal that Haines was almost certainly the peer reviewer.[44] This has a worrying implication. If correct, it would mean the editor of *EHR* sent a highly contentious article about the later life of Edward II to a retired academic whom he *knew* to have a pre-formed judgement on the matter of the death. We can be confident of this knowledge not just because of Haines's many publications maintaining the certainty of Edward II's death but also because the editor was at that point in time – October 2006 – just about to publish Haines's curt three-line dismissal of 'DEII' in the same journal.[45] Moreover, when Haines recommended refusal, the editor accepted this recommendation – even though he knew there was a conflict of interest. This is akin to the official refereeing a boxing match quietly asking the holder of the title whether he would like his opponent disqualified. It may well be that my article did not merit publication. Nonetheless, anyone who is seriously interested in how academic consensus is developed and maintained should take note.

R. M. HAINES, 'SUMPTUOUS APPAREL' (2009)

Given Haines's statement of belief in the traditional narrative, it was something of a surprise that he edited the Melton Letter for *EHR*. Anyone presenting a document in the 'Notes and Documents' section of this journal is expected to provide an introduction which sets the context for the document and raises awareness of its importance for research. Of course, one expects that such introductory material is even-handed in its approach: the editor should not impose interpretations and meanings upon the reader but should facilitate the reader arriving at his or her own judgement. In this case, this called for a careful balancing act, as the Melton Letter (translated in full in the next chapter) includes the line: 'you will want to know that we have certain news [*certeins noueles*] of our liege lord Edward of Carnarvon who is alive and in good bodily health'.[46]

Haines states at the outset that this 'has been invoked as proof that Edward really was alive at the time of writing'. To the best of my knowledge, this is incorrect: the only instance of this document previously being cited in connection with the death of Edward II is in 'DEII' and it was not 'invoked as proof' there. But what is more extraordinary is that Haines does not suggest that this letter might have significance for the survival narrative. He admits that it 'raises a number of issues, some at present insoluble.' He adds: 'if Edward had died at Berkeley in 1327 how could the archbishop be so easily convinced, or should one say deceived?' We have nothing to suggest that Melton was *easily* convinced, let alone that he was deceived. And that is the only line of enquiry Haines suggests. He does not ask the corresponding question of what the letter reveals if Edward had *not* died in 1327, which would seem a far more logical approach as this is precisely what the letter claims. This is hardly a neutral stance.

Here is a key element of the anti-revisionist argument laid bare. Although there are a number of 'insoluble' issues with the traditional narrative, Haines considers it fair to ignore these, to sweep them under the carpet, and to denigrate attempts to explain them as 'conjecture'. Likewise by presenting this letter exclusively in the context of Melton being deceived (rather than well informed) he skews the questions arising from the letter away from the survival of Edward II. This seems rather unsubtle, and indeed it is; but one has to notice that in the same article Haines is even more blatant in his praising the excellence of the research of another academic whose views concur with his own in denying the survival narrative. In the final footnote Haines states 'Seymour Phillips, in his excellently researched article, "Edward II in Italy . . . " agrees with me in not believing that Edward survived after 1326.' Such praise for this 'excellently researched' article is also to be found in Haines's 'Roger Mortimer's scam', where he writes that Phillips, 'like the present author, does not believe that Edward II was alive after 1327.' He adds that Phillips's 'article is impressively researched and makes much use of Italian and French material . . .'. Laying aside the quality of Phillips' piece (in which he missed a number of pieces of evidence that run counter to his argument), Haines's eagerness to accentuate the 'excellence' of some work which supports his own view, while denigrating my own, is a deeply unwise mode of argument. He fails to note that Phillips's 'excellently researched' article was actually written two years before my 'DEII' was published, and therefore takes no note of the basis for the survival narrative.

Haines's skewed view of this letter, and his single-mindedness in exploring only the question of how Melton could have been 'deceived', means that he missed many of the subtle implications of this letter, not least its timing in relation to the Kent plot (discussed in the next chapter). However, it was an unfortunate piece in one regard more than any other. Melton's letter demonstrates his entire confidence that Edward II *could* have been alive in 1330. Indeed, unless one wishes to suggest that it is a forgery (which Haines does not), it proves that Melton believed Edward II's survival was entirely plausible in 1330. If a loyal, capable archbishop believed the ex-king could still be alive in 1330 (despite the royal funeral), more recent commentators are in no position to dismiss the survival narrative as 'impossible'.

J. R. S. PHILLIPS, *EDWARD II* (2010)

The final commentary that needs to be considered here is Seymour Phillips's long-awaited volume on Edward II in the Yale University Press 'English Monarchs' series. In this work Phillips follows Haines in setting aside 'DEII' as a narrative which he does not, or will not, accept. To be specific, he acknowledges on pages 578–9 that Lord Berkeley lied in announcing the death of Edward II from natural causes, as showed in 'DEII'; but he disagrees regarding the nature of that lie. Like, Haines, Carpenter and Hamilton, he interprets *nec unquam scivit de morte sua* as meaning that Lord Berkeley did not know the circumstances of the king's death. He tries to strengthen this by claiming that, because Berkeley said in the preceding sentence that 'he was never an accomplice, a helper or a procurer in his death', the phrase *nec unquam scivit de morte sua* 'can only mean that he knew the death had occurred but that he claimed he had no part in it.' This 'can only mean' is a non-sequitur. Just because Berkeley said he was not an 'accomplice, helper or procurer' in the death does not imply that his denial of knowledge of the death or its circumstances 'can only mean' he lied in one particular way in 1327 rather than another.

Phillips's line of argument is consequently very similar to the three previous commentators who do not wish 'DEII' to affect our understanding of Edward II's death. In his examination of the causes of death he never once explains how any of the chroniclers were supposed to have access to accurate information concerning the Berkeley Castle plot. With regard to the question of why Sir John Pecche believed Edward II was alive in 1330, he speculates that, contrary to the evidence, he had no way of finding out. To make this argument possible he suggests that Sir John Maltravers was really put in charge of Corfe before the date of his formal appointment in 1329, and assumes that, because of this, Pecche had no links after 1327 with the men who had until that date served him in the castle (where Pecche had been resident for a number of years and for which he was still, in theory, financially accountable). On the basis of this suggestion and assumption, he concludes that Pecche would not have found out whether the treasonable plot on which he was risking his life was based on truth or not (even though he was still officially the constable) and so Pecche 'may have been as much influenced by rumour and disinformation as anyone else'. This is deeply dubious as a method: to look for cracks in an argument with which one does not agree, and, having failed to find any, to use speculation in the place of evidence in a counter argument.

This is a shame, as Phillips is probably the most experienced historian of the reign of Edward II. But, in this particular matter of the death, he has let methodological standards slip. On page 580 he quotes his own inability to understand Roger Mortimer's motives as an argument against the narrative I outlined in 'DEII'. As stated before, motive is a means of understanding why someone acted in a certain way, not a means of proving what did or did not happen. It is even more disappointing that the fundamental basis for Phillips's belief in the traditional narrative turns out to be his preference for a simple interpretation, as opposed to a complicated one. On page 581 he states: 'the simplest explanation is surely the best one: that Edward II did die at Berkeley on 21 September and that he was murdered or helped on his way to death, either from a pre-existing illness or from physical decline and depression'. That is the basis of his argument for ignoring the implications of Edward II's survival after 1327: not wanting things to become too complicated.

Can it really be the case that an experienced scholar is prepared to set aside peer-reviewed research and in-depth argument just because of his personal preference for a simple interpretation of the evidence? Yes, it would appear. Without presenting any stronger argument, he concludes definitively that 'Edward II died in September 1327' (p. 582). By page 596 this preference has become a matter of certainty: Phillips declares that 'Edward II was certainly dead' by 1336. To state things are 'certain' when they are a matter of personal opinion, and there is plenty of evidence to the contrary, is the sort of rhetoric that has brought academic history into disrepute with philosophers and critical theorists over the last forty years. The fact is that the simplest interpretation is not always the best. It certainly is not in this case, as it leaves so many objective inconsistencies, results in a narrative in which we have to invent reasons why the earl of Kent died and close our eyes to the means by which the chroniclers and members of the court heard that the ex-king had died. One is reminded of the analogy at the start of this chapter. It may well appear that the Sun orbits the Earth but that 'simplest' interpretation is not a good one, and certainly not 'the best'. It is just the easiest, most facile one, based on a face-value acceptance of the preferred evidence and a refusal to question the evidence that does not accord with what was previously thought.

There is a methodological lesson in this, and a warning to us all. Too much experience can hamper one's openness to new ideas. Historians regularly draw attention to bias in their sources but rarely do they draw attention to their own biases. These are equally dangerous, for they slowly become fixed over time, so that by the time they are emeriti, historians are working within hardened shells of pre-formed opinion, unable to reflect the new thinking or adapt to it. While Phillips's book is the best overview of the reign of Edward II, the end section is a classic example of the hardened shell of pre-formed opinion inhibiting alternative thinking. For example, the part in which he deals with the later life of Edward II is almost identical to his 2003 paper 'Edward II in Italy', published in 2005. His verdict on the Fieschi Letter in both works is the same: it is 'superficially plausible but ultimately unbelievable'. Between 2003 and 2010 his thinking has not changed, even though the appearance of 'DEII' in 2005 shows that the survival is distinctly possible, at the very least. In this context it hardly comes as a surprise to see that Phillips names this whole section 'Edwardus Redivivus' after Haines's 1996 paper of the same name. Indeed, Phillips praises Haines's piece as 'excellent'.[47] How coincidental is it that Haines, in 'Roger Mortimer's Scam', describes Phillips's work in its original 2003 form as 'excellent'? Senior common room colleagues mutually praising one another's work as 'excellent' may temporarily preserve the façade of academic authority in the face of an intellectual attack but this sort of behaviour brings the profession into disrepute. Scholars should *demonstrate* excellence, not mutually assign it to their friends and colleagues. The truth is that, on this particular matter of the death and survival of Edward II, neither Haines's work nor Phillips's is 'excellent'. Both writers ignore the salutary lessons of postmodernism; both are seemingly unaware of the epistemological fragility of their narratives, adopting an unjustifiable default position (that Edward II died in 1327). Both assume that contradictory evidence may be disregarded, or discussed in isolation. Both consider chronicle and record evidence as static texts rather than having a deeper temporal dimension; consequently both ignore the need to show how the information in their preferred evidence is rooted in past reality. Their consensus on the death of Edward II is an example of history as academic ritual: it has nothing to do with the past.

CONCLUSION

It is fair to say that 'DEII' has had more than its fair share of detractors. That so many of them have seen fit to dismiss the argument *in principle* is a significant indicator of the still very unscientific way that many historians determine the details of what happened in the past. Many do not see that they are vulnerable to the criticisms of theorists and postmodern philosophers who would belittle the ability of the historian to know the past. Perhaps they see these threats as largely external, and regard themselves safe from theory, cocooned in academic departments or, even more safely, in academic retirement. Either way, to fail to address historical questions adequately is not just negative in theory, it is also to obstruct valid research from within the history community.

I have yet to read any comment, criticism or observation that causes me to want to revise 'DEII'. The information on the death-narrative side of the balance is simply too weak for us to have any confidence in the traditional account. The information on the survival-side is too strong, the four pertinent information streams being corroborated by men like Archbishop Melton who were in a good position to know the truth. Considering that the survival narrative solves a number of questions that the traditionalists are prepared to ignore as 'at present insoluble' – there is no point in maintaining a polite ambivalence. I am as confident that Edward II did not die in 1327 as I am that his father did die in 1307 and his son in 1377.

The historiographical analysis reveals a great deal, however, about how historical consensus is formed, and how a historical peer group will attempt to resist paradigm change. Certain trends are common to a number of attacks on 'DEII'. The first and most obvious is the tendency simply to presume that the survival narrative is wrong. Although it might seem strange for me to say so, this is actually quite a healthy starting point for it indicates a natural questioning. However, in this context it also has a very unhealthy side-effect because in no instance above has it been accompanied by a reflexive self-questioning, that the death narrative might be wrong. This assumption of the correctness of the tradition has led to some readings of evidence that cannot be termed good practice. One cannot approve of the tendency of the historians mentioned above to filter Latin words and phrases such as *superficialiter* and *nec unquam scivit* through their own prejudgements, and to present a series of translations of these words that are all, in one way or another, apart from the literal meaning of the original. Likewise one cannot approve of misrepresentations of evidence – such as Hamilton's rhetorical question concerning the burial of the king in his coronation robes, or Haines's repeated mistake as to what Roger Mortimer confessed to on the gallows – which follow on from assumptions of 'correctness' and the consequent failure to adjust one's beliefs to examine the evidence for what it actually says.

Considering Carpenter, Hamilton, Haines and Phillips are all professors of history, it is not surprising that they feel they have great authority to pronounce verdicts upon the past. However, it is worrying that they all regularly issue superficial verdicts such as 'unconvincing' and 'implausible' on arguments with which they do not agree, instead of tackling the arguments. All four historians resort to this practice and it seems in each case that they are 'unconvinced' largely because of their predisposition not to be convinced, rather than anything I have written. It is idle and weak to dismiss as 'speculative at best' the argument that John Pecche took advantage of his constableship of Corfe Castle to check whether Edward II was in that castle prior to staking his life and lands on the fact. One can say the same for the refusal to accept serious points because they are 'incapable of proof'. This is facile – not least because it is impossible to prove that Edward II died in Berkeley Castle on 21 September 1327. It brings us back to Hayden White's observation about science and art quoted at the start of this chapter. To dismiss something as incapable of proof without stating how and what test of proof is required is not a good scientific approach. It is not even logical. Nor is it justifiable to resist the survival narrative on grounds of 'implausibility'. The Melton Letter shows very clearly that the archbishop of York believed Edward II might still be alive in 1330: if he could believe it then what is the basis for a modern historian declaring it 'implausible'? Only a predisposition to maintain the traditional narrative.

The above three methodological weaknesses (skewed or filtered translations of source material, misrepresentation of evidence, dismissal of arguments as 'unconvincing', 'speculative', 'incapable of proof' or 'implausible') are all common methodological weaknesses, regularly encountered in traditionalists' analyses. Another is the practice of relying on rhetorical questions to cast doubt upon a historical reading. This is bad practice, especially when it is used to cover up a lack of hard evidence with which to counter what is being proposed. If one does not answer one's own rhetorical question, all one has done is to cast aspersions on a statement. For example, take Hamilton's rhetorical question,

> if indeed the corpse of an imposter was immediately embalmed, sealed in cerecloth and never viewed by any independent witness, what was the point of burying this fake with

the coronation robes of the former king in addition to the outward display of the regalia with the effigy?

This is a question easily countered (as above) but for the historian to leave it hanging like this is actually a failure of the questioner to think through the argument for himself. One could raise rhetorical questions about anything. Such questioning superficially detracts from the opponent's historical argument but the questioner has not actually presented an alternative. He has simply implied that he does not wish to accept it. This is protest, not argument.

Another worrying trend in the recent historiography of this subject is the tendency to resort to reductionism to discredit revisionist arguments. Four examples of this will illustrate. To state that an examination of the corpse buried at Berkeley took place because there is no evidence that an examination did *not* take place is to invent an unsubstantiated narrative. There is no evidence to say that Edward II could not turn a triple somersault but that does not permit us to say in the context of a scholarly argument that he could, or even that he might have been able to. A second reductionism is that anyone claiming to be Edward II after 1327 was a pretender and thus comparable to all other pretenders, i.e. not whom he claimed to be. Edward II's case must not be conflated with those of John of Powderham (who claimed to be a son of Edward I) or Thomas Warde of Trumpington (who claimed to be Richard II) or Perkin Warbeck or anyone else. To make pronouncements on this basis is as illogical as saying that, because almost all squirrels in the UK are grey, a squirrel cannot be red. A third form of reductionism is that a simple narrative is automatically preferable to a complicated one. Simplicity has its virtues but it is not always correct. The fourth form of reductionism is the practice of praising the work of like-minded academics as 'excellent', thereby promoting the 'excellence' of one's own views by association. This strikes me as scholarly propaganda.

Finally, the reason for the title of this essay should be explained. Obviously it derives from the title of the 1957 film, *Twelve Angry Men*. The drama takes place almost entirely in a jury room after a murder trial in America. At first, eleven of the jury are convinced that the accused is guilty. One man (an architect by profession) raises some resistance – and convinces one or two of the others to start reviewing the evidence that they have heard. Gradually they find more and more errors in what seemed at first a watertight case. Other jurors start to change their opinions, persuaded by the architect's logical arguments. But it is not by logic alone that the shift takes place. Some are moved by the integrity of the architect and his compassion for a fellow human being. Two or three, it turns out, only voted for a guilty verdict in the first place because everyone else said the accused was guilty and they did not want to stand out from the crowd. Soon those in favour of a guilty sentence are reduced to a hard core of those who have their own arguments in favour of guilt (and refuse to accept the arguments proposed by the architect), and those who have a prejudice because executing such murderous individuals, as they suppose the accused to be, will somehow improve society. The matter is only resolved when the logical arguments in favour of guilt are called into question, and revealed as superficial, and the deepest prejudice of the strongest individual character is exposed – with the result that the other jurors want to disassociate themselves from the man in question, and consequently isolate him.

Human beings in all walks of life are much more than just creatures of logic, and that is true for the scholars noted above as much as for the characters in the film. I do believe the matter of Edward II's death will follow a similar path, albeit much more slowly. Max Planck wrote that 'a scientific truth does not triumph by convincing its opponents and making them see the light but rather because its opponents eventually die, and a new generation grows up that is familiar with it'.[48] That may well be the case: I suspect that a number of years will pass before the questions I have raised about Edward II's death are accepted as orthodoxy. It might not happen within the next ten or twenty years, or even within my lifetime; but one day it will. And when it does, the majority of scholars will have the means to reconsider not just Edward II's death but the certainty of many other established 'facts'. It is ironic but it is perhaps a truism of historical research that a sincere and ardent quest for certainty is more likely to reveal provable falsehoods than undisputed facts.

Notes

1 White, 'Burden', 112.
2 *Brut*, i, 267. This judgement no longer exists in the original (official) version – the roll for that parliament is no longer extant – but it appears in a number of the contemporary chronicles, most notably the many copies of the longer continuations of the *Brut* and *Murimuth*, 60.
3 These two were John Gillingham, 'Fathers and sons', *TLS* (19 May 2006), 28, and

the review in *The Economist* (20 April 2006). Professor Gillingham wrote: 'What is distinctive about this book is the space it gives to Edward III not as any sort of a father, but as a son. In his recent (2003) biography of Roger Mortimer, *The Greatest Traitor*, Ian Mortimer caused shockwaves by arguing that the murder of Edward II at Berkeley Castle in 1327 had been faked. In consequence, as he explains here, he spent a considerable amount of time in 2003–4 revisiting the subject, and writing it up in still greater detail.' The review in *The Economist* stated 'Mr Mortimer believes that Edward II, Edward's father, was not murdered in 1327 but survived well into his son's reign – and that Edward knew it, and that many of his actions and attitudes were conditioned by this knowledge. This theory, first advanced in Mr Mortimer's study of Roger Mortimer, *The Greatest Traitor*, is forcefully reprised here, with extra evidence . . .'

4 Jonathan Sumption, 'A glorious road to ruin', *The Spectator* (25 February 2006), 42.

5 Jonathan Sumption, 'Plotting the past', *Guardian* (5 April 2003). To be fair to Sumption, he had previously attempted a rebuttal (in the *Guardian*) of the argument as presented in my book *The Greatest Traitor*, and so perhaps felt he would be repeating himself unnecessarily. In this he described the ex-king's death as fact and states 'on the whole, medieval kings did not survive for 10 or 15 years into the reigns of their successors.' He then incorrectly claimed that my argument in *Greatest Traitor* 'turns on four points'. He identified these as the earl of Kent's plot, Berkeley's testimony in parliament, William Norwell's reference in his account book to the king's father arriving at Cologne as William the Welshman, and the Fieschi Letter. In each case he treated the matter in isolation and dismissed my argument preferring his own. In the case of Kent he states 'it was a common occurrence in the late middle ages, after the violent death of a king, for the enemies of his successor to spread reports that he was still living. The earl may well have believed them but he was a famously stupid man . . .'. The earl's behaviour was not standard practice, as here made out. Nor was he 'famously stupid', his lack of intelligence being invented by T. F. Tout, a twentieth-century historian. With regard to Berkeley's testimony, Sumption declared that my translation of *nec unquam scivit de morte sua usque in presenti parliament isto* as 'nor had he ever heard of his death until this present parliament' 'is plainly not the correct translation of the text'. The other two points were (Norwell and Fieschi) not germane to the argument as set out in *Greatest Traitor*, being only discussed later, in the wake of my conclusion that in 1330 Edward II 'was not believed to be dead, and known not to have died in Berkeley's custody' (p. 251).

6 Helen Castor, 'Edward III lived too long to be great', *Sunday Telegraph* (26 February 2006).

7 Michael Prestwich, 'A warrior who lifted the Crown', *Times Higher Education Supplement* (22 December 2006).

8 Prestwich, Britnell and Frame (eds), *Thirteenth Century England X*. In the preface the editors stated as fact that Edward II's 'afterlife' in Ireland, France, Germany and

Italy was 'imagined'. Alarmingly, they then wrote: 'It may be too much to hope that his [Seymour Phillips's] paper will put an end to speculation that the king survived his supposed murder in September 1327 . . .'

9 Mortimer, 'Revisionism revisited'.

10 Kuhn, 64.

11 Kuhn, 5.

12 In view of the importance of this unpublished correspondence in the current context, it has all been deposited in the library of the University of Exeter (EUL), where it is available for public inspection under the reference MS 371.

13 EUL MS 371/5/o.

14 EUL MS 371/5/o. The reviewer's comment that a 'hermit' was presented to Edward III as his father is a conflation of the entries concerning William le Galeys with the subject of the Fieschi Letter – a conflation of identities which is ironically the opposite of what this referee says he believes. The rest of the report comments favourably on my work on the Fieschi family and made some minor points

15 The reviewer stated: 'This paper is not suitable for publication in *EHR*. It is possible that a substantially reworked version might be acceptable at some future point, but not in the near future . . . The purpose of the paper is entirely negative: the author deliberately eschews any attempt to explain what *did* happen if the old interpretation is not longer tenable. Presumably, the point is to 'clear the ground' so that the debate can proceed to this next stage once historians have accepted that the traditional view is incorrect. For this reason alone, *EHR* is not the appropriate forum for this paper: even if the argument put forward was watertight, it would be too narrow in character to justify publication.' See EUL MS 371/3/c.

16 EUL MS 371/3/c.

17 EUL MS 371/5/o.

18 EUL MS 371/7/c.

19 Haines, 'The Stamford Council', 142, n. 8.

20 *PROME*, November 1330, items 11 and 12.

21 Carpenter, 'What happened to Edward II?', 32–4.

22 Fryde, *Tyranny*, 203.

23 Carpenter was sent a copy of the chapter at the time, and stated in an email that he would read it 'with great interest'. I did not receive any further response.

24 'Uncertain death'.

25 Apart from 'Uncertain death', his publications include one book-length study, *Piers Gaveston*, and an edition, *The Charter Witness Lists*. His shorter publications include 'Edward II and the murage of Dublin'; 'Piers Gaveston and the royal treasure'; 'Apocalypse not'; 'Charter witness lists'; and 'Character of Edward II'. A recent monograph, 'Plantagenets', covering the five kings 1216–1399, was published in May 2010 – after the completion of the text of this book.

26 'Uncertain death', 1270.

27 Burden, 'Re-writing', 17.

28 With regard to the aspersions on the present author, refer to the sequence of notes on page 1276 for a sample of instances. Note 43 reads: 'Mortimer himself admits that the cerecloth was removed from the face of Edward I when it was examined in 1774'. Reference to the relevant section of 'DEII' (see p. 67) shows that I noted the cerecloth was still in place in 1774, not that it was removed. The next note, no. 44, states 'Mortimer omits this official proclamation from his process of dissemination.' The proclamation that I omitted was (in Hamilton's words) that 'the death of Edward II was announced in the public forum of parliament.' This is noted in several chronicles; but checking the date of the break-up of that parliament reveals that it ceased to sit on the 23rd September. As Edward III only received the news of the death on the night of the 23rd (as stated in his own letter dated the following day), he could not have had it announced 'in the public forum of parliament' during the day of the 23rd. Rather there must have been a more informal announcement to those who had attended parliament after it broke up, which I referred to in 'DEII' as 'the more general announcement at Lincoln' (see p. 68). In note 47, Hamilton states: 'Mortimer follows a line of argument originally developed by Fryde although Fryde is not cited', insinuating that I have failed to mention a source. This turns out to be the reading that *nec unquam scivit de morte sua* might mean what it literally means: that Lord Berkeley had not heard of the death. Hamilton is thus reprimanding me for translating an important piece of evidence literally and not citing someone else who happened to translate it literally. Note 52 is the explanation about Edward III knowing Berkeley was lying when he said he was at Bradley at the time he reported the death at Berkeley (mentioned above). And note 57 is an even more wilful aspersion. Hamilton labels my assertion in 'DEII' that 'The argument that Agnes received this money for work her father did does not hold water as he died in 1349, nine years before Isabella' as 'disingenuous as debts of this order went unpaid for years on end in Exchequer accounts.' While debts did go unpaid for years on end, unless Hamilton has some evidence that Isabella started building her tomb in the 1340s, and that it was constructed by a man who died in 1349 (even though she herself lived until 1358), my comment is hardly 'disingenuous'.

29 *Murimuth*, 255. It also appears mentioned in *Brut*, i, 263.

30 Carr, 23.

31 He completed a DLitt at Oxford on 'The administration of the diocese of Worcester in the first half of the 14th century' in 1959 and, by the time he was elected a Fellow of the Society of Antiquaries (March 1967), he had published this thesis as a monograph and an accompanying calendar of the register of Wolstan de Bransford, as well as three articles on the ecclesiastical history of medieval Worcestershire. Since then he has published monographs on the political churchmen Adam of Orleton and John Stratford (*The Church and Politics* and *Archbishop John Stratford*) another book on English ecclesiastical history (*Ecclesia Anglicana*), and two further

calendars of entries in episcopal registers (*Calendar of the Register of Adam de Orleton* and *Calendar of the Register of Simon de Montacute*). In addition, since 1967 he has published approximately forty articles in journals such as the *Journal of Ecclesiastical History*, *Canadian Journal of History*, *Mediaeval Studies*, *Bulletin of the Institute of Historical Research*, *Studies in Church History*, *Revue Bénédictine*, *Transactions of the Worcestershire Archaeological Society*, *Archives*, and *EHR*.

32 'Afterlife'.

33 Haines, *King Edward II*, 219–38.

34 Haines, *Death of a King*.

35 See Haines, 'An innocent abroad'; 'Looking back in anger'; 'Sir Thomas Gurney'; and 'The episcopate during the reign of Edward II'.

36 This was originally published in 'Documents'.

37 On page 141 Haines suggests that Moore's assertion that Beaukaire might have been 'a royal officer independent of Berkeley and Maltravers' should not be ruled out, and thus it was not the case that the ex-king was 'at the mercy of his keepers'. However, as Beaukaire was there at the command of either Mortimer or Berkeley, we can be sure he was not independent. Had he dropped by as a matter of coincidence, he would hardly have been given sole guardianship of the ex-king in the wake of him supposedly being killed that same day. Although Haines states that Beaukaire's presence at Caerphilly in 1326 'suggests he was not a Mortimer adherent', this does not mean he had not found favour with the new regime over the course of the year.

38 'Scam', 144.

39 Supporting his interpretation, Haines states that 'in view of the distance involved, the announcement in parliament was apparently made on the 23rd'. Although he mentions the letter of the 24th (TNA DL10/253), it does not look as though he has read the text which clearly states the news reached the king during the night – and, given the distance from Berkeley, as well as the context of the letter, that can only be the night of the 23rd.

40 'Scam', 144–5. The section in square brackets is given by Haines in Latin.

41 'Scam', 146, n. 43.

42 'Scam', 152.

43 'Scam', 153–4. For the sake of completeness, brief responses to his objections follow. With regard to the first (that one cannot accept that Mortimer spread the word about Edward II being alive) he states that it 'overrides the testimony of reliable chroniclers'. No chroniclers are reliable in all respects: to suggest that they were in a matter of political intrigue is to place undue faith in those writing in Edward III's reign, to assume they all had reliable information sources in central government (which they did not) and to fail to address my specific points on the matter in 'DEII'. With regard to the second (that no charges were brought against John Pecche) he makes the mistake of stating that this was *after* Mortimer's fall (his italic). As

noted in 'DEII' Pecche was restored to favour in August 1330, before Mortimer's fall: Haines has not followed note 109 in 'DEII'. On the third issue, he disputes that Edward III consciously allowed Berkeley to lie in November 1330 concerning his whereabouts because 'one wonders about the "consciously"; it was only much later that the truth about Thomas Berkeley's whereabouts was discovered from the record.' Herein he ignores my point about Edward III receiving the letter from Lord Berkeley about an event that occurred at Berkeley Castle while Lord Berkeley was there in person (see comments on Hamilton's article). Haines's 'wondering' is not a good basis to presume Edward III believed Lord Berkeley was elsewhere. The fourth point (*nec unquam scivit*) he flatly denies is an anomaly, even though it has proved the basis of so much discussion for the last century and therefore clearly is problematic. The fifth inconsistency he objects to on account of Berkeley's trial in parliament and 'the verdict of the country': Edward III did not need a jury to empower him to take Berkeley's lands, titles and life, if he felt he was guilty. My point stands. The sixth point (about the writs to capture the guilty men being issued so late) is countered with rhetorical questions, not evidence.

44 'Scam' states 'it assumes what is as yet unproved: that the king did not die at that time' (p. 146). The *EHR* peer reviewer wrote in 2006 'It assumes what is as yet unproven: that Edward II was kept alive'. The similarity of the phrases might be a coincidence, but in the wake of the arguments being so similar, that is unlikely. Further checking reveals that the peer reviewer commented on the Fieschi Letter as being 'an acephalous copy'. In 'Scam' (p. 142) Haines also used the unusual word 'acephalous' to describe it (he called it an 'acephalous transcript'). I know of no one else who has used this word 'acephalous' (Greek for 'headless' or 'unheaded'), let alone in the context of this letter. It seems highly likely that Haines was the peer reviewer of my work in 2006.

45 The lead-in time for *EHR* is between a year and a year and a half: so when I sent my article to *EHR* in October 2006, the editor knew he had a note by Haines coming out in February 2007, rejecting the research on which my second article built.

46 The original is in Warwickshire County Record Office: CR 136/C/2027. A translation is given in the next chapter.

47 Philips, *Edward II*, 582, n. 28.

48 Kuhn, 151, quoting Max Planck, *Scientific Autobiography* (New York, 1949), 33–4.

5

The plot of the earl of Kent, 1328–30

The conclusion of 'DEII' raises two important questions. The first is that of the nature, scope and ambitions of the plot of the earl of Kent; the second concerns the consequences of Edward II's survival after 1327 – not just in respect of his own fate but also for the effect it had on English politics after 1330. The first of these is important because more nonsense has been written about the earl of Kent's plot by scholars in the twentieth century than perhaps any other medieval subject. As noted in 'DEII', the explanation of how the earl of Kent came to believe that his half-brother was still alive in 1330 – because he was 'stupid' – is a modern invention. A survey of the earl's career reveals a number of positions of responsibility and trust. In addition to those noted in 'DEII' (see pp. 83–4), he was appointed to lead an embassy to the pope at Avignon in 1320, was given the important position of constable of Dover Castle and warden of the Cinque Ports in 1321, and took a large number of commissions to suppress uprisings and capture rebel castles.[1] He was a counsellor of the king in the war of 1321–2 and a lieutenant in Scotland in 1323. He was ordered to recapture Roger Mortimer after his escape, was an ambassador to France in 1324, was commander of the English army in France the same year, and was a member of the royal council of regency in 1327. He was widely trusted at the end of his career – by the archbishop of York and the bishop of London, among others. There is nothing here to warrant dismissing him as a 'gullible' man who was 'strangely credulous' (as Haines refers to him in various publications), or one who was 'dignified but stupid' or 'famously stupid' (as Jonathan Sumption has described him in two separate publications), or 'stupid and gullible' as Phillips describes him.[2] The only negative charge that the *ODNB* lays against him is Murimuth's line that the men of his household were greedy and paid for nothing wherever they went. This is hardly evidence of the earl's gullibility or stupidity. Also it is an isolated point of view – and one that contrasts strongly with the verdicts of other contemporary writers, who described him as 'the good earl' and mourned his passing.[3]

The first indication that the earl of Kent may have known of the survival of his half-brother comes in the reference in the Memoranda Rolls of London, where it is noted that the earl of Lancaster wrote to the mayor of London on 5 November 1328 stating that, after the parliament at Winchester (which ended on 31 October 1328 but which neither Kent nor Lancaster had attended), 'the earl of Kent had made certain communications to him [Lancaster], which he could not put into writing, but which the bearer would report by word of mouth.'[4] As other writers have noted, this probably relates to the ex-king's survival.[5] The next reference in the official records is similarly guarded: this is the order, dated 7 December 1329, for an inquiry into the rumours that certain English lords had invited foreign lords to invade. Anyone found to be spreading them was threatened with imprisonment.[6] Although it was not specific, this was almost certainly a consequence of Archbishop Melton's message to Donald, earl of Mar, concerning the survival of Edward II (discussed below). The chroniclers were less coy. The *Brut* and the *Annales Paulini* overtly noted that people were talking about the possible survival of the ex-king.[7] Clearly this had nothing to do with agents provocateurs from Mortimer and Isabella trying to lure the earl of Kent into a bizarre plot (as Haines maintains); it was a rumour that Mortimer and Isabella were trying to quash.[8]

The Melton Letter of 14 January 1330 is the next piece of evidence we have. The full text is as follows:

> William by the permission of God Archbishop of York primate of England to our dear valet Simon de Swanland [Swaneslond] citizen of London greetings, with the blessings of God and ourselves. Dear friend, we have learned from people of our private acquaintance that we are able to reveal to you our privy business safely in all things. By which we pray you, on the blessing of God and ourselves, that this thing that we send to you be secret, and that you do not reveal it to any man or woman in the world until we shall have spoken together. You will want to know that we have certain news [*certeins noueles*] of our liege lord Edward of Carnarvon that he is alive and in good bodily health and is in a safe place of his own will, at which we are more joyous than ever, no better news we could hear. On which account we pray you as dearly as we trust in you that you procure for us a loan of £200 in gold, if you are able to get it easily, to be taken privily towards the said lord for us, and that you will seek out two half cloths of different colours, a good [whole] cloth and privy vesture and a good fur of miniver for six garments, and three hoods of miniver, and two coverlets of different colours of the larger size, with hangings, and two belts and two pouches of the best [quality] that you can find on sale and twenty ells of linen cloth

of ['lak'?] and ask his shoemaker to ensure we may have six pairs of shoes and two pairs of boots; and package up the things abovementioned in a bundle like merchants do with their wares, and we are sending you a horse and the brother of Sir William Clyf, bearer of these [letters], to whom we wish that you will deliver the same bundle packaged in the manner abovesaid; and we are sending you our bond of £200 to be paid eight days after the Purification next coming [10 February] at our manor of Cawood; put the other things abovesaid in writing and you will be promptly reimbursed. These things dear friend may you wish to do at our request for your great honour and profit and our own, if God pleases. Such are the robberies on the road towards our parts that we have been advised to send you our letters for doing these things, that you should deliver to the bearer of these [letters] cloth for one robe and one fur and these will be allowed to you in your account with us; and if he shows to you that he has further expenses, discharge them for him and the other things that he asks of you on our behalf and ensure that it be quickly delivered; and when it is delivered, come yourself towards us as soon as you are able, in order to inform us how we will procure a great sum of money for the said lord as we will wish, that he may be helped as far as we and you are able to arrange. May God protect you. Written at our manor of Cawood on the day after St Hilary [14 January].[9]

Certain significant things are to be noted from this letter. The plot was already sufficiently well developed by 14 January 1330 for Melton to specify what clothes were to be delivered for Edward and how they were to be wrapped to be conveyed to him. Simon de Swanland was not described as mayor of London but as 'our dear valet' – a description he had been given by Melton at least as early as 1328 and which he continued to enjoy after 1330.[10] His role in providing clothes is explained by the fact he was a draper.[11] It is also noteworthy that, like Lancaster's letter to the mayor of London of 5 November 1328, Melton was communicating with the mayor about a secret matter and urging him to keep it secret. In addition, Melton was keeping quiet about where the ex-king was being held. Three other things are noteworthy: that the ex-king was 'in a safe place of his own will' – a line that foreshadows the Fieschi Letter and suggests that Edward had managed to communicate with the outside world; that the £200 was to be provided in *gold*, with no silver, which suggests the plan was to remove him from England (where coins were silver); and that a key agent was 'the brother of Sir William Clyf', who was definitely involved in the plot.[12]

Eleven days after Melton's letter was written, writs were issued for parliament to assemble at Winchester on 11 March. The purpose of the parliament was given as 'great and arduous affairs touching the king and the state of the realm in many ways'. In the interim, on 18 February 1330, Queen Philippa was crowned at Westminster. Thus many of the nobles, prelates and knights would have travelled to Winchester from London, Westminster and the southeast (including the earl of Kent, who had been at the coronation). On 13 March Kent was arrested at Winchester.[13] The following day his pregnant wife Margaret was ordered to be taken into custody, she then being at Arundel.[14] Soon afterwards Kent was indicted. The Parliament Roll for this parliament is no longer extant but, according to the longer *Brut*, he was tried before Robert de 'Hamond' (*recte* Howel), coroner of the king's household, who accused him of being the king's deadly enemy and a traitor and a common enemy to the realm for having

> been about many days to make privily deliverance of Sir Edward, sometime king of England, your brother, who was put down out of his royalty by common assent of all the lords of England, in impairing of our lord the king's estate and also of his realm.[15]

The earl replied that he 'never assented to impair the estate of our lord the king, nor of his crown' and demanded to be judged by his peers. The chronicler claims that Roger Mortimer did not allow this, producing a letter written to the ex-king and sealed with the earl's seal. Mortimer asked the earl if he recognized the letter and as the earl saw his own seal, he acknowledged it as his. Then Mortimer undid the letter and 'began to read it in the hearing of the court'.

> Worships and reverence, with a brother's allegiance and subjection. Sir knight, worshipful and dear brother, if you please, I pray heartily that you are of good comfort, for I shall ordain for you that soon you shall come out of prison, and be delivered of that disease in which you find yourself. Your lordship should know that I have the assent of almost all the great lords of England, with all their apparel, that is to say, with armour, and with treasure without number, in order to maintain and help your quarrel so you shall be king again as you were before, and that they all – prelates, earls and barons – have sworn to me upon a book.[16]

According to the chronicler, Howel then delivered judgement:

> Sir Edmund, since you have admitted openly in this court that this is your letter sealed with your seal, and the tenor of the letter is that you were on the point of delivering the body of that worshipful knight Sir Edward, sometime King of England, your brother, and to help him become king again, and to govern his people as he was wont to do beforehand, thus impairing the state of our liege lord the present king, whom God keep from all disease . . . the will of this court is that you shall lose both life and limb, and that your heirs shall be disinherited forevermore, save the grace of our lord the king.

The same chronicler then notes that the sentence was reserved for the king to confirm, and that the earl was executed on the following day, due to Queen Isabella being determined that he should die. In all probability this is a compressed timeframe. In his confession, made before Robert Howel on 16 March, Kent referred to the letter that Mortimer read aloud in the court, which he (Kent) had sent to John Deveril, castellan of Corfe Castle (acting under John Maltravers, the custodian). He stated that it (and perhaps another) had been written by his wife, Margaret Wake. This reference to the letter indicates that the trial took place before his confession was made. Thus there was at least a two-day wait until the sentence was confirmed, at prime (about 6 a.m.) on the 19th. He waited at the gate of Winchester Castle until vespers (about 3 p.m.) until someone could be found to behead him.[17]

It is astonishing that these things were openly said. What is even more surprising is that such a detailed account of what went on in that court room found its way into a popular chronicle. But as the confession of the earl of Kent shows, the details of the plot were not only rehearsed in this form in a court, they were repeated in full parliament. Hence not only the *Brut* but several other chronicles note that the earl of Kent was charged with trying to procure the release of the supposedly dead ex-king.[18] Several other details in the *Brut* account are corroborated by Kent's confession, such as the trial being conducted by the coroner of the king's household, Howel, and there being an incriminating letter to Edward II written on behalf of the earl and sealed with his seal. As the earl's confession takes on a wholly different meaning in the context of Edward II not dying in Berkeley Castle, it is worth revisiting it in detail here.

> This acknowledgement was made before Robert Houel [Howel], coroner of the king's household, and afterwards before the great men and peers of the land at Winchester, on the sixteenth day of March in the fourth year: namely that Edmund earl of Kent acknowledges that the pope charged him on his benison that he should use his pains and diligence to deliver Edward, his brother, sometime king of England and that thereto he would find his costs. And he said that a friar preacher of the convent of London came to him at Kensington, near London, and told him that he had raised up the devil, who declared to him for certain that his brother Edward, formerly king of England, was alive. And he said that the archbishop of York sent to him by a chaplain, one Sir Aleyn, a letter of credence, which was that he would aid him in the deliverance of his brother with five thousand pounds and moreover with as much as he had and as much as he could give. And he said that Sir Ingelram Berengar told him in London on behalf of Sir William Zouche that he would give as much as he could for the deliverance of his brother. And

he said that Sir William Clyf came to him on the same message, by these signs [*par celes enseignes*] that they were riding together between Woking and Guildford and he told him that he should avoid the town of Guildford because his [Zouche's] niece Despenser was in the same town of Guildford; and this same Sir William told him of the alliance between the son of Richard, earl of Arundel, and his daughter, and said moreover that this would be the greatest honour that ever befell him and that he would aid him as much as he could to do this thing. And he said that this same Sir William came to him from Hugh Despenser, who told him that he would be well pleased to be with him, for he said that he would be sure of the deliverance in short time. And he said that Sir William of Derham, clerk of his letters, and Brother Thomas of Bromfield were those who most abetted him and stirred him to do these things aforesaid. And he said that Sir Robert of Taunton, from the archbishop of York, brought a message of these things aforesaid, and told him that he had ready five thousand pounds to do this business aforesaid, and this of the money of Sir Hugh Despenser. And he said that this same Sir Robert and two friars preacher who have left their order, of whom one is called Edmund Savage and the other is called John, were the chief dealers in this matter. And he said that Sir Fulk Fitzwarin came to him at Westminster and prayed him and stirred him to begin this thing, and encouraged him to do these things, and told him that this would be the greatest honour that ever befell him, and told him that he would aid him with body and heart and whatsoever he had. And he said that Sir Ingelram Berengar came to him from Sir John Pecche [saying] that he was of that mind and thereto would bestow body and heart and whatsoever he had. And he said that Sir Henry Beaumont and Sir Thomas Roscelyn spoke to him in Paris, in the chamber of the duke of Brabant, that they were ready to come to England in aid of these things aforesaid; and that they stirred him to do these things; and that they would land towards the parts of Scotland with the countenance of Donald of Mar, and that he would aid them to uphold these things and with all his strength. But the time of their coming is passed. And he said that Sir Richard of Pontefract, confessor of Lady Vescy, came to him at Kensington, at the coronation, and afterwards at Arundel, from the archbishop of York, for these things aforesaid. And he said that a monk of Quar and John Cymmynges [*recte* Gymmynges], his cousin, had fitted out a ship and a barge and a boat to bring his brother and him to his castle of Arundel and from thence wherever should have been appointed. And he said that of these things aforesaid he opened himself unto Sir E. de Monchiver [*recte* Monthermer] and to George Percy. And he said that the letters that he sent to Sir Bugues de Bayeux [Bogo de Bayouse] and to John Daverill [Deveril], sealed with his seal, he sent – and the one letter was written by the hand of his wife. And he said that Ingelram Berengar, Maucelyn Musarde, and John Cymmynge [Gymmynges] did travail and take pains to accomplish these things. And he said that Ingelram Berengar came to him at Arundel, in his chamber above the chapel, and said that the bishop of London would aid him in the deliverance of his brother with whatsoever he had. And these things he acknowledged to be true and yields himself guilty that he has borne himself evilly for the undoing of his liege lord and of his crown, by countenance of these men aforesaid, and he wholly submits himself to the king's will to come, in his shirt, to London or in this city, barefoot, or wherever the king shall appoint, with a rope around his neck, to do with him as he wishes.[19]

The confession was read aloud in full parliament. The confession itself states this and it can be corroborated. The statement that Kent himself had heard of his half-brother's survival from a London friar who had 'conjured up the devil' is repeated in a letter to the pope written shortly afterwards.[20] It also appears in *Lanercost*, which names this friar as Thomas Dunheved.[21] It is also worth noting that the *Lanercost* writer confirms a number of other points in the *Brut* account; it states that the earl of Kent made a 'confession' that

> both by command of my lord the pope and at the instigation of certain bishops of England, whom he named expressly, and by advice of many great men of the land, whom he also named and proved by sure tokens, and especially at the instigation of a certain preaching friar of the convent of London, to wit, Friar Thomas Dunheved, who had told the said earl that he had raised up the devil, who asserted that my lord King Edward, lately deposed, was still alive, and at the instigation of three other friars of the aforesaid order, to wit: Edmund, John and Richard, he intended to act, and did act with all his power, so that the said Lord Edward the deposed king should be released from prison and restored to the kingdom, and that for such purpose my lord the pope and the said lord bishops and nobles aforesaid had promised him plenty of money, besides advice and aid in carrying it out.[22]

Kent's confession also shows how deeply Archbishop Melton was involved in the plot, and corroborates Melton's own letter in a number of respects. It emphasizes the role of William Clyf – a long-standing companion of Melton's – as a go-between. In the Melton Letter Clyf's brother was the bearer of the letter to de Swanland in London. In Kent's confession Clyf himself obtained access to Sir Hugh Despenser (then in prison at Bristol Castle) to hear his views on the matter. As for the archbishop's direct communications to Kent, these were by three other men: one 'Sir Aleyn', a chaplain; Sir Robert of Taunton; and Richard de Pontefract. The first two made promises to the earl concerning sums of money and reveal Melton as the treasurer of the conspiracy, both with regard to his own money and that of Hugh Despenser. This corroborates his role in the Melton Letter, in which Melton records his borrowing from de Swanland and adds a promise that together they will raise more.

The confession also reveals much about the timing of the plot. It appears that, after hearing the news in or before October 1328, Kent did not act immediately. Presumably he sought clarification of the ex-king's situation. Even so, speaking to Lancaster seems to have been the limit of his action. Although he and his brother, Thomas, had both joined Lancaster in boycotting the Salisbury parliament of October 1328, and had at first joined Lancaster's confederation against Mortimer, the two royal brothers split from Lancaster in January 1329 and joined the young king. Kent remained at court from 15 February to 1 March 1329.[23] In late March 1329 there is evidence of his preparations to go to the pope at Avignon.[24] Then he was delayed. On 23 April his travelling companion John de Asphale appointed as his attorneys Ralph de Bocking and William de Derham (the latter being Kent's clerk of letters and one of the two men who 'most abetted' Kent and 'stirred him' to rescue Edward II).[25] Kent himself appointed attorneys on 29 May – William de Hoo and Ralph de Bocking – to deal with his affairs until 11 November, while he was out of the country.[26] However he did not leave until after 11 June, on which day John de Asphale and Hugh, son of John St John of Basynges, received letters of protection while travelling overseas with Kent.[27] He was in Gascony at the end of September, and certainly communicated with the pope; thus there is reason to believe the statement in his confession that he visited Avignon in person.[28] If he did, he may well have spoken to Cardinal Fieschi, who was as closely related to him as to Edward II.[29] In all probability he saw Henry de Beaumont and Thomas de Roscelyn in Paris on the journey to or from Avignon.

While Kent was away, William Montagu and Bartholomew Burghersh also set out for Avignon, leaving on 15 September or soon afterwards. They had a two-fold mission. On behalf of Mortimer and Isabella they were to offer the pope 1,000 marks a year, in renewal of the pledge of King John: as this had not been paid for more than thirty years it is tempting to see this offer as a bribe or 'hush money' inducing the pope not to repeat what the earl of Kent had told him.[30] On the same mission, Montagu almost certainly carried Edward III's letter with his famous hand-written cipher 'Pater Sancte' by which the pope was to know which instructions were genuinely the king's own and which were Mortimer's.[31] Very shortly after their departure, on 24 September, Sir John Maltravers was appointed custodian of Corfe Castle.[32] Thus there would appear to have been some covert manoeuvres concerning knowledge at Avignon of the ex-king's survival, and a growing sensitivity at court to the vulnerability of the prisoner at Corfe.

According to a court case in April 1330, it was also during this period of Kent's journey overseas that Archbishop Melton learned of the ex-king's survival. One John of Lincoln declared that William de Kingsclere spoke to the archbishop at Sherburn in Yorkshire on 10 October 1329 'stating and emphatically asserting that Edward II . . . was then alive in the prison of Corfe Castle and asking him if he would assist in releasing him'.[33] The archbishop replied that he would sell all he had in the world, except one vestment and a chalice, in order to effect the ex-king's release. He then sent de Kingsclere to Donald, earl of Mar, in Scotland 'to get his advice and aid'. De Kingsclere returned to Melton stating that Mar promised to come boldly with forty thousand men when instructed to do so by Melton. Unsurprisingly, Melton bided his time until the return of the earl of Kent. Kent was back in England by the end of November, being with the court at Kenilworth on 3 December.[34] But not long afterwards, Mortimer and Isabella heard about Melton's message to Mar. The writ to the sheriffs of 7 December 1329 specifically referred to lords of a foreign power being invited to invade by English lords. It seems unlikely that other lords besides Melton and Kent were requesting foreigners to invade, in force, at this juncture.

By 14 January Archbishop Melton had arranged for the clothes and money for the king from de Swanland. Kent went to Westminster for the coronation on 18 February 1330, when he took a leading role in the procession. Considering that Kent must have known that the news about Donald of Mar had reached Mortimer and Isabella, it must have been a very tense occasion. It is very likely that the second message from the archbishop to Kent, carried by Robert of Taunton, had been sent and received by this time, for Kent's confession shows that, on or about 18 February, he received a third message from the archbishop, brought to him by Richard de Pontefract. Kent went down to Arundel afterwards and there met his wife, who wrote the letter to Edward II quoted above, which was delivered to John Deveril. At the same time he arranged for the boats that would take him and Edward II from Corfe with de Swanland's money and the clothes, and thence abroad – perhaps to the lands of the duke of Brabant, Edward II's cousin and loyal supporter, or to the papal court, where Cardinal Fieschi could have vouched for Edward II to the pontiff.

As the narrative outlined above reveals, the plot that we have come to associate with Kent was planned in a relatively short space of time. Although it is likely that de Kingsclere went to Melton on Kent's instructions, probably after Kent had visited the papal curia and was on the way home, there is no indication that there was any degree of coordination in their activities before Kent returned to England, shortly before 3 December 1329. Melton's letter shows that the plan to remove Edward II from custody was in place by 14 January 1330; and that he had agreed with Kent when and how this was to be done: Kent must have agreed with Melton that he (Kent) would arrange the shipping and the actual extrication of the ex-king from Corfe Castle. The speed of the arrangements suggests that the involvement of the exiles in Paris, de Beaumont and de Roscelyn, was not directly related and merely aspirational. This is supported by the fact that they never arrived. Likewise the Scots invasion under Donald of Mar was a side issue, and not part of Kent's plot as such. But much more importantly, the swiftness of the organization shows that it was not simply a reaction to Mortimer and Isabella's government. It was not a slow build-up over the course of 1329. Kent set about arranging his visit to the pope in March 1329 – very shortly after he and his brother Thomas abandoned Henry of Lancaster and were *reconciled* to Mortimer and Isabella. When Kent returned from seeing the pope, and obtaining his blessing, he and Melton went straight into action. Theirs was a response to the unlawful imprisonment of Edward II, and a conspiracy of loyalty to the ex-king, not primarily a reaction to Mortimer and Isabella's government.

On 18 March 1330, two days after Kent's confession, all the secular lords and knights whom he had mentioned were ordered to be arrested.[35] At least three of these – Lords Fitzwarin, Zouche and Pecche – should have been present for the parliament; the fact that orders had to be issued to the sheriffs for their arrests suggests they did not attend. Fitzwarin fled the country. Zouche was arrested soon afterwards and imprisoned temporarily. Pecche evaded arrest for a while but eventually submitted to the king's will and lost his lands.[36] The other men named by Kent who were ordered to be arrested the same day were Ingelram de Berengar (who had acted as a go-between between several lords and Kent), William Clyf (another go-between), John Gymmynges (organizer of the boats), and two men whose only involvement was to know what Kent was plotting: George Percy and Edward de Monthermer.[37] Those secular lords mentioned by Kent who were not arrested were either in exile (de Beaumont and de Roscelyn) or locked up in Bristol Castle (Despenser). Lady de Vescy seems to have played no part in the plot herself, although, as the sister of Henry de Beaumont, it is probable that she sympathized with its aims.[38]

From Reading on 24 March a letter in the king's name was sent to the pope to explain what had happened to the earl of Kent (thereby further confirming the earl's visit to Avignon). This condemned the friar who had 'conjured up a devil' and requested that the pope pay credence to what would be explained to him by the bearer of the letter, John Walwayn.[39] The last element is interesting: the government's explanation of recent events was kept secret – as secret as the information that Kent had given to Lancaster in 1328 (in that it could not be written down). And well the government might have regarded it as secret, for what is most remarkable about Kent's confession are the things that the earl did *not* say. Although scholars have frequently remarked on the fullness of his confession, even going so far to say his eagerness to name names is evidence of his supposed 'stupidity', it was only partial. In addition, it is highly likely that it was extracted through an interrogation process after his appearance in court.

Kent did not name half of his supporters. On 31 March 1330, at Woodstock, the government issued orders for the arrests of the following men:

Fulk Fitzwarin	John Harsik	John de Asphale
Sir John Pecche	Benet de Braham	Giles de Spain
Nicholas Pecche	William de Mareny	*John Gymmynges*
Nicholas Dauney	Stephen Donheved	John de Toucestre
John Coupeland	Ivan ap Griffyn	John Hauteyn
Thomas de Staunton	Robert de Wedenhale	*George Percy*
Walter de Woxebregg	Peter Bernard	*Bro. Richard de Pontefract*
Adam de Wedinhale	John de Mosden	Bro. William Vavasour
Thomas Crannok	Richard de Hull	Bro. Henry Domeram
Richard de la Chambre	Roger de Rayham	Bro. Thomas de Burne
Nicholas de Sandwich	John del Ile	*William Clyf*
Roger de Audeley	William Daumarle	Rhys ap Gruffydd
Henry Wygood	Henry de Canterbury	Richard de Wuselade
Wadin Crok	John de Everwyk	

Of these forty-one men, Kent had named only six (those in italics). One might argue that Mortimer and Isabella herein were taking advantage of the opportunity to round up all those who opposed them, regardless of whether they were involved with Kent's plot or not. But that cannot be the whole explanation. When Kent had gone to visit the pope at Avignon he had been accompanied by John de Asphale, whom he did not name in his confession but who is named in the above list. Kent was also accompanied by two men whose names are *not* on the above list: John de Langeford and Hugh St John, who probably were equally close to the earl and privy to his secrets. Nor were these three the only adherents missing from Kent's confession. Later it turned out that William de Digepit, abbot of Langdon, was also a co-conspirator.[40] Some men who were definitely involved in the plot – like Simon de Swanland – were never named. De Swanland may even have acted to protect two of the Londoners on the above list in the aftermath of Kent's death.[41] If one puts the figures together, Kent named twenty-three co-conspirators (not including Lady Vescy or the monk of Quar, or the friar who 'summoned up the devil'). But he failed to name at least forty-one men: the order of 31 March named a further thirty-five, and de Swanland, de Kingsclere, de Digepit, de Langeford, Hugh St John and Thomas Dunheved are another six. Clearly Kent did not simply lose his self-control and name everyone he knew who was involved.

This raises the question of why Kent named most but not all of the most important men. (We can be confident he did not name others because of the close correlation of the arrest orders of 18 March and the principal secular lords named in his confession.) With de Swanland, de Kingsclere and the abbot of Langdon, the answer may be that he did not know they were involved: they reported to Melton. With men like Archbishop Melton, the man's ecclesiastical position may have rendered him immune from Mortimer and Isabella's authority. However, with men like de Asphale, de Langeford and St John, who had travelled with Kent, such explanations do not hold water.

The realization that Kent certainly and knowingly supplied a partial confession causes us to re-examine the confession itself for the structure of the information it contains. It is noteworthy that in every case of a named conspirator, the go-between between Kent and the conspirator is also named.

Adherent	Go-between
William Melton, archbishop of York	1. 'a chaplain, Sir Aleyn'
	2. Sir Robert of Taunton
	3. Richard de Pontefract, at Kensington
	4. Richard de Pontefract, at Arundel
William, Lord Zouche	Sir Ingelram de Berengar, at London
Sir William Clyf	Kent, in person (riding to Guildford)
Hugh, Lord Despenser	Sir William Clyf

(continued)

Adherent	Go-between
Fulk, Lord Fitzwarin	Kent, in person, at Westminster
Sir John Pecche	Sir Ingelram de Berengar
Sir Henry de Beaumont	Kent, in person, in Paris
Sir Thomas de Roscelyn	Kent, in person, in Paris
Sir Edward de Monthermer	Kent, in person
George Percy	Kent, in person
Stephen Gravesend, bishop of London	Sir Ingelram de Berengar, at Arundel

The recording of an intermediary in every case is evidence of a systematic search for individuals who knew the nature of the plot. It is a sign of a interrogatory process. That this process was not due to Kent's desire to be comprehensive is evident in his failure to name a number of men. It follows that the regular recording of messengers' names was not his initiative but the result of someone else systematically asking 'by what signs' he knew an important adherent was loyal. This was emphasized by the *Lanercost* chronicler: Kent did not just name the men involved, he 'proved' their involvement 'by sure tokens'. The very words 'by these signs' are used in Kent's confession (in conjunction with William Clyf). Whether or not his 'confession' was forced out of him we cannot tell; but, on reflection, it should not surprise us that it was drawn up by a clerk in response to a line of questions put to the earl, given that he had already appeared in court and been incriminated. By the time of his confession (16 March) the authorities had no need for further evidence against him; they already had the letter by which he had been condemned. The government could only have wanted Kent questioned further in order to discover more information about the plot.

The evidence that Kent's 'confession' was the result of a systematic questioning puts his inquisitors in a far more chilling light. These were the people who judged his crime so serious that he deserved to die for it. But the worry at court in the wake of Kent's confession did not diminish with his execution. On 13 April the government sent a royal writ to all the sheriffs in England and the two justices of Wales. This stated that

> In our parliament held at Winchester certain letters of Edmund of Woodstock, formerly earl of Kent, touching on treason and matters of defiance of our estate, were shown to us, which letters the said earl did not deny were his and on which account he was arrested.
>   And the earl himself, of his good will and without any manner of distress made it known before the coroner of our household that he had made alliance . . . to assemble a

power of men-at-arms in defiance of our estate and our royal dignity, against his homage, fealty and allegiance.

Taking colour falsely under this: that Sir Edward of good memory, formerly king of England, our very dear father (at whose funeral he had been with other great men of our realm) ought to be alive.

And we, the said things having been shown to us, asked of those earls, barons and other great and noble men of our kingdom in the said parliament, before whom the said treason and wrongdoing, put in writing, was made known a second time; by the assent of the said earls, barons and other great and noble men in this parliament, with the judgement of the same, the said earl was sentenced to death as a traitor to us and our realm.

We command you, strongly enjoining that, throughout your area of authority or to the limits of your affairs – within as well as outside franchises – you should make known the death of the said earl for his treason and misdeeds aforesaid.

And if you find anyone who preaches or says, in private or in public, that the aforesaid earl was put to death other than by the assent of the said great men and the judgement of parliament, and this on account of his treason and wrongdoing, as is laid out above; or, in order to make a disturbance in this realm, preaches or says that our father be still alive, then have them arrested and safely guarded in prison, until you are commanded otherwise by us, both within franchises and without.

And send to us the names of those whom you will arrest, and the reason as well, from time to time, certified under your seal.

Given at Woodstock the thirteenth day of April [1330].[42]

Very clearly, the government knew that the twenty-three individuals named in the confession and the thirty-five other men ordered to be arrested on 31 March did not include everyone who was an adherent of the earl. In addition to the above writ, a commission was issued the same day to Robert Howel, Thomas de Hindringham and John de Loudham 'to make inquiry into the names of those who were adherents of the earl of Kent' in the counties of Norfolk and Suffolk.[43] This specified that the government had heard that many other people throughout the kingdom were adherents of the earl and involved in 'the same sedition'. The commissioners were empowered to imprison those men whom they heard repeating this 'sedition' and were not to let such men go without a special warrant from the government. And yet certain individuals were never arrested, especially plotters among the clergy. Some secular lords had even been released already. William, Lord Zouche, for instance, was released three days before this writ was issued.[44] This is a sign of a dilemma in government. On the one hand, there was extreme anxiety about anyone else believing Edward II was alive – and a determined wish to suppress any such talk 'in private or in public' and to imprison those circulating such rumours – and, on the other, there was an increasingly relaxed attitude to the identified associates of the earl of Kent. Most of all, the need to have the sentence on the earl proclaimed in every county in England and Wales, together with the threat of arresting everyone who maintained that Edward II was still alive, reveals that the principal purpose of this writ was propaganda.

Archbishop Melton was summoned by a privy seal writ to appear before the King's Bench on 23 April 1330. In answer to the charge that he had sent William de Kingsclere to Donald of Mar encouraging him to invade in the name of Edward II, he responded with a refusal to reply until he was informed as to when and where he was supposed to have sent this message. A week later John of Lincoln provided this information, giving the place and date. The archbishop then denied the charge and orders were given for a jury to be empanelled; but the case was never heard.[45] However, the accusation proved to be a continuing inconvenience to Melton. Two Suffolk men – John de Haltbe of Ipswich and Martin Love – took advantage of his adherence to the earl of Kent to indict him and have him arraigned before the council.[46]

The fates of some of the other men involved in the earl of Kent's plot are known. In August 1330 Sir John Pecche was restored to favour. The same month the government commissioned Roger Mortimer to take action against one of the Welsh rebels named on the list of the adherents of the earl of Kent, namely Rhys ap Gruffydd.[47] The earl of Kent's family lost control of his lands. Arundel Castle was taken into the king's hands on 18 March (although the pregnant widow was allowed to stay there) and the rest of the earl's lands were confiscated on 20 March. Many others lost lands too: inquisitions into the lands of John Gymmynges, Ingelram de Berengar and John Pecche are extant, as well as the orders to confiscate them.[48] For most of those caught up in the plot, restitution of estates did not take place until the parliament of November 1330, after Mortimer's arrest. With Mortimer dead, having confessed on his deathbed that the earl of Kent had been 'wrongfully' put to death, the way was clear for the archbishop of York, the bishop of London, the abbot of Langdon, Lord Zouche and others to petition that the adjourned case brought against them in the King's Bench might be dropped.[49] They were all acquitted and those who had lost their lands had them restored, including the earl of Kent's widow and heir. The king demonstrated his complete trust in Archbishop Melton – and, one might add, his confidence that the prelate was neither 'stupid' nor 'gullible' – by appointing him treasurer of the realm on 1 December 1330, two days after Mortimer was hanged. Giles of Spain was similarly trusted despite his role in the plot: he was commissioned to track down those adherents of the earl as well as those involved in the supposed death. He eventually arrested William de Kingsclere in 1332 and sent him to the Tower – ironically for his role in the death of Edward II.[50]

In conclusion, this new approach to the earl's plot reveals two important aspects that previously have not been noted. The first is the timing of the plot and the implications for its nature. Kent set about making his plans to go and see the pope in 1329 – only a few weeks after his reconciliation with Mortimer and Isabella – and not as the result of long unease with the Mortimer regime. Within six weeks of his return with the papal blessing, he and Melton made detailed plans for Edward II's rescue. Again, this was not the result of a long-standing growing antipathy to the Mortimer regime. On this basis, and given the closeness to Edward II of many of those involved, it would appear that the Kent plot was a pro-Edward II one rather than an anti-Mortimer and Isabella one (contrary to the line normally taken by historians), and this is reflected in the leniency with which all the plotters except Kent himself were treated by Mortimer and Isabella. Further research is needed on all the various less-important men involved; but it is to be expected that a close inspection of their careers will reveal that many of them owed much to Edward II personally, and that their involvement in the Kent plot was primarily to help their king, not to destroy Mortimer and Isabella.

The second important new finding is that the 'certain news' of Edward II's survival was circulating far beyond the control of the government in 1329–30. Given that Kent returned from Avignon not very long before 3 December 1329 (when he witnessed a charter at Kenilworth) and that just four days later a royal writ was issued attempting to suppress a certain seditious rumour connected with Melton's message to Donald of Mar, it seems that Kent returned to England to find the previously secret news of the ex-king's survival had become more widely known. If this is correct, then it is likely that this public rumour forced him and Melton into rescuing the ex-king as quickly as they could – the urgency increased in the wake of Pope John XXII giving them his blessing.

However tense the months between late September 1329 and March 1330 were – and the coronation of Philippa must have been excruciatingly awkward, with Kent in the procession, knowing the government had suspected something was afoot for more than two months – the Kent plot was a powerful lesson in propaganda for the young Edward III. In this respect it was useful preparation for the show trials of November 1330. Not only was there the obfuscation of the writ of 7 December 1329, there were also the widespread threats of imprisonment for those acting in concert with the earl. There was the battle for the acquiescence of the pope between Mortimer and Isabella's agents and Kent – with Edward III co-opting one of the former to carry his own 'Pater Sancte' letter. Then there was the aftermath of that episode. An official letter from the pope was procured in early September 1330 stating that he had not believed that Edward II was still alive due to the proper manner of his funeral. This explanation has been taken by many historians to be proof that the pope never believed Kent' story. However, it seems to have been dictated by the English ambassador sent to him to obtain this statement, John Walwayn. The same reason not to believe Edward II was still alive was given in the government's proclamation of 13 April 1330.[51]

Mortimer's harsh treatment of Kent for the 'crime' of trying to rescue a supposedly dead man, imprisoned without trial, led to the mood of the country turning very quickly and harshly against him. At the start of 1329 Mortimer had been strong enough to see off a challenge to his authority from Lancaster. Kent and Norfolk had defected to him. But Kent's execution destroyed any magnate support Mortimer might have enjoyed except his own personal contacts, family and friends. Awareness among the magnates that Edward II actually was alive and being secretly detained can only have exacerbated the sense of injustice felt at seeing the earl of Kent waiting to be beheaded outside the gates of Winchester Castle.

One last point needs to be drawn from all this: why was it the earl of Kent's plot? Why not the earl of Lancaster's or Norfolk's? Since Tout's time the assumption that Kent was 'stupid' automatically implied the answer. However, as neither Melton nor Kent can be regarded as stupid, the matter requires some thought. One answer is that Pecche informed him before anyone else, in the summer of 1328, and he felt honour-bound to follow through with the rescue. Alternatively Lancaster or some other early recipient of the information might have seen Kent as the natural champion of Edward II, being not only the ex-king's half-brother but a more noteworthy and honourable man than Thomas, earl of Norfolk. If this is correct, it is nothing short of a historical injustice that the man who took on the chief responsibility for rescuing Edward II from Corfe Castle, and lost his life in the process, has been condemned as 'stupid' and 'gullible' by historians. Rather we should see him as honourable, conscientious, loyal and courageous – and just very unfortunate in that the man at Corfe Castle whom he trusted to deliver a message to Edward II turned out to be an agent of the increasingly frantic and ruthless Roger Mortimer.

Notes

1 See Scott Waugh, 'Edmund of Wooodstock', in the *ODNB*.
2 For 'gullible' see 'Scam', referred to in the previous chapter; for 'strangely credulous' see Haines, *King Edward II*, 212. For Jonathan Sumption's comments, see 'Plotting the past', *Guardian* (5 April 2003); *Hundred Years War*, 113. For Phillips's condemnation, see Phillips, *Edward II*, 567, n. 274.
3 For instance, Henry Blaneford called him 'mighty among great men' (*ODNB* under 'Edmund'); the author of the *Anonimalle Chronicle* states 'because out of pity, no one wanted to behead him' (see *Anonimalle*, 143). Another, unpublished *Brut* continuator referred to Kent as 'the good earl' and stated there was a great sadness at his death (BL Harley 200, fo. 78v ('*le bon counte de Kent . . . donc grant doel*'). The longer *Brut* puts emphasis on the young king's personal distress at his uncle's death (*Brut*, i, 267).
4 *CPMR*, 72.
5 Doherty, 'Isabella' (DPhil thesis), 263; Redstone, 'Some mercenaries', 161.
6 *Foedera* (Rec. Comm.), ii, 775.
7 *Brut*, i, 263; *Chronicles*, i, 349.
8 For Haines's repeated use of the description 'bizarre' to explain the plot of the earl of Kent, see his *Edward II*, 211, 233.
9 Warwickshire County Record Office: CR 136/C/2027. Haines's transcription refers to 'William' Clyf as 'Wilham' – although the form of the letters in this word resembles other appearances of 'li' in the letter just as closely as 'h'. Haines also introduces a spurious section break in front of the words '*Honis soit*' in his transcription; there is no break in the original. Note that the transcription of these words is doubtful: others have suggested '*Hom fet*' (one does). See 'Sumptuous apparel', 893–94. I am very grateful to Dr Paul Dryburgh for advice in producing this translation.
10 See Hill (ed.) *Register of William Melton*, vol. 3, no. 171 for a reference to de Swanland as '*dilectum vallettum nostrum*', dated 27 December 1328. The same

volume, no. 200, has a similar description of him dated 1332. De Swanland, in fact had had many dealings with Melton over recent years. He was a draper, described as king's esquire in 1328 (*CMR 1326–7* (1968), 375). On 8 June 1327 he acknowledged a debt to William Melton of £200 (receipt of which was acknowledged by Melton on 15 April 1331: *CMR 1326–7*, 214). Together with others he acknowledged a debt to Melton of £1,200 in August 1328, and in July 1329 he (alone) acknowledged a debt to Melton of a further £100 (*CCR 1327–30*, 406, 561).

11 TNA C241/113/8. Note that this is a record of debts from John Pecche.

12 On this last issue, Haines presumes 'the brother' denotes that Clyf was a friar, rather than Sir William Clyf himself. 'Sumptuous apparel', 886–7. One 'William de Clif' had protection to travel to Scotland on the king's service with William Melton in 1310 (*CCW*, 325).

13 In 'DEII' I dated the arrest to 14 March. However, *CP*, vii, 146 gives the date 13 March but does not cite a source. *Anonimallle*, 143, does give the date as the 13th.

14 Harding, 'Regime', 194.

15 *Brut*, i, 266.

16 This is from the mid-fourteenth century English translation of the French longer *Brut* chronicle. The original letter would have been in French, but it is not known on what authority the author of the chronicle quoted it.

17 For 'prime' as the hour of sentencing, see *Anonimalle*, 143.

18 For instance *Murimuth*, 59–60.

19 Thompson (ed.), *Murimuth*, 255–7.

20 *Foedera* (Rec. Comm.), ii, 783.

21 Thomas Dunheved had previously acted to procure Edward II's temporary freedom from Berkeley Castle prior to his supposed death in 1327. See Doherty, 'Isabella' (DPhil thesis), 225–26; 'Captivity', 85–6; Tanqueray, 'Conspiracy of Thomas Dunheved', 119–24.

22 *Lanercost*, 264–5.

23 TNA C53/116 nos 3, 49–52.

24 Harding, 'Regime', 188.

25 *CPR 1327–30*, 385.

26 *CPR 1327–30*, 391.

27 *CPR*, 397. Note also that on 1 June, at Canterbury, John de Langeford, travelling with the earl, appointed his attorneys to act until 11 November (*CPR 1327–30*, 397).

28 Harding, 'Regime', 189, quoting *CEPR*, ii, 308.

29 The relationship is implied by their father, Edward I, describing Cardinal Luca Fieschi as his kinsman in 1301. See *CPR 1292–1301*, 608.

30 Lunt, ii, 66–7, 75. They also backdated their payments to the start of the new reign. The agreement for paying off this sum was reached on 3 January 1330.

31 For the letter, see Crump, 'Arrest', 331–2. For the period out of the country, see Harding, 'Regime', 298.

32 *CFR 1327–37*, 149.

33 Sayles (ed.), *Select Cases*, 44.

34 Harding, 'Regime', 188, quoting *CPR 1327–30*, 379; TNA C53/116.

35 *CFR 1327–37*, 169–70. The men to be arrested were: Fitzwarin, Zouche, Pecche, de Berengar, Percy, Clyf and Gymmynges. Note that *CPR 1327–30*, 557, has the date of these arrests as 10 March (Zouche, Fitzwarin and Percy) and 22 March (de Berengar).

36 *CP*, v, 498–9 (Fitzwarin); ibid., x, 343 (Pecche); ibid., xii/2, 959 (Zouche).

37 *CFR 1327–37*, 169.

38 This presumes that the Lady de Vescy in question was Isabella Beaumont, second wife of John de Vescy (d. 1289). See *CP*, XII/2, 280, 283–4.

39 *Foedera* (Rec. Comm.), ii/2, 783.

40 *PROME* November 1330, text 2, item 7.

41 John Hauteyn, Henry de Canterbury and John de Everwyk were arrested in London. The sheriffs of London refused to send Hauteyn and de Everwyk from London to the king at Woodstock on account of the fact that they were free citizens of London and could not be moved from the city. It is probable that the sheriffs of London consulted with the mayor, de Swanland, before deciding on this strategy. See Harding, 'Regime', 195.

42 *Foedera* (Rec. Comm.), ii/2, 787.

43 *Foedera* (Rec. Comm.), ii/2, 787. 'Loudham' appears here as 'Londham' – the former is a well-known name, the latter not; hence the change.

44 *CP*, xii/2, 959 (Zouche).

45 Sayles (ed.), *Select Cases*, 43-5.

46 TNA SC8/172/8555.

47 *Foedera* (Rec. Comm.), ii/2, 796.

48 For instance TNA E199/39/10 and E199/15/11.

49 *PROME*, November 1330 (C65/2), item no. 7.

50 William de Kingsclere was arrested at Rochester on 25 July 1332 and sent to the Tower on account of his role in the death of Edward II (with which he had never been charged, even in his absence), and not for his actual crime of informing Archbishop Melton that the ex-king was still alive. Two other men never charged with the murder were also arrested on the same charge by Spain, an adherent of Kent's, namely Sir Richard de Well and John le Spicer. It is possible that these men also were guilty of spreading news about the ex-king's survival. See Hunter, 'Measures Taken', 283.

51 On 5 September 1330 the pope replied to the accusation, brought by John Walwayn, expressing surprise that he, the pope, could believe such an 'incredible thing, namely that he for whom solemn funerals had been made, was alive. The pope

believes and holds firmly that those who were present at the funeral were not deceived and did not attempt to deceive. If the funeral had been secret there might have been some palliation for the report but as it was public there is none'. See *CEPR*, ii, 499.

6

Edward III, his father and the Fieschi

What did happen to Edward II? The inevitability of that question in the wake of the preceding pages is not matched by an equally inevitable answer. The principal source for Edward II's life after 1330 – the Fieschi Letter – has been dismissed as a fraudulent document by scholars in the past, and it is right to approach it with caution. Just because Edward II did not die in 1327 does not mean that any documents claiming to account for his later life should automatically be trusted. We could draw up a hypothesis that it was created by a blackmailer who knew about Edward II's survival – a disaffected adherent of the earl of Kent, for example. So, while ignoring it would obviously be counterproductive – and no wiser than ignoring any other piece of contemporary evidence – it seems sensible to start by setting it aside and considering what we know of Edward II's possible survival from other sources.

Three lines of enquiry present themselves at the outset, namely (1) Edward III's attempts to resolve the problem of his father's survival; (2) matters connected with Edward II's supposed death that were still pending after 1330; and (3) the one official piece of direct evidence that referred to Edward II as alive after 1330 – at least in the minds of the English royal household. It goes without saying that, even collectively, these do not amount to very much. However, it equally goes without saying that this is not surprising, given Edward III's evident determination to allow no public discussion of his father's possible survival and his systematic destruction of certain records that would have proved useful to historians in researching his secret activities after 1330. For a start, he personally burnt the chamber accounts for the whole period of Thomas Hatfield's responsibility on 4 December 1344, so none survive between John Flete's account of 1333–34 and that date.[1] In addition, a royal clerk attempted to eradicate the official record of the reference to a meeting of Edward III and the woman who embalmed the body supposed to be that of his father.[2] The destruction of all the Parliament Rolls between September 1327 and March 1330 – the entire period of the dominance of Mortimer and Isabella – is probably no coincidence.[3] We can say the same regarding the lack of an official copy of the Fieschi Letter. Edward destroyed any records that might cast doubt upon his regnal legitimacy.

Edward III's quest for information relating to the events of 1327–30 would have involved men whom he knew and trusted, like Archbishop Melton and Lord Berkeley. However, such conversations have left nothing in terms of evidence. Thus we need to turn to the king's several attempts to track down William de Kingsclere, Thomas Gurney and Sir John Maltravers. De Kingsclere was arrested in Rochester in 1332; his fate is unknown. Gurney was arrested, escaped, was recaptured, fell sick, and then was nursed back to health, and interrogated before being beheaded by Oliver Ingham, seneschal of Gascony, in 1333. A key agent in both arrests (and the arrests of two other men connected with the Berkeley Castle plot) was Giles of Spain: an adherent of the earl of Kent and thus a man who believed Edward II to be alive.[4] That Gurney was given medicines until he could be interrogated in Bayonne – and only after that interrogation or 'confession' was he beheaded and brought back to England in June 1333 – suggests that Edward III was still seeking information about the events of 1327–30, three years after Mortimer's fall. The other person from whom Edward III can be shown to have sought information was Sir John Maltravers, who had been at Corfe Castle around the time of the fake death in September 1327 and thus probably assisted with the transfer of the ex-king from Berkeley to Corfe.[5] In March 1334 Maltravers wrote to the king from Flanders notifying him that he had information about the 'honour, estate and well-being of the realm'.[6] Edward responded by sending his most trusted man, William Montagu, to him. Within a year (by 29 March 1335) Maltravers had been allowed secretly to return to England to take part in a series of meetings with several friends of the king, including Sir William Montagu; Sir Nicholas de la Beche; Sir John Molyns; Thomas, Lord Berkeley; Sir Maurice Berkeley; Sir William de Whitefield; the abbot of Malmesbury; and Edmund Bereford.[7] Lack of information about his father made Edward uneasy, and he did all he could to find out what he could from Mortimer's surviving adherents.[8]

The second area of enquiry possible is that of the delay in some functions that one would have thought dependent on Edward II's death. The one title that Edward II did not resign in his lifetime was that of 'prince of Wales'.[9] Had

Edward III wanted to invest his son with that title while his father was still alive, few would have tried to stop him; but he did not. Instead, in the parliament of 1337, he created him duke of Cornwall. Not until the parliament of 1343 did he create him prince of Wales: a delay which suggests that, if he was putting off the creation on account of Edward II bearing the title, he did not learn of a change in the circumstances (death or, less probably, forfeiture) until after the parliament of 1341.

Another area of delay relates to certain foundations for priests to pray for the soul of the late king. There are a number of curious foundations for chantries for masses to be sung for the soul of Edward II in the 1340s. Two in particular stand out: Bablake and Sibthorp. In 1342 Queen Isabella founded a chantry at Bablake in Coventry to pray for various souls, including that of her late husband. She took special pains over this foundation, creating a gild of St John the Baptist to perform the masses in 1343 and endowing it with land in 1344, and further endowing it in 1345.[10] Even more intriguing is the foundation history of the collegiate church at Sibthorp, founded by Thomas Sibthorp in the 1320s (during Edward II's reign) to say prayers for the well-being of his friends, family and Edward II during their lives, and for their souls after death. In 1335 the ordinances of the church were rewritten by Archbishop Melton, and in this revision it was made very unclear whether Edward II was among the living or the dead. The passage in question is *et nostra ac inclite memorie domini Edwardi filii regis Edwardi secundi*.[11] This has to relate to Edward II somehow (as Edward III's charter of July 1338 states that it does) but that would require it to read *domini Edwardi secundi, filii regis Edwardi*, which it does not. It is quite possible, of course, that the elision of the two kings' names was a mistake; but it is worth noting that the rector of this chantry in 1335 was serving in the household of Manuele Fieschi, the author of the Fieschi Letter, at Avignon. The matter was only sorted out when the ordinances were rewritten yet again in February 1343: this time Edward II was clearly placed among the dead.

These observations – in particular, that the princely title was not passed on to Edward of Woodstock until the parliament of 1343, and that Queen Isabella's principal foundation for her husband's soul was not made until 1342 – draw attention to Edward III's own pattern of behaviour with regard to his father's memory. As he was keen to establish a firm public belief in his father's death, it is not surprising that he licensed many prelates and magnates to endow chantries for the souls of his ancestors, including Edward II, throughout the period; but it is noticeable that, after Mortimer's fall, Edward himself did not visit his father's supposed tomb in Gloucester until September 1337. On that occasion he made a small distribution of alms at a mass held in his presence in the cathedral; and he made a donation to the friars of the town during a royal procession: 31s to thirty-one Dominican friars, thirty-one Carmelites and thirty-one Franciscans (4d each). The reason for the emphasis on the number thirty-one is not known but it is possible that it was a recognition of it being the thirty-first year since Edward II had come to the throne.[12] What is far more certain is that Edward III's gift-giving was a very public affair at Gloucester, and comparable to that in memory of his late brother, John, made just afterwards (which was triggered by 'bad dreams').[13] After that he did not visit Gloucester again until making a very hasty visit there on 10 August 1342, when he made an assignment to repay Henry Whissh, king's yeoman, money that was owing to him since 1339.[14] His next visit was a pilgrimage made after surviving a storm at sea in 1343 (one of five), when he donated a gold ship to the altar of the cathedral.[15] With the sole exception of the 1337 visit, Edward III's attendance on the church containing his father's grave did not start until 1342, nearly fifteen years after the man's death.

The foregoing framework suggests a few initial parameters for considering the later life of Edward II as perceived by Edward III and his mother. Inquiry into the events of 1327–30 continued to take place until early 1335. Edward paid little attention to his father's grave until 1342–3, and did not pass on Edward II's last remaining title to the young Edward of Woodstock until the parliament of 1343, which suggests that the king was not known to be dead at the time of the April 1341 parliament. This is supported by Isabella's principal foundation for the soul of her late husband being made in 1342. However, these circumstantial details allow very little progress beyond this point, and they suggest no secure leads and nor do they come close to suggesting any certainty about Edward II himself. For this reason it is necessary to examine in detail the only known official English record indicating Edward II's possible whereabouts after 1330, namely the account of William Norwell, keeper of the royal wardrobe.

THE ACCOUNT OF WILLIAM NORWELL

Norwell states twice in his wardrobe account book for 1338–40 that one 'William le Galeys', who was brought to Edward III at Koblenz in September 1338, claimed to be the king's father. The first of these two references is an undated payment:

> To Francisco the Lombard sergeant at arms of the king for the money by him spent on
> the expenses of William le Galeys who asserts that he is the father of the present king,
> previously arrested [*arestati*] at Cologne and by the said Francisco led to the king at
> Koblenz by his own hand, 25s 6d.[16]

Judging from the king's itinerary derived from the same volume, this delivery
of 'William le Galeys' must have been while the king was staying at Werde
near Koblenz, between 30 August and 7 September 1338. The second entry is
specifically dated 18 October, when the royal party was at Antwerp. Francisco the
Lombard – now fully and less formally named as 'Francekino Forcet' – was paid:

> For the money received by him for the expenses of William Galeys remaining in his
> custody, who calls himself king of England, father of the present king, namely for three
> weeks in December of year twelve [1338] by his own hand 13s 6d.[17]

This entry was first published by Cuttino and Lyman in their seminal 1978 article,
'Where is Edward II?', having been brought to their attention by Pierre Chaplais.[18]
Chaplais suggested that it was a 'demonstration during a royal visit'. There are
a number of reasons why this suggestion cannot be accepted – not the least
being that 'William le Galeys' had to be taken 57 miles to see the king by a royal
sergeant-at-arms. But over and above the specific suggestion of a demonstration,
if this entry relates to Edward II himself, it tells us several very interesting details
about the ex-king's later life. Therefore the question must be asked at this point:
was 'William le Galeys' actually the father of Edward III or a pretender?

Only two scholars have attempted to tackle this problem – R. M. Haines and
J. R. S. Phillips – and both have done so in the firm belief that Edward II died in
1327, so they do not consider the possibility that 'William le Galeys' was the ex-
king. Haines simply comments that, while Edward III was at Koblenz, 'a certain
William le Galeys . . . was arrested at nearby Cologne'. He offers no explanation
of the meeting except to observe that 'impersonations of kings were not that rare
and in 1318 a man (of unsound mind?) had been put to death for claiming to be
the real king.'[19] This is a reference to John of Powderham, who believed that he
was the true heir of Edward I. John publicly claimed this at Oxford, where the
tale gained some credence, because Edward II was so unlike his father. On that
occasion Edward II had John brought to him at Northampton and mockingly
addressed him as his 'brother'. John denied that he was Edward's brother as

Edward II had no royal blood in him. John was then arrested and the council determined that he should be executed for treason.[20] Phillips's consideration of 'William le Galeys' at Koblenz also considers he was an impostor. Phillips points out that Edward III attended masses for his father's soul and comments that 'Edward III would scarcely have done this if he had any doubt about the real identity of William le Galeys, unless he was being extraordinarily devious'.[21] Phillips seems to forget that this situation was forced on the young king by Mortimer, and thus Edward had no option but to be 'extraordinarily devious' (unless he wished to acknowledge his wrongly deposed father was still alive). Phillips's own theory is that Edward III knew that his father had been murdered in 1327 but responded to the Fieschi Letter by 'saying, in effect, "I should like to meet the impostor, send him to me by return. By the way I shall be in Germany, so send him there."'[22]

In considering the Norwell account, the first point to note is the meaning of the word '*arestati*'. It has a wider meaning than the modern English 'arrested'. Not only men were 'arrested', ships and bales of wool could be too. The word was regularly used to relate to workmen: when masons and carpenters were required to work on a royal building or to accompany an army to war, the writ was sent to the sheriff to 'arrest' such men. Likewise mariners were 'arrested' to sail ships. Second, it has to be noted that there was a well-known royal servant called William le Galeys at this time. He was in royal service by 1328.[23] In 1347 he obtained permission to found a memorial college for the benefit of the souls of the king and his late brother John, their mother and late father Edward II, and the king's eldest son.[24] This in itself shows that the real William le Galeys was close to the queen; the fact that the said college was in the grounds of Isabella's own manor of Cheylesmore, near Coventry, shows just how close. When he died, both William and his son were buried in the same church as Isabella, the London Greyfriars, 'between the choir and the altar'.[25] Therefore the identity assigned to the man who claimed to be Edward II was that of an established royal servant. It is unlikely that we will ever know why this identity was assigned to the claimant but we might speculate that he was assigned this identity because of a resemblance between the real William le Galeys and the ex-king.

The third point arises in connection with the place where 'William le Galeys' was *arestati*: Cologne. Edward III had originally planned a very high-profile journey from Antwerp to Cologne, with special robes made for the journey.[26] On arrival, however, the changing political situation forced him immediately to go to the Holy Roman Emperor at Koblenz, and so he left Cologne the next morning by barge.[27] Hence 'William le Galeys' (or whoever sent him) knew in advance where the king had planned to be on a certain date, which in turn suggests there had been some prior communication. In addition, the initiative for the meeting lay with the king, as the claimant was brought a long distance to the king by a royal sergeant-at-arms at a cost to the royal purse. So, 'William le Galeys' met Edward III not as a consequence of his will but as a consequence of the king's.

This is where Phillips's theory of 'William le Galeys' as royal impostor sent to Edward III on the king's orders starts to fall apart. The theory relies on 'William le Galeys' being brought to Edward III's attention by a third party, on account of his being an impostor. The circumstances differ fundamentally from the pretender archetype in three respects: publicity, respect and fate. With regard to publicity: people pretending to be royal personages did so with as high a profile as possible; there was no point in pretending to be a king quietly, without any show. Those promoting pretenders also wished them to have a high profile: no one would support a humble claimant. Even impostors from humble backgrounds (like John of Powderham) made a public statement of their assumed identity. So it is significant that the appearance of 'William le Galeys' is only known from a private royal account involving the reimbursal of expenses. His claim, made in a foreign kingdom, where he was vulnerable and had no hope of whipping up popular support, could not possibly benefit him politically.[28] Second, Norwell knew Edward II well as he had served the king twelve years earlier.[29] He also would have known the real William le Galeys. In this context it is significant that Norwell did not describe 'William le Galeys' as 'the man who *falsely* claims to be the father of Edward III' but felt the need to distinguish him in some way from the real William le Galeys. In addition, the man's expenses were paid. The record is respectful of the man's claimed identity (as is Manuele Fieschi's letter). Third, as amply demonstrated in Chapter 10, medieval kings usually took two courses of action with pretenders. The first was to prove the impostor's real identity. The second was to have him publicly killed. In the case of John of Powderham, his parents were summoned from Exeter to affirm who he was in truth; then he was publicly executed. Continental pretenders were normally hanged or burnt at the stake. Later pretenders were publicly humiliated and declared traitors after their 'real' identities had been exposed; it was the necessary response of an established ruler to a public threat to his sovereignty. In marked contrast, even though 'William le Galeys' claimed to be Edward II in Edward III's own household, he was not killed, exposed or otherwise humiliated. He was concealed under the name of a member of the royal household and entertained at the king's expense in Antwerp, where the royal family was staying after the birth of Edward II's second grandson, Lionel. In these respects 'William le Galeys' falls wholly outside the pattern of the pretender.

The foregoing strongly suggests that past commentators have been wrong to refuse to consider that 'William le Galeys' was Edward II. Therefore it is reasonable to compare the record of his appearance with what we have already determined about Edward II's possible later life. The arrival of 'William le Galeys' at Cologne in 1338 would accord with the circumstantial evidence that suggests Edward II was alive until the early 1340s. His meeting with Edward III in the autumn of 1338 accords with Edward III searching for details as to his father's fate for a limited period (until 1335). His behaviour fits the pattern of what we might expect of a living Edward II in 1338: sent for and welcomed by his son, then accommodated at royal expense, and taken to see his newly born grandson, Lionel, at Antwerp. The information stream from 'William le Galeys' to Norwell (and thus to us) is only certain to the effect that he *asserted* that he was Edward II but, as far as the extant evidence allows us to judge, the theory that 'William le Galeys' was Edward II is a much stronger one than that he was an impostor.

THE FIESCHI LETTER

The Fieschi Letter was written by Manuele Fieschi (d. 1348), a papal notary until he was elected bishop of Vercelli in 1343. It is known from a single copy in a cartulary of a mid-fourteenth century bishop of Maguelonne, discovered by the French scholar Alexandre Germain and announced by him in a paper read to the Académie des inscriptions et belles-lettres in Paris on 21 September 1877.[30] It was first published by the Société Archéologique de Montpellier the following year and has subsequently been published several times, in Latin and English, as well as in three photographic reproductions.[31] The text in translation is as follows:

> In the name of the Lord, Amen. Those things that I have heard from the confession of your father I have written with my own hand and afterwards I have taken care to be made known to your highness. First he says that feeling England in subversion against him,

afterwards on the admonition of your mother, he withdrew from his family in the castle of the Earl Marshal by the sea, which is called Chepstow. Afterwards, driven by fear, he took a barque with lords Hugh Despenser and the earl of Arundel and several others and made his way by sea to Glamorgan, and there he was captured, together with the said Lord Hugh and Master Robert Baldock; and they were captured by Lord Henry of Lancaster, and they led him to the castle of Kenilworth, and others were [held] elsewhere at various places; and there he lost the Crown at the insistence of many. Afterwards you were subsequently crowned on the feast of Candlemas next following. Finally they sent him to the castle of Berkeley. Afterwards the servant who was keeping him, after some little time, said to your father: Lord, Lord Thomas Gurney and Lord Simon Bereford, knights, have come with the purpose of killing you. If it pleases, I shall give you my clothes, that you may better be able to escape. Then with the said clothes, at twilight, he went out of the prison; and when he had reached the last door without resistance, because he was not recognised, he found the porter sleeping, whom he quickly killed; and having got the keys of the door, he opened the door and went out, with his keeper who was keeping him. The said knights who had come to kill him, seeing that he had thus fled, fearing the indignation of the queen, even the danger to their persons, thought to put that aforesaid porter, his heart having been extracted, in a box, and maliciously presented to the queen the heart and body of the aforesaid porter as the body of your father, and as the body of the said king the said porter was buried in Gloucester. And after he had gone out of the prisons of the aforesaid castle, he was received in the castle of Corfe with his companion who was keeping him in the prisons by Lord Thomas, castellan of the said castle, the lord being ignorant, Lord John Maltravers, lord of the said Thomas, in which castle he was secretly for a year and a half. Afterwards, having heard that the Earl of Kent, because he said he was alive, had been beheaded, he took a ship with his said keeper and with the consent and counsel of the said Thomas, who had received him, crossed into Ireland, where he was for nine months. Afterwards, fearing lest he be recognised there, having taken the habit of a hermit, he came back to England and proceeded to the port of Sandwich, and in the same habit crossed the sea to Sluys. Afterwards he turned his steps in Normandy and from Normandy, as many do, going across through Languedoc, came to Avignon, where, having given a florin to the servant of the pope, sent by the said servant a document to pope John, which pope had him called to him, and held him secretly and honourably more than fifteen days. Finally, after various discussions, all things having been considered, permission having been received, he went to Paris, and from Paris to Brabant, from Brabant to Cologne so that out of devotion he might see The Three Kings, and leaving Cologne he crossed over Germany, that is to say, he headed for Milan in Lombardy, and from Milan he entered a certain hermitage of the castle of *Milasci*, in which hermitage he stayed for two years and a half; and because war overran the said castle, he changed himself to the castle of *Cecime* [Cecima] in another hermitage of the diocese of Pavia in Lombardy, and he was in this last hermitage for two years or thereabouts, always the recluse, doing penance and praying God for you and other sinners. In testimony of which I have caused my seal to be affixed for the consideration of Your Highness. Your Manuele de Fieschi, notary of the lord pope, your devoted servant.

Past interpretations of this letter have been understandably skewed by seeing it in the context of the certainty of Edward II's death in 1327. In Tout's eyes, the letter was a forgery created by a dissident from Edward III's regime. But as he said, it was unusual, bearing 'none of those marks by which a gross medieval forgery can generally be detected'.[32] Several early twentieth-century Italian writers were eager to take on the story that Edward II had died in their country, but they had no further direct evidence or methodological advances to contribute. Not until Cuttino and Lyman published 'Where is Edward II?' in 1978 did the letter receive serious consideration. The authors observed the unreliability of the chronicle accounts of the death, that the person murdered in Berkeley Castle was not necessarily Edward II, that the use of a mannequin at the ex-king's funeral was novel, and that the document could be dated to the period 1336–43. They concluded that there was 'a strong documentary case against a king's body residing in the unexplored leaden coffin in Gloucester Cathedral'. Although much of this work was basic in its methods – the analysis of the chronicles, for example, was largely a matter of traditional source criticism – it was a constructive questioning of received wisdom in the light of the problems posed by the document. In addition, in a footnote Cuttino introduced readers to the Norwell account, thus alerting them to the fact that the Fieschi Letter was not the sole piece of evidence that Edward II might have been alive in 1336.

Since 1978 scholars have not probed deeply into the questions posed by the Fieschi Letter. R. M. Haines, in an article published in 1996, commented on 'the wealth of circumstantial detail it contains' and acknowledged that it is 'by no means impossible' that Edward II escaped from Berkeley Castle to Corfe in the manner described, but, despite this, he did not explore the possibility that the letter was genuine and written in good faith.[33] Instead, he recapitulated much previously published evidence supporting the traditional interpretation of the death, and highlighted the apparent discrepancies between that tradition and the Fieschi Letter. Such a method was prone to be self-supporting: the process of contrasting any problematic document with the evidence for the orthodoxy with which it conflicts is bound to isolate that document and to present it as odd, idiosyncratic and unreliable. Haines concluded that the document was 'a competent forgery' created in Italy as a result of information from England, with the name of Fieschi perhaps being 'borrowed' to lend it weight.[34] Extraordinarily, he suggested the purpose of the forgery was to encourage a 'cult' sympathetic to Edward II. He did not explain how an Italian statement that the ex-king was alive and well in Italy was supposed to create sympathy in England for the supposedly dead king in England, or help his political canonization.

Phillips, in his discussion of the Fieschi Letter in 2003 (published in 2005), adopted a similar position. His starting point was an affirmation of his belief in Edward II's death in Berkeley Castle, without commenting on the argument put forward for his survival.[35] In so doing, he restricted himself to considering whether the letter was a hoax in itself or a description of the activities of an impostor. After making a number of interesting observations about the correlation between Fieschi's 'Edward II' and 'William le Galeys', Phillips decided that the two men were probably the same, that the Fieschi Letter was written in good faith, but that Manuele Fieschi was deliberately trying to reveal the antics of a pretender. He postulated the theory that the Fieschi Letter led Edward III to write back to Fieschi asking for the impostor to be brought to him in Germany (as outlined above). However, the theory is fundamentally flawed. Nowhere in the letter did Manuele Fieschi refer to his subject as an impostor or pretender. He acknowledged him to be whom he claimed to be and described him throughout in respectful tones, even describing the man to Edward III as 'your father' – something he would not have done if he believed the man was a fraud.[36] Phillips ended his piece even more strangely than Haines did his: by speculating that the man who pretended to be Edward II to Fieschi and travelled as 'William le Galeys' to Cologne might have been one William le Walsh of Woolstrop, even though Phillips himself admitted that he had no evidence for the identification and that le Walsh died in 1329, six years before the earliest possible date for the Fieschi Letter and nine years before 'William le Galeys' arrived at Koblenz.[37]

The prejudgements of past scholars against the document are unfortunate, for there is much within it of interest to the student of Edward III's reign as well as Edward II's later life. The letter was informed by someone who had a good knowledge of the events of 1326–30 as well as the geography of England and Italy. The person who confessed to Fieschi knew about the politics of the rising against Edward II, his flight from Chepstow, the individuals with him when he fled, his capture, his captor, his first place of imprisonment (Kenilworth) as well as his second (Berkeley), his deposition, the date of Edward III's coronation, the men who personally served Mortimer, Edward II's later shelter in Corfe Castle, Lord Maltravers's presence at Corfe in late 1327, and the earl of Kent's plot. Much of this was public knowledge but some was not. Few would have known correctly who was with Edward II when he fled, and the list of his companions given – Hugh Despenser, the earl of Arundel and Robert Baldock – is accurately described, as is Edward's capture by Henry of Lancaster and his transfer to Kenilworth.[38] Fewer still would have known that Maltravers was at Corfe Castle in an unofficial capacity in the autumn of 1327 – a fact that is only known to us from Lord Berkeley's accounts.[39] Probably no one but Edward II himself knew *all* these details. If the letter was the result of an impostor's work, the man in question had to learn about Italian geography – or at least enough to convince Manuele Fieschi, an Italian – and to visit Avignon to see Fieschi, by way of Languedoc. Fieschi's Edward II also would have had to know the significance of the visit to the shrine of the Magi at Cologne.[40] There is only one obvious slip in the entire narrative – the length of time Edward II was at Corfe Castle must have been two and a half years, not one and a half – but given that this is contradicted by the internal evidence of the letter, it turns out to be a miscalculation by Manuele in drawing up his letter to Edward III, and so is not suspicious.[41]

There is a second unfortunate consequence of the prejudgements of past scholars and the emphasis on the presumed falsehood of the Fieschi Letter. Attention has focused exclusively on the author, Manuele Fieschi. Although Phillips has commented on the wider relationships of the family, commentators generally have failed to note that, at the time that the supposed Edward II made his confession in person to Manuele Fieschi, Manuele was a member of the household of his powerful kinsman, Cardinal Luca Fieschi (his second cousin once-removed: see Appendix 6.1). Manuele had the status of a papal notary but his direct superior was the cardinal.

In order to demonstrate the implications of this, a distinction needs to be made concerning the date of the Fieschi Letter and the date of the information it contains. On internal evidence, the letter was written no earlier than December 1335. It accounts for the period of nine months after the discovery of the earl of Kent's plot (March to December 1330, which coincides with Mortimer's fall); then for an indeterminate period while the subject travelled to Avignon. At an average of 85 miles per week (12 miles per day, the days being short), the earliest he could have arrived in Avignon would have been the second half of February 1331. After two weeks with the pope, and a journey of a further 1,000 miles to Milan, via Paris, he cannot have reached Italy before May 1331 at the very earliest. So the two and a half years near *Milasci* plus the two years near *Cecime* mentioned in the letter cannot have come to an end before December 1335. However, almost 80 per cent of the detail in the letter relates to Edward II prior to his arrival at Avignon in 1331. The period in question – approximately September 1326 to about March 1331 (four and a half years) – occupies thirty lines of the original letter; the remainder (amounting to at least four and a half years) occupies only eight lines. This strongly suggests that the 'confession' which Manuele received from the ex-king was not one which reflected on the events of 1331–6 but one based on the period prior to his appearance at Avignon in 1331, which was brought up to date when the letter came to be written, after December 1335. This is supported by the specific details given in the letter. Manuele claimed at the outset to have received the 'confession' in person, and as he was resident at Avignon throughout the period and no subsequent return to Avignon by the subject is recorded, the confession must have been made in the spring or early summer of 1331. Manuele also notes that the subject of his letter spent 'fifteen days' in Avignon (not an approximate period) and he bribed the servant of the pope with 'a florin', and 'was summoned' and kept 'secretly and honourably'. The specific details contrast with the remainder of the letter, which is a very brief description of places that Edward visited (or was taken to) afterwards.

This distinction between the date of the information given to Manuele in the spring of 1331 and the writing of the letter to Edward III in or after 1336 is important. Cardinal Fieschi died at the end of January 1336 – Manuele Fieschi was probably not acting under his guidance when he wrote the letter (sometime after December 1335). However, when Manuele received the 'confession' of the supposed Edward II at Avignon in the spring of 1331, he was still first and foremost Cardinal Fieschi's own notary and a member of his *familia*.[42] So, if Manuele Fieschi believed that the man who confessed to him in 1331 was Edward II in person, Cardinal Fieschi also believed him to be the genuine ex-king. And Cardinal Fieschi was not only a kinsman of Edward II, he also knew Edward personally, having resided for two or three protracted periods in England (see below). Thus the Fieschi Letter contains within its own text a verification of the man's identity, being created by a servant of a cardinal who knew Edward II reasonably well and who was present at Avignon at the time he supposedly arrived. Unless one wishes to speculate that Cardinal Luca Fieschi himself was the architect of a fraud – and that Edward III never discovered this fact but continued rewarding members of the Fieschi family for ten years, even after he had met his supposed father – then the Fieschi Letter is nothing less than what it seems to be: a letter telling Edward III where his father had been for the previous eight years, and how he came to be there. In addition, as the man who claimed to be Edward II at Avignon in 1331 could demonstrate knowledge about Edward II's experiences in 1326 and 1327 which were probably not known in their totality to any other individual, we have two good information streams that, taken together, indicate Fieschi's Edward II was almost certainly the ex-king himself. One of these information streams started with Cardinal Fieschi's recognition of the man at the papal court in 1331 and passed to Manuele Fieschi in the form of the instruction to take down his story, the information later being enshrined in the Fieschi Letter copied into the Maguelonne cartulary. The other started with the claimant himself, who had access to information about events at Chepstow, Corfe and elsewhere in 1326–7.

The foregoing passages allow us to answer the key question of whether the Fieschi Letter is a hoax or the result of the work of an impostor. Clearly it is neither. It follows that we have good reason to believe that the real Edward II was not just alive in November 1330 (as concluded in 'DEII') but still alive at the end of 1335. This tallies with the circumstantial evidence discussed at the beginning of this chapter and with the details of 'William le Galeys' given in Norwell's account. Furthermore it may be observed that the Edward II of the Fieschi Letter matches the 'William le Galeys' character in a number of respects. Both men were in the control of Italians – the Fieschi Edward II was at a hermitage in Italy and 'William le Galeys' was brought to Edward III by an Italian, Francisco or Francesco Forzetti, described as a Lombard. Both the Fieschi Edward II and 'William le Galeys' were living modestly: the former in a hermitage and the latter on about 7½d per day for him and his guardian. Both men kept a very low profile: neither man was paraded publicly – one living as a recluse in a hermitage and the other travelling under an assumed name and with no household, only his Italian escort. Both texts are respectful of the identity of the claimant. Lastly, both men *personally* claimed to be the king, they were not promoted by other agencies. Neither man sought to replace Edward III, as pretenders usually did.

Neither claim to be Edward II was made in England and thus neither was made in the hope of triggering a popular movement. In both cases the claim was for nothing more than to be recognized as Edward III's father.

There is one very important respect in which the central character in the Fieschi Letter corresponds with the claimant in the Norwell account: custody of the ex-king. As Manuele Fieschi knew *where* Edward was in Italy after November 1335, even though he does not mention seeing him since 1331, it follows that Edward II's whereabouts were being monitored if not controlled by the Fieschi. Thus the role of an Italian in bringing Edward II as 'William le Galeys' to Edward III in 1338 is significant: the ex-king was not free to wander where he pleased: he was in the custody of Italians. Obviously this includes his journey to Italy in 1331 from Avignon via Paris, Brabant and Cologne: this explains how he travelled so far without being discovered. It also applies to his journey to Cologne and Koblenz in 1338. In this light, the Fieschi Letter reveals that Edward II never 'escaped' from custody but was almost continually a guarded man. He was taken from Berkeley to Corfe by his keeper, maintained at Corfe by the same man, taken to Ireland by him, and only released on the fall of Mortimer and Isabella. After his journey to Avignon he was in the keeping of Italians and never seems to have evaded their watchfulness. His period of freedom after 1327 thus amounted to a mere two or three months in early 1331, when he was travelling to Avignon.[43]

EDWARD III AND THE FIESCHI

The origins of the Fieschi lay in the area directly to the north and to the east of Genoa in the eleventh century, but it was not until the mid-thirteenth that the family came to occupy an important place in English affairs. This was principally because of the election of Sinibaldo Fieschi (d. 1254) as Pope Innocent IV in 1248, and his consequent preferment of members of his family. He created cardinals of his nephews Guglielmo (d. 1256) and Ottobono, later Pope Adrian V (d. 1276). As the family gained a grip on the papal appointments system, many of its members were given English missions and English benefices. In 1249 the three principal secular branches of the Fieschi received the right to call themselves counts of Lavagna. This right extended to younger sons, so all branches in later years could, and often did, use the title. One therefore finds Giacomo, grandfather of Manuele Fieschi, described as count of Lavagna in 1256, and Federico, uncle of

Cardinal Luca Fieschi, described likewise in 1266.[44] Even ecclesiastical members of the family referred to the title, styling themselves 'of the counts of Lavagna'. Consequently, various thirteenth-century Fieschi men appear in English records not as 'de Flisco' but as 'de Lavania', such as 'Percevalle de Lavania, brother of Pope Adrian' in 1290.[45]

As noted above, there was a family connection between Edward II and the Fieschi. The exact nature of that relationship has proved elusive. The marriage of Thomas II (d. 1259), count of Savoy, and Beatrice Fieschi (d. 1283), which took place in about 1250, has been suggested as the link.[46] However, this is demonstrably incorrect, for that marriage would not have resulted in a blood connection and never led to claims of royal kinship by Beatrice's brothers when they came to England in the late thirteenth century.[47] Laying aside the equally misleading royal consanguinity of a woman who married into the Fieschi family,[48] the first direct reference to a blood relationship was made in connection with Cardinal Luca Fieschi in 1301, when he was described as 'the king's kinsman'.[49] In later years his brother Carlo and the two sons of their deceased brother, Federico, were also described as 'king's kinsmen'.[50] Manuele Fieschi, however, was never described as a royal kinsman.[51] These details, and especially the failure to describe Luca's uncles as royal kinsmen, indicate that the relationship was through the mother of Cardinal Luca Fieschi and his brothers, namely Leonora or Lionetta, whose surname is unknown. As Federico's sons (the next generation after Luca) were also described as royal kin, the relationship of Cardinal Luca Fieschi to the English royal family was probably that of a third cousin (fifth cousins being outside the usually noted degrees of kinship). Luca claimed to be connected to James II of Aragon when he was appointed a cardinal (in 1300), so it is probable that Leonora was descended from the house of Savoy.[52] Support for this is in the list of members of Cardinal Fieschi's household in 1305, which includes two men surnamed as 'of Savoy' (de Sabaudia).[53] Therefore, if Cardinal Fieschi and Edward II were third cousins, their common ancestor was most probably Thomas I of Savoy. Alternatively, if Leonora was, like her sister-in-law, Brumisan, the daughter of Giacomo del Caretto, then Luca would have been a fourth cousin of Edward II. Whichever genealogy is correct, Cardinal Luca Fieschi and his brothers and nephews were habitually recognized and acknowledged as royal kinsmen in England.[54]

Any discussion of the prominence of the family and its relevance to the English royal family in the early fourteenth century has to begin with Luca Fieschi, son of Niccolo Fieschi, count of Lavagna. He was born in the early 1270s, and was made a cardinal by Pope Boniface VIII in March 1300. He visited England in 1301.[55] He returned to England for a protracted period in 1317–18, when he was a papal emissary facilitating negotiations between Edward II and the Scots.[56] In 1325 he twice obtained protection from Edward II – on 5 March (for three years) and on 4 May (for one year) – but he did not necessarily visit England.[57] He owned many English items, especially vestments, as specified in the inventory of his possessions at the time of his death.[58] His ecclesiastical contacts were to be found throughout Europe; and his family links, especially with the Malaspina family, his Fieschi nephews and the Visconti of Milan, gave him great influence with both the church and nobility in the regions where Edward II is supposed to have been maintained.

This is a starting point for understanding why the Fieschi became involved in the story of Edward II's later life. Depending on how fit Edward II was as a forty-six-year-old, he would have arrived at Avignon in February or March 1331. His reason for going there was no doubt partly that of the supposed independence, moral virtue and power of the pope; but equally it was because his late half-brother, the earl of Kent, had made the same journey for a similar purpose twenty months earlier. Even if he was unaware that the pope already knew of his plight, he could be confident of proving his identity in the presence of Cardinal Fieschi, Cardinal Gaucelin de Jean d'Eauze and other cardinals. But the pope could hardly maintain an ex-king secretly at the papal curia indefinitely, so he entrusted Edward to the safekeeping of his kinsman, Cardinal Fieschi, who also happened to be well positioned to conceal him safely in Italy.

Cardinal Fieschi was not only familiar with Edward II, he was familiar with Archbishop Melton too. Melton had been commended to the cardinals in 1312, and went to Avignon in February 1316. He stayed there for eighteen months, until his confirmation as archbishop on 25 September 1317.[59] Cardinal Fieschi was probably in Italy when Melton arrived at Avignon but he returned on 17 November 1316 and was there until the following May, when he left for England on his papal commission, landing at Dover on 22 June 1317.[60] Thus the two men would have spent six months at the papal curia together. Cardinal Fieschi's business included negotiating peace with the Scots, and so would have come into close contact with men from Melton's province. It was noticeable that the prebend of Beverley, held by William Melton before his elevation to York, was given to Cardinal Fieschi's nephew Bernabo Malaspina, who was in his household at the time.[61] Cardinal Fieschi did not leave London to return to Avignon until 18 September 1318, having spent fifteen months in England, and thus would have met Melton again after the latter returned from the papal curia at the end of 1317. They would have probably met again at court if Cardinal Fieschi's permission to return to England, in 1325, was enacted: Melton witnessed all the royal charters issued between 26 June and 30 October 1325.

Cardinal Fieschi was thus familiar with both of the men who plotted to release Edward II from Corfe Castle in 1330. When Kent arrived at Avignon in 1329, he probably spoke to Cardinal Fieschi (as mentioned in the previous chapter). If so, Cardinal Fieschi might not have been wholly unprepared for Edward II's arrival at Avignon. He would have heard about the fake death from Kent and perhaps suggested that Melton too might do something about Edward's false imprisonment. This is important, for Cardinal Fieschi communicated with Melton not long after Edward II arrived in Avignon. On 26 April 1331 William Aslakeby, rector of Sibthorp, was licensed by Melton to leave his living in order to spend two years in the service of Cardinal Fieschi.[62] It is possible that the message was carried by Antonio Pessagno and Richard Bury (discussed below). Melton was a constant companion of Edward III until 1 April 1331, while he was treasurer, so it is interesting that his communication from Cardinal Fieschi at Avignon also coincided with Edward III's letter to the pope in the spring of 1331 asking whether he should visit Ireland.[63] Given Lord Mortimer's powerful position in Ireland, it would have been natural for Edward III to suppose his father had been taken there for safekeeping. The Fieschi Letter narrative states that he had indeed been removed to Ireland after the earl of Kent tried to rescue him. A communication from Cardinal Fieschi to Archbishop Melton about the ex-king would have alerted Melton to the fact that Edward II's location was known at Avignon; this in turn would explain why Edward III asked the pope whether he should visit a part of his own domain – probably the only time an English king ever asked such a thing of a French pope.

Edward's question indicates that, whatever information passed between Cardinal Fieschi and Archbishop Melton in early 1331, it did not amount to the current location of the ex-king. Edward III was thus somewhat on the back foot: he knew his father was under the protection of distant Italian kinsmen based at Avignon; but he did not know where he was, nor could he limit those to whom the Fieschi made this information available. He had to trust them. Hence the next appearance of a member of the Fieschi family in the English records is interesting. Later in 1330 Edward III became aware of a dispute between a royal clerk, John Melburn, and Guglielmo Fieschi, son of Niccolinus Fieschi, a kinsman of Manuele Fieschi.[64] Guglielmo Fieschi had been given the prebend of Strensall in 1326 but the government of Mortimer and Isabella had appointed Melburn to it on 28 September 1329, thereby ousting Fieschi.[65] Edward learned that Guglielmo Fieschi was attempting 'to draw John into a plea outside the realm concerning certain matters which ought to be brought to the king's attention'.[66] Edward prohibited John from leaving the country and did not relent until 15 October 1331. Even when he did let him go to Avignon to pursue the case, he gave him strict instructions not to engage in other matters apart from his right to the prebend. It would appear that this business involving the Fieschi caused Edward III some anxiety.

The above dispute might have been coincidental. The series of messengers that Edward started sending to Avignon on his private business was not. The first of these consisted of Richard Bury, king's clerk, and the Italian merchant Antonio Pessagno. They were sent in March 1331 to the court at Avignon to conduct negotiations on behalf of the king. Extraordinarily, they were empowered to borrow the enormous sum of £50,000 in the king's name.[67] They returned in April and there is no indication that they borrowed a large sum at that time.[68] However, the despatch of William Aslakeby to Cardinal Fieschi by William Melton on 26 April 1331 (mentioned above) may well have been a result of information they brought back about the ex-king. The following year, on 22 July 1332, Antonio Pessagno was sent again to Avignon with John de Shordich 'to further certain arduous affairs there touching the king specially'.[69] This embassy returned to England on 14 December. Two months later, in February 1333, Edward III had his first direct meeting with a member of the Fieschi family, when he gave 'two robes for Cardinal & his companion'.[70]

'Cardinal' was Niccolinus Fieschi, *dicti Cardinal*, the father of the Guglielmo Fieschi mentioned above.[71] He was probably the same age as Cardinal Fieschi, about sixty, and perhaps born in Lucca.[72] He was more closely related to Manuele's side of the family than the cardinal's, probably being a second cousin of Luca and an uncle or first-cousin-once-removed of Manuele (see Appendix

6.1). He and Manuele were associated in other ways too. Both men used the same legal representatives, Adam of Lichfield and Anthony Bacche of Genoa, in England.[73] A document relating to a French plot to kidnap Niccolinus from the papal court in 1340 appears in the same cartulary as Manuele Fieschi's letter, so whoever was interested in the Fieschi Letter at Maguelonne was also interested in Niccolinus' mission in 1340.[74] Unlike Manuele, however, Niccolinus was a man of the world: he had at least four sons and considerable ambassadorial experience. He had trained in civil law, and by 1319 was described as 'ambassador of Genoa' at Avignon.[75] In May 1320 King Henry of Cyprus was directed to receive him as 'ambassador of the Commune of Genoa'.[76] In 1329 he negotiated a trading pact between Genoa and Henry's successor, King Hugh of Cyprus.[77] Thus he had at least thirteen years international diplomatic experience when he first met Edward III in February 1333.

Following Niccolinus' arrival at court, Edward III sent a special delegation to the pope, headed by Richard Bury and John de Shordich 'for the secret negotiations of the king and touching the state of the kingdom and to expedite such business with the pope and the cardinals'.[78] Bury and de Shordich remained at the papal curia for more than six months, not returning to England until 20 November 1333, their expenses amounting to more than £542. But that was a fraction of the cost of the expedition. Edward directed at the outset that three papal kinsmen should be given valuable goblets and asked to help Richard Bury and John de Shordich on their mission, but many more gifts and pensions were made.[79] The section of the account headed, 'Gifts made at the Curia by the view and testimony of John de Shordich, knight, and by indenture' notes the gift to the pope of 'a silver gilded goblet worth £66 13s 4d purchased at Avignon'. Various cardinals were given gifts 'for the swifter expedition and promotion of the king's affairs at the curia'. The cardinal vice-chancellor received 'a goblet worth £15 and 200 florins' (£33 6s 8d). Similar goblets worth between £5 and £20 were given to Arnold de Osa, the pope's kinsman; Peter de Via, the pope's nephew; Arnold de Trie, the pope's kinsman and marshal; Bernard Jurdan de Insula, the pope's nephew; Arnold Neopolitano, the pope's proto-notary; and Bertrand de Mari, knight of the pope's chamber. Similar goblets were given to all their 'knightly companions'. Master Robert de Adria received 18 florins for making and writing a royal petition. Two knights, master-ushers of the papal chamber, received two plain silver goblets with lids and bases worth 40s each, four ushers of the papal chamber received four such goblets worth 64s; two squires of the cardinal vice-chancellor received 12 florins for taking letters of petition, granted by the pope to the king, to the keeper of the wardrobe; and John Rygald, the pope's chamberlain, received 30 florins (£6 13s 4d). A further 157 florins were distributed to 'the *familia* of the papal chamber, sergeants-at-arms, porters and other ministers within the papal palace'. On top of all these gifts, pensions were awarded to several cardinals, each of whom was 'retained as a member of the king's council at an annual pension of fifty marks'. These included Anibaldo Ceccano Gaetani, cardinal-bishop of Frascati (letter of acquittance dated 8 June 1333); Bertrand de Montfavez, cardinal-priest of St. Maria in Aquiro (22 September 1333); Neapoleone Orsini, cardinal-deacon of St Adrian (22 September 1333); Peter Mortemart, cardinal-priest of St Stephen in Celiomonte (5 October 1333); and Gaucelin de Jean d'Eauze, cardinal-bishop of Albano (21 September 1333).[80] In addition a payment of sixty florins (£10) was made 'to Master William de Veraco, doctor of law, retained for a certain annual pension as a member of the king's council' (22 September 1333). Given all these payments to cardinals and members of the papal *familia* in the papal chamber – the pope's most intimate companions – and given the petitions to the pope and the long duration of the mission, Bury's 'secret business' is unlikely to have related simply to the £1,000 paid to the pope on 7 July 1333 as a contribution towards the arrears of the annual sum of 1,000 marks per year, agreed to be paid by Mortimer and Isabella in late 1329.[81] Despite this, it was not until the payment of the majority of the pensions at the end of September that they received a response from the pope. As Lunt put it in examining relations between the papacy and the king: 'what favours the king received in return is not explained.'[82] All that is certain is that on 21 September the pope wrote back to Edward, stating that he had received his ambassadors and was 'prepared to give a favourable answer to the petitions presented'.[83] Edward's 'secret negotiations' with the cardinals resulted in a positive answer from John XXII – and remained secret.

In late 1333 or early 1334 William Aslakeby came to the end of his two years service in the household of Cardinal Luca Fieschi. Whether he returned to England in person to renew his permission to be absent from his living is not clear.[84] Either way, he was licensed to spend the next two years in the service of Manuele Fieschi. If he did return in person, any information about Edward II he had picked up in Cardinal Fieschi's household would have probably been passed to the king, via Archbishop Melton. We can have greater confidence that Edward III learned something from Maltravers, who wrote to him the same year eager to impart information (as noted above). But presuming that these two lines of communication did not reveal Edward II's location, it would appear that the first that Edward knew about the whereabouts of his father was either the delivery of the Fieschi Letter or the second visit of Niccolinus Fieschi in April 1336, depending on which happened first.

On 15 April 1336 Niccolinus Fieschi was made a king's councillor at the Tower and given a pension of £20 per year and robes befitting a knight.[85] This is the most likely date for the delivery to Edward III of the Fieschi Letter.[86] Although the information contained within the letter relates to the years 1326–31, the temporal accounting period in the last few lines suggests a *terminus post quem* of December 1335 (as noted above). As for the latest date, Edward III would have had no need for the information contained in the letter after the arrival in England in August 1337 of Antonio Fieschi and Giffredus di Groppo (the legal representative of Bernabo Malaspina, bishop of Luni).[87] Both Antonio and Bernabo were nephews of the late Cardinal Fieschi (who died on 31 January 1336) and, like Manuele Fieschi, long-standing members of his household at Avignon (as indeed was Giffredus di Groppo himself). Antonio Fieschi was also a papal chaplain and a co-executor (with Manuele Fieschi) of Cardinal Fieschi's will, written at Avignon. Bernabo had been a witness of the cardinal's will.[88] So the information available to these men would have obviated the need for Manuele to put these things in writing at a later date. Either Antonio brought Manuele's letter with him in 1337 (as trustworthy evidence for the king, being written by a papal notary) or the letter preceded his arrival. This narrows the possible window for the letter to have been written to December 1335–July 1337. Given the attention to dates in the letter, and the comprehensiveness of periods covered, it is more likely to have been written towards the beginning of the period in question, as otherwise a period of time is left unaccounted for. If the letter was written in February 1336, just after the death of Cardinal Fieschi, then this would tally with Edward III rewarding its likely bearer on 15 April.

Niccolinus Fieschi's fortunes rose dramatically from that day on. On 4 July 1336 Edward agreed with him that the English treasury would pay to the Commune of Genoa 8,000 marks in lieu of damage to a ship of Yvanus Luccani, which had been the victim of Hugh Despenser's piracy more than fifteen years before.[89] In addition to his pension of £20 per year, Edward also started to pay Niccolinus a daily wage. It is not certain when this commenced but from 12 July 1338, the first day of William Norwell's account (and thus probably from some time earlier), he was paid 12s per day.[90] This lasted until the end of Norwell's accounting period, 29 January 1340, when his payments went up to one mark per day, which he was paid until 24 November 1341 (the end of Thomas Crosse's accounting period).[91] He then reverted to 12s per day for the duration of Richard Eccleshale's period as controller of the wardrobe, that is until 1 April 1344.[92] In all, between 12 July 1338 and 1 April 1344, he was assigned more than £1,300 – an average of more than £220 per year – in addition to his expenses, his £20 annuity, 20 marks annuity granted in early 1339, and his knightly robes. In addition to the rise in his own fortunes, his sons benefited from prebends and favours.[93] A pension granted to Niccolinus in January 1339 was directed to be paid to his sons even after his death.[94] There is consequently no doubt that Edward III thought highly of Niccolinus, and his being an associate and kinsman of the author of the Fieschi Letter seems to have done him no harm at all.

Whatever the reason for the extraordinary promotion of Niccolinus Fieschi, it is clear that the political stakes were high in 1336–40. Edward II's survival thus raises a series of questions, not the least of which is whether someone threatened to expose him and have him recognized at Avignon if Edward III continued to press his claim on the throne of France. But first the basic question needs to be answered of who was directly controlling Edward II in Italy. As we have seen, Manuele Fieschi was resident at Avignon, and yet he knew where Edward II was supposed to be living, so we can be sure that the ex-king was not simply 'a wandering hermit' (as Sumption refers to him).[95] How did the Fieschi keep control of him and manage the 'political stakes'?

EDWARD II IN ITALY 1331–5

The two places in which Edward II is supposed to have stayed for protracted periods are 'a certain hermitage of the castle of *Milasci*' and another hermitage near the castle of *Cecime* 'of the diocese of Pavia in Lombardy'. The second of these, *Cecime*, is easily identifiable as Cecima sopra Voghera, for, although it falls in the diocese of Tortona, it was a possession of the bishop of Pavia.[96] *Milasci* could be any one of a large number of places. It was identified by the Italian writers Constantino Nigra and Anna Benedetti as Melazzo d'Aqui, but this is very unlikely because the medieval Latin name for Melazzo was *Melagius*, not *Milasci*.[97] More likely candidates are Milazzo in Sicily, the Torre delle Milizie (in the centre of Rome) or, strikingly, Mulazzo, a castle in the Val di Magra 4 miles from Cardinal Fieschi's inheritance of Pontremoli. This was in the hands of Manfredo Malaspina, marquis of Giovagallo, a nephew of Cardinal Fieschi, in the 1330s. If this identification is correct, then it needs to be realised that the ex-king was removed from a region dominated by one of Cardinal Fieschi's nephews, Manfredo Malaspina, and delivered to a hermitage in a region dominated by another of his nephews, Niccolo Malaspina, marquis of Filattiera and Oramala, known as 'il Marchesotto'.[98]

Various writers have identified the hermitage in the vicinity of Cecima as Sant' Alberto di Butrio. The earliest identification was that of Constantino Nigra in 1901. Cuttino and Lyman noted a record dating from 1958 – that an eighty-eight-year-old man, Zerba Stefano, remembered his grandfather telling him about an English king who had taken refuge in the monastery.[99] Of course, one old man's testimony in such matters is easily disputed: Phillips simply stated that it 'does not carry conviction'. Accordingly, he declared that

> the tradition that Edward II was at Sant' Alberto goes back no further than the decade between 1890, when Constantino Nigra visited the castle of Melazzo and 1901, when he published his findings and the alleged tomb of Edward II was first examined . . . The history of the abbey of Sant' Alberto, which was published in 1865 by Count Antonio Cavagni Sangiuliani, before Alexandre Germain revealed the Fieschi letter [in 1877] has no mention of Edward II. Neither is there any reference in the second edition of Sangiuliani's book, published in 1890.[100]

This is not the full story. Sangiuliani would not necessarily have mentioned an old tradition which he could not substantiate; historians are quick to dismiss any argument which is not supported by evidence, so they should be sensitive to the same carefulness in other historians, even nineteenth-century ones. And although Phillips does mention in a footnote that the alleged 'first tomb' of Edward II was opened in 1900 (when a piece of bone was found), he does not mention that it was first opened and examined many years earlier, before the discovery of the Fieschi Letter.[101] A pair of very high-quality early thirteenth-century Limoges candlesticks were found in the grave; these were eventually acquired by the renowned collector and geologist Gastaldi Bartolomeo, and later given by him to the Museo Civico di Torino, which accessioned them in 1874, three years before the discovery of the Fieschi Letter.[102]

There is some previously overlooked contemporary evidence demonstrating a direct link between Cardinal Fieschi and a castle very close to Sant' Alberto, which supports the theory that Edward II was at that hermitage. This comes from a letter of Niccolo Malapsina, marquis of Filattiera and Oramala, addressed to Cardinal Luca Fieschi (his uncle). It is dated November 1335 and was sent from Oramala, across the valley from Sant' Alberto and clearly visible from the grounds of the hermitage, being less than two miles away. It begins:

> Reverend father and lord, so that your fathership might have notice of the condition of these parts from me. I signify by this [letter]: leaders of La Scala [Scalagleri] within the last few days have entered the city of Lucca, as I learnt from the information related to be by Barrete F . . . [*damaged words*] . . . ei, who joined William de Caynacio, a companion of the said lords, with a great number of armigerous people in order to enter and munition the aforesaid city. Why he was there, God knows, but if I find out I will write and tell your paternal lordship. Of John Nero, your pious son, I notify your paternal lordship that he was with me in Oramala and truly I found him to have worked about the promotion of the pious negotiations of your fathership in the land of Lombardy not like a man young in age; on the contrary, certainly as if a mature and discreet man, very expert in this type of negotiations, just as any wise and mature man would have done in the aforesaid work . . .[103]

The significance of this letter lies partly in realizing how remote the Oramala region is, in very hilly territory, sparsely inhabited, a long way from any major settlement. Oramala Castle had been the chief residence of Niccolo Malaspina's ancestor who had founded Sant' Alberto di Butrio in the eleventh century; Cecima itself is 3.5 miles to the west of the monastery. The letter shows that in late 1335, Cardinal Fieschi's nephew was resident in this remote place, and supplying 'notice of the condition of these parts' to the cardinal. Most significantly he had met at Oramala a young man, John Nero of Florence, a goldsmith (according to Cardinal Fieschi's bequests to him), who had been sent by the cardinal to act for him in delicate negotiations in the area in late 1335.[104] This shows how the Fieschi could have monitored the whereabouts of Edward II in Italy: by direct liaison through men like John Nero with the man's guardians, Cardinal Fieschi's kinsmen. Moreover, because Niccolo Malaspina was Cardinal Luca's nephew through Fiesca Fieschi (*Flisca de Flisco*, Luca's sister), Niccolo was also a kinsman of the English royal family. It is worth noting too that John Nero was not the only means of contact between Cardinal Fieschi and Oramala in 1335: on 24 June that year, Cardinal Fieschi gave a canonry to three of his nephews, two of these being Antonio Fieschi and 'Bernabo son of Niccolo, marquis Malaspina, *dicti Marchesotto de Oramala*'.[105] So the hermitage to which Edward II had been moved in 1334 for his security was not just one of the most remote places in Northern Italy, it was a place watched over – literally – by one of his most powerful Italian kinsman, 'il Marchesotto', a man with direct links to Cardinal Fieschi at Avignon.

Given this strengthened identification of the *Cecime* hermitage, we need to consider more seriously whether *Milasci* was Mulazzo, a small town with a castle in the Val di Magra.[106] As mentioned above, the lord of this place was Manfredo Malaspina, marquis of Giovagallo, who would also have been a kinsman of Edward II (being the son of another of Cardinal Fieschi's sisters, Alagia Fieschi).

Figure 6.1 View of Oramala Castle, residence in 1335 of Niccolo Malapsina, il Marchesotto, nephew of Cardinal Fieschi and kinsman of Edward II, taken from the grounds of Sant'Alberto di Butrio, near Cecima, where the Fieschi Letter states Edward II was maintained in 1334–5. *Reproduced by kind permission of Paul Lizioli.*

In fact, the whole region was dominated by Cardinal Fieschi's relatives. Mulazzo was near Pontremoli, a town that had belonged to the cardinal but which he had lost in 1314. It had been recaptured in 1328 by Pietro Rossi (d. 1337), the husband of Ginetta Fieschi, one of Cardinal Fieschi's nieces (and thus also a kinswoman of Edward II). In addition, the part of the Val di Magra which was *not* under the authority of Manfredo Malaspina, being on the other side of the River Magra, was dominated by another nephew of Cardinal Fieschi and kinsman of Edward II – the same Niccolo Malaspina, marquis of Filattiera, 'il Marchesotto', who was lord of Oramala, Godiasco and the district around Cecima. To be precise, Mulazzo is about 3 miles from Filattiera, Niccolo Malaspina's seat in the Val di Magra. If Edward II was taken from a hermitage near here to Cecima, this would have entailed a journey of about 50 miles, ending up at a hermitage less than 2 miles from Niccolo Malaspina's other seat of Oramala. And Niccolo Malaspina represented Cardinal Fieschi's interests in both places: the same letter of November 1335 urges him to look towards making moves to reclaim Pontremoli.

Cardinal Fieschi's influence in the Val di Magra was not just secular; it was ecclesiastical too. The sequence of bishops of the local diocese of Luni, centred on the city of Sarzana, reads like a list of Cardinal Fieschi's favoured kinsmen. His nephew Gherardino Malaspina (brother of Niccolo) was made bishop of Luni in 1312. Gherardino was succeeded in 1321 by another of Cardinal Fieschi's nephews, Bernabo Malaspina (brother of Niccolo and Gherardino), who had been in the cardinal's household for many years. Bernabo had in fact accompanied Cardinal Fieschi on his visit to England in 1317–18 and thus also had met Edward II.[107] On Bernabo's death in 1338 the title of bishop went to another of the cardinal's nephews, Antonio Fieschi – the cardinal's co-heir and co-executor. Nor were these men mere placements: they had close connections with the region. When this Antonio Fieschi came to England in 1337 he was accompanied by at least two other men from the Val di Magra. Giffredus di Groppo, who has already been mentioned, was from Groppo San Pietro in the Val di Magra. The other was Francesco Fosdinovo – Fosdinovo being another Malaspina lordship in the same region.[108] The strength of Cardinal Fieschi's association with the Val di Magra would have made it an obvious first choice for a place in which to hide a political refugee from England.[109]

This reckoning permits a fuller – albeit tentative – reconstruction of Edward II in Fieschi custody to the end of 1335. After arrival in Avignon, he passed into the guardianship of his kinsman, Cardinal Fieschi, who sent him by way of Paris and Brabant (home of his loyal cousin, the duke of Brabant) to Cologne (shrine of the Three Kings), and then to Milan (ruled by Azzo Visconti, nephew of Luca's niece, Isabella Fieschi). From there he was taken to a hermitage near *Milasci*, possibly Mulazzo, where he would have been under the political authority of one of Cardinal Fieschi's two nephews in the region, either Niccolo Malaspina at Filattiera or Manfredo Malaspina at Mulazzo itself; and the ecclesiastical authority of another nephew, Bernabo Malaspina, bishop of Luni. However, in 1334 troops began to gather for an attack on Pontremoli, which came under siege in 1335; hence the ex-king's removal to the hermitage of Sant'Alberto, between Cecima and Oramala, an area also under the political influence of Niccolo Malaspina. The bishop for the area – the bishop of Tortona – was Percevalle Fieschi, another member of Cardinal Fieschi's extensive family.[110] Through this network of politically and ecclesiastically powerful kin, Cardinal Fieschi kept control of the ex-king. Finally, although this is a hypothetical reconstruction, it is only hypothetical with respect to the ex-king's presence in the Val di Magra. The Fieschi Letter allows us to be confident that Cardinal Fieschi was monitoring Edward II in Italy; and Niccolo Malaspina's letter shows that in late 1335 he sent a trusted agent to Oramala, near Cecima, where the Fieschi Letter states Edward II was staying at the time.

EDWARD III AND EDWARD II'S KEEPERS 1336–8

The foregoing section provides an answer to the question of who was guarding Edward II in 1334–5: Niccolo Malaspina, on behalf of Cardinal Fieschi. But on whose behalf was Niccolo Malaspina guarding the ex-king after the cardinal's death on 31 January 1336?

The starting point for considering this is the presentation of Edward II as 'William le Galeys' to Edward III in 1338. Soon after Edward III met his father in this guise he issued a series of letters in favour of Niccolinus Fieschi. Most significantly, on 6 September 1338 at Koblenz – the same week as Francisco Forzetti led 'William le Galeys' from Cologne to meet Edward III, and perhaps on the same day – he praised one sea captain Niccolo Bianco di Fieschi ('*Blanco de Flisco*'), nephew of Niccolinus Fieschi, adding that he 'released him from the covenants which he made in the city of Marseilles with Niccolinus Fieschi, called "Cardinal" of Genoa.[111] We need to consider whether this could have been the means by which Edward II was taken to Cologne: a galley commanded by Niccolinus Fieschi's nephew.

The arrival of Niccolo Bianco di Fieschi's two galleys in early September 1338 was Edward III's second attempt to arrange for a galley to come to him from the Marseilles/Nice region under the auspices of the Fieschi. The first was in late 1336, when he had sent his clerk, an Italian named Paul Montefiore, on a mission to Avignon. Montefiore had been assigned 3,000 marks by Edward at the Tower on 15 April 1336 – the same day that Niccolinus Fieschi was made a king's councillor.[112] Montefiore then went to Avignon, where he paid £412 to the cardinals in part payment of the pensions promised by Richard Bury in 1333, which had not been paid in the interim.[113] He also had an audience with the pope. On 25 September 1336 papal envoys were given a letter saying that the pope had received Edward III's letters by Paul Montefiore and Laurence Fastolf, papal chaplain, and that 'the answer will be brought back by word of mouth'.[114] Before this, however, Montefiore had sent money to Nice in an attempt to contract with one Jacobo or Giacomo de Sarzana (James of Sarzana in *CPR*) to provide galleys for the king's service; but the money was sequestrated at Monaco by Gherardo Spinola, marshal of Robert, king of Naples, titular king of Jerusalem and Sicily. Edward's attempted contract with Jacobo de Sarzana is known from two later commissions to investigate the business, issued to none other than Niccolinus Fieschi. To be precise, on 30 November 1338, at Antwerp, Edward commissioned Niccolinus and John Petri

> as the king's proctors to require and examine accounts by James of Sarzana of money delivered to him by Paul Montefiore for fitting out galleys for the king's service; and money sent by the same Paul to Nice for fitting out such galleys, which was impounded by ministers of the king of Sicily in the counties of Provence and Forcalquier.[115]

The key point here is that Jacobo de Sarzana was another long-standing member of the *familia* of the late Cardinal Fieschi. He was a citizen of Genoa and an officer in the cardinal's household by 1317.[116] In October 1336 he received some of the late cardinal's books and pearls (along with John Nero, Manuele Fieschi and others of the late cardinal's household).[117] It is thus significant that Paul Montefiore was trying to arrange with him in the early autumn of 1336 what Niccolinus Fieschi later arranged with his nephew: to bring galleys from the Nice/Marseilles region to Northern Europe, in line with Edward III's instructions.

On the latter occasion the number of galleys was two, and 'William le Galeys' appeared. On the former, the number of galleys was probably the same: a larger number would have required Edward to have contracted with the government of Genoa, not an old servant of Cardinal Fieschi.

Paul Montefiore was back in England by 10 November 1336, when the king ordered that his payment of the cardinals be reimbursed. Eight days later he promised to repay him the sum of £9,590 lent to him 'for his war in Scotland'.[118] Edward soon took up the matter of the money lost at Monaco with his seneschal in Aquitaine. On 12 December he sent a messenger, William de Radnor, to Oliver Ingham, the seneschal. The reply came by Hugh Starky, whom Edward sent back to Ingham sometime before 1 May 1337.[119] On 12 July, Edward wrote directly to the marshal of King Robert of Naples, explaining that he had seen the marshal's letters to the constable of Bordeaux which had been sent in reply to Oliver Ingham's enquiries, and that he had received further information on the matter from Antonio Bacche (the lawyer representing Niccolinus and Manuele Fieschi). In his own letter Edward drew attention to the sequestration of money by the marshal and stated that

> with regard to the arrangement made by Master Paul Montefiore, his clerk, with certain adversaries and rebels of Gherardo, this was done without the king's knowledge and much to his annoyance, chiefly because Paul was not charged with that affair by him.[120]

This denial was obviously a lie – given Edward's continued trust of Montefiore, his subsequent delivery to him of more than £100,000, and his later commissions to find out what had happened to the money. But Edward's demonstrable untruth is not the only interesting thing about this letter. It was copied to a Genoese sea captain named Giovanni Doria ('John Aurie'). Edward's subsequent attempt to bring two galleys from the Mediterranean under the auspices of the Fieschi also involved this man.

After Paul Montefiore's failure to contract the galleys, Niccolinus Fieschi took up the task. Sometime in 1337, at Marseilles – exactly when is unknown – he 'covenanted' with his nephew Niccolo Bianco di Fieschi to provide the galleys. Niccolo Bianco and Giovanni Doria accordingly received safe conducts to take two galleys to Scottish waters on 3 January 1338.[121] The plan seems to have been for them to meet Edward III at Berwick. Edward certainly made a secret dash north to Berwick in late March and perhaps another in May–June 1337 but he failed to meet the ships conducted there by Bianco and Doria.[122] On 21 July

Niccolo Bianco di Fieschi, 'master of galleys', was paid £366 for his wages and those of his men by the English treasurer.[123] A receipt dated to this year confirms that Niccolo Bianco and Giovanni Doria came with just two galleys and received in return £1,000 from the merchants of Bardi on behalf of the king.[124] That there were just two ships is confirmed by the entry in the Bardi accounts.[125] If we are right in thinking that Niccolo Bianco di Fieschi brought with him Edward II then he delivered him by ship to Cologne in compliance with Niccolinus' contract, and the man was taken to Edward III at Koblenz by Forzetti on Edward III's orders. Edward III gave presents to Niccolo Bianco di Fieschi, letters of acquittance to present to his uncle, and sent messengers to Niccolinus Fieschi, whom he immediately started to employ on his most important diplomatic business at Avignon and in France.

Although the evidence for this maritime project is often assumed by historians to be Edward's attempt to employ the Fieschi to provide him with a fleet for his war, this explanation is simply wrong. Niccolo Bianco di Fieschi arrived in British waters with just two vessels and was hugely reimbursed nonetheless. No other ships arrived at the same time – no other Genoese sea captains were named in the same Bardi account. And Niccolo Bianco di Fieschi was not retained in royal service. If Edward went to such expense over every pair of galleys temporarily to enter his service he would have emptied the royal purse very rapidly, with nothing to show for it. This was a one-off arrival, and the high value placed on this arrival can only reasonably be associated with an important delivery. Edward's repeated attempts to arrange for the Fieschi to send a pair of galleys from the Mediterranean may well have been connected with his wanting to see his father in person. Much of the process by which this was brought about remains shadowy and doubtful; but there is no doubt that in the same week in 1338 that Edward III met 'William le Galeys' the Fieschi were richly rewarded and applauded for a service to the king which involved them bringing two galleys from the Mediterranean. Given that this was the second time Edward had tried to arrange this under the auspices of the Fieschi, and as *someone* had to have brought Edward II to Cologne from Italy (as 'William le Galeys'), then it seems highly likely that the relatives of Manuele Fieschi who were rewarded by Edward III at the time were the ones who did it. This means that either Edward II was taken to Nice or Marseilles in 1336, or ships from those places took him from Lombardy to the Low Countries. Thus it seems that the Fieschi remained in control of Edward II until at least September 1338, and very probably thereafter.

EDWARD III AND NICCOLINUS FIESCHI 1338–43

By September 1338, nearly five and a half years had passed since Niccolinus Fieschi had first met Edward III, and nearly two and a half since he had been made a royal councillor. His stature had constantly grown at court. However, his diplomatic position assumed a more important position after the delivery of 'William le Galeys' in September 1338. In November of that year Edward sent Niccolinus – now described as an 'intimate confidant' – with the lawyer John Petri to lay 'certain matters' before the pope.[126] At the same time he charged him to investigate the sequestration of the money intended for Jacobo de Sarzana (as mentioned above). On 6 January 1339 he confirmed Fieschi's yearly fee of £20 and granted him a further annuity of 20 marks at the exchequer.[127] In December 1339 Niccolinus was empowered to take verbal messages from Edward to King Robert of Naples and to petition him for the return of the money intended for de Sarzana.[128] On 30 January 1340 Niccolinus went abroad for 'certain negotiations' on the king's behalf, appearing at Avignon shortly afterwards.[129] He then was appointed one of Edward's delegates in April 1340 to negotiate peace with France.[130] Such was his importance that he, his son Gabriele, and a servant, Andrea of Genoa, were abducted from the papal city in Holy Week and taken into France for five days.[131] This abduction – stage-managed by the pope's own steward – was profoundly worrying to Pope Benedict XII, who responded by placing the whole of France under an interdict, even though he himself was French. King Philip responded on 21 May that this was too harsh, and by the 30th had restored Niccolinus to freedom.[132] Philip was quite right: this was an extraordinary act by the pope, indicating Niccolinus' involvement in matters far more serious than merely hiring galleys.

Niccolinus' unusual set of responsibilities did not change with his kidnapping. When Pope Benedict XII secured his release, he automatically added him to the list of Edward III's representatives at Avignon, without consulting Edward.[133] Although this seems high-handed, Edward thanked Benedict for doing so. Thereafter Niccolinus appears in the records closely associated with the embassies discussing peace with France. His importance to the negotiations at the outset of Edward III's war with France may be judged from the pope's letter written in December 1340, in which he specifically stated that 'neither what the envoys, nor what Niccolinus [Fieschi], knight of Genoa, offered in explanation, seem to make for peace, but rather to light up the fires of dissension'.[134] From Edward's point of view, whatever Niccolinus brought to the debate was clearly an asset, for in 1341 he was again representing Edward's interests at the papal curia. He was also commissioned to treat with the French king, and was summoned to Edward III in Flanders 'for the making of a treaty at Antoing'.[135] The following year he was again commissioned to treat with Philip de Valois on Edward III's behalf – an extraordinary position for a Genoese lawyer.[136] In 1343 Edward wrote to the pope about Niccolinus' abduction, and the punishment of the wrongdoers, and again related this to the discussion of peace with France. In 1344 Niccolinus took part in the second embassy to inform the pope of the merits of Edward's claim on the French throne. In September that year he received his last safe-conduct for a journey to Avignon 'as an envoy from the king to treat of peace with France'.[137] Edward equipped him with £200 towards the arrears of his wages and a pension, and a bundle of letters to foreign rulers, namely Luchinus Visconti, duke of Milan; Giovanni Visconti, archbishop of Milan; Andrew, king of Naples; Simon Boccanegra, doge of Genoa; his brother Giles Boccanegra, admiral of the king of Castile; and Pope Benedict XII.[138] Soon after 7 September 1344 Niccolinus left England.[139] After the inevitable failure of the peace mission to the papal curia in December 1344, he returned to Italy.[140] Thereafter his business in England was dealt with by his attorneys, Master Adam of Lichfield and his son, Giovanni Fieschi. His other son Guglielmo departed for the papal curia earlier in 1344 on royal business.[141] However, Niccolinus and his sons continued to do business overseas occasionally for Edward after 1345; his son Antonio was acting as an agent for Edward III in Italy as late as 1352.[142]

With the exception of Phillips, no historian has given this extraordinary diplomatic career more than passing notice. Sumption mentions Fieschi a few times in his first *Hundred Years War* volume, appropriately refers to him as 'conspiratorial' and states that from 1340 he was in semi-permanent residence at the papal court and was largely concerned with hiring warships in Southern France.[143] This does not adequately explain Fieschi's role in Edward III's 'secret business' – and certainly not his role in discussing peace with France. Phillips writes that

It is hard to resist the conclusion that [Niccolinus'] services to the English crown did not consist only of the hiring of Genoese galleys, however important these were to the English war effort, and that he was centrally involved in the events which led both to the writing and delivery of the Fieschi letter and to the custody and delivery of William le Galeys.[144]

Quite. That a Genoese ambassador could represent Edward III in his secret business with the papacy, and in his negotiations over the throne of France, and that he could negotiate peace on behalf of the English when his countrymen – some of them at least – were fighting as mercenaries on the French side, are challenging anomalies in the pattern of international relations. That Niccolinus could do this without losing the credibility of his own people, the Genoese, is remarkable. That the pope could add him to Edward's delegation knowing that he would be acceptable to Edward, and that he himself and his son were so important that their kidnapping warranted an interdict on the whole of France, goes far beyond all the usual analysis of diplomatic relations. It is hardly surprising that his presence in the English missions to Avignon in the period 1340–44 has been downplayed by historians: his role was just too secretive and complicated. But historians should not ignore his role, which appears to have been due to some authority which he was able to wield on Edward's behalf at Avignon, and which the pope understood, and yet which did not threaten his Genoese compatriots. That he was also a kinsman and associate of the author of the Fieschi Letter, and was very much in Edward III's favour when Edward II was presented to him as 'William le Galeys' in December 1338, suggests that his authority was connected with the continued custody of Edward II. It is perhaps in this context that we should understand the wording of Edward III's reappointment of Niccolinus as a member of his council on 6 January 1339, in which he drew attention to 'the purity of his [Niccolinus'] affection for Edward III and his royal house and the circumspection with which he had carried out royal business'.[145]

EDWARD III'S RELATIONS WITH THE PAPACY

The career of Niccolinus Fieschi, and his role at Avignon in particular, shows that he was more than just 'conspiratorial'. He was clearly an important ambassador. But was he really the agency in control of Edward II from 1336? Did the ultimate authority over the ex-king change with the death of Cardinal Fieschi in 1336? Or were Cardinal Fieschi, Niccolinus, Antonio and Manuele Fieschi, and their Malaspina cousins, all acting on behalf of the pope?

As soon as we start to reflect on this question, many other aspects of the later life of Edward II point to papal influence. It was to Avignon that the earl of Kent went in 1329 to seek help, and where he was promised unlimited aid by Pope John XXII. On the embassy to Avignon following this visit, Mortimer and Isabella offered to renew payment of 1,000 marks per year – for no apparent gain (unless it was 'hush money', to suppress news of Edward II's survival). It was to Avignon that Edward II himself made his way in 1331, and where he made his 'confession' to Manuele Fieschi. According to Manuele, John XXII received Edward II in person at Avignon in 1331, when he had 'held him secretly and honourably'. The Fieschi Letter then states that *permission* was obtained for Edward II's journey to Paris, Brabant, Cologne and Italy; in other words, Edward's journey had papal blessing. It was to Avignon that Edward III addressed his enquiry about whether he should go to Ireland or not in 1331, and it was to Avignon that Antonio Pessagno, Richard Bury and John de Shordich were sent on the king's 'secret business' in 1331–3. After John XXII's death, it was from Avignon that Manuele Fieschi wrote to Edward III giving details about Edward II since 1326. It was to Avignon that Edward III sent Paul Montefiore in 1336 to pay money to a member of the late Cardinal Fieschi's household to hire galleys. Several exchanges of diplomatic messages took place after this between Edward and the pope, none of which was to be written down.[146] It was from Avignon that Antonio Fieschi came to Edward III in the summer of 1337 – it is perhaps significant that he was not just an executor of Cardinal Fieschi's will but also a papal chaplain. It was to Avignon in 1338 that Edward III sent back Niccolinus Fieschi to meet with Pope Benedict XII, and where he asked him to remain throughout 1339. It was from Avignon that Niccolinus Fieschi and his son were kidnapped by the French in 1340. It was by papal intervention that Niccolinus was released and joined the English embassy, regularly staying there until 1344. In most of the official dealings touching on Edward II-related issues, Avignon was the principal place of negotiation and the main channel of information and decision-making. As a result, it looks highly likely that John XXII and, after John's death, Benedict XII, exercised the greatest level of control of Edward II, and were the focus of the major part of Edward III's 'secret business'. The Fieschi – first Cardinal Fieschi and then other members of the Fieschi family at Avignon – were simply entrusted with the actual custodial and carriage services, at least until 1338.

Papal influence over Edward II's concealed location in the development of relations between England and Avignon on the eve of the outbreak of war between England and France is obviously an important issue. The Fieschi Letter marks a crucial turning point in that it revealed to Edward III new information about his father. No doubt Benedict XII hoped that sending it would dissuade Edward from continuing on his path to war; and for a while the ploy was successful. If it was delivered in April 1336, as seems likely, it would explain why Edward did not go to war that summer. Although there were many occasions when it looked as though fighting might break out – beyond the usual acts of piracy committed on both sides – Edward prevaricated. Clifford Rogers has pointed out that Edward tried to stave off the outbreak of direct war with France in the spring and summer of 1336, even though he knew the French were planning to send troops to assist the Scots.[147] Edward did not rise to the bait, even though he probably wanted to.

Despite Benedict XII's intentions, the delivery of the letter was never going to stop a man as determined as the young Edward III. It simply slowed his march to war. In fact, it may even have helped him make more careful plans. In 1336 and 1337 Edward would still have been diplomatically vulnerable but he would have been better equipped to control the situation, having good information as to where his father was and with whom he had to negotiate for ensuring the man was kept securely and secretly. This explains the gradual shift of his military and diplomatic endeavours from Scotland to the continent. In the autumn of 1336 he made preliminary enquiries about the readiness of the German states, including the Low Countries, to form a confederacy against Philip. The following January, he openly proposed such a course of action.[148] Edward's treaties with the German states were ratified on 26 August 1337. Two days later he granted a safe conduct for the papal chaplain Antonio Fieschi and the lawyer representing Bernabo Malaspina. A few days after that, he set out for his father's supposed burial place at Gloucester, despite the urgency of the impending war, making his first visit there since the fall of Mortimer and Isabella. Immediately on his return to London, on

6 October 1337, he pressed his claim to be king of France, styling himself 'king of France and England' and 'king of England and France' in official letters (a claim he had not otherwise pressed since the fall of Mortimer and Isabella).[149] That same day he ordered £500 to be delivered by the bishop of Exeter to Antonio Bacche – the legal representative in England of Manuele and Niccolinus Fieschi – 'for the furtherance of some secret business beyond the seas'.[150] The claim to France was soon dropped, probably on account of some persuasion brought to bear on Edward III by the pope and two cardinals hurriedly sent to England at this time.[151] It is possible that Antonio Fieschi and the cardinals between them managed to convince Edward to suspend his claim on the throne of France by assuring him of his father's planned delivery the following year.

Following this, there was a period of delay as Edward III waited for his father to be brought to him and while he made arrangements for his expedition to the Low Countries in 1338. But after the presentation of the ex-king to Edward III at Koblenz in October of that year, the diplomatic negotiations with Avignon heated up, as Benedict XII was not only displeased at the continued moves to war but also at Edward's acceptance of a vicarial crown from the Holy Roman Emperor, Ludwig of Bavaria, who had been excommunicated by John XXII. Thus Niccolinus Fieschi's role became more important, as the principal intermediary between Benedict XII and Edward III. It is possible that Niccolinus helped neutralize the effect of Edward III's eventual claim to the throne of France, made on 26 January 1340. Philip of France received a copy of Edward's new seal as king of both kingdoms on 8 February; the French kidnapping of Niccolinus Fieschi from Avignon took place in Holy Week (Easter Day falling on 16 April 1340). We have no direct evidence that Niccolnius' kidnapping and his possible knowledge of Edward II's whereabouts were connected, but the timing of the action, orchestrated by the pope's steward, is highly suspicious. Benedict XII seems to have wanted Edward II to remain *secretly* in the custody of the Fieschi. No doubt it gave him a hold over Edward III which he wanted to keep to himself. Perhaps he reasoned that, if the French king had access to the same information, it would soon be wrongly used. Benedict XII seems to have considered Philip of France unwise, to say the least.

If the pope was the ultimate authority controlling the ex-king, how long did this situation continue? It may have started to come to an end with the visit of Edward as 'William le Galeys' to the king in 1338. However, presuming that even after this he remained under the aegis of the Fieschi and, by implication, the pope, the situation did not change until Edward II actually died. As shown at the outset of this chapter, this was probably not before the Crisis parliament of 1341. Elsewhere I have suggested that the Dunstable tournament of February 1342, at which Edward III paraded twelve large banners bearing the motto 'It is as it is', was a confirmation of his father's death to those in the know.[152] This suggests that news of his death probably reached Edward III between May 1341 and February 1342. The Fieschi evidence supports this. Edward III ratified Manuele Fieschi's estate in 1342.[153] Manuele became bishop of Vercelli in 1343 and retired from the papal curia. As for Niccolinus Fieschi, he came back to London at the end of 1341 and stayed there until the time of Dunstable tournament.[154]

Things were not entirely at an end with the death of Edward II, however. It seems likely that his body was still overseas. The reason for suggesting this lies in Edward III's secret journey to Gloucester in August 1342. He made a dash there via Portsmouth on 10 August 1342, dating letters in both places on the same day.[155] While at Gloucester he ordered the sheriff of Hampshire to pay the arrears of the wages of Henry Whissh, as noted above. The recipient is significant, for Henry Whissh was a trusted 'king's yeoman' who had been the recipient of a grant made at the Tower on 16 April 1336, the day after Edward made Niccolinus Fieschi a king's councillor there.[156] Throughout the intervening period he had been in Edward's service, travelling back to see the king at various times. He was with Edward in the Low Countries in December 1338 (at the same time as Edward II qua 'William le Galeys') and again in November 1339, when he was rewarded 'for his faithful service and for welcome solace many times afforded by him'.[157] Therefore Edward's sole grant in the few hours he can have spent at Gloucester on 10 August 1342 was to a man whose service correlated at certain key points with that of Niccolinus Fieschi. Moreover, immediately on returning to London two days later, Edward ordered the abbot of Eynsham to acquit Manuele Fieschi of a debt on account of it already having been paid, 'whereupon Manuele has asked the king to provide a remedy'.[158] Edward III's sudden, private journey to the church containing his father's intended tomb when he had just been in direct communication with Manuele Fieschi, at a time which corresponds with his already having received news of the ex-king's death, suggests that he was making arrangements for his father's interment. A death in the second half of 1341 or early 1342 would indicate that Edward II died at the age of fifty-seven.

CONCLUSION

This study has revealed several crucial points about Edward II and Edward III after 1330 and raised some important questions. It is clear that the appearance of 'William le Galeys' falls wholly outside the pattern of the pretender, and therefore it is not reasonable to dismiss the man's assertion that he was Edward II. Likewise the one serious attempt to explain the Fieschi Letter (by Phillips) has been shown to be wrong, due to the respectful way Fieschi refers to the claimant as Edward III's father. The letter itself shows that it was based on information gathered by Manuele Fieschi in 1331 at Avignon under the auspices of Cardinal Fieschi, who knew Edward II. The very detailed information in the letter allows us to say with some confidence that there are two independent information streams underpinning it. This fact, combined with the Malaspina letter (which shows direct links between the cardinal and the area in which Manuele Fieschi stated that Edward II was being held), allows us to place a great deal of confidence in the narrative of the Fieschi Letter. If we then consider the abundant evidence for the high favour shown to several members of the Fieschi by Edward III, we can see we have a narrative that is potentially very important. There is no evidence that Edward II was anywhere else but in the keeping of the Fieschi after 1331 and a high likelihood that members of the Fieschi family arranged the delivery of Edward II to Edward III in 1338. Finally, it seems certain that crucial decisions about Edward II were made by the popes at Avignon and it is reasonable to suppose that the ex-king was used as a diplomatic bargaining chip – a situation that persisted at least until 1338 and perhaps did not end until his death.

This last point is undoubtedly the most important aspect of Edward II's survival. His continued existence was not a quiet problem simmering away on the far side of Europe, out of sight and out of mind. Throughout the 1330s Edward III worked hard to rebuild the royal dignity which had been brought low by the deposition of Edward II and the execution of the earl of Kent. He did all he could to maintain the fiction that his father was dead – publicly celebrating the anniversary of the man's 'death' on 21 or 22 September each year and never mentioning his survival once, and destroying any documents in which the man might have been mentioned. Edward II's continued existence in a foreign land was a deeply troublesome factor for it threatened Edward III's regnal legitimacy. If the ex-king had been produced at Avignon and had publicly acknowledged that he had been forced to abdicate against his will, the effect on Edward III and the English political classes would have been dramatic. Some magnates and prelates (like Archbishop Melton) would probably have felt ties of loyalty to Edward II even after 1330. Although Edward III was no doubt strong enough to withstand such a challenge, it would have hugely damaged his reputation at home and abroad, for he had not only acquiesced in the deception for some years, he had permitted the execution of his own uncle rather than see his father reclaim the throne. In addition, he had ordered the execution of Roger Mortimer for murdering Edward II (among other things). The implications of taking the throne of a man who reigned by God's will, and who many believed could not have been legally dethroned, and killing a man whom he knew to be innocent of murder, and allowing his own uncle's execution, would all have appeared ungodly acts in themselves.

The answer to the question of what happened to Edward II beyond 1330 is therefore not simply a matter of whether the Fieschi Letter narrative is true. It is rather a matter of what political and geographical factors allowed him to survive. This requires us to pay attention to a wealth of other evidence, not just the Fieschi Letter. The powers that controlled the ex-king and monitored him were not static forces but politically powerful players whose interests changed and periodically came under threat. Understanding Edward II's situation, therefore, is very much a case of understanding theirs. Whatever the full extent of the survival narrative (and the next chapter will suggest that it might have been far more damaging to Edward III than outlined here), the most significant outcome was that Edward III was able to overcome it. It is fair to say that his achievement in this regard has not been fully appreciated.

APPENDIX 6.1

THE FIESCHI FAMILY

The simplified genealogy here is taken from *DBI*, Battilana and Sisto. The three lines of the Fieschi who were given the right to call themselves counts of Lavagna in 1249 by William II of Holland were (1) Tedisio Fieschi, (2) Niccolo Fieschi (d. c.1304), who was the son of another Tedisio (d. 1248), and (3) Opizzo Fieschi (d. 1268).[159] Their names are capitalized below. Individuals important to the narrative of this chapter are in bold.

Ugo Fieschi (d. pre-1211), the first to use the name Fieschi[160]

A. Alberto Fieschi (d. pre-1226)

    1. Macia or Mazia (fl. 1251)[161]

    2. Simona, m. Taddeo Grimaldi

    3. Ugone (d. pre-1282), m. Caracosa

?uncertain

    4. TEDISIO FIESCHI, COUNT OF LAVAGNA (d. pre-1288)[162]

        m. Simona della Volta

        a. Clarisia m. Manuele Zacaria in 1268

        b. Vittoria m. Ottobono del Caretto

        c. [*daughter, name unknown*] m. Simone del Carmadino

B. Tedisio Fieschi (fl. 1209, d. pre-Feb. 1248)[163] m. Simona Camilla

    1. Alberto (fl. 1232, d. 1278) m. Argentina

        a. Manuele

        b. Egidio, canon of Paris

        c. Leonardo, archdeacon of Genoa 1270–88, bishop of Catania

        d. Andriolo (fl. 1288)

            i. Leonardo

            ii. Edoardo (had daughter Isabella).

        e.–i. [three other sons, two daughters]

    2. Ugo (d.c.1274)[164] m. Brumisan, dau. of Giacomo del Caretto,

        marquis of Noli, second cousin of Eleanor of Provence

        a.–h. [*eight sons*]

    3. NICCOLO FIESCHI, COUNT OF LAVAGNA (d. 1304x10)[165]

        m. Leonora or Lionetta [of Savoy?]. She was a kinswoman of

        Edward I, probably a second cousin.

        a. Federico, count of Lavagna (d. pre-1334)[166]

            i. Adriano, archdeacon of Cleveland to 1334

            ii. Innocento, archdeacon of Cleveland 1334[167]

        b. Carlo, count of Lavagna, count of Savignone, lord of Torriglia

            (fl. 1324)[168] m. Teodora (d. c.1325).

            i. Luchino (d. pre-1336), prebendary of Lafford 1322;

                m. Constanza Orsini[169]

                α. Niccolo (d. pre-1386), lord of Torriglia[170]

                    • Ludovico (d. 1423), bishop-elect of

                      Vercelli prior to becoming a cardinal in

                      1384 (see Chapter 7).

                β. Giovanni (d. 1381), bishop of Vercelli (1349)[171]

            ii. Giovanni (d. 1339), lord of Torriglia, m. Donatella da

                Corregio in 1319

> > > *iii.* **Antonio Fieschi (d. 1343)**, papal chaplain 1337,
> > > canon of Paris, bishop of Luni 1338 and co-heir of
> > > Cardinal Luca Fieschi 1336[172]
> > > *iv.* Gabriele
> > > *v.* Ginetta m. **Pietro Rossi** (1301–37) lord of Pontremoli
> > > from October 1328[173]
> > > *vi.* Eliana
> > > *vii.* Isabella (d. 1331x39) m. **Luchino Visconti** (d. 1349),
> > > lord of Milan
> > > *viii.* Soborgia, m. Geoffroy de Challant
> > > *ix.* Luciana m. Daniele Usodimare
> > c. Ottobono[174]
> > d. Brancaleone (d. 1297), rector of Tirrington[175]
> > e. **Luca Fieschi** (c.1272–1336), cardinal of St Maria in Via Lata
> > 1300, lord of Pontremoli 1313–21[176]
> > f. Alberto, archdeacon of Rome[177]
> > g. Alagia (d. post-1344), m. Moroello Malaspina (1269–1315),
> > marquis of Giovagallo and Lusuolo[178]
> > > *i.* **Manfredo Malaspina of the Spino Secco**
> > > (d. after 1344), marquis of Giovagallo
> > > *ii.* Luchino Malaspina (d. 1340)
> > > *iii.* Beatrice Malaspina m. Alberto Torelli di Ferrara in 1308
> > > *iv.* Giovanni Malaspina
> > > *v.* Fiesca Malaspina (d. 1338)
> > h. Fiesca, m. Alberto Malaspina (d. after 1320), marquis of Oramala[179]
> > > *i.* **Niccolo Malaspina of the Spino Fiorito, 'Il
> > > Marchesotto'** (d. 1339), marquis of Oramala and
> > > Fillatiera[180]
> > > *ii.* Gherardino Malaspina (d. 1318), bishop of Luni 1312
> > > *iii.* **Bernabo Malaspina** (d. 1338), bishop of Luni 1321[181]
> > i. Ginetta m. Obizzo d'Este (1247–93)
> 4. Ottobono Fieschi (d. 1276), Pope Adrian V[182]
> 5. Rolando, proctor from Henry III to the pope 1267[183]
> 6. Percevalle (d. c.1290), canon of Parma, archdeacon of Buckingham
> 1270[184]
> 7. Federico (d. 1303)[185] m. (1) Teodora Spinola; (2) Clara
> > a. Eleonora m. Bernabo Doria
> > b. Andriola m. Antonio del Caretto
> 8. Beatrice (d. 1283), m. Thomas II of Savoy
> 9. Agnese m. Ottone III del Caretto
> 10. Caracosa, m. (1) Bonifacio Grimaldi; m. (2) Bonifacio del Caretto

C. **Sinibaldo Fieschi (d. 1254), Pope Innocent IV**

D. OPIZZO FIESCHI, COUNT OF LAVAGNA (d. c.1268) m. Simona

   1. Gugliemo (d. 1256), cardinal of St Eustace 1244

   2. Andrea, archdeacon of St Lorenzo, Genoa 1259–69[186]

   3. Enrico called 'Cardinal' (fl. 1282)

       a. Petrino, cousin (*consobrinus*) of Niccolinus Fieschi, called 'Cardinal' 1319 (see below)[187]

   4. Tedisio, parson of Sibet', canon of Exeter (fl. 1251–81)[188]

   5. Ugolino, count of Lavagna (d. pre-1281)[189] m. Alasia

       a. Percevalle, m. Orietta Doria

       b. Simona, m. Salado Doria

       c. Bonifacio, archdeacon of Ravenna

       d. Giacomo, *dicti Re di Sicilia*

       e. Sorleone, canon of Brugnato

       f. Pietro m. Cattarina Grimaldi

   6. Argentina m. Corrado Spinola

   7. Giacomo, count of Lavagna (d. pre-1288) m. (1) Bertolina (d. pre-1258); m. (2) Bellavia (fl. 1292)

       a. Opizzo

       b. Guglielmo (d. pre-1312) m. Floria del Mare

           i. **Percevalle Fieschi**, bishop of Tortona[190]

       c. Andrea (fl. 1288)[191] m. ? Zaccaria

           i. **Manuele Fieschi** (d. 1349), papal notary, bishop of Vercelli 1343[192]

           ii. Opicino m. Aiguina Falcone

           iii. Gabriele m. Mencia Usodimare

               α. Lazarinus, canon of Lincoln 1330[193]

               β. Papiannus, prebendary of Lincoln 1332[194]

               γ. Lorenzo m. Cattarina

               δ. Selvaggia m. Simone Bestango

               ε. Isabella

       d. Manfredo (fl. 1288) m. Cicalina Cicala

       e. Francesco (fl. 1288)[195] m. Giacoma

           i. Paride

           ii. Ettore m. Tobietta Lionelli

           iii. Luca

       f. Luchino (fl. 1288)

       g. Claretta m. Guido Pallavincini

       h. Fiesca m. Andreolo del Mare, admiral

           i. Albertino, chaplain of Cardinal Luca Fieschi 1316, prebendary of Tournai[196]

?uncertain

i. **Niccolinus Fieschi, called 'Cardinal'** [see note* below]
   i.   Antonio, called 'Cardinal'[197] fl. 1352
   ii. Gabriele[198] fl. 1343
   iii. Giovanni, called 'Cardinal', prebendary of
          Fridaythorpe 1327, prebendary of Kingsteignton and
          Yealmpton 1334, fl. 1356[199]
   iv. Guglielmo (d. c.1357)[200]
   v.   ? Niccolo, fl. 1346[201]

* Exactly how Niccolinus Fieschi was related to Luca and Manuele Fieschi is not clear. Niccolinus Fieschi was a descendant of the first Fieschi, Ugo (d. pre-1211), and so at least a second cousin of Luca Fieschi. This is supported by the family title of 'count of Lavagna'. As indicated above, three lines of the family were entitled to call themselves counts by an Imperial decree of 1249, and Niccolinus appears so described in a letter of Pope John XXII in 1316.[202] The three lines were those descending from Ugo's son, Opizzo Fieschi (d. 1268); Opizzo's nephew, Niccolo (d. 1304x10, son of Tedisio); and Tedisio, also described as Opizzo's nephew. The identity of this last man has proved a problem to Italian historians; he appears in no Italian genealogies except where he is confused with Tedisio Fieschi, father of Niccolo: in the above genealogy he has been tentatively identified as a son of Alberto. The *DBI* associates three daughters with him (one whose name is not known) and possibly one son, Rolando.[203] In considering these possible lines of descent, it is clear that Niccolinus was not a son of the wife of Niccolo (d. 1304x10) as he was never described as a king's kinsman in England. It is also noticeable that his sons were not advanced significantly by Cardinal Luca, and nor did Niccolinus receive any of the goods from Luca's estate at his death, both of which one might expect if Niccolinus and Luca were brothers.[204] So he was almost certainly not 'of the counts of Lavagna' by virtue of being a son of Niccolo. As for Rolando, the *DBI* seems to have misplaced Rolando, who was described as a brother of Cardinal Ottobono in the English records (and thus was not descended from a line designated 'count of Lavagana' in 1249). Thus Niccolinus was unlikely to have been a son of Tedisio, who seems to have had no male offspring. It follows that he was most probably descended from Opizzo. In support of this we should note that Niccolinus' son Giovanni acquired the prebend of Yealmpton (Devon) which had previously been held by Andrea [Fieschi] de Lavagna (d. 1270), son of Opizzo.[205] Even more significantly, another of Opizzo's sons, Enrico Fieschi, '*dicti Cardinal*', had a son Petrino, who was described as the cousin (*consobrinus*) of Niccolinus Fieschi, '*dicti Cardinal*' in 1319.[206] If 'consobrinus' here means cousin on father's side (it normally means cousin on the mother's side but can be non-specific regarding gender), then Niccolinus was a grandson of Opizzo Fieschi (d. 1268)

and thus a son of either Ugolino (who died before 1281), or Manuele's grandfather, Giacomo (who died before 1288), or some other son of Opizzo's.[207] Thus Niccolinus was either a first cousin once-removed or an uncle of Manuele Fieschi, and a second cousin of Cardinal Luca Fieschi.[208]

APPENDIX 6.2

JOHN DE GALES, ROYAL BASTARD

Why was Edward II presented to Edward III as 'William le Galeys'? The explanation suggested above is that he was assigned this identity by Edward III in order to conceal his identity under that of a real member of the English court – perhaps a man who looked like the ex-king. However, there are alternatives. One is that the soubriquet was chosen to reflect the fact that he had been born in Wales. This tallies nicely with his un-resigned title 'prince of Wales'. Alternatively it might have been a code used in conjunction with the Fieschi, alluding to the man as a thorn in the king's side – 'William le Galeys' being the contemporary way in which the English referred to William Wallace of Scotland. Alternatively we might observe that it was simply a common name in use at the time. The name was proportionately as common and had much the same meaning as 'Welsh' and 'Walsh' do today.

One possible reason to think that Edward II may have adopted the name himself, perhaps as a result of the 1338 meeting, is to be found in the Navarrese royal accounts for 1392. In that year, a gentleman called John de Gales or de Galas was knighted by the king of Navarre, he having with him a company of men at the time. He was described as 'the bastard brother of the king of England', 'the bastard of Wales [Gales]' and 'the bastard of England'. Logically this suggests an illegitimate brother of Richard II, a son of Edward the Black Prince, prince of Wales. But Prince Edward never acknowledged an illegitimate son of this name. The prince named his only known surviving illegitimate son (Roger of Clarendon, not 'Wales') in his will and he acknowledged his other known illegitimate son Edward in his register – but he never acknowledged John de Gales. It is difficult to see why the king of Navarre would have acknowledged an illegitimate son of the Black Prince if the prince himself had never done so. It is of course possible that John de Gales was a bastard son of the Black Prince who has escaped the historical record; but equally it is possible that he was a son of Edward II as 'William le Galeys', and thus a half-brother of Edward III by some unknown woman.[209] It is to be hoped that, having been identified as a royal English bastard, further information about this shadowy character will emerge allowing us to identify his father.

Notes

1 Tout, *Chapters*, iv, 287–8, discussing *CPR 1343–5*, 371. In the latter it states that 'the king accepting his [Thomas Hatfield's] account has received from him the rolls and memoranda relating to such account and has caused them to be burned that they may not again come in demand.'
2 See 'Documents', 226; *Greatest Traitor*, 293.
3 *PROME*. The Parliament Rolls are extant from Mortimer's fall until 1334, when there is a second period of lacunae, covering September 1334–February 1339. Thereafter the rolls are complete until April 1357.
4 Hunter, 'Measures taken', 274–97; Galbraith, 'Extracts from the Historia Aurea', 207, 217.
5 BCM Select Roll 39.
6 Harding, 'Regime', 332.
7 *CPR 1334–7*, 88, 89, 111, 112.
8 As regards Bogo de Bayonne or de Bayouse – the man who had received the first of the earl of Kent's letters at Corfe Castle – he fled to Italy with his wife Alice and died there on 26 July 1334. His death there was not a secret in England, however, as this information was gleaned from a Yorkshire inquest held at Helperby in the year after his death, and it notes that both the king and council were informed (who had previously understood that Bogo de Bayonne had died at Vienne in the Rhône valley). See Phillips, 'Edward II in Italy', 210.
9 Edward II had resigned the earldom of Chester to Edward III soon after the boy's birth in 1312. He had given him all his French titles in 1325, on sending him to France. But when he had acceded to his own deposition – thereby abdicating – in 1327 he had not resigned the title of prince. As the Melton Letter suggests, 'Edward of Carnarvon' was how he remained in his supporters' minds.
10 Knowles and Hadcock, *Medieval Religious Houses*, 328. The endowment of 1344 makes the purposes clearer. See TNA C143/274/14; *CPR 1343–5*, 40, 479.
11 Hamilton Thompson, *English Clergy*, 258.
12 For similar royal age-related payments, including those made by Edward I in respect of his son, see Mortimer, 'Henry IV's date of birth', 567–76.
13 TNA E101/388/5 m. 4, m. 14.
14 *CCR 1341–3*, 378.
15 Ormrod, 'Personal religion', 860, 871.
16 *Norwell*, 212

17 *Norwell*, 214.
18 'Where is Edward II?', 530.
19 'Afterlife', 74.
20 Haines, *King Edward II*, 43–4.
21 Phillips, 'Edward II in Italy', 223, n. 74.
22 Phillips, 'Edward II in Italy', 220.
23 *CMR*, 375.
24 *CPR 1345–48*, 428.
25 C. L. Kingsford, *The Greyfriars of London* (1915). The relevent entry reads: '*Et ad sinistram eius sub lapide jacet Willelmus Galeys, valens armiger Regine Isabelle, et Robertus filius eiusdem Willelmi*'.
26 TNA E101/388/8 m. 1. 'A special robe made of eight ells of mulberry cloth in grain and an ell of scarlet and trimmed with two miniver furs . . . at this time for his journey from Antwerp to Cologne . . .' Another entry on this membrane records the manufacture of fifteen tunics and fifteen mantles for the persons of the king of England, the Emperor, the duke of Brabant and twelve other magnates of England and Germany.
27 *Perfect King*, 150–2.
28 He was certainly not sent from England to Edward, otherwise the royal accounts would note the transportation costs and the English chronicles would have recorded his claim.
29 Norwell had served Edward II since 1313. See Tout, *Chapters*, iv, 80.
30 The text of the letter is on fo. 86r of register G 1123 in the Archives départementales d'Hérault. See 'Afterlife', 80, n. 6, and Phillips, 'Edward II in Italy', 214–15, for its early historiography.
31 In its English translation, it appears in 'Where is Edward II?', 526–7; *Greatest Traitor*, 251–2; and Paul Doherty, *Isabella and the Strange Death*, 186–8. A readable black-and-white photograph of the original registered text appears in *Greatest Traitor*, facing p. 189; another (in colour) appears in Alison Weir, *Isabella: She-wolf of France* (2005), facing p. 335. A wider black and white photograph appears in Phillips, *Edward II*, plate 23. A Latin version appears in *Chronicles*, vol. 2, ciii–cviii, and a 'fresh transcription' appears in 'Where is Edward II?', 537–8.
32 'Captivity', 103.
33 'Afterlife', 67, 72. Haines did not substantially revise this view in writing his *Edward II* (2003).
34 'Afterlife', 66–7 (for the Italianate style), 79 (information from England), 80 ('borrowing' Fieschi's name).
35 Phillips, 'Edward II in Italy', 211.
36 For Phillips's theory that Fieschi was reporting an impostor, see Phillips, 'Edward II in Italy', 220.
37 Phillips, 'Edward II in Italy', 225.

38 Phillips, in *Edward* II, 516, argues that this is not accurate, stating that the earl of Arundel had previously departed and was captured in Shropshire. However, Edward II was at Chepstow on 19 October 1326 and was at sea for six days while he tried to escape (Haines, *Edward II*, 181); there is no indication that Arundel had been captured before that date. Phillips cites three sources. Two (*Anonimalle* and the *Annales Paulini*) note that Arundel was beheaded on 17 November at Hereford. The third (*Knighton*), states that he was arrested that day. Neither version of events is inconsistent with his attempted departure by boat with Edward from Chester, his landing in Glamorgan, his departure from the king on 26 October and his arrest in Shropshire between one and three weeks later. Besides, the Fieschi letter is explicit in stating that Arundel was not caputured with the king, Despenser and Baldock in South Wales. So the Fieschi Letter and Phillips's sources are in agreement.

39 Letters were sent to Maltravers at Corfe from Berkeley. See BCM Select Roll 39. Maltravers was not made constable of Corfe until September 1329; hence the reference to his being there in an 'unofficial capacity'.

40 This was where the Prophecy of the Six Kings had foretold Edward III would be buried. See *Perfect King*, 21.

41 The slip is in line 22. However, lines 13–19 indicate that the 'escape' in the custody of his keeper took place before the official burial at Gloucester in December 1327; and in line 22 it is clearly stated that it was after the beheading of the earl of Kent that he was taken to Ireland (March 1330). The slip is thus an error of calculation, not of information.

42 Manuele was regularly described as Luca's kinsman (*nepos*), and had become Luca Fieschi's own notary at Avignon by 1329. All of Luca's Fieschi kin were described as his *nepoti*, regardless of their actual relationship with him; this is presumably what confused Phillips into thinking Manuele was his actual nephew. See Phillips, 'Edward II in Italy', 219, and ns 49 and 55. For Manuele being Luca's *nepos* see Mollat (ed.), *Lettres Communes*, i, no. 2140. For Manuele as Luca's notary see Timmins (ed.), *Register of William Melton*, vol. 5, 107 (no. 311).

43 For the possibility that he was recognized on this journey, see *Perfect King*, 90–2.

44 Sayer, *Original Papal Documents*, 244; *CPR 1258–66*, 624, 635, 676.

45 *CEPR*, i, 512.

46 'Where is Edward II?', 544.

47 At least three of Beatrice's brothers appear in the English records: Cardinal Ottobono Fieschi (d. 1276), later Pope Adrian V, from whom Edward I took the cross in 1268; Rolando Fieschi, proctor from Henry III to pope, 1267 (*CPR 1247–58*, 616; *CPR 1258–66*, 28); and Percevalle Fieschi, archdeacon of Buckingham (*CPR 1272–81*, 427, 456). Many other members of the family also appear, including her uncles and cousins, but none are described as royal kinsmen.

48 In July 1278 Brumisan, widow of Ugo Fieschi (d. *c*1274), claimed that she was a kinswoman of Edward I's through her father (*Foedera* (Rec. Comm.), i/2, 559).

She names him as Giacomo del Caretto, who was the son of Enrico del Caretto (d. 1231) and Agate, daughter of William II (d. 1252), count of Geneva, William II's sister, Margaret of Geneva, married Thomas I of Savoy and was the grandmother of Eleanor of Provence, Edward I's mother.

49 *CPR 1292–1301*, 608.

50 *Foedera* (Rec. Comm), ii/1, 274 and *CPR 1313–17*, 340 (Carlo Fieschi); *CPR 1317–21*, 14; Timmins (ed.), *Register of William Melton*, vol. 5, 6, 148 (nos 15, 433–4) (Federico's sons Adriano and Innocento Fieschi).

51 In both redactions of his work on the later life of Edward II in Italy, Phillips states that Manuele Fieschi was Edward II's third cousin once-removed ('Edward II in Italy', 219, n. 55; *Edward II*, 590, n.63). This is incorrect; there was no blood connection between Manuele and Edward II (see Appendix 6.1). It would appear that Phillips has misread the genealogical table in 'Where is Edward II?' (on p. 544).

52 James II's mother, Constance (d. 1302), was the daughter (by her second husband) of Beatrice of Savoy (d. 1257), granddaughter of Thomas I of Savoy (d. 1233), count of Savoy. This would in turn connect her to the earls of Lincoln as well as the English royal family, and some evidence of this consanguinity exists: a member of the Malaspina family (related to the Fieschi), was described as a kinsman by the earl of Lincoln in 1309. See *CEPR*, ii, 56.

53 *Raccolta Praghese*, 101.

54 For example, Johnstone, *Letters*, 54; *CCW*, 388, 511; *CPR 1292–1301*, 608.

55 *CPR 1292–1301*, 608.

56 Haines, *King Edward II*, 106–111.

57 *CPR 1324–7*, 119.

58 Sisto, 194–9, 231, 239, 265.

59 *ODNB*, under 'Melton'.

60 For his absence from the curia, see *DBI*, xxxxvii, 488–9. For the date of his arrival in England, see Haines, *Edward II*, 107.

61 *CPR 1317–21*, 61. This is dated 21 November 1317. See also *Raccolta Praghese*, 101.

62 Brocklesby (ed.), *Register of William Melton*, vol. 4, no. 638. Aslakeby was late setting out, still being in England in December 1331, but presumably he went shortly after that, as nothing more is heard of him for the next two years. He was back in England in October 1334, for on the 28th of that month he received licence to be absent for another two years, this time in the service of Manuele Fieschi (Brocklesby (ed.), *Register of William Melton*, vol. 4, no. 757).

63 Melton witnessed almost every charter from 30 November to 28 March 1331. Edward's question is known from the pope's reply, dated 1 July 1331. *CEPR*, ii, 499.

64 Guglielmo may have visited England in Cardinal Fieschi's household in 1317–18. See Timmins (ed.), *Register of William Melton*, vol. 5, A18; *CPR 1317–21*, 197.

65 *CPR 1327–30*, 446. This ousting had been confirmed in May 1330 by the bureaucracy

of York diocese. See Timmins (ed.), *Register of William Melton*, vol. 5, 115–16 (no. 336).

66 *CCR 1330–3*, 366.

67 *CPR 1330–4*, 98.

68 *AEC*, 184, 199.

69 The sums for this seem to have been acknowledged as royal debts in advance: 200 marks acknowledged as owed to Pessagno on April 1332 (*CPR 1330–4*, 270) and £350 on 29 July 1332 (*CPR 1330–4*, 321). In the letter close relating to his final account, the advance payment of £350 is noted. The nature, date of setting out and returning are from this same letter – see *CCR 1333–7*, 34.

70 TNA E101/386/9 m. 12. Writ dated 23 February 1333. The 'Cardinal' here is not a proper cardinal but rather relates to the soubriquet borne by Niccolinus. The original reads: '*deux robes pour cardinal & son compaignon*'.

71 The name 'Cardinal' was a family one: as well as his cousin and uncle, at least two of Niccolinus' four sons bore the name. Niccolinus appears as 'Cardinal' in the majority of the many references to him in England and Avignon. His son Giovanni appears as 'Cardinal' in 1346 and 1351 (*CCR 1343–6*, 148; *CCR 1349–54*, 374). His son Antonio Fieschi appears as 'Cardinal' in 1347 and 1352 (*Foedera* (Rec. Comm), iii/1, 127; TNA E40/14744).

72 For his possibly being raised in Lucca, see *Murimuth*, 159, where he is described as 'Niklaus de Luca'. As regards his age, it is noticeable that his son Giovanni received a prebend in York in December 1327 (*CEPR*, ii, 266), and his other son Guglielmo had Strensall in 1326. It is likely these sons and their non-ecclesiastical siblings Antonio and Gabriele were born around 1300.

73 See *CEPR*, ii, 322, for Manuele being resident at the papal curia. Adam of Lichfield regularly represented both Niccolinus and Manuele in English business, as well as Niccolinus' sons. See *CPR 1334–8*, 116, 302, 470, 484; *Grandison*, ii, 770; Timmins (ed.), *Register of William Melton*, vol. 5, 107 (no. 311); *CPR 1343–5*, 341. All these cover the period 1329–44; Adam continued to represent Giovanni Fieschi, Niccolinus's son, in the 1350s.

74 This is an account of the kidnapping of Niccolinus at Avignon in 1340, so the recipient – presumably Arnaud de Verdale, the then bishop of Maguelonne, who also was a papal emissary – had an interest in both Manuele's letter and Niccolinus' fate. See Phillips, 'Edward II in Italy', 219.

75 Fayen, no. 745, for his description as 'ambassador'. For his legal training see Augustino Oldoini, *Atheneum Ligusticum*, 435. See also *Foedera* (Rec. Comm.), ii/2, 1191 for his description as '*juris civilis professoris*' in 1342.

76 Mollat (ed.), *Lettres Communes*, i, no. 11484.

77 Epstein, *Genoa*, 198.

78 TNA E101/386/11 m. 2. His letters of protection were dated 26 February. See *CPR 1330–4*, 408–9.

79 *Foedera* (Rec. Comm.), ii/2, 854.

80 The original acquittance from Gaucelin, bishop of Albano survives: TNA E42/318. It is dated 21 October, not 21 September.

81 These appear in the account as 'delivery to the Pope [John XXII] of 4000 gold florins, each worth 3s 4d, the annual payment due to the Roman Curia in 1330, acknowledged by a papal bull of acquittal dated at Avignon on 7 July 1333 [£666 13s 4d]. Like payment of 2,000 gold florins, the sum due for Easter term 1331 [£333 6s 8d]' TNA E101/386/11 mm. 1–2. See also Lunt, 67.

82 Lunt, 68.

83 *CEPR*, ii, 512. Significantly, these petitions were not written up in England and carried to Avignon but written up in the papal city itself. Master Robert de Adria was paid eighteen florins (60s) for writing a petition on Edward's behalf. TNA E101/386/11 m. 1.

84 Brocklesby (ed.), *Register of William Melton*, vol. 4, no. 757. If he did return to England, it is possible that he encouraged the rewriting of the ordinances of the chantry at Sibthorp, where he was rector.

85 *CPR 1334–8*, 247; *Foedera* (Rec. Comm), ii/2, 937.

86 Alternatively, Manuele Fieschi sent one Leoneto de Malonibus of Genoa to England and France to announce the death of Cardinal Fieshci and to pay his debts in England and France in 1336. See Sisto, 320.

87 *CPR 1334–8*, 487. Bernabo was the brother of Niccolo Malaspina, 'il Marchesotto', mentioned above. Giffredus was a canon of Beverley and a doctor of canon law. For his presence as a chaplain in the Fieschi household, see *Raccolta Praghese*, 103.

88 Sisto, 163–8.

89 *CCR 1333–7*, 686 (payment to be in silver, dated 4 July 1336); *CPR 1334–8*, 328 (payment to be allowed on their trading, dated 12 October 1336). That this sum was not direct compensation is demonstrated by the alteration of the means of payment from sterling to an allowance against import duties for Genoese merchants bringing wares to England: an arrangement that can hardly have benefited Yvanus Luccani. Yvanus had in fact still received no reparations in January 1338, when the constable of Bordeaux was ordered to discuss the matter with him. See *Foedera* (Rec. Comm.), ii/2, 1011.

90 *Norwell*, 343, 355, 356.

91 TNA E101/389/8 mm. 7, 25.

92 TNA E36/204 fo. 83r.

93 For Niccolinus' son Giovanni, called 'Cardinal' as prebend of Fridaythorp, see *CEPR*, ii, 266; *CPR 1334–8*, 470; as prebendary of Kingsteignton see *CEPR*, ii, 297; *Grandison*, ii, 770; as parson of Tarring, 1346 (*CPR 1345–7*, 70. For the ratification of his estates, see *CPR 1334–8*, 323. For his other son in holy orders, Guglielmo Fieschi (d. c.1357), see Jones, *Fasti (Monastic Cathedrals)*, 32; *CPR 1345–7*, 70. Guglielmo's estate was ratified in 1336 (*CPR 1334–8*, 323), he was in England with

his brother Antonio Fieschi in 1347 (*CPR 1346–8*, 531; *Foedera* (Rec. Comm.), iii/1, 117).

94 *CPR 1338–40*, 197; *Foedera* (Rec. Comm.), ii/2, 1068.

95 Jonathan Sumption, 'A glorious road to ruin', *The Spectator* (25 February 2006), 42.

96 Phillips, 'Edward II' in Italy', 216, n. 37; *Edward II*, 586, n. 43.

97 *Dizionario di Toponomastica Storia e Significando dei Nomi Geografici Italiani*, 388. Other variants given in this source are *Melacius, Melaxus* and *Melaçus*.

98 Niccolo was the son of Luca's sister Flisca and Alberto Malaspina, marquis of Oramala. See *DBI*, xxxxvii, 502; Fayen, no. 203. Note that Niccolo and Manfredo Malaspina were not closely related, Niccolo and his brothers being of the Spino Fiorito line of the family and Manfredo being of the Spino Secco. The division of the family had taken place in the thirteenth century, with the River Magra being the dividing line between the lands of the Spino Fiorito and the Spino Secco Malaspinas.

99 'Where is Edward II?', 531.

100 Phillips, 'Edward II in Italy', 218; *Edward II*, 588.

101 Phillips, 'Edward II' in Italy', 217, 218; *Edward II*, 587, n. 49.

102 The candlesticks have the inventory number 0381 and are described in the register as '*Coppia di candelieri a tre piedi a testa di drago, con base a faccia trapezoidali raffiguranti due leonesse affrontate con rosoncino in mezzo. Corpo cilindrico a losanghe puntinate e due nodi percorsi da girali. Scodellino con bordo a petali.*' I am very grateful to Paul and Arabella Lizioli and John Earle for drawing my attention to this detail. Cuttino and Lyman refer to Anna Benedetti's article claiming Sant' Alberto was the first burial place of Edward II, and discuss her work in 'Where is Edward II?', 532; but they fail to note the potential significance of the date of accession of the candlesticks to the museum. Phillips dismisses the candlesticks but does not give a reason in his *Edward II*, 188.

103 *Raccolta Praghese*, 125–6.

104 Nero appears as *Iohannes Nerii de Florentia aurifex* in the distribution of Cardinal Fieschi's goods on 4 September 1336. Sisto, 225–6, 240, 245, 294.

105 J. M. Vidal (ed.), *Benoit XII*, nos 832–4. Note: '*Marchesotto*' has been rendered as '*Machefoci*' by Vidal.

106 One obvious candidate for the hermitage near Mulazzo is the Sanctuary of Madonna del Monte on Mount Carbone, overlooking the town.

107 William de Cornazano di Parma, Tedisio de Malocelli and Bernarbo Malaspina were in the household of Luca Fieschi in 1303. See *DBI*, xxxxvii, 484. See also the list of Fieschi's household in *Raccolta Praghese*, 101, which is headed by Bernabo.

108 *CPR 1334–8*, 467. The original MS (TNA C66/190 m. 11) reads '*ffos de novi*'.

109 Also note the presence at court of Tedisio Benedicti de Falcinello in the Val di Magra, in 1336, a few weeks after the arrival of Niccolinus Fieschi. Queen Philippa wrote to the Bardi merchants on 22 May 1336 requesting a loan for the purchase

of draperies etc. by Thadys Fauchmel [Tedisio Benedicti de Falcinello] her valet. The receipt by Tedisio of this and other money, to the sum of £65 from the Bardi is TNA E43/664/(i and ii). Benedict's origin is made clear by the appointment on 3 November 1344 of Francisco Forzetti to guard the manor of Eure, Bucks, belonging to 'Thedicius de Folchmello' (CPR 1343–5, 565). Theodicius Benedicti de Folchinello appears in CEPR, ii, 3, 11, 23 as a papal sergeant-at-arms and esquire of Queen Philippa (1343–4). Falcinello is near Sarzana, south of the Fieschi lordship of Pontremoli, about 3 miles from the Malaspina lordship of Fosdinovo. The reason for Forzetti guarding this manor was that Benedict was about to go on pilgrimage on behalf of Queen Philippa (Foedera [Rec. Comm.], iii/1, 18).

110 Phillips, 'Edward II in Italy', 219. He was a first cousin of Manuele Fieschi, being the son of Guglielmo. See Fayen, nos 202, 247.

111 CPR 1338–40, 190; Foedera (Rec. Comm.), ii/2, 1058. Note that Niccolo Bianco di Fieschi, who died in 1346, was not actually a member of the Fieschi. The family of Bianco took the suffix 'di Fieschi' on account of the legend that they were descended from Robaldo, an ancestor of the Fieschi (see Battilana, under the introduction to 'Bianco' and the first chart for 'Fieschi'). The description of Niccolo Bianco as Niccolinus Fieschi's nephew may be literal – in which case, either Niccolinus was married to an unknown sister of Facino Bianco or Facino was married to a sister of Niccolinus Fieschi – or it may be a loose use of the word, in the sense of 'any acknowledged kin', as Luca Fieschi used it of his kinsmen.

112 CCR 1333–7, 566–7. Edward arranged to pay Montefiore any money owing to him, according to a bill drawn up by Montefiore, at the same time. This stated that he had paid money at the request of the chancellor and the treasurer, as well as the king.

113 CCR 1333–7, 625.

114 CEPR, ii, 561. For Fastolf as a papal chaplain, see CEPR, ii, 547. He was also an executor of Simon, archbishop of Canterbury. CCR 1333–7, 231, 593.

115 CPR 1338–40, 195; Foedera (Rec. Comm.), ii/2, 1066–7. The detail about the money being sequestered at Monaco is from CPR 1338–40, 404.

116 Raccolta Praghese, 102, 104 n. 323. Note: he also served the cardinal's nephew Bernabo Malaspina.

117 Sisto, 244, 249, 287 (where he is described as a citizen of Genoa, acting in conjunction with Antonio Fieschi).

118 CPR 1334–8, 336.

119 CPR 1334–8, 340, 425.

120 CCR 1337–9, 135.

121 Foedera (Rec. Comm.), ii/2, 1008.

122 For Edward's dash to Scotland, see Perfect King, 148–9.

123 Norwell, 3.

124 TNA E43/716. This is dated 12 Edward III.

125 *AEC*, 202.

126 *CPR 1338–40*, 195; *Foedera* (Rec. Comm.), ii/2, 1067.

127 *CPR 1338–40*, 197; *Foedera* (Rec. Comm.), ii/2, 1068

128 *CPR 1338–40*, 404; *Foedera* (Rec. Comm.), ii/2, 1104. The money had been appropriated from Jacobo de Sarzana, to whom some of Luca Fieschi's goods were distributed after his death in January 1336. See Sisto, 244, 249, 317.

129 *Foedera* (Rec. Comm.), ii/2, 1107.

130 *Foedera* (Rec. Comm.), ii/2, 1156.

131 *Melsa*, ii, 386–7; Barnes, *Edward III*, 157. Barnes notes his son as Andrea; this is a mistake. The son is named as Gabriele in Benedict's register. See J. M. Vidal (ed.), *Benoit XII: Lettres Communes*, 295 (nos 3235–6).

132 Barnes, *Edward III*, 158.

133 *CEPR*, ii, 583–4.

134 *CEPR*, ii, 588.

135 *CPR 1340–3*, 109; *Foedera* (Rec. Comm.), ii/2, 1168–9; *CCR 1341–3*, 268.

136 *Foedera* (Rec. Comm.), ii/2, 1191.

137 *CPR 1343–5*, 341.

138 *CCR 1343–6*, 341, 351, 447. These letters were dated 4 August, 6 August and 1 September 1344.

139 *CPR 1343–5*, 341 (appointing his attorneys).

140 Sumption, *Trial by Battle*, 444.

141 *CCR 1343–6*, 378.

142 TNA E101/391/4 (1345x1348, payment of £10 to son Niccolo for arranging provision of galleys and 20 florins as a gift to Niccolinus for going to Flanders on the king's business); TNA E40/14744 (1352, Antonio accounting with the king for 13,205 florins received by him on the king's behalf).

143 Sumption, *Trial by Battle*, 319, 437–8.

144 Phillips, 'Edward II in Italy', 223; *Edward II*, 595–6.

145 Phillips, 'Edward II in Italy', 223; *Edward II*, 595, both times quoting *Foedera* (Rec. Comm.), ii/2, 1066.

146 For instance, the message sent in September 1336 stating that the pope had received Edward III's letters and that 'the answer will be brought back by word of mouth'. See *Cal. Papal Regs*, ii, 561. This is in addition to secret messages like the purpose of the money given to Anthony Bacche on 6 October 1337. Similarly, in June 1337 an English bishop was found with secret letters in France in June 1337 (*Cal. Papal Regs*, ii, 564).

147 Rogers, *War Cruel and Sharp*, 114–15.

148 Rogers, *War Cruel and Sharp*, 122, 124.

149 *Foedera* (Rec. Comm.), ii/2, 1001. This was in his letters appointing the duke of Brabant, the marquis of Juliers, the earl of Hereford and the count of Hainault as his vicars general in Europe.

150 *CPR 1334–8*, 537. Bacche was appointed one of the two legal representatives in England of Giovanni, son of Niccolinus Fieschi, on 21 July 1337. See *CPR 1334–8*, 470. His fellow agent appointed at this time was Adam de Lichfield, who was the agent of Manuele Fieschi and Niccolinus throughout the period. See *CPR 1334–8*, 484 (as 'Aidan'); *Grandison*, ii, 770; *CPR 1334–8*, 116 ('Master Adam'); Timmins (ed.), *Register of William Melton*, vol. 5, 144n. (no. 418); *CPR 1334–8*, 302; *CPR 1343–5*, 341; *CCR 1346–9*, 404.

151 On 28 September 1337 Benedict XII wrote to Philip expressing his hope that there should be no war unless Edward invaded France or Scotland. The same day he wrote to his cardinal envoys stating that they should go directly to Edward III before he left England, on the grounds that he would have to start paying his allies once he was in Germany, and then he would want to see some military return on his financial investment. See *CEPR*, ii, 565.

152 *Perfect King*, 199–201.

153 *CCR 1341–3*, 639; *CPR 1340–3*, 417. Ratification of one's estate often happened as a result of a change in circumstances, in case the positions one held might be considered doubtful.

154 Niccolinus probably returned from Avignon before 3 December when an order to pay him the arrears of his wages was made. See *Foedera* (Rec. Comm.), ii/2, p. 1183. He was still in London on 22 December 1341 when he dated a receipt for fifty pounds at London (TNA E40/508 i). He remained in London while the knights were all at Dunstable. Another receipt of his is dated 11 February 1342 at London (TNA E40/508 ii).

155 *CCR 1341–3*, 578–9.

156 *CPR 1334–8*, 248. This was an enlargement of a grant of a royal messuage made the previous summer (ibid., 116). See also TNA E156/28/133 which notes his presence there on the same day.

157 *Norwell*, 16, 48, 259, 305 (1338); *CPR 1338–40*, 399–400 (1339). See also *CPR 1340–3*, 17 (1340).

158 *CCR 1341–3*, 639.

159 *DBI*, xxxxvii, 528.

160 *DBI*, xxxxvii, 526.

161 *CEPR*, i, 273.

162 *DBI*, xxxxvii, 528–9. Note: Tedisio's place in the family tree is not at all certain. The reason for placing him here is that he must be descended from the first Fieschi, Ugo, but cannot have been a brother of his exact namesake, Tedisio Fieschi (d. 1248), father of Niccolo. It is not impossible that he was a son of Tedisio (d. 1248) but that side of the family is better recorded, so his neglect would be surprising if he was Niccolo's brother.

163 *DBI*, xxxxvii, 527–8, 425–6, 499, 526–9.

164 *DBI*, xxxxvii, 428, 528, 531–2; *Foedera*, I, ii, 559.

165 *DBI*, xxxxvii, 428, 438, 450, 488–9, 498–502; Sisto, 119.

166 *CEPR*, ii, 403; Sisto, 143; *DBI*, xxxxvii, 502. Named in his father's will (Sisto, 158).

167 Described as a royal kinsman (as was his brother). *CEPR*, ii, 403; Timmins (ed.), *Register of William Melton*, vol. 5, 423.

168 *DBI*, xxxxvii, 438–40, 489, 502. Named in his father's will (Sisto, 158).

169 *DBI*, xxxxvii, 440, 466; King, *Fasti (Lincoln)*, 72; *CEPR*, ii, 241. He resigned his prebend in 1324.

170 *DBI*, xxxxvii, 431, 438; co-heir of Cardinal Luca 1336 (Sisto, 165).

171 *DBI*, xxxxvii, 438, 466–8; co-heir of Cardinal Luca, 1336 (Sisto, 165). Bishop of Vercelli, 12 January 1349 (Eubel, *Hierarchia Catholica*, vol. 1, 521).

172 *CPR 1334–8*, 467; *DBI*, xxxxvii, 440; Sisto, 165. Prebendary of Lincoln 1328 (*CEPR*, ii, 269; *CPR 1330–4*, 48; *CPR 1334–8*, 467) and prebendary of Toledo and Noyon 1331 (*CEPR*, ii, 341); prebendary of Lichfield 1335 (*CEPR*, ii, 518). Beseiged in Pietrasanta by the Pisans in September 1343, where he died. See also Villani, book xiii, chapter 26.

173 *DBI*, xxxxvii, 440.

174 *DBI*, xxxxvii, 438, 489, 502. Named in his father's will 1304 (Sisto, 158).

175 *DBI*, xxxxvii, 488, 502; *CPR 1281–92*, 483; *CPR 1292–1301*, 123, 213.

176 *DBI*, xxxxvii, 438, 440, 444, 488–91, 502), parson of Tirrington (*CPR 1313–17*, 382, 622). Lord of Pontremoli until it was seized by Castruccio degli Antelminelli. Named in his father's will 1304 (Sisto, 158). Regularly described as a royal kinsman.

177 *DBI*, xxxxvii, 502. Named in his father's will 1304 (Sisto, 158).

178 Malaspina is mentioned in book xix of Dante's *Purgatory* (*DBI*, xxxxvii, 502). Note Alagia or Alasia received some of Cardinal Fieschi's goods after his death: Sisto, 288, 290.

179 *DBI*, xxxxvii, 502; Fayen, no. 203.

180 Lord of Filattiera, Bagnone, Treschietto, Castiglione del Terziere, Malgrate (all in the Val di Magra), as well as Oramala, Godiasco, Piumesana, Cella, Cigno and Cignolo (Val de Nizza). In 1339 his estates were divided between his five sons into five lordships. Each lordship had a town in the Val di Magra and each a town in the Val di Nizza. For the date of his death, see Burla, *Malaspina di Lunigiana*, 118, 121. I am grateful to Susan Earle for directing me to this reference. Note: his son Bernabo Malaspina was one of three of Cardinal Luca Fieschi's nephews given a canonry on 24 June 1335. The others were Antonio, son of Carlo Fieschi, and Italiano Fieschi (J. M. Vidal (ed.), *Benoit XII*, nos 832–4).

181 Fayen, 203, 1094. See also *DBI*, lxvii, 763, where it is explained that Barnarbo was not of the Mulazzo branch as long thought but a brother of Niccolo Malaspina (d. 1339).

182 *DBI*, xxxxvii, 428, 442, 499–501, 509, 514, 532. Edward I accepted the cross from him in preparation for his crusade in 1268, when Ottobono was a papal legate.

183 *CPR 1247–58*, 616; *CPR 1258–66*, 28.

184 *DBI*, xxxxvii, 442, 500, 502, 513–16; King, *Fasti (Lincoln)*, 40–1, 49; *CEPR*, i, 512.

185 *DBI*, xxxxvii, 442–4, 501; Sisto, 146; *CPR 1258–66*, 60, 624, 676).

186 *DBI*, xxxxvii, 450; Sisto, 16. Probably to be identified with Andrea Fieschi, canon of Chartres and prebendary of Kingsteignton, who died in 1270 (Horn, *Fasti (Salisbury)*, 100–2).

187 Fayen, 745.

188 *DBI*, xxxxvii, 450, 499. In England 1258 where described as 'Parson of Sibet-' and brother of Ugolino (*CPR 1247–58*, 626). Appointed attorneys November 1281 (*CPR 1281–92*, 1). Given 'Sibet-' as 'Cibezeya' in 1251 by Innocent IV; also given a prebend and canonry in Exeter Cathedral (Sisto, 49).

189 In England 1258 (*CPR 1247–58*, 626).

190 Fayen, nos 202, 247.

191 *DBI*, xxxxvii, 451; *CEPR*, ii, 187; Sisto, 119, 143.

192 Timmins (ed.), *Register of William Melton*, vol. 5, 107, 311, 433; papal notary 1329, 1335, 1336 (*CEPR*, ii, 291, 518, 533); rector of Paulesholt 1329, which he resigned the same year in favour of his attorney Adam Woodward of Lichfield (*CEPR*, ii, 291); prebendary of Salisbury 1319, described as son of Andrea (*CEPR*, ii, 187), prebendary of Ampleforth 1329 (*CEPR*, ii, 291; Timmins (ed.), *Register of William Melton*, vol. 5, 107,); prebendary of Liège in 1329 and 1334 (Fayen, 2527 and 3622); archdeacon of Nottingham 1329–31 (*CEPR*, ii, 314; Timmins (ed.), *Register of William Melton*, vol. 5, 591; *CEPR*, ii, 359); prebendary of Milton Manor, dioc. Lincoln (*CEPR*, ii, 359; Timmins (ed.), *Register of William Melton*, vol. 4, 657); provost of Arnhem 1332 (Fayen, 3193); prebendary of Renaix 1333 (Fayen, 3193); ratification of estate (*CPR 1340–43*, 417; 'Where is Edward II?', 542); bishop of Vercelli, 16 June 1343 (Eubel, *Hierarchia Catholica*, vol. 1, 521).

193 *CEPR*, ii, 319.

194 *CEPR*, ii, 363.

195 *DBI*, xxxxvii, 451; Sisto, 119, 143. Possibly the 'nephew' of Cardinal Luca and count of Lavagna on his visit to England with the Cardinal in 1317 (*CPR 1317–21*, 10). In which case his wife was probably Arterisia (Sisto, 233).

196 Fayen, 204, 248

197 *CPR 1338–40*, 197; *Foedera* (Rec. Comm.), ii/2, 1068. He wrote to Edward III 1352 referring to his own services and those of Giacotto and Saladino [Provana] (TNA E40/14744). Probably the Andre incorrectly mentioned in Barnes, *Edward III*, 157–8. Probably visited England 1347, as the '*germanus*' of Guglielmo Fieschi (d. 1357).

198 *CPR 1338–40*, 197; *Foedera* (Rec. Comm.), ii/2, 1068). He was, according to the papal registers, kidnapped with his father from the papal court at Avignon in April 1340.

199 *CEPR*, ii, 266; *CPR 1334–8*, 470; *CEPR*, ii, 297; *Grandison*, ii, 770 (Kingsteignton and Yalmpton). Estate ratified (*CPR 1334–8*, 323). Parson of Tarring 1346 (*CPR 1345–4?*, 70).

200 Jones, *Fasti (Monastic Cathedrals)*, 32; *CPR 1345–8*, 70; possibly in household of Cardinal Luca de Fieschi 1318 (Timmins (ed.), *Register of William Melton*, vol. 5, A18; *CPR 1317–21*, 197); removed as prebendary of Strensall 1330 (Timmins (ed.), *Register of William Melton*, vol. 5, 336); estate ratified 1336 (*CPR 1334–8*, 323); in England with 'germanus' Antonio de Fieschi 1347 (*CPR 1346–8*, 531; *Foedera* (Rec. Comm.), iii/1, 117).

201 TNA E101/391/4, m. 1–2. This is the only source I have found for him. It could be that he has been described incorrectly as a son, being actually Niccolinus' nephew, Niccolo Bianco di Fieschi.

202 Fayen, no. 745; *DBI*, xxxxvii, 528.

203 *DBI*, xxxxvii, 529. It should be noted that the Roland who visited England in 1258 was described as a brother of Cardinal Ottobono, and thus not a son of Tedisio the nephew but Tedisio the uncle. See *CPR 1247–58*, 616; *CPR 1258–66*, 28.

204 Some sources claim that his son, Guglielmo, was in the household of Cardinal Luca Fieschi in 1317 but this is supposition; the Guglielmo in Luca's *familia* in England is not given a surname. See Timmins (ed.), *Register of William Melton*, vol. 5, 181 (no. A18); *CPR 1317–21*, 197. None of the many preferments of the ecclesiastical sons (Giovanni and Guglielmo) can be associated with Luca, although this does not mean that they were not due to his influence. See for example *CEPR*, ii, 266, 297; *CPR 1334–8*, 470; *Grandison*, ii, 770.

205 Battilana, cart.i; *DBI*, xxxxvii, 450; Horn, *Fasti (Salisbury)*, 100–2. The Fieschi had a habit of keeping certain benefices in the family, whether in England (for example, the prebend in Lincoln which passed between three sons of Carlo Fieschi in the 1320s), France (Liège, which came to Niccolinus from his cousin; see next note) and Italy (for example, the diocese of Luni, which was held by three of Luca's nephews in succession from 1312–44, and the that of Vercelli, which was held in turn by Manuele and Giovanni Fieschi).

206 Fayen, no. 745.

207 *DBI*, xxxxvii, 428, 449–52, 498–9, 508, 528, 531; Battilana, cart. i and xiv; Sisto, genealogical tables between 40–1; *CPR 1247–58*, 626; *CPR 1281–92*, 1; Sayer, *Original Papal Documents*, 244.

208 Jonathan Sumption has suggested that Niccolinus was the brother of Francesco Fieschi, which would tally with this, as Francesco was Manuele's uncle. See Sumption, *Trial by Battle*, 163.

209 Castro, *Archivo General de Navarra*, vol. 19 (1957), nos 356, 383, 856. These three references are payments to or on behalf of '*un escudero de la compañia del hermano bastardo del rey de Inglaterra*' (no. 356, May 1392), '*Johan de Galas, bastardo de Inglaterra*' (no. 383, June 1392), and for '*una hopalanda de paña de oro que se le tomó cuando el rey hizo caballero al bastardo de Gales*' (no. 856, November 1392). The first and last references rule out the possibility that it was John de Southeray, illegitimate son of Edward III, who was not a brother of a king of England and

had been knighted by Edward III on 23 April 1377. The use of the name 'de Gales' suggests we should consider the last years of Edward II's life, the 1330s or early 1340s, for any illegitimate son of his would indeed have been a 'bastard brother of the king of England' (but a brother of the deceased Edward III, not Richard II). That Edward III did not recognize such a half-brother (as far as we can tell) does not militate against such a child being born and being recognized by the authority protecting Edward II in his exile.

7

Edward III and the moneylenders

Narratives of intrigue or secret plotting, by definition, tend to leave little or no evidence that directly relates to the plot in question. So any history of secret business based exclusively on direct evidence is bound to be partial. If we want to test the limits of a political intrigue or a king's 'secret business' we have to move away from the assumption that direct evidence relating to the intrigue must still exist. Indeed, we have to shift, cautiously, to a position in which certainty is impossible – circumstantial details being the only means to reconstruct a possible narrative. What follows is therefore an exploration of a series of possibilities and probabilities arising from the preceding chapter.

Niccolinus Fieschi was not the only man to meet Edward III at the Tower of London on 15 April 1336. As noted in the previous chapter, Paul Montefiore was also probably present, as on that day Edward ordered his chamberlains and the exchequer to repay £2,000 that Montefiore had lent him 'for his secret affairs' and to pay the outstanding amounts owed to him by the king.[1] In addition, that same day a patent letter was drawn up in which the king acknowledged 'his indebtedness to John [Giovanni] Baroncelli, Guy [Guido] Donati and John [Giovanni] Juntyn and the other merchants of the Society of the Peruzzi of Florence in £3,666 13s 4d (5,500 marks) lent for the furtherance of some urgent matters'.[2] This was the first large financial deal that the Peruzzi had made with a king of England, and only the second loan of any sort they had made to Edward III.[3] The following day, 16 April, Henry Whissh was present, as mentioned in the previous chapter. So too were members of the Bardi – Edward ordered his debts to them to be cleared in a similar fashion to those he owed Montefiore.[4] Three of these five parties were connected with the outline narrative of Edward II's later life: Montefiore's arrangements with Jacobo de Sarzana, a member of Cardinal Fieschi's household, have been mentioned in the previous chapter, as have Whissh's and Niccolinus Fieschi's careers. But there is reason to suspect that the Bardi and Peruzzi may also have been connected with the later life of Edward II. If they were, we have to address a question which many people have asked in the past without coming to a specific answer: was the Fieschi Letter part of an attempt to blackmail Edward III, and were the Italian bankers part of that blackmail attempt?

This question directly relates to the matter of Edward III's finances in the period 1336–41, while he was notching up huge expenses on account of his war. Shortly after the meetings at the Tower, on 8 May 1336, the first council of merchants was summoned to advise the king on how he could raise enormous sums of money by using the English wool trade. Two more such councils followed in 1336 before the establishment of the English Wool Company in August 1337.[5] By then, Edward was already in the red. Over the next five years his debts mounted – and had several important knock-on effects. They led to him having to pledge the crown of England, two of Queen Philippa's crowns and other jewels as security for his financial dealings. The earl of Derby – a royal cousin – had to stand security for royal loans, submitting to detainment in 1340–1 and a hefty ransom. Edward III himself was practically detained for debt at Ghent in 1340. The archbishop of Canterbury was similarly made to stand as security, having to stay within the precincts of Canterbury Cathedral in order to avoid arrest. There was the 'Crisis of 1341' too: a stand-off between Edward and the archbishop in which the latter directly drew attention to the fate of Edward II as a warning to Edward III.[6] There can be little doubt that Edward III's indebtedness was the single greatest hindrance to his military progress against France in the period 1338–41. Even countries that were not directly involved in the war felt the effects. The Florentine chronicler, Giovanni Villani, whose brother was a member of the Peruzzi, famously blamed Edward III's failure to pay 900,000 florins (£135,000) to the Bardi and 600,000 florins (£90,000) to the Peruzzi as the reason why both banks failed, so there were further international consequences.[7] The question of whether payments in respect of his father's survival added to Edward's financial problems is thus a hugely important one. Indeed, if Edward's authorization to his envoys to Avignon in March 1331 to borrow up to £50,000 (see the previous chapter) is an indication of how far he was prepared to go to keep his father hidden, and if their failure to conclude a deal at that rate is taken as an indicator that he may have paid an even larger sum, then it may be that Edward II's survival in the custody of the Fieschi, under the auspices of the pope, was an extremely important factor – one which no one has previously taken into consideration.

ACKNOWLEDGEMENTS OF INDEBTEDNESS 1335–7

Although the Bardi and Peruzzi are normally linked together in discussing Edward III's financial dealings, they did not actually work together until an agreement in March 1338, when they extended loans to Edward III in the ratio of 60:40 (the Bardi being responsible for the larger share). The Bardi lent money to Edward III from the start of the reign, and it is important to gain an idea of the nature and scale of payments at this time to appreciate the subtle differences from those of 1335–40. The following schedule (Figure 7.1) shows the pattern of 'acknowledgements of the king's indebtedness' after the fall of Isabella and Mortimer (their government having borrowed heavily from the Bardi from 1326, especially in the year 1330):

Date	Amount	Purpose	Ref.
29 March 1331	£8,000 [or £800[8]]	A loan 'received in the king's chamber'	CPR 1330–4, 96.
21 May 1331	£45 16s 8d	Paid by them to Richard Bury, king's clerk for his expenses overseas	CPR 1330–4,122.
21 May 1331	£22	Paid by them to Thomas West for two cups	CPR 1330–4, 122
2 April 1332	200 marks	Paid by them to Antonio Pessagno for his expenses in going to Avignon to further the king's business	CPR 1330–4, 270
8 May 1332	£80	Paid by them to Nicolas D'Aubridgecourt at the king's request	CPR 1330–4, 301
29 July 1332	£350	Paid by them to Antonio Pessagno for his expenses in going to France, Gascony and Avignon to further the king's business	CPR 1330–4, 321
1 Aug. 1332	200 marks	Paid by them to Hugh de Palice for a release of two manors in Norfolk	CPR 1330–4, 323
16 Dec. 1332	£200	Paid by them to Henry de Beaumont	CPR 1330–4, 380
3 Feb. 1333	£633	Acknowledgement made at the same time as a loan of £213 6s 8d from the Peruzzi and £800 from Antonio Bacche	CPR 1330–4, 397
2 May 1333	£1,071	For the expenses of the household	CPR 1330–4, 431

Figure 7.1 'Acknowledgements of the king's indebtedness' to the Bardi, 1331–June 1333

It needs to be emphasized that the above is strictly 'acknowledgements of indebtedness' on the Patent Rolls – not all debts and promises. Edward's total indebtedness at this time was much greater. The Bardi accounts with the English Crown for these years reveals that in the account dated 25 April 1331, they had spent a total of £30,092 8s 11½d on Edward's behalf since 10 December 1328; over the same period Edward had paid or assigned to them £25,368 12s 3½d, leaving him owing £4,723 16s 8d, plus a further £1,500 which had been assigned to them and not paid.[9] On 19 May 1332 the total debt of £6,223 16s 8d had been revised to £7,493 13s 9½d, which may be considered a much better indicator of his indebtedness as a whole.[10] However, concentrating on this specific form of wording allows for some exactness and comparison with similar payments in a later period. It also reveals a gap of two and a half years, to November 1335, when he made no such 'acknowledgements of indebtedness' to the bankers in letters patent.

November 1335 was clearly a significant month. Not only did Edward III start acknowledging his indebtedness to the Bardi on a much larger scale, the Peruzzi took their 'first tentative steps' towards lending to the English Crown that month (to use Edwin Hunt's phrase).[11] This followed the reformation of the Peruzzi in Florence on 1 July 1335.[12] Obviously the regular deals of the Bardi over the previous ten years may have inspired the Peruzzi to emulate them, but not until 15 April 1336 and the appearance of Niccolinus Fieschi were they successful.

Figure 7.2 includes only specific 'acknowledgements of indebtedness' by the king to the Bardi and Peruzzi, so the reasons and amounts can be compared with those in Figure 7.1. The amounts are of a different character – not so much specific payments to named individuals (the sum handed to Queen Isabella being the exception) but payments for vaguely defined overseas business, often of a specifically 'secret' nature. The sums are also considerably larger. At a total of £44,533 6s 8d, the acknowledgements of indebtedness to these two companies were made at a rate of more than £2,226 per month – five times the rate in 1331–3. But even this high rate is an underestimate of the amount of Edward's total indebtedness to the companies. At the beginning of September 1337 he made two recapitulations of 'indebtedness': one for £28,000 to the Peruzzi (1 September), another for £50,000 to the Bardi (2 September).[13] These seem to be totals of everything owed to the companies on those dates: the Peruzzi sum was justified as 'by memoranda of the Exchequer and other evidences in their

Date	Co.	Sum	Purpose	Ref.
19 Nov. 1335	Bardi	2,500 marks	'for the furtherance of some important business'	CPR 1334–8, 180.
20 Nov. 1335	Bardi	2,500 marks	'for the furtherance of his affairs'	CPR 1334–8, 197.
27 March 1336	Bardi	2,000 marks	'lent for the furtherance of some important business'	CPR 1334–8, 240.
15 April 1336	Peruzzi	5,500 marks	'lent for the furtherance of some urgent matters'	CPR 1334–8, 249
15 April 1336	Peruzzi	£1,000	'Loan'	CPR 1334–8, 249
6 May 1336	Bardi	£7,200	'Paid at his request to Queen Isabella'	CPR 1334–8, 261
28 Aug. 1336	Peruzzi	£1,000	'lent for his service'	CPR 1334–8, 312
16 Jan. 1337	Bardi	£2,000	'lent by them for the furtherance of some secret business'	CPR 1334–8, 348
26 Jan. 1337	Bardi	£10,000	'which they have undertaken to pay for him as well beyond the seas as within'	CPR 1334–8, 379
26 Jan. 1337	Peruzzi	£8,000	'lent for the furtherance of some secret business beyond the seas and within'	CPR 1334–8, 388
3 May 1337	Peruzzi	£2,000	'paid by them on some secret business wherein they were employed by the king'	CPR 1334–8, 430
29 June 1337	Peruzzi	£5,000	'lent for the furtherance of his affairs in parts beyond the seas'	CPR 1334–8, 466

Figure 7.2 'Acknowledgements of the king's indebtedness' to the Bardi and Peruzzi, 1335–June 1337

hands'. The Bardi sum was specifically calculated at their request, relating to debts acknowledged 'since the feast of the Purification last' (2 February 1337).[14] Shortly afterwards, both of these grand totals were revised to take account of interest and other expenses, with Edward acknowledging that he owed the Peruzzi £35,000 (a 25 per cent increase) and the Bardi £62,000 (a 24 per cent increase).[15] Several other promises-to-pay and discharges which were included in these totals were similarly for the king's 'secret business'.[16] But after the totalling in early September 1337, such payments almost entirely disappeared from the rolls. Thereafter there is just one acknowledgement of indebtedness to the Bardi for the king's 'secret business' – for 800 marks 'paid in parts beyond the seas for the furtherance of his secret business' – dated 15 February 1338.[17] Shortly afterwards, Bonifazio Peruzzi, chairman of the Peruzzi Company, arrived to take charge of the English operation in person, and in March 1338 the two companies merged for the business of lending to, and recovering from, the Crown.

The months from November 1335 to the totalling up of liabilities in September 1337 thus seem to be a distinct period during which the banks undertook to pay for Edward III's secret business overseas on a regular basis. During this same period Edward discussed with his councils of merchants and parliament how he was going to be able to raise the money to pay them back. At the end of the period, Edward's indebtedness to the companies was totalled and interest added. Soon afterwards he started making arrangements to pay in a new way: by allowing the merchants to export consignments of wool to the Mediterranean and making grants out of the customs of various ports.[18] In this he was acting against the interests of the recently established English Wool Company, whose principal members had undertaken to provide Edward with a loan of £200,000 in return for a monopoly on the wool trade. To recapitulate: a period of acknowledgement of indebtedness for 'secret business' 1335–7 was followed by a period of payment, involving the two banking companies joining forces in March 1338, under the direct supervision of Bonifazio Peruzzi in person, in London.

The payments in respect of Edward's secret business are just the start of the secretiveness. Hunt in his study of the Peruzzi remarks on the distinctiveness of this period and states that

> it is riddled with anomalies. Here is a company weakened by persistent losses lending on a lavish scale to a monarch from whom it must gain prompt recompense to recover its fortunes . . .[19]

To grasp the full importance of this statement it is necessary to understand that the 'super-companies' were not super-rich. The Bardi – the larger of the two – could only afford to loan the king as much as £30,000 between 1328 and 1331 because of the regular repayments by collectors and receivers amounting to five-sixths of that sum. According to Hunt, at the end of June 1335 the Peruzzi company had equity of 52,000 *lire a fiorino* (li.); net borrowing in Florence of li. 118,000; and net borrowing from foreign branches of li. 53,000.[20] All this adds up to li. 223,000 – or approximately £22,000 sterling – for the whole company, which had many other business interests besides its English office. Given that the Peruzzi business in England was always assessed as two-thirds of that of the Bardi, it would be reasonable to assume that the Bardi's assets were not a great deal more than one and a half times this sum – across all their branches. Both companies needed swift repayments to stay in business if they made large loans. However, the totalling up of the payments to the Bardi and Peruzzi on 2 September 1337 suggests that none of the 'acknowledgements of indebtedness' had been paid for a considerable time – at least since 2 February 1337 in the case of the Bardi. Nor were the sums then owed paid straightaway. Although a writ on the Liberate Rolls for 15 October 1337 states that the whole amount of £35,000 should be paid to the Peruzzi 'immediately', on 5 November 1337 the king made provision to pay just £10,000 of the Bardi's £62,000 and £9,000 or the Peruzzi's £35,000.[21] Even after making these payments, Edward still supposedly owed the Peruzzi a sum considerably larger than the wealth of their entire company. In short, Edward III had 'acknowledged his indebtedness' for sums of money that the Peruzzi could not possibly have loaned him.

This is perplexing, for it was not the way the Peruzzi worked prior to 1336. Similarly mysterious is the fact that the Peruzzi's account books do not mention these sums. They record the expenses of Giovanni Baroncelli and the other Peruzzi members in London in 1336 but they do not record any loans to the king. Neither the 15 April 1336 record of indebtedness nor the £1,000 loan of the same date (which Hunt states was effectively a 'gift' from Edward III, probably a form of interest acknowledged in advance) appears in the Peruzzi accounts. Nor do any other royal loans for 1337. Records of court fees in 1336 and expenses in pursuing a case in London to clear the Peruzzi of any responsibility for the outstanding debts of Hugh Despenser are acknowledged, and the quittance is confirmed in the English records; but no loans are included in the Florentine book.[22] As and when they were paid the £35,000 that Edward had promised, they could have lent back to Edward his own money; but prior to this they did not have the resources.

As Hunt states in his study of the Peruzzi, 'the only remaining possible way to reconcile the records with reality is that the companies gave the king promises instead of money'.[23] While some of the smaller payments were 'real' (in that the bankers did hand over sums of money on the king's behalf), Hunt's statement can hardly be wrong with regard to the major sums. Edward's acknowledgements were promissory, that he would pay the bankers at some later date, because their services were also promissory – in that they had underwritten his secret business with a promise to pay at a future date. However, the promissory nature of the debts raises questions regarding the nature of the business, and why it needed to be secret. Inevitably we are forced to consider either bribes (such as to a foreign power) or blackmail, for promissory debts on such a massive scale can only have been undertaken for a promissory service or the suspension of a threatened act. We might speculate that the promises of money by the bankers on Edward's behalf were to encourage the German states to back him in his bid for the Imperial vicarial crown and a league against the French. However, Edward did not start to form his grand strategy until the end of October 1336 at the earliest – a year after his first 'acknowledgements of indebtedness' to the Bardi and six months after his first promises to the Peruzzi.[24]

EDWARD'S RELATIONSHIP WITH THE BANKERS, 1337–46

Whatever the causes of the debts, Edward started to pay the bankers huge amounts of money and to show them extraordinary favour. According to a memorandum in a Bardi account, Edward repaid on 27 May '1337' [sic] all the money he had received from the Bardi at the receipt of the Exchequer between 15 July 1335 and 11 December 1337.[25] Obviously this does not necessarily include 'acknowledgements of indebtedness' that were of a promissory nature. But he paid these too over the period 1338–40. According to Fryde, between May 1338 and March 1340 Edward paid the Bardi £66,000 and the Peruzzi £38,000 – a total of £104,000 – towards a total debt of £126,000 (£86,000 and £40,000 respectively), not including two huge gifts to the two companies totalling £50,000.[26] This is no doubt why Bonifazio Peruzzi, chairman of the Peruzzi, came to London in person in 1338, leaving the centre of operations in Florence to others.[27] His company, which had been losing money in 1335, depended on Edward III's payments in order to stay afloat.

At first both companies were very well treated. Not only were they assigned many large gifts of between £1,000 and £10,000, the partners and employees were exempted from Edward's order to arrest all foreign merchants and to confiscate their goods and jewels in the late summer of 1337.[28] They were exempted from a similar order the following summer.[29] They were permitted to carry on their wool trade irrespective of Edward granting a monopoly to the English Wool Company. In September 1337 they were exempted from a general suspension of payments to royal creditors and officers; and similarly, in May 1339, the king ordered that 'no fees be paid to any justices, barons of the Exchequer, clerks promoted or other minsters who have other means of support' with the sole exceptions being the defence of castles and towns in Scotland and moneys assigned to the Bardi and the Peruzzi.[30] The massive gifts of £30,000 (to the Bardi) and £20,000 (to the Peruzzi) which they were first promised in 1338 and secondly in 1339 – despite the king's shortage of cash – mark a high point in their relations with the king.

In 1340 both companies slowly started to fall from favour. Contracts with the two companies were renegotiated in April and May 1340, which entailed them advancing 2,000 marks per month for the royal household in return for a portion of the ninth.[31] But the sums were not paid fully and nor were the large gifts promised by Edward III. Parliament issued a call for all the merchants' accounts to be examined in June 1340. On 15 June Edward ordered an account of what was owed to them to be drawn up, ostensibly so he could pay the companies more quickly; and to that end he sent a schedule of his debts to the treasurer. On 2 July he commissioned various prelates and lords to audit the accounts of the wool merchants, where these were submitted; but as yet no full enquiry was launched.[32] A number of prests or loans made to them at an earlier date were allowed to them on 22 July 1340; but thereafter these almost cease.[33] Two days later the main account with the Bardi was drawn up to establish what the king owed.[34] There was no punitive action, and still it was years before an enquiry would be launched; but the companies had suddenly lost their high standing. The Bardi and the Peruzzi were assigned a grant of 20,000 marks, three-quarters in wool, in July 1341 'for the relief of their estate, much depressed in these days by large payments made and undertaken on [the king's] account.'[35] All Edward's favours to them then ceased. Safe conducts and writs to customs officers to allow wool exports were still issued but Edward's business with them henceforth became one of strict accounting, limiting his liabilities. The commission of *oyer et terminer* drawn up on 19 October 1342 to examine the accounts of both the Bardi and the Peruzzi marked the start of the process of disentangling the 'super-companies' from English royal affairs.[36]

The actual winding up of the royal involvement with the Bardi and Peruzzi was slow. In January 1343 the strength of the commission of enquiry was increased, with the addition of five more judges. On 7 March 1343 Edward wrote to his clerk, William Stowe, ordering him not to leave London until the 'final accounts' of the Bardi and Peruzzi and other alien merchants were complete.[37] On 27 October 1343 the Peruzzi declared itself bankrupt in Florence and ceased to trade in the city. Most of its agencies closed down.[38] In England, however, it continued to act – as did the Bardi – questioning the audit. On 5 February 1344 a new committee of enquiry was commissioned.[39]

The accounts of the companies with the Crown, created as part of the winding-up process, suggest that for the regnal years 12–17 (25 January 1338–24 January 1344) the Bardi's wool receipts were valued at £72,878 8s 9d and those of the Peruzzi at £17,732 13s 8d. In addition the two companies received £10,277 10s 2d and £6,851 13s 5d respectively in their joint account. The Bardi received a further £20,399 18s 3½d in cash on their own account, and the Peruzzi £54,591 0s 4½d. This meant Edward was supposed to have paid the immense sum of £182,731 4s 8d to the two companies. This figure seems only to have been disputed in respect of the bankers not realizing the full value of consignments of wool assigned to them. The total payments by the Bardi on Edward III's behalf were assessed by Edward's commissioners at £76,583 9s 10d and the total payments by the Peruzzi £31,184 8s 6d.[40] The result was, according to this account, that the Bardi owed Edward III £26,972 7s 4½d and the Peruzzi owed him £47,990 18s 11½d.

The bankers responded with an account listing further payments and debits for which they sought recompense, including (among many other payments) the corrections to the wool account, Edward III's unpaid 'gift' of £20,000 to the Peruzzi and £63,665 10s 6½d for many parcels paid to the receipt of the exchequer between 17 November 1336 and 2 March 1340. The total of payments, unpaid gifts and allowances they claimed – to set aside the money that Edward III's commissioners said they owed – amounted to £126,395 19s 6d, so by their reckoning Edward still owed them money. Various members of the Peruzzi were in the Fleet Prison by 10 June 1344 and they remained under scrutiny for the next two years – some being lodged in the Tower in March 1346 although they were allowed to come and go under a safe conduct.[41] The Peruzzi never received their gift of £20,000 but did get a final payment of £6,375 in June 1346.[42] The Bardi were treated slightly differently: their account with the king to

24 July 1340 was presented on 20 April 1345, when the king declared his will to make good what had not been paid of £50,493 5s 2½d entered on the rolls of the receipt of the Exchequer.[43] In March 1346 he promised to repay the outstanding sum of £23,082 3s 10½d, this sum being reduced by payments to creditors of the Bardi, so that by 1348 it was £13,454 2s 11½d. This debt was finally discharged by Richard II in 1391.

WHERE DID ALL THE MONEY GO?

The totals owing in September 1337, which indicate debts far beyond the capabilities of the Peruzzi (and very probably the Bardi too) suggest that the money Edward had promised the bankers for most of his overseas affairs had not been paid. Thus the payment of the money Edward promised for his overseas 'secret business' took place after this date, between October 1337 and July 1340, mainly from the bankers' sale of English wool. There is just one payment stated to be for the king's 'secret negotiations' in these accounts: £10,000 in the Bardi accounts for Michaelmas term 1339–40, which probably should be dated to March 1340.[44] Obviously Edward's acknowledgements for his 'secret business' went a lot further than this (as seen above). Thus the recipients of the bulk of the debts incurred on Edward's behalf in 1335–37 were the other beneficiaries named in the accounts. In this respect it is significant that a large proportion of the money was handed over to Paul Montefiore.

It has not previously been appreciated quite how much of Edward III's money was placed in the hands of this Italian clerk. In the regnal years 12 and 13 (25 January 1338–34 January 1340) the Bardi gave him £62,380 5s 3d in gold florins for the king's negotiations under the writ of the privy seal, which Montefiore acknowledged in three letters patent.[45] The Peruzzi handed over £25,173 7s 9d in gold florins, acknowledged in six patent letters by Montefiore and authorized by a privy seal writ for the 'king's negotiations'.[46] The total of these two entries alone is £87,553 13s. In addition there were additional payments of smaller amounts to Montefiore, in both cash and wool, such as the 2,848 florins (£427 4s) that the Bardi paid him, in accordance with a royal writ of 22 August 1338, and many shipments of wool.[47] In addition there were large payments by Edward III directly to Montefiore: for instance the £10,000 paid to him in March and May 1337, as a result of an earlier loan.[48] Several large rebates from the final sum of £23,082 3s 10½d owed to the Bardi in 1346 were sums owed by them to Montefiore. It seems Montefiore was acting as a sort of paymaster general for Edward's overseas affairs. Of course, he was not alone in this role; many other merchants from the Low Countries, Italy and England made over significant amounts of money to Edward's German allies. But he was by far the most significant: more than £100,000 was paid to him, either directly or via the Bardi and Peruzzi.

Montefiore's role in the later life of Edward II was touched upon in the last chapter; but the above financial issue demands that we know more about him. He was an Italian clerk from the diocese of Fermo, in Italy, who first came to England as the proctor of Cardinal Neapoleone Orsini, cardinal-deacon of St Adrian, in 1323.[49] He had entered Edward's service by 1329 and quickly found favour, being given a prebend of Lincoln in 1332 (which he held until about 1338).[50] In 1335 he took two royal crowns into his safekeeping in return for a loan of 8,000 marks, which was repaid that June; and in 1336 he made a loan of £9,590 6s 8d towards the king's war in Scotland.[51] But, as mentioned at the start of this chapter, Montefiore had by this stage started lending money for the king's 'secret business', commencing on the day when Edward III made Niccolinus Fieschi a king's councillor. Later that year Edward III sent Montefiore to pay Jacobo de Sarzana to arrange for galleys to be sent to him (a task later arranged by Niccolinus Fieschi which was clearly of a secret nature as Edward III denied he had done it in his letter to the marshal of the king of Naples). Edward also sent him to Avignon that year (1336) to discuss his secret business with the pope, bringing the answer back by word of mouth. Thus Montefiore was conducting some aspect of Edward's 'secret business' at the same time as the Bardi and Peruzzi were undertaking to pay for it. If Edward III's unpaid acknowledgements of indebtedness for his secret business in the period 1335–7 were also due to Montefiore's activities, it is possible that Montefiore was passing some of Edward III's money to individuals directly or indirectly concerned with the keeping of Edward II. A stray account entry for £400 that escaped the auditors indicates that the Bardi were indeed paying Genoese men at Montefiore's direction. The entry states that 'by the view and testimony of Master Paul Montefiore they [the Bardi] delivered £400 to divers men of the parts of Genoa, by the king's order, for his affairs'.[52]

On 20 November 1338, not long after the delivery of 'William le Galeys' and a week before Edward III's massive gifts to the Bardi and Peruzzi and his commissions to Niccolinus Fieschi, the king issued an acquittance for all previous sums paid to Montefiore, who had provided the king with a full account of his expenditure in his service.[53] Montefiore continued to serve Edward after this, and undertook much wool business and other payments for the king, probably connected with the payment of Edward's German allies – who seem to have preferred payment in florins. But his fall from favour mirrored that of the Bardi and the Peruzzi. The parliament of June 1340 called for Montefiore's accounts to be investigated along with those of the bankers. On 12 May 1341 Edward summoned Montefiore from abroad to deliver his accounts personally, sending a safe-conduct the same day.[54] At that time Montefiore was staying in Bruges, attending to the residual payments connected with Edward's war in the Low Countries: he presumably did return by Michaelmas for the first commission to investigate his accounts was dated 4 October 1341. He was still trusted by the king as he was sent back to Germany to arrange for the redemption of the great crown, which Edward had pawned. But on the same day that the strengthened commission was ordered to investigate the Peruzzi and Bardi (5 February 1344) a similar commission of enquiry was set up to investigate his accounts.[55] Montefiore protested that he could not be called to account fairly because some of the payments he made did not have legal receipts which would be recognized by the Exchequer; accordingly a separate commission was ordered on 5 March 1344 to investigate his accounts since 20 November 1338.[56] The commissioners seem to have decided in his favour at first, for on 12 April 1346 Edward promised to pay Montefiore £716 3s 10d.[57] But by 4 February 1348 he needed royal protection from creditors, being 'held to the king in a great sum payable at certain terms'. He remained in that unfortunate state for the rest of his life.[58]

THE INDEBTEDNESS NARRATIVE

The foregoing sections collectively allow us to draw up a narrative of Edward III's indebtedness for his secret business. The first thing to note is that, from the outset, there was a financial element to English dealings with the papacy. In September 1329, in the wake of Kent's journey to Avignon that summer, Mortimer and Isabella sent ambassadors (William Montagu and Bartholomew Burghersh) offering to resume paying the 1,000 marks per year to the papal camera that King John had promised more than a century earlier and which had remained unpaid for more than thirty years (resulting in a debt of £22,000).[59] Then in March 1331 Edward built on this financial element, when he equipped two more diplomats to go to the pope and, if necessary, borrow £50,000 for his business. One of those same diplomats, Richard Bury was sent back to Avignon on 'secret business' in 1333, and paid the arrears due on the 1,000 marks for 1330 and 1331 and undertook further discussions, which resulted in the pope declaring he was minded to agree with Edward III's secret petition. Thus there seems to have been an agreement by the time of John XXII's death in 1334.

Benedict XII probably built on his predecessor's agreement. He had been part of the curia since 1327, so he would have known about the nature of Edward III's 'secret business' in 1333. Determined to prevent the war between England and the Franco-Scottish alliance, in August 1335 he equipped envoys with letters of credence for Edward, Queen Isabella, Queen Philippa and King Philip of France, and authorized the envoys to make peace between England and Scotland. All these letters of credence imply word-of-mouth messages.

Benedict XII's messages were followed in November 1335 by Edward III's renewed and enlarged acknowledgement of indebtedness to the Bardi. Soon afterwards, in April 1336, Edward started to acknowledge his indebtedness to the Peruzzi. Clearly the meetings at the Tower on 15–16 April 1336 were important, for they brought together the Peruzzi, the Bardi and Paul Montefiore, all of whom Edward acknowledged as undertaking his secret business over the next two years. Montefiore went to Avignon later that year and saw the pope, and tried to arrange for Genoese galleys to sail to Edward III from Nice; but he was stopped by King Robert of Naples. In the meantime Edward acknowledged more indebtedness for his secret business until late August 1337, when he ordered his accounts with the bankers and Paul Montefiore to be drawn up. Thereafter he set about starting to pay these debts, partly through assignments on subsidies, partly through cash payments and prests, and partly through the wool trade. In order to maximize their exploitation of the business arising, and perhaps to safeguard themselves against Edward III, the Peruzzi and Bardi joined forces and the head of the Peruzzi came to England.

In November 1338, Edward III acknowledged the services of the Bardi and Peruzzi through massive gifts: £30,000 to the Bardi; £20,000 to the Peruzzi; 500 marks to the daughter of Bonifazio Peruzzi; 500 marks to each of the wives of the two leading Bardi; £200 to the wife of Dino Forzetti; and £200 to the wife of Tommaso Peruzzi.[60] He also received Paul Montefiore's account for all the expenditure he had incurred on behalf of the king and acquitted him of all further liabilities arising from his account to 20 November 1338. After this he continued to pay the bankers through the wool business and to employ them to ransom the earl of Derby and to redeem the great crown; but in effect his need of them had passed by 1340.

In reviewing this 'indebtedness narrative', it is the temporal correlations with the survival narrative (as outlined in the previous chapter) that demand attention. To be specific:

1. In March 1331, at the same time or very shortly after Edward II arrived there (according to the Fieschi Letter), Edward III was prepared to offer someone at the papal court a sum of up to £50,000.

2. On 26 April 1331, a matter of days after Richard Bury returned from the abovementioned mission to Avignon, Archbishop Melton authorized a priest to serve in Cardinal Fieschi's household.

3. In February 1333 Niccolinus Fieschi arrived in England. Very shortly afterwards Richard Bury was sent again to Avignon on the king's secret business; and remained there until October, negotiating a secret deal with John XXII on Edward's behalf.

4. On 15 April 1336, the very day that Edward III began to acknowledge his indebtedness to the Peruzzi and Paul Montefiore for his overseas 'secret business', he created Niccolinus Fieschi a king's councillor at the Tower. This followed not long after the earliest date for the composition and despatch to England of the Fieschi Letter, which Niccolinus Fieschi may have brought with him.

5. In the autumn of 1336 Montefiore attempted to have galleys sent from Nice to Edward III by paying a large sum of money to Jacobo de Sarzana: a member of the household of the late Cardinal Fieschi. Edward later denied any responsibility in this contract, even though he was the instigator. This shows that at least some of the king's acknowledged indebtedness for his overseas 'secret business', for which Montefiore was later reimbursed by the Bardi and Peruzzi, was intended by Edward to be given to a long-standing connection of the Fieschi.

6. On 1–2 September 1337 Edward drew up final sums for what he owed the bankers and Paul Montefiore: this was just four or five days after he

had granted a safe-conduct to Cardinal Fieschi's co-heir and co-executor, Antonio Fieschi and the legal proctor of another of the cardinal's nephews, Bernabo Malaspina, to make their only known visit to England.

7. In early September 1338, Niccolinus Fieschi's nephew was paid at least £1,366 by the Bardi – for business that had been entrusted by the king to Niccolinus Fieschi and which involved bringing two galleys from Marseilles. His arrival and the completion of the mission coincides with Edward II being brought to Edward III as 'William le Galeys'.[61]

8. In late November 1338, one week after Paul Montefiore's account was signed off by Edward III, Niccolinus Fieschi was given a new commission and the Bardi and the Peruzzi were promised 'gifts' of more than £50,000 – far beyond the normal form of gift-giving to merchants.

9. In December 1339, one of the two men whom Edward commissioned to investigate the sequestration of the money which Montefiore was meant to have paid to Jacobo de Sarzana was Niccolinus Fieschi.

10. All the bankers, including Montefiore, began to fall rapidly from favour at about the time that Edward II was known to have died.

Six of these correlations between the 'indebtedness narrative' and the 'survival narrative' could be coincidental. Nos 1–4, 6, 8 and 10 are simply instances where an important meeting or development in the 'indebtedness narrative' happens to coincide with the 'survival narrative'. It may have been a coincidence that Edward III acknowledged his first indebtedness to the Peruzzi on 15 April 1336 – the same day that he granted £2,000 to Montefiore, the eventual recipient of much of the money he would hand over to the Peruzzi. Similarly it could be entirely coincidental that the king made Niccolinus Fieschi a royal councillor in the Tower that same day. However, the possibility that these six instances were coincidences does not mean that they were. This is especially the case as three of the above points are direct links between the separate agencies of 'survival' and 'indebtedness'. No. 5 shows that a portion of the money that Edward was promising to pay for his overseas 'secret business' in 1336 was intended to be handed to a recent employee of the late Cardinal Fieschi, Jacobo de Sarzana. No. 7 reveals that some of the money which Edward III paid to the Bardi went to Niccolinus Fieschi's nephew. No. 9 underlines the fact that Edward III's secret business involved Niccolinus Fieschi, for it shows that Edward knew Niccolinus understood the circumstances in which Montefiore had lost the above-mentioned money while dealing with Jacobo de Sarzana in 1336.[62]

In addition to the seven temporal correlations and three direct connections, there is one further piece of evidence that directly links the 'indebtedness narrative' and the 'survival narrative'. This is the identity of the Italian man who took the ex-king as 'William le Galeys' to Edward III at Koblenz. Forzetti is not a common name: it only occurs once in the *DBI* – in respect of Dino Forzetti, the English agent of the Bardi. Another Forzetti of roughly the same age, Francesco, was the Sicilian agent for the Peruzzi at this time. Two of Francesco's sons worked for the same company: Giovanni Forzetti (as a Sicilian factor) and Andrea Forzetti (in England).[63] It is likely that the Francisco or Francesco Forzetti who guarded the ex-king was some kin of this Florentine family. In fact it is highly likely – considering his links with the Bardi and Peruzzi. After the delivery of 'William le Galeys' in September 1338 his name does not appear in the English records until October 1340. Between that date and June 1342, Forzetti was authorized exclusively with respect to the joint venture of the Bardi and the Peruzzi to oversee the transportation of wool from England to the Mediterranean.[64] Although officially an English sergeant-at-arms, his duties were primarily to assist the Italian banking houses.[65] After June 1342 he only appears twice in the Patent Rolls and Close Rolls. In one of these entries he was ordered on 20 December 1342 to go to Haverfordwest and take a ship and its cargo intact to Bristol, as it had been seized by Rhys ap Gruffydd.[66] The last instruction to him was his appointment on 3 November 1344 to guard the manor of Eure, Bucks, belonging to Tedisio Benedicti of Falcinello in the Val di Magra, who was going on a pilgrimage on behalf of Queen Philippa.[67]

CONCLUSION

Most of the critical evidence on which one can assess Edward III's secret business has been destroyed – if it was ever written down. The schedule of payments for the bankers' liabilities drawn up in June 1340 names no names. Not one of Paul Montefiore's accounts is extant. It seems that Edward was as thorough in destroying these as he was in destroying his own chamberlain's accounts for this exact period, 1338–44. But as the investigation has gone on, and in the light of all of the above observations, especially the payments to Niccolo Bianco di

Fieschi, the role of Francisco Forzetti, and the channelling of large sums of money through the bankers to Paul Montefiore (and from him to Jacobo de Sarzana and other men of Genoa), it seems that Edward II's secret custody in Italy and Edward III's 'acknowledgements of indebtedness' in respect of his overseas secret business were more likely to have been connected than completely separate intrigues. Of course the bankers were paying other agencies by 1338 – such as the German princes and mercenaries – but this was not the limit of their activities, and they were not doing this before 1337. There can be little doubt that some of the indebtedness acknowledged by Edward III in 1335–7 was a consequence of the Fieschi's activities – and not just for providing a couple of galleys in 1338 but for providing reassurance to Edward III that his father was not going to fall into the hands of the king of France.

The combination of the 'indebtedness' and 'survival' narratives as outlined above would answer several important questions. It would explain why the Fieschi Letter was written: to convince Edward III his father was alive and not in danger of falling into the wrong hands. It would explain the nature of some of Edward III's overseas 'secret business'. It would explain the king's employment of an Italian, Niccolinus Fieschi, as one of his principal ambassadors at the papal court and in negotiations with the French, and why he became so important to Edward, and why the French kidnapped him. It would go some way to explaining why Edward pawned the royal crowns, including the great crown, to foreign merchants (mainly Italians); and why he redeemed them in 1342–4 (using the services of Italians: Paul Montefiore and Francisco Drizacorne).[68] Most of all, it would explain Edward III's acknowledgements of indebtedness, and especially how he could have acknowledged such huge debts to the Bardi and the Peruzzi in 1335–7 even though they did not have the funds to make payments on this scale on his behalf.

Lastly, the connection of the bankers with Edward II's custody would explain why Richard II settled his grandfather's debts to the Bardi in 1391. The settlement of the account coincided with Richard II's attempt to have Edward II recognized as a saint.[69] In 1390 Richard summoned several prelates and had a book of miracles that had been performed at Edward II's tomb drawn up and sent to the pope.[70] The business was entrusted to a monk of Gloucester, William Brut, but the pope did not immediately acquiesce to Richard's request. In November 1391 Richard drew up a close letter instructing the fifty-year-old Bardi debt to be paid in full and delivering a patent letter to the Bardi pardoning and discharging them of all money due from them to the king: in return for the payment they had to surrender all letters of obligation – including Edward III's letter patent of 1339 promising to give them £30,000.[71] The same month, Richard II gave a clerk, William de Storteford, a letter of protection for conducting 'certain business touching the king and realm' at Avignon.[72] De Storteford had not left London by 2 December 1391 but set out soon after, the Issue Rolls explaining that his mission was to petition the pope to recognize Edward II as a saint.[73] Thus the final payment to the Bardi, fifty years later, happens to coincide with Richard's second attempt to have Edward II canonized.[74] If Edward III's debts to the bankers were connected with papal custody of Edward II, it is possible that the outstanding Bardi debt had to be cleared first if the canonization was to go ahead. It is perhaps significant that one of the cardinals at Avignon at the time was one Ludovico Fieschi, son of Luca Fieschi's great-nephew and co-heir, Niccolo Fieschi. Although half a century had passed, it can hardly be doubted that the Fieschi experience had lived on. Ludovico was the third consecutive Fieschi to be bishop of Vercelli. His direct predecessor as bishop was Cardinal Fieschi's other great-nephew and co-heir, Giovanni Fieschi, and *his* direct predecessor was Manuele Fieschi himself.

We are left with the problem of scale. Although some 'secret business' money can be traced through the bankers and Montefiore to Niccolinus Fieschi and Jacobo de Sarzana, allowing no room for doubt that Edward II's survival cost Edward III financially, we have no way of knowing how much money was involved. We do not have Edward III's 'secret business' accounts – whether drawn up by the Bardi, the Peruzzi or Montefiore. We cannot say how much of Edward III's money, via the bankers, went from Montefiore to the pope (if any) and how much went to Jacobo de Sarzana, or other 'men from Genoa' (including Niccolinus Fieschi). We do not know how much of Montefiore's colossal budget was spent on German mercenaries – an intrigue of a relatively open nature. Much more research is required into the Italian bankers' links with the papacy and the Fieschi, and where Montefiore actually spent Edward III's money.[75] The 'combined narrative' should alert readers to the possibility of a considerable financial dimension to the pope's use of Edward II against Edward III, and maybe even that he tried to prevent war by extorting money from the warrior king, reducing his ability to pay an army. But the evidence that it exceeded the

£50,000 that Richard Bury and Antonio Pessagno were authorized to borrow is circumstantial. Only two things are absolutely certain. The first is that Edward III's secret business involved a number of royal intrigues and concerns in 1330–40 that academic historians have not previously dreamed of, let alone studied. The second is that, by 4 December 1344, when Edward destroyed his chamberlain's accounts, the two problems of his father's survival and his financial exploitation in respect of his 'secret business overseas' had both come to an end. From that point on he could concentrate on putting his resources fully towards his war with France. Suddenly that conflict became considerably more successful.

Notes

1 *CCR 1333–7*, 566–7.

2 *CPR 1334–8*, 249.

3 The first was a loan of £213 6s 8d acknowledged by Edward III on 3 February 1333. See *CPR 1330–4*, 397.

4 For Whissh, see the previous chapter. For the Bardi, see *CCR 1333–7*, 566.

5 Unwin, 'Estate of merchants', 183–4.

6 *Perfect King*, 187.

7 Villani's condemnation was broadly accepted by historians until Hunt demonstrated the fallibility of the argument in *Super-companies* in 1994. On p. 6 Hunt draws attention to Ormrod, Sumption and Waugh, all of whom have blamed the banking collapse on Edward III's failure to pay his debts.

8 This appears as £800 in *AEC*, 180–1.

9 *AEC*, 178–83. Note: the heading of this document (TNA E101/127/27) states it ended on '25 April 1332'. Reference to the text states '*anno quint*' (25 April 1331) which seems to be correct. There are no payments after that date in the document.

10 *AEC*, 184–5, 198.

11 *Super-companies*, 188 n. 17.

12 *Super-companies*, 184, 188 n. 11. This was for reasons that 'are not immediately apparent', according to Hunt. It is worth noting that in May 1335 Edward summoned representatives of the Peruzzi as well as the Bardi to him at York, to advise him on the papal tenth granted in 1333 and to advise the king and council 'because the king expects that their advice will be most opportune for the completion and happy disposition of the said affair'. *CCR 1333–7*, 486. However, given the distances involved, and the time taken in travel, this summons is unlikely by itself to have triggered the restructuring of the Peruzzi.

13 *CPR 1334–8*, 515, 517.

14 *CCR 1337–9*, 196, 205–6.

15 *CPR 1334–8*, 517, 541. The Church forbade the payment of interest, so the king made 'gifts' or paid 'regard' money, in lieu of losses and service.

16 For instance Edward's promise to pay the Bardi 500 marks for his 'secret business' on 20 August 1337, and his promise to repay the Peruzzi £2,000 which they had paid 'beyond the seas for the furtherance of pressing and secret business' on 1 September 1338. See *CPR 1334–8*, 507, 515.

17 *CPR 1338–40*, 11.

18 Edward gave permission to the Peruzzi to send a ship from Spain to export wool on 2 November 1337 (*CPR 1334–8*, 543). The joint Bardi and Peruzzi wool account begins in 1338. See *AEC*, 225.

19 *Super-companies*, 190–1.

20 *Super-companies*, 192–3.

21 *Super-companies*, 192; *CCR 1337–9*, 206.

22 Sapori, 150; *CPR 1334–8*, 343.

23 *Super-companies*, 202.

24 See Sumption, *Trial by Battle*, 192. He states that the end of October 1336 'almost certainly, was when the plans of the next three years were first mooted. During the first three months of the new year [1337] there were no less than three separate English embassies at work on Imperial territory'.

25 *AEC*, 204. Note the regnal years are inconsistent.

26 *Super-companies*, 209–10, quoting E. B. Fryde, 'Edward III's War Finance, 1337–41: transactions in wool and credit operations' (DPhil thesis, University of Oxford, 1947), appendix B.

27 With regard to the date of Bonifazio's arrival being 1338 and not 1339, see *Super-companies*, 199. With regard to his comments on the move – that it was 'startling' – see ibid., 34.

28 For the Peruzzi immunity see *CPR 1334–8*, 506; for the Fieschi, see *CPR 1334–38*, 487 (dated 28 August).

29 *CPR 1338–40*, 123.

30 *CCR 1337–9*, 467; *CPR 1338–40*, 255.

31 *Super-companies*, 208–11.

32 *CPR 1340–2*, 87.

33 *AEC*, 212–22.

34 *CPR 1343–5*, 467–8; *AEC*, 212.

35 *CPR 1340–3*, 247.

36 *CPR 1340–3*, 558. *Super-companies*, 227, notes that an earlier commission in 1340 had not touched the Peruzzi and Bardi.

37 *CCR 1343–6*, 106.

38 *Super-companies*, 229.

39 *CCR 1343–6*, 360.

40 *AEC*, 242–65.

41 *CPR 1343–5*, 265, 269; *CCR 1346–9*, 53–4.
42 Russell, 'Bardi and Peruzzi', 129, quoting Bond (ed.), 'Liberate Rolls', appendix, cci–ccii.
43 *CPR 1343–5*, 467–8; *AEC*, 212.
44 *AEC*, 209.
45 *AEC*, 252.
46 *AEC*, 264.
47 *AEC*, 254.
48 *CCR 1337–9*, entries under 3 March and 5 May.
49 *CEPR*, ii, 336 (from Fermo); *CPR 1321–4*, 355 (proctor).
50 *CPR 1327–30*, 420; *CPR 1330–4*, 337; *CPR 1334–8*, 29.
51 *CPR 1334–8*, 336.
52 *CCR 1343–6*, 330 (12 July 1344).
53 *CPR 1343–5*, 276, 285; *CPR 1334–8*, 194–5. This notes that Montefiore has rendered a 'reasonable and clear account' of 'sums of money for the furtherance of business enjoined on him by the king' and acquits him of the need to render further account.
54 *CCR 1341–3*, 135; *CPR 1340–3*, 188.
55 *CPR 1343–5*, 154 (crown), 276 (enquiry).
56 *CPR 1343–5*, 276, 285.
57 *CPR 1345–8*, 69.
58 *CPR 1348–50*, 21. His later life may be summarized as follows. Shortly this first protection he was declared to have obtained the prebend of South Cave (which had previously been held by his old employer, Cardinal Orsini) illegally from the pope; and the king revoked his ratification of that estate. Soon afterwards he was in the Fleet Prison. He was eventually released and spent the rest of his life as warden of the hospital of St Katherine in London (*CPR 1350–4*, 357). He had to obtain the king's protection from creditors every year, still being 'bound to the king in a great sum'. The last such protection is dated 18 January 1357, after which he probably died (*CPR 1354–8*, 491).
59 Lunt, 66–7. Note, this was the same mission that carried Edward III's famous letter signed 'Pater Sancte', wishing to disassociate himself from the commands of Mortimer and Isabella issued in his name.
60 *CPR 1338–40*, 195. These 'gifts' enrolled on 28 November were later marked *vacat* (revoked) but identical 'gifts' of £30,000 to the Bardi and £20,000 to the Peruzzi appear on the Patent Roll for the following year (28 June and 30 June 1339) and these are not marked *vacat*, being made 'in remembrance of their timely subsidies for the king's service' (*CPR 1338–40*, 388, 392).
61 TNA E43/716 (receipt for £1,000); *AEC*, 202 (two payments: one of £366 and another of £333 13s 4d).
62 In such circumstances it is perhaps worth noting that among the possessions of Cardinal's Fieschi distributed after his death were several gifts to the head of the

Bardi. See Sisto, 221 (*Gerardus de Bardis unam crucem cum perlis* . . .), 251–2 (*Gerardus de Bardi de societate de Bardorum de Florentia unum breviarum magni unam* . . . *Bibliam magnam* . . .).

63 For Giovani, see Sapori, 11, 28, 43, 53, 120–1, 188, 194, 247–8, 264–5, 310; for Andrea, see *Super-companies*, 237, n. 23.

64 *Perfect King*, 497 n. 7, quoting *CPR 1340–3*, 45, 75, 145, 174.

65 *Perfect King*, 464, n. 56.

66 *CPR 1340–3*, 589.

67 *CPR 1343–5*, 565.

68 For Drizacorne, see *Foedera* (Rymer), v, 316, 341. The latter, which refers to the redemption of the queen's crown, is dated 15 September 1342. For Montefiore, see *CPR 1343–5*, 154 (26 Dec. 1343), 527 (10 July 1345).

69 This was a process that Richard II had begun in February 1385, with the appointment of John Bacon and Nicolas Dagworth as ambassadors to the pope (Perroy (ed.), *Diplomatic Correspondence*, 210). On 7 December that same year Richard II acknowledged that he was indebted to the Bardi to the tune of £4,252 15s 7d, and would give them a further £800 (*CPR 1385–9*, 60). This was replaced by an acknowledgement of indebtedness the same day for £5,000 (*CPR 1385–9*, 74.) The money seems not to have been paid, however, and nor did the canonization take place.

70 Perroy (ed.), *Diplomatic Correspondence*, 210 (95).

71 *Super-companies*, 205 n. 88, 242.

72 *CPR 1389–92*, 513. The original letter patent of protection does not appear on the Patent Rolls.

73 *Issues*, 247–8. De Storteford was given 40 marks and a further 52 marks were handed over to pay certain proctors, notaries and scribes at Avignon

74 This second attempt was, like the first, unsuccessful. So too was the third attempt in 1395–6. See Perroy (ed.), *Diplomatic Correspondence*, 210 (95).

75 For example, it is entirely possible that sums of money were channelled to Avignon via the Hospitallers, who had accumulated £60,000 in deposits with the bankers by 1343 and were routinely passing large sums to the papal treasury. See *Super-companies*, 234.

8

Richard II and the succession to the Crown[*]

The question of the succession in the period 1376–99 has vexed historians for many centuries. In the past it was frequently subjected to historical scrutiny either because it was seen as the cause of the Wars of the Roses – did the house of Lancaster have a greater right to the throne than that of York? – or because the process whereby Henry IV became king (by parliamentary election, by conquest or by succession) was crucial to the debate about the Lancastrian experiment in parliamentary government. Certainly there was discussion about the succession before the end of Richard's reign: it was unavoidable, for the king had failed to sire any offspring in twelve years of marriage, had lost his wife in 1394, and subsequently married a minor. But, with two notable exceptions, historians have construed the question as a legal problem, not a matter of royal nomination or a consequence of political bargaining in Richard's lifetime.[1] To quote Nigel Saul on the subject: 'by tradition, if not by law, the throne of England descended by primogeniture; and if tradition were followed, and Richard were to remain childless, the heir would have been the young earl of March, Roger Mortimer'.[2] Although most writers, including Saul, acknowledge that the situation was considerably more complicated than this, no one has yet tackled the question from Richard's point of view nor identified his strategy for the succession and how he manipulated this to his own political advantage.

It is not difficult to make a case that the royal will was of considerable importance in determining the succession, especially where the matter was in doubt. In 1376, as Prince Edward neared death, the question of the heir to the throne was raised and quickly determined by the king in favour of

---

[*] This essay was first published in *History: The Journal of the Historical Association* in July 2006 (vol. 91, issue 3, 320–36). It is reproduced here in its original form except for the stylistic changes necessary for consistency within this volume and the excision of the final endnote, which has been rendered superfluous by the subject being treated fully in the next chapter.

Richard of Bordeaux in accordance with the popular feeling and parliamentary representations. This is in line with the primogeniture 'tradition' mentioned above. However, even in 1376 the succession was not a foregone conclusion. The dying prince himself seems not to have presumed that his son would inherit the throne, asking both his father and his brother, John of Gaunt, to swear an oath to protect Richard and to uphold him in his inheritance.[3] In the only previous example of a succession dispute between a king's younger son and his grandson by a deceased heir apparent (King John and Arthur of Brittany in 1199), the principle of primogeniture had failed. Although twelfth-century legal writers had been divided over the issue, the events of 1199 did set a precedent which remained unchallenged until Edward III simply disregarded it, albeit with the consent of a parliament which was heavily prejudiced against John of Gaunt. Certainly King Edward and others of the court circle believed that he had the right to establish the line of succession without reference to parliament, as this is implicit in his entail of the throne on his heirs male. This chapter argues that Richard II also believed he had the power to determine his successor and tried to implement it in the early 1390s to eradicate the claim of the Lancastrians.

Any consideration of Richard's views on the succession has to begin with Edward III's entail of the crown. This remarkable document states that in late 1376 or very early 1377 Edward settled the order of succession in tail male, removing the Mortimers (children of Philippa, the only child of Lionel of Antwerp, Edward III's third son) from the line of inheritance.[4] The measure was partly a result of the actions of the Mortimer steward, Sir Peter de la Mare, against several court favourites, including the king's long-standing mistress, Alice Perrers, during the 1376 parliament. It was also a retort to the conclusions of the council, headed by the earl of March, which threw out Gaunt's request during this parliament to bar the succession through females.[5] However, King Edward's motives are less important than his actions: the key point is that he had this document drawn up and witnessed. It may also have been enrolled, for although it does not survive in the original or on any of the relevant rolls, the membrane may have been removed in the fifteenth century when the extant copy was made, or even during Richard's reign.[6] Either way, those who witnessed it were aware that it made Gaunt the heir apparent, and after him, his son, Henry of Bolingbroke. The order after that would have been (in 1377) Edmund of Langley (later duke of York), then his sons, Edward (later earl of Rutland, then duke of

Aumale) and Richard (later earl of Cambridge), and lastly Thomas of Woodstock (later duke of Gloucester).

Who else knew of the entail? It is reasonable to presume that Richard was made aware of it early in his reign, if not before. It is similarly reasonable to presume that Gaunt and Edward's other sons – potential beneficiaries – were privy to its contents. Also in the know would have been the chancellor, treasurer, chamberlain, keeper of the privy seal, steward and all those other members of the court who witnessed the document (including William Latimer, Sir John Burley, Sir Richard Sturry, Sir Philip Vache, Colard d'Aubridgecourt, John Salisbury and Walter Walsh). But beyond that it is very difficult to make a case that this document was accepted or even openly discussed. No chronicler mentions it. Walsingham, who took a particular interest in the succession debate, was certain of the earl of March's claim to be next in line.[7] So too was the Westminster chronicler.[8] It is possible that even the young earl of March himself was unaware of it in January 1394 when he argued against its implications, apparently in ignorance of its provisions.[9] There is also circumstantial evidence of its secretive state: if it was widely known that Edward had effectively determined that Gaunt was Richard's heir, then there would have been uproar because Gaunt was extraordinarily unpopular in the years 1376–81. There is, however, no evidence of uproar against Gaunt on account of the succession after Edward's death. The whole succession question was only relevant if Richard had no children, and there would have been no point in drawing public attention to this document and stirring up the anti-Gaunt discontent while Richard's potency to sire an heir was still unknown. Thus its existence and the potential benefits to the Lancastrians remained virtually a political secret.

Nevertheless, the limited currency of this knowledge does not mean it had little effect. After learning of the contents of the document, Richard would have understood it to mean that in the event of his death without male issue, he would be succeeded by Gaunt, and after the latter's death, by his son, Henry of Bolingbroke. There are at least two further pieces of independent evidence for this. During the parliament of April–May 1384, a Carmelite friar, John Latimer, claimed that Gaunt was planning to murder Richard so that he could seize the throne. Richard instantly ordered Gaunt to be executed without even interrogating him.[10] This shows that Richard could easily believe – with no need for further evidence – that Gaunt stood to inherit. It also suggests that Richard believed Gaunt had a motive for bringing about his death. This awareness in court circles that Gaunt was the heir apparent in 1385 is further supported by the chronicler Jean Froissart, who heard that Michael de la Pole had told Richard in the summer of 1385, 'the duke of Lancaster wishes for nothing more earnestly than your death, that he may be king'.[11] This seems to be reliable and part of a structured political narrative, not mere storytelling by Froissart. Not only did he have access to members of the court for his information, he also reported the conversation between de la Pole and Richard as a prelude to the well-evidenced argument between Richard and Gaunt about whether to advance north from Edinburgh. In this argument Richard stated his fears that he might be killed and voiced his suspicions of Gaunt's treasonable motives in urging him to advance.[12] Richard's propensity to believe that Gaunt stood to inherit the throne is good evidence that he was aware of Gaunt's prior position in the succession over the Mortimers, according to Edward III's entail.

This raises the matter of whether Richard tried to influence the succession question himself. As is well known, in the parliament of October–December 1385 he is supposed to have announced that Roger Mortimer, earl of March, was the heir to the throne.[13] This has become something of an issue in its own right. The author of Mortimer's entry in the *ODNB* dismisses this claim as 'without foundation', and many other well-respected writers in the past have accorded it no greater credibility.[14] G. L. Harriss's volume in the *New Oxford History of England* does not mention it at all.[15] Such refusals to countenance contemporary narratives are potentially misleading. As shown below, the chronicle in question was written by a contemporary whose work is marred mainly by chronological errors (not descriptions of events, about which it is generally accurate). Furthermore, it is supported by a reliable contemporary chronicle written at Westminster and only a few hundred yards from where the declaration is supposed to have been made. Three scholars who have recently considered the matter – Chris Given-Wilson, Michael Bennett and Nigel Saul – have all agreed that Richard may well have declared the Mortimers heirs to the throne.[16] Bennett and Saul have in fact arrived at almost identical conclusions: that Richard preferred the claim of the Mortimers in the 1380s but in the 1390s his liking for them diminished, leaving only doubts about the succession, an outcome which was wholly to Richard's advantage. In Bennett's words, 'Richard II seems to have seen more advantage in creating doubt rather than certainty', or, as Saul would have it, 'his chosen policy appears to have been to keep people guessing. He did everything in his power to prevent the emergence of a front-runner'.[17]

The problem with these analyses is not so much that they are wrong as they lack precision and thus create more problems than they solve. Both Saul and Bennett presume that the date usually assigned to this declaration – 1385 – should be taken at face value. If so, the implication would be that Gaunt dined with the king on the penultimate night of the parliament in which he had been ruled out of the succession. This does not ring true, especially given that Gaunt received at least two personal favours from the king during and after that parliament.[18] Saul's view that Roger Mortimer's claim to the throne was 'better' than that of Bolingbroke cannot be accepted without further evidence, both with regard to law (given the precedent of 1199 and Edward III's entail) and with regard to Richard's intentions (the king did nothing to advance his Mortimer cousins after 1394).[19] Similarly, Saul's statement that 'in the mid 1380s Richard was on particularly bad terms with Gaunt and may have wanted to spite him by promoting the cause of his young cousin' is a broad-brush approach to what is a fine point of detail.[20] Although Richard had attempted to murder Gaunt in February 1385, and they argued bitterly on the Scottish campaign that summer, they had made up their differences by October, as is shown by their dining together during that parliament and the several favours shown to Gaunt mentioned above. They remained on good terms the following March, and they and their wives exchanged precious gifts and said fond farewells when Gaunt and Constance departed for Castile in March 1386.[21] Nor is there conclusive evidence to suggest that Richard deliberately created the confusion as to his successor's identity which clouds historians' minds today. Indeed, given the need for an order of precedence to be observed at almost all formal and informal occasions – courtly as well as parliamentary – Richard could hardly have avoided acknowledging those who stood highest in status and closest to the throne. While Saul may be correct to assert that 'at no time did he [Richard] nominate a successor',[22] it would have been obvious to all those present which lord normally took precedence over the others at court. For these reasons, the broad-brush approach to the specific question of the succession is inappropriate.

Richard's declaration that Roger Mortimer was his heir is mentioned only in one chronicle, the continuation of the *Eulogium Historiarum*. This is not without its problems.[23] First, there is no supporting information on the relevant parliamentary roll. Second, if Roger Mortimer was placed in such a position of prominence, why was he never elevated to a dukedom or marquisate by Richard, to reflect his status? Third, the *Eulogium* is not generally regarded as a reliable source. In particular, if the announcement was made as publicly as the writer of the *Eulogium* says – 'in the hearing of all the lords and commons' – then it is surprising that no other contemporary writer mentions it. These points, together with those mentioned above regarding Richard's relationship with Gaunt during and after the parliament of 1385, are the principal reasons why many writers have felt justified in rejecting this evidence and the event it describes.

Under more intense scrutiny, however, the objections appear superficial. For a start, there is no reason why an announcement about the king's intention should appear on the Parliament Roll. There was no official position of 'heir presumptive' and so the king's expression of will did not necessarily result in a formal enrolment. As for Roger Mortimer's title, it would have been both premature and controversial to advance him to a dukedom in the 1380s. Richard had great difficulty in the parliament of 1385 elevating Robert de Vere to a marquisate and Michael de la Pole to an earldom. Furthermore, if Richard's prime motive for naming Mortimer was to use his royal status to threaten the Lancastrians, there would have been no advantage in increasing his status and potential authority then, especially given that he might become a thorn in Richard's side in later years. In addition, the leader of the Mortimer family during Roger's youth – Sir Thomas Mortimer, his uncle – was the steward of the earl of Arundel, the king's most outspoken critic. Thomas sided with the Appellants in 1387–8, estranging his young charge still further from Richard's circle.[24] Roger Mortimer's value to Richard in the mid-1380s was thus as an alternative to Gaunt and his heirs, who was himself young and weak and therefore unable to threaten Richard.

The third problem with the continuation of the *Eulogium* is the question of its reliability. It suffers from severe chronological inconsistencies and in many places its dating of events is completely wrong. If it was written after 1428, as suggested by the reference to the disinterment of Wycliffe, then it is a late record too. However, although there are several post-1398 entries, there are also phrases which indicate a smaller and more coherent original text, which must have been in progress before 1404.[25] In addition, it has to be stressed that the chronicle's unreliability lies not so much in its descriptions of events as in the dates it assigns to them. In listing the creations associated with the 1385 parliament – an entry often cited as an example of the chronicle's unreliability – it is actually correct in its identifications of all seven men and their corresponding titles and only inaccurate regarding their dates of creation.[26] Similarly the reference to Wycliffe's burial at Lutterworth is quite correct, but the date of his death was 1384, not 1388.[27] With regard to the proceedings of the 1386 parliament, about which it gives a good account, there are no noticeable errors, and it gives several details not found in other chronicles which are either supported by record evidence or so likely that historians have accepted them.[28] Indeed, with reference to the period as a whole, the continuator displays general accuracy in events, if not dates. Like Adam Usk – who is usually accepted as a 'reliable' chronicler of this period – the author had 'more thought for the truth of what happened than for the order in which it happened'.[29]

On this basis it seems most unwise to dismiss Richard's declaration in favour of the Mortimers as 'without foundation'. There are also good reasons to believe that Richard's declaration was not made in the 1385 parliament but in that of 1386, and that a later interpolation has displaced the entry from the description of the parliament to which it originally related. To be exact: the original pre-1404 continuator ignored the parliament of 1385 but described that of 1 October–28 November 1386 in detail, and followed it with the statement that the earl of Arundel was named as Keeper of the Seas (10 December 1386) and that 'by the London crier the king ordered Michael de la Pole to be called earl of Suffolk and restored him to liberty' after the dissolution of the 1386 parliament.[30] Then a later writer (probably the post-1428 copyist) added the entry 'however in the ninth year of Richard's reign [June 1385–June 1386], the king held a great parliament at Westminster in which ... Michael de la Pole was made earl of Suffolk'. With the use of the word 'however' (*autem*) and his reference back to an earlier parliament, this is clearly a later interpolation, included to correct the pre-1404 continuator's dating of Suffolk's creation from 1386 to 1385. This is immediately followed by the entry beginning 'and it was in this parliament' that Roger Mortimer was declared the heir to the throne, which is then followed by an explanation that he 'was later killed in Ireland' in 1398.[31] This second element is also a later interpolation. The later copyist, having just written that Mortimer was named Richard's heir to the throne in the 1380s, anticipated that his post-1428 audience might wonder why he did not inherit the throne in 1399, and so he added the phrase about his death in Ireland. The key point is that the need for such an explanation shows that the entry naming Mortimer as the heir apparent was part of the original pre-1404 continuator's work. Thus the original pre-1404 continuator included the entry that Mortimer was declared the heir 'in this parliament' not in relation to the parliament of 1385 (which the pre-1404 continuator did not mention at all) but to that of 1386 (about which he was well informed).

The re-dating of Richard's declaration to the parliament of 1386 explains many things. Gaunt and Richard did not fall out over this matter because Gaunt was in Castile and not present at the 1386 parliament. The leading Lancastrian representative on that occasion was Henry, earl of Derby, whose outburst took the form of his siding with the Appellants the following year. In addition, Henry was both a blood relation and a close ally of the two men who went to the king from the 1386 parliament to threaten him with deposition, namely Thomas of Woodstock and Thomas Arundel. This gives a context to the declaration, for the accepted process of deposition was to force the king to abdicate in favour of an heir.[32] Richard was hardly likely to acknowledge that he would have to resign in favour of Henry if he had an alternative. Thus, there were good reasons for Richard to declare publicly that his successor would be a twelve-year-old boy. It was a swiping blow to Henry's supporters and a sharp reminder to all at that parliament that his youthful successor's ruling abilities might be no greater than his own.

This new analysis also goes some way to explaining why no other chronicles mention this announcement.[33] The question of the succession was just one of many important developments in the parliament of 1386; the bigger picture was one of parliamentary revolt. In addition, given that the entail was not widely known, an announcement that Roger Mortimer was the heir would simply have confirmed what many of those present at that parliament already believed. If the Crown had passed in the same way as other titles not strictly entailed on male descendants, it would certainly have descended to Lionel's daughter and then to her children, not to his younger brother. The only reason to see the supposed declaration of the succession of the earl of March (Lionel's heir general) as sufficiently worthy of comment in 1386 is if both the chronicler and the bearer of the news to him already knew or suspected that the Crown of England was subject to an entail male. Thus there are two good reasons why no other extant chronicles mention this announcement: it was of little news value except to those few who knew about the entail and it was overshadowed by the most significant and dramatic crisis of Richard's reign before 1399.

There are two further pieces of evidence to back up the *Eulogium* continuator's statement about the declaration. First, the Westminster chronicler recorded that the Mortimer brothers (Roger and Edmund) were the heirs apparent.[34] This was made in relation to a description of the members of the royal family following an entry for June 1387, and thus was temporally located – if not written – just a few months after the October 1386 parliament at which the declaration was made. It was also composed very near to the Palace of Westminster where the declaration would have been made, and by a monk who would have had access to the abbot, who was present in that parliament.[35] The second piece of evidence is the fact that the *Eulogium* continuator took a special interest in the succession question, and accurately reported such matters. In connection with the parliament of January 1394, he recorded that Gaunt requested that his son, Henry, be recognized as the heir to the throne.[36] The strangeness of the request – for his son to be the heir and not Gaunt himself – militates against it being the result of common rumour, and caused the later copyist to introduce another inaccurate explanatory interpolation.[37] But there is a simple explanation for Gaunt making this request. Richard was about to go to Ireland: so who was to be keeper of the realm in his absence? Normally this position indicated who was next in line to the throne (excepting those who were also abroad).[38] Gaunt himself could not have been appointed, as he was about to leave for Aquitaine.[39] According to the entail, it should have fallen to Henry. Thus Gaunt may well have asked that his son be confirmed as the heir apparent or keeper of the realm. According to the continuator, this request met with stiff opposition from the twenty-year-old Roger Mortimer.[40] He goes on to say that Richard did not side with either party, requiring them both to be quiet. Although this failure to support Mortimer appears contrary to Richard's 1386 announcement in his favour, it is in fact an accurate summary of the position he took in 1394. After delaying some months, he appointed neither claimant, preferring instead the duke of York. The unexpected accuracy of the continuator's reporting of this matter supports his other statement touching the succession under the year 1386.

Throughout the foregoing arguments it is important to preserve a clear distinction between two constituencies of knowledge: those who knew about Edward III's entail and those who did not. Those who were in the know were few in number, and of high rank or closely associated with the court. Thus for the majority, who did not know about the entail, it was not of great or lasting importance whether Richard made an announcement about the succession in 1386. They already assumed that Roger Mortimer was the rightful heir, and it was more important to them that Richard had been threatened with deposition. However, for those few who did know about the entail, Richard's declaration was a direct challenge to the Lancastrian position in the order of succession. Given that the *Eulogium* continuator was an accurate reporter of such matters, and that the reasons for dismissing the announcement are without substance, it would appear that Richard did state in the parliament of October 1386 that his heir was the twelve-year-old earl of March. But this was merely a political ruse, and a short-lived one at that. Not only did Richard fail to reverse Edward III's entail in favour of the Mortimers, he accepted it, and tried to work around it. His declaration that Roger Mortimer was the heir to the throne was not a promise to the Mortimers but a response to the threat of deposition and a counter-threat to the pro-Lancastrian opposition, showing them that he could remove Henry from the succession at will.

The evidence for Richard's acceptance of Edward III's entail lies in the Charter Rolls' witness lists. These preserve the order of seniority of the various magnates who were named. Royal peers were accorded precedence over peers of a similar type in relation to their closeness to the Crown so that Edmund of Langley (as a royal earl) was named before Edmund Mortimer (a non-royal earl even though he was married to Edward III's granddaughter) in charters from the 1370s.[41] The order of precedence accorded to the sons of these two earls in the 1390s therefore is significant. Roger Mortimer's name first appears in the witness lists on 5 March 1394: from then onwards it was placed below that of Edward, earl of Rutland.[42] This can only be explained through their relative positions in proximity to the Crown, for the earldom of March (1328–30, restored 1354) was older than that of Rutland (1390), and so Rutland was not preferred on the seniority of his title. That Roger Mortimer was accorded some royal status as heir general of one of Edward III's sons is evident in his title of March being given precedence over older earldoms, for instance Arundel, Warwick and Northumberland. The only earl who took precedence over Rutland in the period 1393–7 was Henry, earl of Derby.[43] This is wholly consistent with Edward III's entail: Derby (heir male of Edward III's fourth son) took precedence over Rutland (heir male of the fifth son), who took precedence over the earl of March (heir general of the third son). It follows that the announcement of 1386 was only a notional or temporary elevation of the Mortimers. By the end of the parliament of January–March 1394 Richard II had decided not to recognize the right of females to pass on a claim to the throne (except in the absence of a male heir). This reverses the traditional understanding of the importance of primogeniture, on which basis Saul suggested that Roger Mortimer was rightfully Richard II's heir.

Such a radical change of attitude on Richard's part – from threatening the Lancastrians with demotion to according them more openly the status of heirs apparent – is exemplified in Richard's change of heart towards Gaunt. By 1389, when he rode out to greet Gaunt on his return from Castile and took the Lancastrian livery collar and put it around his own neck, he had experienced a magnate rebellion – that of the Appellants – and had probably seen his kingship placed in abeyance for a few days in December 1387. The reason for the very short period of his loss of regnal authority is usually said to have been the failure of Thomas of Woodstock and Henry of Bolingbroke to agree on who should be king in his place.[44] This has much to recommend it, but for a more specific reason than that normally given. It is reasonable to presume that Henry maintained that his father should be king. The obvious objections to this were Gaunt's absence in Castile and his unpopularity with the English people in general and parliament in particular. Henry could hardly insist on his own claim, as his father was still in good health and Henry himself not yet twenty-one. So the compromise of Richard's second chance at reigning was agreed. It was either that or the abandonment of Edward III's entail. Hence this decision marks a significant diplomatic success for Henry: he managed to preserve the Lancastrian position in the line of succession through not giving in to his fellow Appellants' attempts to divert the Crown in another direction, presumably towards Thomas of Woodstock. It might even be suggested that Henry did a deal with Richard, especially given the fact that Henry, alone of the Appellants, remained with Richard and dined with him after the crisis was over.[45] Both men would have realized that, after five years of marriage, Richard's prospects for fatherhood did not look good. His union with his queen, Anne of Bohemia, had proved unproductive and yet she was young, and might even outlive him, still in a barren state. He may even have been averse to sexual union, as Nigel Saul has suggested, because he swiftly married a girl so young that she could not have been expected to produce an heir for several years.[46] If Richard was resigned to childlessness, there would have been good sense in him doing a deal with his cousin. Henry might have helped to restore Richard in 1387 on the condition that he thereafter maintained the line of succession implied by Edward III's entail.

Whether as part of a deal or not, Richard did recognize the entail, in so far as it precluded the inheritance of the Mortimers. As mentioned above, the *Eulogium* continuator states that in January 1394 Gaunt petitioned the king to recognize Henry as his heir. If the continuator reported Roger Mortimer's objection correctly, it shows that Mortimer either did not know about Edward III's entail or he believed that it had been set aside in the 1386 parliament or at some other time. Ominously, Richard did not support Mortimer in January 1394, and before the end of the parliament recognized the Lancastrian precedence implied by the entail. Richard gave Mortimer the consolation of possession of his vast English and Welsh estates in February 1394 and sent him on an embassy to Scotland. But he did nothing to support his claim to the throne whatsoever. His policy was to rid himself of the possible threat posed by Mortimer by keeping him away from court. He took him to Ireland himself in September 1394, and left him there, as Lieutenant, for most of the rest of his short life. Wishing to test his loyalty in 1397, he gave him an impossible task, the arrest of his own uncle, Sir Thomas Mortimer, who had brought him up and whom he was protecting from Richard. Of course, Roger Mortimer failed the test, and incurred Richard's anger. He was not elevated to a dukedom on 29 September 1397, when the heirs male of Gaunt and Edmund of York were created dukes of Hereford and Aumale respectively, and his position in the order of precedence sank lower with the creation of three dukes (Surrey, Exeter and Norfolk) and one marquis (Dorset). He was summoned to the prorogued parliament in January 1398 and received a hero's reception when he arrived at Westminster. Twenty thousand turned out to see him, according to Usk, which, even though it is probably a gross exaggeration, is probably sufficient indication to conclude that many of the populace still believed that the rightful line of succession lay in the Mortimer family, and wished to demonstrate in his favour as a protest against Richard.[47] But as far as Richard was concerned, Mortimer did not feature in the order of succession. Shortly before Mortimer's death in Ireland (20 July 1398), Richard discussed the succession with Sir William Bagot: on that occasion Edward, duke of Aumale, and Henry, duke of Hereford, were the alternative candidates, not Mortimer.[48] By then Richard had ordered in parliament that those harbouring or assisting Sir Thomas Mortimer were to be regarded as traitors, and this category included Roger Mortimer.[49] The Mortimer claim was never anything more than an unofficial, popular one, despite the declaration of 1386. It was never recognized, for the king had the right to adjudge his successor where the matter was in doubt. Edward III had ruled the Mortimers out of the succession through his entail, and Richard never officially ruled them back in.

If Richard had accepted Edward III's entail by 1394, does this mean that Henry of Bolingbroke was considered his legal heir (in court circles, at least) in 1399? Logically, if Richard adopted the entail, then after Gaunt's death, Henry was next in line to the throne. If so, then it would follow that, when Richard resigned the throne to him in 1399, he was simply doing so in favour of his legal heir, just as Edward II had done in January 1327.

Although Richard clearly used the entail to bar the Mortimers from the throne, he did not follow it as far as respecting Henry's precedence over Edmund of Langley. Despite Gaunt's plea for his son to be recognized, it was Edmund who was appointed keeper of the realm in September 1394. This deviation from the entail cannot be explained by the prospect of Henry travelling abroad, like his father; he had no official appointments overseas, nor did he travel privately. Rather this seems to be the moment when Richard decided that Edmund of Langley would be his heir. There is further evidence of this from the period 1397–9. As a duke, Edmund was accorded precedence of title over Henry (who was still an earl) until 1397. However, when Henry became duke of Hereford, allowing his royal status to be compared with that of his father's younger brother, Edmund remained above Henry.[50] In two of the last charters which Richard granted, on 20 March 1399 and 6 April 1399, 'Edmund, duke of York, our very dear uncle' appears above the bishops in the witness lists.[51] Such raising of a duke over the religious lords in a charter was unprecedented (although it was common practice in the rolls of parliament), and probably reflects an elevated status after Richard believed that he had finally eradicated the Lancastrian claim to the throne by revoking Henry's pardon and confiscating the Lancastrian inheritance. Even before this, Richard honoured Edmund's son, Edward, with references to the precedence of the house of York over that of Lancaster. He stated to Bagot in 1398 that he would in due course resign the throne to Edward but not Henry.[52] After Edward was created duke of Aumale in September 1397,

Richard habitually referred to him as 'our very dear brother', having apparently adopted him as such (they were actually first cousins).[53] Finally, in his will of 17 April 1399, Richard made arrangements to leave the residue of his money to his 'successor', subject to him observing a number of parliamentary statutes, decrees, ordinances and judgements arising from the parliament of September 1397–January 1398 and specifically adding the decision of 18 March 1399 (the day of the revocation of Henry's pardon and the confiscation of the Lancastrian inheritance). Significantly, he added a clause that 'should the aforesaid successor be unwilling to act', then the payment of his debts was to be undertaken by the dukes of Surrey, Aumale and Exeter and William le Scrope.[54] Thus Edmund of Langley was named as his successor by default, for in April 1399 Edmund was the sole living member of the royal family who took precedence over these dukes.[55]

There were three clear turning points in Richard's view of the succession. The first was his declaration in favour of Roger Mortimer, expressed in the parliament of 1386. The second was his decision some time in the late 1380s (most probably in December 1387) to acknowledge Gaunt, in line with Edward III's entail. The third was his decision to subvert the entail and elevate the duke of York over Henry of Bolingbroke in 1394. Anthony Goodman has suggested that his cool attitude towards Gaunt from 1394 was triggered by his new associations with a younger generation of nobles in Ireland.[56] But with Gaunt's health then on the wane,[57] it seems more likely that Richard realized that Gaunt would soon die and Henry would become the heir. This raised the prospect of Henry succeeding to the throne, and this was anathema to Richard.

The idea that Richard was motivated by a strong desire not to allow Henry to succeed him has sometimes been dismissed as writing history with the benefit of hindsight, presuming too much on the events of 1399. Historians have regarded acts such as Richard's grant to Gaunt of the duchy of Lancaster as a palatinate in tail male in 1390, and his elevation of Henry to a dukedom in 1397, as signs of great favour.[58] The gift of a breastplate to him in 1389 has similarly been seen as a sign of reconciliation between him and Richard.[59] However, none of these was a sign of kindness or reconciliation. As Chris Given-Wilson has shown, Richard was determined to redress what he saw as the wrongdoings against the royal family by the house of Lancaster, in particular, the rebellion of Earl Thomas in 1321.[60] Even this is not the full extent of Richard's antipathy, for while Richard's treatment of his uncle, Gaunt, swung from one extreme to the other, there is no evidence of any affinity between Richard and Henry. It cannot be ignored that Henry had joined the Appellants in 1387, a decision for which Richard never forgave him (according to Henry's own schedule of January 1398).[61] Nor can it escape notice that Henry was never appointed to represent Richard in any embassy except that of 1384, when at his father's suggestion, he accompanied him to Leulinghen. With regard to grants to Gaunt which included Henry, it is likely that long before 1399 Richard was planning to confiscate the entire Lancastrian inheritance and brand Henry a traitor as soon as Gaunt was dead, as he eventually did. When he gave Henry an expensive breastplate in 1389, it was a loaded gift – a warning to Henry to be on the defensive – for it had previously belonged to Richard's great friend John Beauchamp of Kidderminster, whom Henry and the other Appellants had recently impeached and executed.[62] Similarly, when he raised Henry to a dukedom in September 1397 along with many of his friends, it was the opposite of reconciliation, being nothing more than bait to lure Henry and his father to the parliament in September 1397 after which four of the king's friends intended that they should both be murdered.[63] A second assassination plot is indicated by the startling fact that, in early 1398, Sir William Bagot was forced to enter into two recognizances to ensure that he did not attempt the disinheritance or murder of Gaunt or any of his family.[64] Finally, fixing on a patently unjust method of throwing Henry out of the country in 1398, and disinheriting him in an even more unjust move, shows that Richard turned against the Lancastrians not because of some strategic vision of reuniting the Lancastrian inheritance with the Crown (although this is perhaps how he expressed it) but out of personal hatred for the heir.

In conclusion, although there was a widespread feeling in the 1380s that Roger Mortimer was the rightful heir to the throne, this was never an official position, and the king simply used this popular feeling as a means to counter pro-Lancastrian threats to depose him in 1386. After the Appellants had given his reign a second chance, he warmed to his uncle Gaunt and seemed to acknowledge Edward III's entail. But in 1394 he sought to impose his royal prerogative by turning against Gaunt again and raising Edmund of Langley above Henry of Bolingbroke. This remained his preferred order of succession from 1394 to 1399, during which years he was probably planning to charge Henry with treason (for joining the Appellants) as soon as Gaunt died. Had he done so, York would have been in the best position to inherit. Certainly in September 1397, Edmund's claim to the throne was being seen as superior to Henry's. Roger Mortimer was barely even being recognized as a member of the royal family.

The most important implication of this is that Henry's decision to join the Appellants in 1387 was not primarily due to his family ties nor to his Stubbsian 'constitutional' stance but to his ambition to safeguard the position of the Lancastrians in the order of succession.[65] He realized this ambition. Whereas prior to 1387 Richard had viewed a designated heir as a constant threat, after 1387 he recognized that he could use Gaunt's position in the order of succession to bind him into a mutual defence against his political adversaries. The only drawback as far as Richard was concerned was that he had to recognize Henry as second in line to the throne and his most likely successor. In 1394, when challenged to do this, he refused, and shortly afterwards began to prefer Edmund of Langley and his son, Edward. Immediately a period of decline in the relations between Richard and the Lancastrians set in. The situation worsened after Gaunt's third marriage to Katherine, the mother of his Beaufort children, and their consequent legitimization in January 1397. By the end of 1397, the Lancastrians were on the very edge of losing everything. That Henry was invested with the ducal title in the parliament of September 1397 and yet escaped murder on the way home is like the mouse grabbing the cheese from the mousetrap and the trap not snapping shut. Even his pardon for the events of 1387 proved illusory, granted to reassure the Lancastrians during Gaunt's lifetime. As soon as Gaunt was dead and buried, Richard saw Henry as nothing more than a liability, extinguished his pardon and confiscated the Lancastrian inheritance, and with it, all the papers and rolls in the Lancastrian muniment rooms. Did Henry have a copy of Edward III's entail with him in France? It is impossible to be certain about this. But there is no doubt that when Henry returned to England and met Richard in September 1399, he believed absolutely that he was the rightful heir of Edward III. Richard may well have been genuinely confused (as he claimed) as to whom he should resign his throne in September 1399 – whether Edmund or Henry – but Edmund's capitulation proved to everyone aware of Edward III's entail that, whatever Richard had done to promote the interests of the house of York, Henry was the rightful heir. It was only the fog of his own prejudice that had made things seem otherwise to Richard.

Notes

1 The exceptions are Given-Wilson, 'Richard II, Edward II', 553–71, and 'Entail', 580–609.

2 Saul, *Richard II*, 397. See also ibid., 419, where Saul states unequivocally that Edmund Mortimer, not Henry, was Richard's 'nearest male heir'.

3 'Entail', 585, n. 1. See also Froissart's statement about Edward making all his sons swear at Michaelmas 1376 to uphold Richard's right in Johnes (ed.), *Froissart*, i, 509.

4 'Entail', 583. An earlier *terminus ante quem* for the document is provided by John Knyvet's appearance as chancellor: Adam Houghton was appointed on 11 January 1377. It is reasonable, however, on the strength of the witness list, to accept Bennett's preferred date of October or November 1376.

5 *St Albans*, 41.

6 Perhaps because of this lack of enrolment and the extant version being a fifteenth-century copy, G. L. Harriss suggests that the document might never have been more than a draft. There is no evidence for this, and plenty to the contrary. Richard undoubtedly accepted the precedence of the exclusively male succession in 1394 when Henry of Bolingbroke and Edward of York were given precedence over Roger Mortimer. In addition, the appearance of specific witnesses, and the giving of a date and place of witnessing, is good evidence of the document being sealed. It should be noted that Henry IV's statute of 1406 (7 Henry IV, cap. 2) ensuring the succession through his sons is comparable, in that he names each of them in turn, so the idea of such a document was at least acceptable. See Harriss, *Shaping the Nation*, 443, n. 29.

7 *St Albans*, 38–41.

8 *Westminster*, 194–5.

9 *Eulogium*, iii. 369.

10 *Westminster*, 68; *St Albans*, 722.

11 Johnes (ed.), *Froissart*, ii. 54; Goodman, *Gaunt*, 104.

12 *Westminster*, 127–9; *St Albans*, 762–3.

13 For previous discussions of this matter see Tout, *Chapters*, iii. 396; Steel, *Richard II*, 214, 217, 275; Tuck, *Richard II*, 205–6; Pugh, *Southampton Plot*, 73–4; 'Entail', 595.

14 Davies, 'Mortimer, Roger . . . (1374–1398)' in *ODNB*. For the good parliamentary connections of the continuator of the *Eulogium*, see the details supplied regarding the 1386 parliament, *Eulogium*, iii, 359–61.

15 Harriss, *Shaping the Nation*, 443.

16 *PROME*, October 1385, Introduction; Saul, *Three Richards*, 153–6; 'Entail', 595–8.

17 'Entail', 598; Saul, *Three Richards*, 156.

18 For Gaunt dining with Richard at the end of the 1385 parliament see Goodman, *Gaunt*, p. 106. The favours to Gaunt include the pardon of John Northampton, an

ally of Gaunt, and the funding of the Castilian expedition. The latter was confirmed by the council on 8 March 1386; Gaunt left court on the 25th.

19 Saul states that Edmund Mortimer, fifth earl of March, had 'a better claim' than Henry of Bolingbroke to being 'Richard's heir male', which he was not; he was his heir general (as stated correctly on p. 154). See Saul, *Three Richards*, p. 217.

20 Saul, *Three Richards*, 155.

21 Martin (ed.), *Knighton's Chronicle*, 340.

22 Saul, *Three Richards*, 156.

23 *Eulogium*, iii, 361.

24 Gillespie, 'Thomas Mortimer and Thomas Molyneux', 163–73; Goodman, *Loyal Conspiracy*, 26. Thomas Mortimer was the illegitimate son of Roger Mortimer (1329–60), second earl of March. See *Royal Wills*, 115.

25 Philip the Hardy (d. 1404) is described as still being the duke of Burgundy. See *Eulogium*, iii, 355. Antonia Gransden's conclusion is that the work was written by one author fairly contemporarily with the events described, and that the post-1428 reference to Wycliffe is one of a number of late interpolations. See Gransden, *Historical Writing II*, 158, n. 5.

26 *Eulogium*, iii, 361. The correctly given titles are York, Gloucester, Dublin and Suffolk; the incorrect titles are Earl Marshal (*recte* 1386), Huntingdon (1388) and Rutland (1390). The creation of Henry of Bolingbroke as earl of Derby could be correctly associated with this parliament, as this was the first parliament he had been summoned to attend, and although he had previously used the title, so too had his father.

27 *Eulogium*, iii, 367.

28 For example, the author states that the parliament of 1386 sought further information about the 'statute' by which Edward II was adjudged. There was no such statute – Edward II was not actually deposed, he resigned the Crown in favour of his son – but the twenty-fifth article of the Parliament Roll for 1388 includes the proceedings of the council of 25 August 1387, which states that this 'statute' had been invoked. The *Eulogium* continuator is thus wholly accurate on this point of detail.

29 *Usk*, 19.

30 *Eulogium*, iii, 360.

31 *Eulogium*, iii, 361.

32 This process was specifically checked by parliament in October 1386, requiring them to ascertain to whom Richard should resign the throne. See *PROME*, February 1388, pt II, article 25.

33 Obviously it is possible that other chroniclers' work on this matter has not lasted, through accidental or wilful destruction. Bennett points out that a chronicle of Glastonbury, now lost, also supported the Mortimer claim to the throne. See 'Entail', 595, n. 4.

34 *Westminster*, 194–5.

35 The abbot of Westminster was present, as shown by his appointment as a trier of petitions for Gascony.

36 *Eulogium*, iii, 369–70.

37 Clearly the manuscript copyist found the request difficult to understand as he interpolated a later narrative (which Usk dates to 1399) to explain to the reader that Henry's claim was through his mother, not Gaunt, based on the myth that Edmund Crouchback was the first-born son of Henry III. See *Usk*, 65; 'Entail', 599.

38 Edward III had normally appointed his most senior son in England as keeper, even if that meant appointing an infant. In April 1331, when leaving the country at short notice, he appointed his brother, John, but his eldest son at that time had yet to complete his first year. During absences in 1338–40, 1340 and 1343–4 he appointed his eldest son, Edward (eight years old in 1338), and when his heir travelled with him in 1345 and 1346–7, he appointed Lionel regent (six years old in 1345). In 1355 and 1359–60, when his four eldest sons travelled to France with him, he appointed the last one left in England, Thomas, even though in 1355 he was less than a year old. Finally, in 1372 he appointed Richard regent, heir to the throne which Edward then expected his eldest son to inherit.

39 Gaunt was appointed Lieutenant in Aquitaine on 10 March 1394. See *Syllabus*, ii, 526.

40 Although *CP*, *PROME* and *ODNB* all suggest that Mortimer was not summoned to parliament until 1397, the January 1394 parliament did not end until 6 March. Mortimer witnessed his first charter on 5 March. See TNA C53/164 no. 1. In addition, he performed homage for his English and Welsh estates on 25 February 1394 (*CPR 1391–6*, 284, 375), thus showing he was present during this parliament.

41 For example, TNA C53/154, nos 11–13.

42 Rutland took precedence over Roger Mortimer on 5, 10 and 13 March, and 16 June 1394 (TNA C53/164 nos 1–5).

43 Henry, earl of Derby, took precedence over Edward, earl of Rutland on 15 February 1392 (TNA E40/5925), 26 July, 11 and 22 September 1395 (TNA C53/165 nos 3, 10 and 11), 10 and 23 February 1397 (TNA C53/166 nos 1–3), and 5 July 1397 (TNA C53/167 no. 25).

44 Goodman, *Loyal Conspiracy*, 32, quoting a Polychronicon continuation; Given-Wilson, *Chronicles of the Revolution*, 81, quoting the confession of Thomas of Woodstock.

45 *St Albans*, 847.

46 Saul, 'Anne of Bohemia', in *ODNB*.

47 *Usk*, 39.

48 *PROME*, September 1400. For the date see Walker, 'Richard II's Views on Kingship', 50. The earl of March did not die until 20 July so he must have been alive at the time of this conversation.

49 In this same parliament he gave the earl of Salisbury leave to sue for the lordship of Denbigh, a Mortimer possession, and reversed the judgement against the Despensers, whom Roger Mortimer's great-grandfather and namesake had declared traitors and executed.

50 See *PROME*, September 1397–January 1398, items 39 and 72, in which the duke of York is given precedence over the duke of Hereford.

51 TNA C53/167 nos 2 and 4. For a discussion of the relevance of personal epithets in the Charter Rolls see Biggs, 'Royal charter witness lists', 414–15.

52 *PROME*, October 1399, Appendix. In this statement Richard seems to have been envisaging resigning the throne at some point in the future after the deaths of both of his uncles; his preference for Edward of York thus indicates he was already planning to discount Henry's claim in the first half of 1398.

53 Edward duke of Aumale is described as 'our very dear brother' in TNA C53/167 nos 5–10 (23 April, 1 May and 9 May 1399), 16–17 (13 and 24 April 1398). This is also the way he is named in Richard's will. Only Edward was treated to this familiarity: Thomas, duke of Surrey (who was raised to a dukedom the same day as Edward) is correctly described in the will as Richard's nephew. See *Royal Wills*, 196, 199.

54 *Royal Wills*, 198.

55 The order of ducal precedence in the 1397 parliament, as recorded on the parliament roll, was Lancaster, York, Hereford, Aumale, Surrey, Exeter and finally Norfolk.

56 Goodman, *Gaunt*, 157.

57 Goodman, *Gaunt*, 355.

58 Goodman, *Gaunt*, 146; Tuck, *Richard II*, 184–5.

59 Goodman, *Loyal Conspiracy*, 52; Saul, *Richard II*, 203.

60 Given-Wilson, 'Richard II, Edward II', esp. 559–61, 567–71.

61 *PROME*, September 1397.

62 *CCR 1385–9*, 571.

63 Given-Wilson, 'Edward II, Richard II', 563–4. See also the bill of the duke of Hereford against the duke of Norfolk, *PROME*, September 1397, prorogued to January 1398.

64 *PROME*, September 1400, Appendix; Tuck, *Richard II*, 208.

65 For Stubbs's interpretation of Henry IV, see Stubbs, *Constitutional History*, iii, 7–74, and the comments in McFarlane, *Lancastrian Kings and Lollard Knights*, 8–13.

9

The rules governing succession to the Crown, 1199–1399

In introducing Edward III's entailment of the throne on his male descendants, Michael Bennett noted that 'in October 1460, in rather dramatic circumstances, the rules governing succession to the Crown were made a matter of public debate'.[1] He went on to describe 'the dramatic circumstances' – namely Richard duke of York's claim to the Crown and the admission by the royal judges that such matters were beyond the common law and were rightly matters for the peerage and the royal family. The peers for their part resorted to 'dyvers entayles made to the heires male as for the corone of Englond as it may appere by dyvers chronicles and parlementes'.[2] In the same piece Professor Bennett revealed not only an entail male of Edward III settling the throne in favour of Lancaster but set it within the context of its creation, shortly after the death of the Black Prince, when the order of the succession may have been considered in doubt. Here, surely, was the text of the very entailment in the male line referred to by the lords in 1460, albeit in a charred fifteenth-century copy. One could even find a parliamentary equivalent, drawn up by Henry IV in 1406, settling the throne on his sons and their sons in preference to his daughters. But was it drawn up as a result of doubts about the succession in 1376 (as discussed in the previous chapter) or was it a result of John of Gaunt's petition to the Good Parliament to make a law forbidding women from being heirs to the throne? Or was it drawn up for some other reason? As Professor Bennett himself noted, there was an earlier precedent in the entailment of Edward I in 1290. Subsequently, he has drawn attention to two more examples that predate 1376 – one from Scotland, one from France – which seem to demonstrate an influence on the creation of such entailments. These suggest that Edward III's entail was not a one-off document but a part of a wider programme of settling the throne, with a longer tradition behind it and an international scope.

Historians before Bennett did not imagine that there was a tradition of entailments of the throne in the period 1290–1376. The reason is obvious: the texts do not exist anymore. In drawing up a document governing the order of the succession, a king was creating a politically powerful document but one that was deeply partisan and divisive as soon as he died. It was, by definition, in the interests of the potential beneficiaries to preserve it and in the interests of those whom it disenfranchised to destroy every copy. Ultimately every such document was vulnerable: the older ones as much as the newer ones, for all could be used to claim a greater authority, whether newer (more relevant) or older (an earlier precedent). No copy of Edward I's entail survives today: we only know of its contents due to the survival of a charter of one of the king's sons-in-law. The original of Edward III's entailment has also vanished. It is possible that Henry III and Richard II also entailed the throne (as discussed below). If so, those documents too have vanished. The entailment of the throne drawn up by Henry VI has likewise vanished.[3] In the early seventeenth century Robert Cotton was forced to surrender Edward VI's 'device' for the succession so it could be destroyed.[4] Political forces were just as eager to destroy chronicles containing texts of, or references to, entailments contrary to their interests.[5] The chronicles containing one or more settlements of the throne, noted above in respect of the 1460 case, have all disappeared. Therefore it is evident that, in discussing evidence concerning the king's will regarding the inheritance of the throne, we are discussing documents which were doomed, by their very nature, to have been destroyed almost as often as they were created.

In 'Entail', Bennett took as his starting point the claim of John over and above that of Arthur of Brittany in 1199, using that claim to demonstrate the need for a settlement in 1376. As he states, the 1199 question was whether the 'principle of representation' applied. If it did, then a king's deceased heir could pass on his claim to the throne to his son. If not, the sons of the deceased heir were by-passed and the claim transferred to the eldest *surviving* son of the king. Expressing the problem in this theoretical manner, however, slightly over-simplifies the political question. John le Patourel pointed out in 1971 that the kingdom of England had developed piecemeal in Anglo-Saxon times: an accumulation of separate kingdoms with different laws and customs.[6] Therefore there could be no one acceptable 'law of succession' for all the parts of England. Moreover, there could be no 'common law of kingship', for kings were, by definition, unique, and while they had acquired some parts of their kingdom by inheritance, some parts had been acquired by conquest. It did not follow that one law of inheritance would always prove acceptable in all the various parts. One therefore cannot judge what was lawful or not in establishing inheritance. The Saxons surmounted this difficulty by doing away with lawful inheritance as the prime factor in the succession and subjecting the Crown to election. The only absolute priority was that the kingdom should remain intact.[7] This led to a fundamental inconsistency with the common law. In common law inheritance, if there were no male heirs an estate was divided between the heiresses. This was not possible with a kingdom, so the principles of common law could not apply. Nor was it necessarily 'right' if a minor were to inherit the throne in a time of danger; the responsibilities of kingship had to be considered as well as the rights. Therefore kings were sometimes succeeded not by their sons but by their brothers. On the death of Edmund in 946, his two young sons Edwy and Edgar were passed over and their uncle, Edmund's younger brother Edred, was elected king. It seems that Harold Harefoot had a son Aelfwine who did not inherit, being a clergyman; therefore the throne passed to his brother, Harthacnut, in 1040. Nor did Aelfwine inherit two years later on the death of the last of his dynasty: the throne passed instead to Edward the Confessor. As for Harold Godwinson, his accession was more pragmatic than dynastic, his designation as the heir by the dying Edward the Confessor probably being the most significant factor.

William the Conqueror's conveyance of the throne followed a similar pattern – or lack of pattern. If any 'rule of succession' applied, it was that the king could choose whom his successor should be – as the dukes of Normandy had done since 996.[8] Perhaps also there was a measure of *droit d'aînesse* – the division of an inheritance among Norman heirs as equally as possible without dividing any fief – which encouraged the Conqueror to consider dividing Normandy and England.[9] The end result was clear: Robert, the Conqueror's eldest son, inherited Normandy; William the second son, inherited England; and the youngest, Henry Beauclerc, was given a sum of money. The critical factor for those looking back on the Norman succession in 1199 was that an elder brother did not automatically take precedence over a younger one. In 1087 William II inherited England, not his elder brother. In 1100 Henry I inherited England and his elder brother was again deprived. No less significant was the succession question after 1100. Henry I was obsessed with the accession, having only one legitimate son, William, whom the barons collectively acknowledged as the heir in 1116. After William's death in the White Ship, Henry ordered in 1127 that his daughter Matilda be recognized as his heir by the magnates of England (including Stephen); he arranged for her marriage to Geoffrey of Anjou to bolster her right over that of his elder brother's son, William Clito. But on Henry I's death in December 1135 the king's will did not prevail – unlike January 1066 and September 1087. Henry I's nephew, Stephen, took the throne despite having previously sworn an oath to support Matilda's claim, showing that a grandson of William I by one of his daughters could take precedence over a daughter by one of his deceased sons. Not only that, Stephen took precedence even over Matilda's infant son, Henry of Anjou, the first-born grandson of Henry I. One clear implication was that a woman was deemed unsuitable by the lords as a queen in her own right, whatever Henry I thought. A second implication was that the heirs of the body did not at this time automatically take precedence. In this way it can be seen that any lawyer considering the principle of representation in relation to the succession in 1199 would have seen the precedents mostly going John's way. A younger son might take precedence over an elder son on account of the last king's will (as in 1087), or a younger brother might take precedence over a deceased older brother's son (as in 946), or a younger brother might take precedence over his elder brother through simple quick-witted action and diplomacy (as in 1100), or the nephew of a deceased king might succeed over the grandson (as in 1135).

The legality of John's succession was not the decisive factor in 1199. There were no universally recognized rules – only a series of precedents. The issue that had inhibited a law of succession in Saxon England now applied to the whole Angevin empire: it was impossible to satisfy the rules of succession in each place without breaking up the empire. Hence the late king's will remained the principal (although not the only) guidance. Richard I nominated his brother, John, not his nephew Arthur; and the influence of William Marshal probably carried the day.[10] Arthur died in prison in mysterious circumstances and his sister Eleanor, countess of Richmond, was kept under close scrutiny for the duration of her life. Her claim to the throne was not advanced even on John's death – again, possibly due to William Marshal's view on the succession. Thus Henry, an under-age boy, became king.

THE FLANDERS SETTLEMENT OF 1200
AND ITS REPERCUSSIONS

In reviewing John's reign it is important to recognize that his accession was recognized by an increasingly legalistic and literate society on the Continent. In particular, Baldwin, count of Flanders and Hainault, did homage to John for his Norman estates at Rouen in August 1199.[11] The following year Baldwin, who was then preparing to go on the Fourth Crusade, drew up two charters for the county of Hainault. These became the foundations of the feudal and the criminal law of that county. No doubt he also drew up similar charters for Flanders itself or – if he did not – he based the laws for Hainault on those in existence in Flanders, as the prime purpose of the feudal charter was to prevent controversy over his inheritance. The feudal charter established the succession law. As a supporter and vassal of King John, Baldwin and his Hainaulter vassals followed John in preferring a dying king's younger son to the sons of a deceased elder son. Baldwin's charter stipulated that:

> A daughter succeeds if there is no son; the son of a second marriage succeeds rather than the daughter of a first; if an elder son or daughter dies before the parent who holds the fief and leaves a child, this grandchild of the fief-holder is passed over in favour of the next younger brother or sister of the deceased heir, thus keeping the line of succession in the first generation of descendants. If there are no heirs of the body, the fief passes to the nearest living relative of the family from which the fief was inherited by the deceased proprietor . . . [12]

In other words, the principle of representation did not apply in Hainault with respect to either sex. But the principle that the heirs of the body should take precedence over other relatives had become established. Crucially, these principles did not remain localized in their focus. The rest of Europe learnt of Baldwin's rules of succession in colourful detail in 1244, when a war broke out between his grandsons: the sons of his daughter Margaret by two separate husbands. The eldest son by the first marriage, John of Avesnes, had been declared illegitimate after the annulment of his mother's marriage and so, according to Baldwin's rules, her eldest son by the second marriage, William of Dampierre, was declared heir to the whole of Flanders and Hainault. But when John was legitimized by the pope in 1244, he became heir to the both counties. The ensuing war, which led to Louis IX of France settling Hainault on John and Flanders on William, continued well into the 1250s.

The reason why Baldwin's succession rules are significant is because they had a direct effect on later succession questions. In 1281 it was proposed that Margaret of Flanders, daughter of Guy of Dampierre, count of Flanders, should marry Alexander, son and heir of Alexander III of Scotland. In the course of negotiations, the Flemish ambassadors asked whether the children of Alexander and Margaret would inherit the throne in the event of Alexander III having more sons and outliving his eldest son, Alexander. If the principle of representation did apply, then, if Margaret had a son, she would be the mother of the next monarch whether her husband outlived his father or not. If it did not, then she might find herself the mother of an unimportant member of the royal family who would probably prove more of a liability than an asset to the eventual king, and may well disappear like Arthur of Brittany. Clearly, any ruler marrying his daughter to a prospective heir needed to clarify the inheritance. Alexander III referred the question over to a great council of sixteen men: six earls, five bishops and five barons. In their view the principle of representation *did* apply – but only in regard to males. To be precise, if Prince Alexander and Margaret of Flanders were to have a son in Alexander III's lifetime, and then the prince were to die, their son would inherit, regardless of whether Alexander III had gone on to have other sons or not. But if the same thing were to happen with regard to females, then a younger son of the king by a subsequent marriage would take precedence over the daughters of the deceased prince.[13]

Prince Alexander died without issue in January 1284 and, as his brother David had already died, the sole survivor of the dynasty was Margaret of Norway, the one-year-old granddaughter of Alexander III by his daughter Margaret, who had married Erik, king of Norway, in 1281. Despite her extreme youth, Alexander III had the baby girl publicly recognized as his heir in 1284 – there were no other heirs of his body. Alexander III died in March 1286. This left Scotland in the hands of a body of Guardians during the absence and minority of Margaret of Norway.[14] Edward I was just setting out for Gascony at the time; he was absent for the next three years, leaving his brother Edmund as regent. But the thought of unifying England and Scotland cannot have been far from his mind and on 6 November 1289, two months after returning to England, he and his council met the envoys of Norway and Scotland at Salisbury to discuss the possibility of Margaret, queen of Scotland, marrying his eldest surviving son, the future Edward II.[15] The nobles of Scotland were called to Birgham near Berwick to discuss the proposal and gave their assent on or about 17 March 1290.[16] As things turned out, the prospective bride never arrived in England. A letter dated 7 October 1290 conveyed the news that she was believed to be dead – but counter-reports suggested her illness was not fatal. The confusion proved permanent, and the young queen probably died at Orkney. Certainly there was no royal marriage.

EDWARD I'S ENTAIL, 1290

On 17 April 1290, just one month after the Scots' approval of the marriage of Edward of Carnarvon and little Queen Margaret, Edward I held a gathering at Amesbury in which he laid down his own proposals for the inheritance of the realm. Present were family members, such as William de Valence, the king's uncle; Eleanor of Provence, his mother; Edmund Crouchback, earl of Lancaster, his brother; and Gilbert de Clare, earl of Gloucester, his prospective son-in-law. Also present were six bishops, including the archbishop of Canterbury, and three other lords. Edward I drew up his settlement of the throne of England – a document which has, like every other similar document, disappeared. Its text is known, however, from the charter issued by Gilbert de Clare that day, attesting to his oath to observe the provisions of Edward I's settlement, following his betrothal to the king's daughter Joan.

Specifically, there were six clauses governing the inheritance. Gilbert acknowledged that (1) Edward of Carnarvon would be his liege lord after the king's death; (2) if Edward of Carnarvon were to die without heirs of his body during Edward I's lifetime, then the throne would pass to any other sons which may be born to Edward I; (3) if Edward I died without leaving a son and if Edward of Carnarvon died without leaving an heir of his body, then the throne was to pass to Eleanor, eldest daughter of Edward I, and the heirs of her body, she being able to reign in her own right; (4) if any other sons Edward I might yet have died without leaving an heir of his body, then Eleanor was to inherit, and the heirs of her body; (5) if Eleanor died without heirs of her body, then Joan was to inherit; (6) if Joan were also to die without heirs of her body, then the throne was to pass to her nearest sister. At that point Edward I probably had three other daughters: Margaret, Mary and Elizabeth.

As Powicke observed, making the settlement of the throne at Amesbury at this point was very much a family-centred event.[17] Eleanor the queen mother was living at the abbey and so was Edward I's third daughter, Mary, both as nuns. The purpose was to establish the succession before a series of royal marriages. In addition to the betrothal of the infant Edward of Carnarvon to Queen Margaret and the betrothal of Joan to Gilbert de Clare, Edward I's eldest daughter Eleanor was betrothed to Alphonso III of Aragon, and Margaret to John II of Brabant. All four marriages were scheduled to take place over the course of 1290: Joan married Gilbert at Westminster Abbey later that same month; Margaret married the duke of Brabant there in July; Eleanor married Alphonso by proxy there in August; and Edward and Margaret were meant to marry soon after Margaret's arrival, which was specified to be no later than 1 November. Therefore there is an obvious reason why Edward I's settlement of the throne was drawn up at this time: if he died without leaving a son (and he had already buried several), there might be fighting between his daughters' husbands as the kingdom of England should not and could not be divided between co-heiresses. As the common law could not apply, past precedent was all that could govern the succession – and past precedent was useless to Edward I. If he left no sons his brother might inherit the throne instead of the heirs of his body. Edward I's guarding against this possibility emerges clearly when comparing his model of the succession with the Scottish one of 1281. The Scots accepted the principle of representation only for males; Edward accepted it for women too. The crucial clauses are the second and third: Edward I's settlement states that a daughter of Edward of Carnarvon would take precedence over any other sons Edward I might yet have, and they would inherit even if Edward I outlived his eldest son. Even more unusually, he allowed women to inherit in their own right.

Given that Edward I's settlement conflicted entirely with Edward III's entailment of the throne in 1376 and the basis on which the Lancastrians claimed the throne in 1399, it is not at all surprising that the original settlement has disappeared. It probably did not outlast the fourteenth century. But its very vulnerability begs a question: was this the first such settlement of the throne of England? Was there an earlier document that now no longer exists, due to it being destroyed on the orders of a previous monarch?

As Edward I did not simply adopt the Scottish model (despite the anticipated marriage of his son to the queen of Scotland), his settlement was not drawn up to promote harmony between the two kingdoms: it was potentially divisive. Had the marriage between Edward of Carnarvon and Margaret gone ahead and resulted only in a daughter, then England would have been inherited by the daughter but Scotland would have passed to the sons of Edward I by a second marriage. Thus, if Edward I saw this document as a means to secure peace in England, he did not see it as instrumental in securing peace with Scotland. Furthermore, it shows he deliberately sought to secure the succession through the heirs of his body, excluding his brother, who was only mentioned as a witness. Clearly Edward wanted future kings to look back at *him* as their paternal ancestor, not Edmund. His settlement was thus not just a statement that the principle of representation applied in England, regardless of the sex of the heir. It was also a rebuttal of two other principles: that of male-only inheritance (established in 1135 and reinforced in 1153 by the Treaty of Wallingford) and that the heirs of the body did not take precedence (as had happened in 946 and 1135).

Thus between 1153 and 1290 two important precedents had been overturned and the principles of primogeniture and representation established. Given Edward I's strong promotion of the common law, it is not surprising that these reflected shifts within aristocratic society generally. In the late twelfth and early thirteenth centuries there was a move towards entailing estates on the heirs of the body – thereby avoiding the problem of descendants being deprived of their inheritance by a cousin (as in 1135). There was a growing belief that the principle of representation should apply – at least in regard to males (as shown by the Scottish council's decision in 1281). The question which thus arises is whether these changes in the rules directing the royal succession were drawn up *for the first time* in 1290. In short, was Edward I doing something new? Or was he updating a settlement of the throne drawn up by Henry III?

HENRY III'S ENTAILMENT OF THE THRONE?

It is not possible to prove that Henry III drew up a document settling the throne on a specific line of his descendants. No such document exists. However, the fact that it does not exist should not be considered an indication that it was never created. As mentioned above, we are dealing with a very specific class of document – one that is so sensitive and vulnerable that every known original example has been destroyed. The only way to proceed is to recognize that, in the circumstances, it would be just as wrong to presume that such a document never existed as it would to presume that it did. This is especially the case as there is good evidence that Henry III considered the principle of representation in relation to the royal family and applied it to the succession.

The fact that Edward I drew up a succession document that constrained the inheritance to the heirs of his body suggests that he was reacting to, or building on, an understanding of the succession that prevailed in his father's reign. The precedence of Richard over John in 1189, Henry III's own precedence over his brother Richard in 1216 and the regularity with which Edward was described as his father's first-born son and heir (Henry III described him thus four times in his will) allows us to be certain that the principle of male primogeniture was firmly established by the time of Edward's birth, in 1239. Had he died without children, his heir would undoubtedly have been his brother, Edmund. Clearly the understanding in the twelfth century was the throne could not be inherited by a woman, so the key question for Henry III, if he considered the succession (and most monarchs did, at great length), was whether the daughters of Edward I would take precedence over Edmund. In 1267, when Henry III became the first king of England since Henry I to attain the age of sixty, his eldest son had only a daughter, Edmund was yet to marry, and both of his surviving daughters had married and produced sons. The question of representation thus would have been pertinent (in the event of both sons dying) and the question of whether male primogeniture ruled out female inheritance (by Edward I's daughter) no less so. So all the reasons that we may put forward for Edward I making a settlement of the throne in 1290 applied in 1267. In fact, they had applied from much earlier – at least from December 1251, when Henry's daughter Margaret married Alexander III of Scotland.

One particular set of circumstances from this earlier period suggests that Henry III would have made arrangements for the succession. On 24 May 1253, he planned two diplomatic marriages: he instructed ambassadors to negotiate the marriage of his daughter Beatrice with the heir to the kingdom of Aragon, and the marriage of his eldest son, Edward, with Eleanor, half-sister of the king of Castile. Both of these marriages would have led to questions over the principle of representation. If Beatrice bore a son before her husband had inherited the throne of Aragon, and if her husband then predeceased his father, would the child take precedence over the king of Aragon's other sons? And what if she produced daughters? The same questions might well have been asked by the king of Castile about Eleanor's offspring in England. If Edward and Eleanor had a son and Edward died before Henry III, would their son take precedence over Edward's brother Edmund? Or did King John's precedent of disregarding the principle of representation still apply? And what about their daughters? Henry III can hardly have arranged these marriages without offering the ambassadors some safeguards concerning the rules of succession then prevailing in England. But did he formally codify such rules?

In answering this question, and in the absence of an easy answer based on an extant document, one thing is obvious. The value of the Anglo-Castilian marriage was far greater in securing a permanent and lasting peace if it was permanent and lasting itself – in other words, if the Castilian king's sister was guaranteed to be the mother of all future heirs to the throne of England. It would not have been diplomatic to make the royal status of Eleanor's sons by Edward conditional on Edward outliving his father. It is likely therefore that Henry acknowledged the principle of representation by the time the arrangements for the marriage of Edward and Eleanor received his consent on 22 August 1254.

There are further reasons to suspect that the principle of representation was dealt with before the marriage was agreed. The process of entailment itself – settling a property on a specific line of heirs – provides us with further evidence. Henry III started making grants which were essentially fee tail (as opposed to fee simple), to the descendants of the recipient. Normally it is said that granting in fee tail was only established by *De dono conditionalibus* – cap. 1 of the statute of Westminster (1285). However, in that statute Edward I was simply recognizing what had become common practice at an earlier date. Henry III made grants specifically to the heirs of the body with reversion to the Crown as early as 1228. On 13 December that year Henry III made a gift of the manor of Soham to Hubert de Burgh, earl of Kent, and his wife Margaret 'and the heirs of their bodies'.[18] This essentially means that, if they had children, it would pass to one of them or a grandchild. If not, the land would revert to the Crown; it could not be inherited by their brothers, sisters or other relatives. In 1236 he made a similar grant of the manor of Shopland to Henry de Tibetot 'to hold to him and his heirs by his espoused wife'.[19] The same form of wording appears in grants of 1245 and 1246.[20]

The earliest evidence of Henry III making a grant in fee tail to a member of the royal family dates from 1235. That year he gave his brother Richard, earl of Cornwall, 'and his heirs by his espoused wife' the manor of Kirketon.[21] In 1243 he made two more grants to Richard 'and his heirs by Sanchia his wife', with reversion to the Crown, and another in 1252.[22] In March 1249 he made a grant of the manor of Bampton 'to William de Valence, the king's brother, and his heirs by his wife'.[23] Even more significantly, in September that same year he made a gift to his son and heir Edward 'of all the land in Gascony and the island of Oléron, to be held by him and the heirs of his body'.[24] This meant that Gascony would have passed to Edward's children in the event of his predeceasing his father – and Edward was at this date still only ten years of age. If any document demonstrates that Henry III accepted the principle of representation in the royal succession in defiance of the basis on which his father had succeeded to the throne, it is this charter in which he entailed the lordship of Gascony on his eldest son, Edward, and his heirs. Had he not done so at that time, no doubt he would have been required to do it before Alphonso of Castile consented to hand over to Edward all his lands in Gascony in 1254: Alphonso's charter stresses that it was for the benefit of his own heirs and successors.[25] This could not have been agreed without settling the question of who would inherit the said lands if Edward were to predecease his father, leaving no issue by Eleanor.

The foregoing passages allow us to be certain that Henry III entailed the lordship of Gascony on his eldest son in 1249 and reasonably confident that he gave some undertaking that the throne would pass to the heirs of Edward by his wife Eleanor at some point before their marriage in the summer of 1254. The marriage contract itself does not specify any such settlement but nor would one necessarily expect it to: the succession was not a matter to be enshrined in a marriage contract but was worthy of a separate document, for it had a wide range of social and political applications. The question thus becomes one of what sort of settlement might it have been? Four options present themselves:

1.   the Flanders model of 1200, which rejected the principle of representation;
2.   the Scots model of 1281, which allowed representation but only in respect of males;
3.   a variation on the Scots model, which allowed representation in respect of females as well as males but did not allow females to inherit;
4.   Edward I's model of 1290, which treated male and female heirs of the body alike, allowing females to inherit in the absence of sons.

Given that Henry accepted the principle of representation with respect to his subjects, including his own son's tenure of Gascony, we can rule out the possibility that he would have accepted his father's mode of succession, codified in the Flanders model. The question is thus one of whether Henry recognized the principle of representation in respect of women.

Male-heir entails were certainly known to Henry III. The earliest one noticeable in the Patent Rolls is that of a Jew, Elias Ridel, lord of Bergerac. Having had his lands entailed upon him in the strict line of male primogeniture, in 1250 Elias sought the king's permission to pass his them to his younger son, Rudel, 'in case his brother Elias withdraw from the king's fealty or die without heir male'.[26] In 1253 Henry III granted to Peter of Savoy that, if he had a male heir by his wife, he could bequeath the wardship of his lands to whomsoever he willed.[27] Clearly the lands held from Henry III by Peter – a kinsman of the queen and of Sanchia, Henry's sister-in-law – were held in tail male. Although grants in tail male to members of the royal family were rare at this period they were not unknown: in 1253 Henry III granted to his brother Richard that 'on the hill above his manor of Mere he may build and fortify a castle of stone and lime, to hold for his life, with reversion to the male issue of him and Sanchia his wife and failing such to the king or his heirs, without claim or hindrance of the heirs of the said earl'.[28]

While we can only guess at why he entailed Mere Castle on Richard's male descendants rather than the heirs of the body, the fact that he did so is significant. It suggests that Henry saw different forms of entailment as serving different purposes. He may have seen the Crown itself as being subject to male primogeniture and lordship of royal estates as descending to the heirs of the body. It is possible that the Scots were copying Henry's own pattern of inheritance in 1281. Indeed, this is probable, as the queen of Scotland was Henry's daughter and Henry had meddled a great deal in Scottish affairs at the time of her marriage. Just after her marriage, on 1 July 1253, Henry drew up a will in which he specified that 'custody of Edward my first-born son and heir, and of my other boys [*puerorum*] and of my kingdom of England and of all my other lands of Wales and Ireland and Gascony, I leave and entrust to my illustrious queen Eleanor until my heirs reach legal age'.[29] It could be that *puerorum* was used instead of *liberi* to refer to all his children, but it is more likely that this was a emphasis on his sons because of the succession. Finally, it is possible that a reference to a lost entail of Henry III was known to the lawyers advising Henry IV on how he should formulate his accession in 1399. If Edward I's settlement was not to hand, and lacking the original of Edward III's settlement, they may have believed Henry III's settlement

– which he may have drawn up in a charter, like Baldwin – provided the strongest legal basis for Henry IV's claim (discussed below).

While it is impossible to be certain that Henry settled the throne on his sons in a specific way, he must have done so informally, and almost certainly did so formally, before the end of his reign.[30] In looking for a date, we might note the period of the marriages of 1251–54, including the making of his will of 1253, as being likely. Alternatively we might look to his serious illness in 1262–63, after which (on 22 March 1263) he summoned a great council and made them recognize Edward I as their future king, demanding from them oaths of loyalty. Perhaps both occasions were significant. Given the circumstances, it seems as likely as not that he outlined a mode of succession that was followed by that of Scotland nine years after his death. If so, then his overlooking the principle of representation in respect of females would have given Edward I an even greater need to draw up his own entailment of the Crown in 1290.

EDWARD III'S ENTAILMENT OF THE THRONE, 1376

The circumstances and consequences of Edward III's entailment of 1376 have been discussed in the previous chapter and in 'Entail', and so only an outline of the development of the form need be added here. Clearly it was not a one-off document but an example of a rare and vulnerable but highly important political instrument. Whether any memory of earlier English settlements remained among the official classes in 1376 is a moot point: it is probable that only the historically literate users of monastic libraries were aware of past precedents. Any settlement made by Henry III was replaced by that of Edward I in 1290 and then this too dwindled in the memory as the male line of the royal family continued unbroken. The Scottish model of the succession, however, was not forgotten. Robert Bruce called upon the principle in 1315 when he drew up his first entailment of the Scottish throne.[31] His priority was to preserve the independence of the kingdom and so this entailment stipulated that, if he should die without a male heir, his brother Edward was to inherit the throne, rather than his daughter Marjorie, his sole child by his first marriage. This was confirmed by the Scottish parliament and supposedly had Marjorie's blessing. The following year she gave birth to a son, Robert Stewart (the future Robert II of Scotland); but she died in 1317. Edward Bruce was killed at the Battle of Faughart in Ireland in 1318. Thus a new entailment of the Scottish throne was drawn up in December 1318 by which the throne passed to his grandson, Robert Stewart, if Robert Bruce died without male heirs. The future David II was born in 1324 and Bruce had a third entailment of the throne drawn up in 1326 acknowledging David as heir. In every respect, the rules of succession followed those drawn up by Alexander III on the advice of his council in 1281: male-only entailment, with male inheritance through females only being considered when the male line failed. When Robert II finally inherited on the death of David II in 1371 he had sons and daughters by both his first and second wives: a new entailment was necessary. In this entailment, drawn up in 1373 and ratified by the Scots parliament in the same manner as Robert I's entailments, Robert II settled the succession on the male line of his eldest son, with each of his surviving younger sons and their male lines mentioned in turn. It was a blueprint for Edward III's own entailment. According to Walsingham, John of Gaunt petitioned parliament in the parliament of 1376 to make a law on the pattern of the French: that no woman be heir to the kingdom'.[32] But Edward III's entail was not a law as such: its model – or models – were rather the tradition of Scottish entailments, starting in 1315 and going back at least to 1281.[33]

There is another context to this. By 1376, the male entail had been long established as a means of passing on the estates and titles of the higher nobility. The process of lords surrendering their earldoms to the king and having them re-granted in fee tail male had begun under Edward I; by 1377 it was almost complete.[34] With regard to lesser estates, grants in fee tail male represented between 10 and 20 per cent of the total entailed grants for each decade, hitting a high of 20 per cent in the decades of 1381–90, 1411–20 and 1471–80.[35] As most estates were not entailed, even in a general sense, it is clear that male entailments were perceived to be of great importance only for the aristocracy, and of course this included the Crown itself. Edward III's male entail may have been influenced by the Scots example of 1373 but it was also a reflection of general aristocratic practice.

RICHARD II'S SETTLEMENT OF THE THRONE

As the previous chapter shows, Richard II did not feel bound to recognize the provisions of Edward III's entailment. Nevertheless he seems to have observed the principle of exclusively male primogeniture, recognizing Henry of Lancaster as having precedence over Roger Mortimer from 1394–8. He also elevated his uncle, the duke of York, to the position of heir apparent. Therefore the question is: did he formally recognize York in a settlement of the throne?

Although no such document exists today, there is good reason to believe that one was drawn up. The first piece of evidence is Henry IV's failure to cite Edward III's entail when claiming the throne in 1399. As a result of Adam Usk's chronicle, we know there was a high degree of confusion as to the process whereby Henry IV could claim the throne. Even if Henry did not have possession of Edward III's actual letter patent – which Richard II might have destroyed – there were men living who could have attested to its creation. It is likely therefore that there was a legal reason why it was not used. One such legal reason would have been a more recent entailment by Richard II, which would have rendered it void. There is evidence in Jean Creton's chronicle that Richard's intentions for the throne were widely known in court circles (discussed below). Given the Scottish, French and English entailments of the throne, it would have been very unlikely for Richard to have drawn up his will in April 1399 and *not* made provision for the inheritance of the throne.

The second piece of evidence that Richard II entailed the throne is not so much a 'piece' of evidence as a series: namely, his use of male entailments. A survey of all the grants in tail mail in the last three years of the reign is very instructive on this point. Laying aside four pardons to widows for continuing to enjoy estates settled on their late husbands in tail male,[36] and laying aside also six licences granted to men to entail their existing estates on their male descendants,[37] the patent letters include just forty-seven new grants in tail male. Of these forty-seven, thirty-seven (79 per cent) were to men of the rank of duke or earl, including eighteen to members of the royal family. To be specific: five were to Richard's uncle, the duke of York.[38] Five more were to York's son and heir, Edward earl of Rutland and duke of Aumale.[39] Six were to Richard's half-brother, John Holland, duke of Exeter; and two to their nephew, Thomas Holland, earl of Kent and Surrey.[40] Of the remainder, three were to Thomas Mowbray, earl of Nottingham and duke of Norfolk; six were to William le Scrope, earl of Wiltshire; three were to Ralph Neville, earl of Westmorland; three were to Thomas Percy, earl of Worcester; three were to John Montagu, earl of Salisbury; and one to Thomas Despenser, earl of Gloucester.[41] The other ten were all to five knights.[42] This shows a definite propensity to grant lands in tail male to the more senior members of the aristocracy, especially Richard's own family and the house of

York. It is evident that Richard II's understanding and that of his legal advisers was that male entailment was increasingly necessary the closer the grantee was to the throne. There can be little doubt that, with regard to the throne itself, the right form of inheritance was understood to be that of male-line primogeniture – with the exception that the heirs of John of Gaunt were passed over after 1398 on account of the so-called treason of Henry of Lancaster. Given this conclusion, it would be reasonable to suppose that this was not just believed by Richard but written down by him at the same time as he made his will, in April 1399.

The third piece of evidence that Richard drew up an entailment lies within his will itself. As the previous chapter noted, he made provisions for a successor in his will but did not enter the man's name, presumably leaving this to be governed by a separate document. However, he did make provision for his debts to be paid if his successor failed to act, naming in this capacity the dukes of Surrey, Aumale and Exeter and the earl of Wiltshire. In so doing he implied the duke of York was his intended successor (York being the only man who took precedence over these other named men). The reason for not naming York directly was that York was old and immobile, being very arthritic in his back, with several fused vertebrae. It was no doubt perceived that he would probably die before long, perhaps while Richard was in Ireland (as it turned out, he died in 1402). So there was a need for the succession beyond him to be clearly delineated. This was especially the case as the next-in-line after the duke was his eldest son Edward, duke of Aumale, who travelled with Richard to Ireland in 1399. Had Richard II and Edward of York died in Ireland, and Edmund died before or soon after, there would have been doubt as to whether the duke of York's grandson by his daughter Constance should inherit or his second son, Richard of Conisburgh, who was suspected to be the illegitimate son of John Holland. Richard's propensity for male entailments leaves little doubt he would have specified Richard of Conisburgh, who happened also to be Richard II's godson (as well as his nephew, if he was illegitimate).

The foregoing evidence suggests Richard's settlement would have designated Edmund of York as the heir apparent, followed by Edward, duke of Aumale. Richard of Conisburgh, was probably named as well, as third-in-line and a potential keeper of the realm in case Edward became king while still in Ireland. A fourth piece of evidence that this was indeed the case, and was well known in court circles, comes from the chronicle of Jean Creton, an eye-witness of the events of 1399. He noted that the assembly of 30 September 1399 was asked whether they would prefer any of these three – Edmund of York, Edward or Richard of Conisburgh – to be king instead of Henry.[43] This not only suggests that a settlement had been drawn up by Richard II which named York as his heir but that it also named York's two sons. It also suggests it was known well enough for its contents to be put to the test. It met with disapproval.

Given all these circumstances, it is very likely that Richard drew up a settlement of the throne in conjunction with his will in April 1399, in much the same way as Edward III had drawn up his entail in conjunction with *his* will in October 1376. In both cases, the royal settlement was not treated as permanently binding.

THE SUCCESSION IN 1399

Much has been written on the political situation of 1399, and it is not the intention here to repeat what has already appeared in print. But the foregoing passages mean a few further points need to be made. It may seem obvious why Richard II's settlement of the throne was set aside in 1399; but the reality is that the mechanics of that act were both complicated in their own right and also led to further complications.

Clearly Edward III's settlement had led John of Gaunt and his son, Henry of Lancaster, to believe that, in the event of Richard not having a son, the throne would pass to the house of Lancaster. Henry's return to England in 1399 and his success was only made possible by the agreement of the one person who could have rightfully challenged him for the title, Richard's designated heir, Edmund, duke of York. Edmund Mortimer, earl of March, was a mere eight-year-old and in no position to fight. Thus Henry's path to the throne was unopposed. But when it actually came to claiming his inheritance, he ran into difficulties. First there was the question of whether Henry should be recognized as the heir, and rule the kingdom while Richard was allowed to continue as nominal king for his lifetime. The situation in Scotland may well have been a precedent for this, Robert II having been removed from power in 1384 and left as a titular king for the last six years of his life, real power passing to his son and heir, the future Robert III. However, this possibility was ruled out by 10 September, when official documents stopped being dated according to Richard's regnal year. With parliament due to assemble on the 30 September, there was a limited time to find a solution to the problem of how to make Henry of Lancaster a legitimate king.

As is well known, Henry relied heavily on his legal advisers, especially Justice William Thirning, who dissuaded Henry from claiming the throne by right of conquest. Equally well known is the fact that Henry set up a committee to discover whether his maternal ancestor, Edmund Crouchback, was in fact the elder brother of Edward I.[44] Hardyng states that he heard from the earl of Northumberland that Henry IV had produced a chronicle on 21 September 1399 that claimed that Edmund Crouchback was actually the elder brother.[45] It is likely that he did so, for the matter was checked in 'all the chronicles of Westminster and of all the other well-known monasteries' by a committee at this time. Adam Usk, who served on this committee, repeats the various sources he found for dispelling any possibility of the story being true.[46] There can be no doubt therefore that Henry was informed that it was a myth. And yet this belief is often stated as the reason why he claimed the throne as the heir of Henry III. Herein we have an objective inconsistency: we have good information that Henry was looking for a legal basis on which to base his claim to the throne, and we have good information that he was told the Edmund Crouchback legend was false. So it does not make sense for historians to claim that, despite the legal advice, he went ahead and based his claim to the throne on a known falsehood. It would have been better for him if he had claimed right of conquest.

Given the findings above, there is every likelihood that in 1399 there was some other reason why Henry IV mentioned Henry III in his claim to the throne. It could be that Thirning knew that Henry III had entailed the throne of England on his heirs male. In support of this it may be noted that, when Richard of York claimed the throne in 1460, the lords put forward more than one entail in support of the Lancastrian claim: 'dyvers entayles made to the heires male as for the corone of Englond'. Obviously the 1406 parliamentary settlement was one. But how many others were there? The entailment of Edward I would not have helped the lords' case, nor would Richard II's settlement (had it survived). So there were only two other English settlements that can have been relevant, so far as we know and suspect: those of Edward III and Henry III.

Stronger evidence that the Lancastrian claim depended on an entailment drawn up in the thirteenth century lies in the fact that Henry IV is noted in several sources as claiming the throne as the *heir male* of Henry III. There are two forms of evidence for this: implicit and overt. The implicit evidence lies in the wording of the Parliament Roll for 1399, which states that Henry issued a 'challenge' for the throne (in English) 'in as much as I am descended by right line of the blood from the good lord King Henry the third'. Reference to this 'right line of the blood' implies that he believed that his was the pre-eminent claim, not because he was the heir general of Henry III (which he was not – unless one believes the Crouchback legend, which even Adam Usk had given short shrift) but because he was the heir male. Thus the official line itself supports the 'heir male' aspect of his claim. It is worth noting that the official wording of Henry's claim is closely followed in a number of contemporary accounts, both in English and in Latin (*tanquam per regium sanguinem veniens de rege Henrico*), suggesting the official version was included in a newsletter circulated at the time.[47]

At least three contemporary sources overtly state that Henry claimed the throne as the 'heir male' of Henry III. One, published as *An English Chronicle*, states that Henry in parliament 'redde in a bille how he descendid and cam doun lynealli of kyng Harri the sone of king Johan, and was the nexte heir male of his blod, and for that cause he chalanged the croune'.[48] The continuation of the *Eulogium* states that Henry '*legebat quamdam cedulam in qua ostendebat quod ipse descendebat de rege Henrico filio Johannis, et proxima masculus erat de sanguine suo; et istis de causis regnum vendicabat*' ('read a certain document which showed how he was descended from King Henry son of John, and was the next [or 'nearest'] male of his blood; and on this account he challenged the kingdom').[49] As can be seen, this is simply a Latin version of the *English Chronicle* text. In much the same way as the officially enrolled version of the claim circulated and was copied in English and Latin, so too this specifically 'male heir' version of the text circulated and was copied in English and Latin. However, the third chronicle which specifically states that Henry IV claimed to be the male heir of Henry III is slightly different.[50] This records that Henry claimed the throne as 'the nearest male-heir and worthiest blood-descendant of the good King Henry the third, son of King John'. As this was probably written by an eye-witness (the editor suggests Thomas Chillenden, prior of Canterbury Cathedral) and as the core of the *Eulogium* continuation was completed by a friar in the Canterbury area before 1404, the three documents suggest that contemporaries in the south-east of England (and probably elsewhere) understood that Henry had claimed the throne overtly – rather than implicitly – as the 'male heir' of Henry III.

One thing revealed by Adam Usk's details concerning the Crouchback legend is the level of desperation felt by Henry and his advisers in September 1399. It was no doubt this desperation that forced Henry to resort to what was apparently an unorthodox claim from a long-dead king. But as hinted at above, this unorthodox solution was a highly sophisticated one. It solved two problems: how Henry could claim the throne of England and how he could maintain the English claim to the throne of France at the same time, the latter having already passed through the female line in 1328.

This needs some further explanation as it would naturally strike any reasonably informed historian that Henry IV claimed the throne of France as the *heir general* of Philip IV (in preference to the heir male) at the same time as claiming that of England as the *heir male* of Henry III (in preference to the heir general). He could not have it both ways, surely? Indeed, several historians – including myself – have stated that, if Henry's claim to England was justified, then his claim to France was wholly spurious.[51] It turns out we have probably not given Justice Thirning sufficient credit: Henry *could* have it both ways. If Henry III had outlined the rules of the succession exactly as the Scots did in 1281, then Henry IV's claim was good in respect to France as well as England. To start with England: the throne of England could not pass through Lionel to Philippa, and from her to the Mortimer family, because Lionel predeceased his father and the principle of representation only applied if the grandchild was male. It did not matter that Philippa had a son, Roger Mortimer; the 1281 model clearly ruled that the principle did not apply in the case of a female grandchild. Thus the male heir after Richard II's death should have been John of Gaunt's eldest son and heir, Henry IV. The elegant part of this solution was that the same rules could be applied to pass on to Henry the claim to France legally.[52] The 1281 model indicated that, despite the emphasis on male primogeniture, the daughter of a king passed on a claim to the throne if she had no brothers. This was the basis on which Margaret of Norway was acknowledged as heiress to the throne of Scotland in 1284 and proclaimed queen in 1286, and on which Edward III claimed the throne of France in 1328, and Robert II inherited the throne of Scotland in 1371. However, Edward III's claim to the throne of France could not be conveyed to the Mortimers by his granddaughter Philippa for the same reason as above: the principle of representation did not apply in respect of female grandchildren. Therefore it is likely that these rules for the succession – extant now only in the form outlined by the Scots in 1281 but possibly formulated at an earlier date by Henry III – were the legal basis for Henry IV to claim he was rightfully king of both England and France.

The complexity of the problem would explain why, although royal family trees were produced in parliament to explain his descent, the exact details were not recorded by chroniclers. The matter was too complicated; only the essential details were important at the time. It would also explain why few people in England understood Henry's claim. As noted above, male entail itself was a particular feature of aristocratic life – it lay outside most normal landholders' experience, so it was far beyond the experience of most citizens, clerics, monks and the peasantry. A study of feet of fines in four counties has revealed that, in Richard's reign, only 1 per cent of grants were in tail male.[53] Thus the sense of 'rightness' about a male-only entailment was shared only by a very small proportion of the population. As for the necessary deviation from the common law – implicit in the indivisibility of the Crown – this was probably understood by even fewer people. Finally, the technical detail of the principle of representation being applicable only in the case of male grandchildren would have gone over the heads of most contemporaries. If the reckoning put forward here is correct, then Justice Thirning permitted Henry IV to claim the throne of England and the lordship of Ireland, together with the titles of Scotland and France, on a legal basis which very few people in England could have understood and which would have alienated the majority, who believed the common law should apply to succession in the royal family.

CONCLUSION

At the end of this exercise there is no proof that Henry III drew up a settlement of the throne, nor that Richard II did. But it is very likely in Richard II's case, and probable in Henry III's. Certainly it would be foolish to rest an argument on the fact 'there is insufficient evidence'. We are dealing with a class of records that was habitually destroyed. However, we can be certain that magnates and prelates formulated rules governing succession that, if they were derived from an English model developed by Henry III, would account for how the Lancastrian kings could claim the throne of England as the heir male in preference to the heir general, and the throne of France as the heir general in preference to the heir male. Indeed, no other formulation drawn up before 1400 would have permitted this. While Henry IV himself might have put some faith in the story of Edmund Crouchback being the eldest son of Henry III, only to be told it was nonsense, his legal advisers came up with a far more sophisticated solution. Whether they actually possessed a copy of Henry III's entail, however, or simply theorized it, or borrowed it from some other source (for example, the Scottish model of 1281 or a legal precedent book), we cannot say.

More generally, it is clear that the accession of King John had consequences for understandings of the rules of succession right across Europe. It set in motion a process whereby kings and independent dukes and counts had to consider the succession law in their domains. The principle of representation was rejected altogether by Baldwin of Flanders in 1200. It was not rejected in England or Scotland, both of which kingdoms seem to have accepted the principle in relation to males but not females after 1216. This is the reason why Edward III paid no attention to the succession potential of the marriage of his granddaughter Philippa. The common law did not apply, as every monarch had realized, even Edward I. In permitting the principle of representation in respect of females, Edward I's settlement was the exception, not the rule, and even this was outside the common law as it implied female primogeniture, not division among co-heiresses. This is no doubt why Gilbert de Clare was required to swear an oath to uphold the terms of the settlement before he married the king's younger daughter. Not until 1404 would another settlement be drawn up that tolerated the idea that the principle of representation should apply in the case of females, and even then it was contentious, as the two cases on the 1406 Parliament Roll reveal.[54] No doubt the second of these, agreed on 22 December 1406, entailing the succession on Henry V and the heirs of his body, was one of the documents produced in defence of the Lancastrian claim against the duke of York in 1460. Very probably a copy of Edward III's entail was another. But behind them lay a royal tradition of considering the touchy business of the inheritance – a tradition which has now almost entirely vanished.

Notes

1 'Entail', 580.
2 'Entail', 581, quoting *RP*, v, 376.
3 'Entail', 604.
4 'Entail', 606.
5 See 'Entail', 595, n. 4, for reference to the destruction of a chronicle that supported the Mortimer claim to the throne.

6 Le Patourel, 'Norman succession', 228, 236.

7 As early as Ethelwulf's reign (839–55) this principle of integrity is found to be a consideration. See Le Patourel, 'Norman succession', 241.

8 Le Patourel, 'Norman succession', 235.

9 Le Patourel, 'Norman succession', 226.

10 Warren, *King John*, 48–9.

11 Warren, *King John*, 53.

12 Wolff, 284.

13 Barrow, 'Kingdom in crisis', 122.

14 There was a precedent for this, arranged during the minority of Alexander's daughter, Margaret of Scotland (d. 1283), at Windsor in 1261. See Watt, 'Minority of Alexander III', 22.

15 *Foedera* (Rec. Comm.), i/1, 720.

16 *Foedera* (Rec. Comm.), i/1, 730, has Friday 17 March. Barrow, 'Kingdom in crisis', 132 has 14 March.

17 See Powicke, *Thirteenth Century*, 268, 512.

18 *CChR 1226–57*, 81.

19 *CPR 1232–47*, 154; *CChR 1226–57*, 220.

20 *CChR 1226–57*, 287 (Dec. 1245), 290 (Feb. 1246).

21 *CChR 1226–57*, 193.

22 *CChR 1226–57*, 276, 392; *CPR 1232–47*, 437.

23 *CChR 1226–57*, 339.

24 *CChR 1226–57*, 345.

25 *Foedera* (Rymer), i, 509.

26 *CPR 1247–58*, 72.

27 *CPR 1247–58*, 220.

28 *CPR 1247–58*, 208.

29 *Royal Wills*, 15.

30 Chris Given-Wilson has pointed out that the continuator of the *Eulogium*, in putting forward the Crouchback legend, 'preserves some interesting ideas', including there being a compromise between Edward I and his brother as to whom should inherit. See Given-Wilson, 'Legitimation, designation', 94.

31 Barrow, *Robert Bruce*, 293–4.

32 Bennett, 'Royal succession', 12.

33 The words '*sez heirs masles de soun corps loialment engendrez*' appear in Edward's entail – and the words 'male heirs of the king's body lawfully procreated' in the Scots entail of 1318. See 'Entail', 583; Barrow, *Robert Bruce*, 294.

34 For Edward I's re-grant in tail male to the earl of Warwick on 25 June 1306, see *CPR 1301–7*, 447. For Edward converting earlier grants to royal family members in tail male, see 'Entail', 589, quoting *CPR 1374–7*, 327, 337, 355, 359. For the completion of the process, see McFarlane, *Nobility*, 72, 272–3.

35 Biancalana, *Fee Tail*, 175.
36 *CPR 1396–9*, 8, 39, 122, 265.
37 *CPR 1396–9*, 35, 150, 164, 176, 340, 402.
38 *CPR 1396–9*, 213 (2), 400, 404, 424–5.
39 *CPR 1396–9*, 201, 205, 281, 415 (2).
40 *CPR 1396–9*, 266, 280–1, 290, 266, 458, 467 (John Holland); 215, 429 (Thomas Holland).
41 *CPR 1396–9*, 209–10, 220, 249 (Thomas Mowbray); 196, 200, 207, 209, 267, 269 (William le Scrope); 39, 61, 267 (Ralph Neville); 213, 250, 449 (Thomas Percy); 213–14, 264, 275 (John Montagu); 219 (Thomas Despenser).
42 *CPR 1396–9*, 361, 543 (Walter Styward); 196, 217 (John Bussy); 196, 221, 226, 322 (Henry Greene); 405 (Thomas Camoys); 579 (Simon Felbrigg).
43 Creton, 201.
44 An entry in the *Eulogium* states that this was raised in the parliament of 1394, when John of Gaunt had sought confirmation that Henry was the heir apparent. However, this may be one of the many post-1399 interpolations. *Eulogium*, iii, 369–70.
45 Given-Wilson, *Chronicles of the Revolution*, 196.
46 *Usk*, 65–7.
47 For example, Riley (ed.), *Chronica et Annales*, 281 (English); *Historia Anglicana*, ii, 237.
48 Davies (ed.), *English Chronicle*, 18.
49 *Eulogium*, 383.
50 Corpus Christi College MS 59, published in Given-Wilson (ed.), *Chronicles of the Revolution*, 166.
51 My own comments to this effect appear in the *Bulletin* of the Richard III Society (Autumn 2008), 20–4. Another historian who has made a similar presumption is McNiven in 'Henry IV and the Lancastrian Title', 476–7.
52 With reference to the legal emphasis, it should be noted that most of the discussions in Edward III's reign concerning the English claim to France had been carried on by lawyers. See Taylor, 'Edward III and the Plantagenet claim', 155–70.
53 Payling, 'Social mobility', 71. He studied feet of fines for the counties of Essex, Sussex, Warwickshire and Wiltshire.
54 *PROME*, 1406 March, items no. 38 (7 June 1406) and no. 60 (22 Dec. 1406).

10

Regnal legitimacy and the concept
of the royal pretender

Historians discussing 'the pretender' in medieval Europe have tended to regard it as an unchanging concept: a continually repeating feature of political life. This lack of nuance is perhaps a symptom of the awkwardness that historians feel when treading on such uncertain ground as medieval royal identity theft. The best study of pretenders yet, Gilles Lecuppre's *L'imposture politique au Moyen Âge* (2005), treats all royal claimants safely, as impostors or 'pseudos', preferring not to discuss whether any of them might have been the genuine article. Such caution reflects the treatment pretenders have received in the English-speaking world, where the tendency has been to lump all post-mortem claimants and 'once and future kings' and 'sleeping kings' together and to regard them all as an archetype or an element of folklore, if they cannot easily be dismissed as political opportunists. Pretenders are much safer subjects when relegated to the margins of history. This is unfortunate for no one pretender is exactly like any other: each one's 'pretender' status owes as much to the king's regnal legitimacy as to his own claim and the political context in which his or her alternative royal status was promulgated. Furthermore, there are fundamental differences between living 'hidden kings' – *les rois cachés* – and the deceased 'sleeping heroes' of folk legend. Some may have been genuine claimants, like Edward II. Thus a key question emerges from the foregoing chapters: how does the survival of Edward II fit in with the development of the pretender in Europe in the Middle Ages?

ORIGINS OF THE CONCEPT

Pretenders were nothing new in the fourteenth century. They had been known in the ancient world. According to Tacitus, an ex-slave had once pretended to be Drusus Caesar after his death in captivity. Thirty years later, at least one man bearing a striking resemblance to Nero claimed to be the post-mortem emperor.[1] However, pretenders remained rare – the stories of kings surviving their deaths tended to follow the archetype of heroic leaders sleeping within caves or hills, ever-ready to return from their personal Valhallas to protect their people (but never actually doing so). In England the best-known 'once and future king' was, of course, Arthur, whose 'survival' was firmly believed in Cornwall in 1113.[2] Folktales from Wales, Cornwall and Brittany suggest a variety of literary attempts to rouse the sleeping king; but only in one respect does this archetype bear upon a real English figure. The undying king as popular hero corresponds with the story of Harold II, who, according to the *Vita Haroldi* (written around 1205), did not die at Hastings but was carried to Winchester where he was nursed back to health by a Saracen woman. After going into Germany and trying in vain to raise support for his restoration, he travelled around Europe as a pilgrim and visited Jerusalem, finally dying at Chester (or Canterbury) as an anonymous hermit.[3] According to Gerald of Wales, writing in the late twelfth century, the Holy Roman Emperor, Henry V (d. 1125), similarly lived out his days at Chester, equally penitent. Gerald's near-contemporary, Walter Map, also mentions Henry V, the last of his dynasty, surviving incognito as a hermit.[4]

The story of Harold II so neatly foreshadows that of the Fieschi Letter that at least one writer has seen the two as developed from a single literary archetype.[5] The similarities are, however, superficial. The *Vita Haroldi* was written for a public audience by a literary creator for the glorification of the dead king 150 years after Harold existed. In marked contrast, Manuele Fieschi was dealing with the personal account of a real man whom he had met and whom he knew still to be alive. As a papal notary, writing for the private information of the king of England, he cannot be compared to a hagiographer writing about a man he only knew from stories and chronicles. Nevertheless, the development of the pretender tradition before the writing of the letter is significant for two reasons. First, it forms a model for a dethroned medieval king to follow, if he found himself as an anonymous individual without resources, respect or throne, and thus it allows us to see more clearly why Edward II went as a pilgrim to Avignon – and why Edward III and his companions followed him into France in 1330 as pilgrims.[6] And, second, it permits us to understand the cultural context which produced post-mortem kings.

Gilles Lecuppre begins his study with an example from eleventh-century Spain, Hisham II al-Hakam, caliph of Cordoba, who was overthrown in 1009. Hisham II returned to power the following year and ruled for three years before being overcome by the Berbers. Then he disappeared, supposedly murdered on 19 April 1013. But rumours of his survival in the East lived on. The governor of Ceuta claimed he knew nothing of the death but had heard that Hisham was a prisoner, and accordingly seized Malaga on Hisham's behalf in 1014. For more than twenty years Hisham continued to be a potent force in the politics of the region, one ruler after another claiming to be acting in his name. Lecuppre uses Hisham to express two basic 'characteristics' of *les rois cachés*: that they represent an alternative ruler or 'leader of the opposition' and that they confer on another family a degree of dignity or orthodoxy that would not extend to a rebellious subject. He uses numismatic evidence to illustrate the power of the post-mortem Hisham II: over the next twenty years no fewer than five rulers invoked Hisham's authority, whether in genuine belief of his survival, or as a pretender, or as a legend.[7]

POST-MORTEM CLAIMANTS BEFORE 1330

The first *active*, living pretender we know of was a man who claimed to be Alphonso I of Aragon, 'the Battler'. Officially, Alphonso the Battler died in the battle of Fraga (1134); but the mid-thirteenth century chronicle of Rodrigo Jimenez de Rada shows that legends were then in circulation that he had survived. That this was not only a legend but a real pretender had indeed claimed to be Alphonso, is evident from other sources, most notably two letters sent by Alphonso II of Aragon to Louis VII of France, between 1163 and 1179, in which he requested Louis's help in arresting the old man, who was then in Catalonia.[8] The author of the *Annales de Teruel*, covering the years 1089–1196, recorded that the pretender was executed by Alphonso II's brother, Raymond Berengar, outside the walls of Barcelona. The disappearance of several local lords at the same juncture suggests the old man gathered political support as an opposition figure.

The next European pretender, Baldwin IX, count of Flanders and Hainault, met a similar fate in 1225. The original Baldwin had been crowned king of Jerusalem and emperor of Constantinople in May 1204 but, in April 1205, he was captured near Adrianople by Ioannitsa (John II) Kaloyan, king of the

Vlachs and Bulgarians.[9] Those in the East were in considerable doubt as to what had happened to him: those in Flanders were left wholly in the dark. The pope wrote to Ioannitsa asking for his release; Ioannitsa replied with the news that the emperor had died in prison.[10] For the next few years, during the minority of his daughters, Joan and Margaret, Flanders and Hainault were ruled by their guardian, Philip of Namur, as regent. When the daughters came of age and married, neither endeared herself to the people of Flanders. Joan, the elder of the two, managed to make herself particularly unpopular. Thus there was a strong popular will for the pious, chaste, crusading Baldwin IX to return. In 1222 one of his old companions arrived back in Flanders dressed as a Franciscan friar, and made himself known to his nephew, Arnoul de Gavre, a councillor of Joan of Flanders. This old crusader announced that several companions of Baldwin were returning in similar guises, having served in the company of Baldwin's brother, Henry, until 1216, after which they fought the Moors in North Africa. In February 1224 a friar appeared in Mortaigne, Flanders, who at first denied that he was Baldwin – dismissing such thoughts as no less ridiculous than the return of King Arthur – but later admitted that he was the genuine count and emperor. The populace was delighted; even Joan's most trusted counsellor believed the man was the returned Baldwin. The returned Baldwin dubbed knights and issued charters, using a seal that employed all his titles, including that of emperor of Constantinople. Henry III of England wrote to him on 11 April 1225 from Westminster congratulating him on his release from prison.[11] Eventually Baldwin met the king of France, Louis VIII, at Péronne. There he failed to answer satisfactorily some questions put to him by the king. Various clergymen identified him as a *jongleur*, Bertrand de Rais. Fleeing to Valenciennes by night, the claimant continued to divide Flanders until the French king captured him. Louis sent him to Joan, requesting that she deal with him mercifully; but she had him tried at Lille, pilloried, tortured and hanged, with his body being exposed on a pole in a field after his death.[12]

The post-mortem Alphonso I and the post-mortem Baldwin IX were both individuals whose deaths were doubtful and whose continued existences would have been of political importance to a faction. The next post-mortem rulers all fall into the same category, and they all concern the inheritance of the iconoclastic Frederick II of Hohenstaufen, king of Germany and Sicily, Holy Roman Emperor, who died in 1250. As is well known, his family struggled unsuccessfully to keep his empire together. His eldest surviving son by Yolanda of Jerusalem, Conrad, died of malaria in 1254, leaving a two-year-old son, Conradin. Conrad's younger half-brother, Manfred, prince of Taranto, acted as regent and refused to surrender Sicily to Pope Innocent IV (Sinibaldo Fieschi, d. 1254). Manfred was promptly excommunicated and went to war with Innocent IV – a war which was continued by Innocent's successors: Alexander IV (d. 1261) and Urban IV (d. 1264). In 1258, having heard that Conradin was dead, Manfred had himself crowned king of Sicily – and did not abdicate when he learned that Conradin was still alive. Nor did he give in to repeated papal demands that he cede the kingdom. When Urban sold Sicily to Charles of Anjou, brother of Louis IX of France, Manfred found himself fighting the French as well as the pope: he was killed at the battle of Benevento in 1266. Charles of Anjou thus gained the throne of Sicily. However, Conradin pursued the throne for another two years until he was seized by Charles at the battle of Tagliacozzo on 23 August 1268 and beheaded in prison at the end of October that year. With no Hohenstaufen heirs of sufficient prominence to continue the fight, the kingdom of Sicily remained in Charles's hands until the Sicilians murdered all the French people on the island during the Sicilian Vespers of 1282.

This was the political backdrop to a succession of pretenders in Italy. The first of these was John de Cocleria: a hermit who bore a marked resemblance to Frederick II. Knowing much about royal affairs in the kingdom of Sicily and elsewhere in the empire, he left his Sicilian hermitage in 1261 at the instigation of various conspirators, especially one Philippe de Catane, a member of the imperial chancery, who had remarked regularly on his likeness to the emperor. John was captured, tortured and executed by Manfred.[13] That did not dissuade men from pretending to be Hohenstaufens – some even claiming to be Manfred himself. According to Salimbene, after Manfred's death, 'King Charles had a large number of men who claimed to be Manfred killed one after another. For these men pretended to be Manfred in order to gain money, and thus exposed themselves to the danger of death.'[14] In 1269, a young man called Hans Stock from Ochsenfurt (Bavaria), who had travelled to Italy, was advanced as a post-mortem Conradin, on account of the fact that he bore a striking resemblance to the beheaded boy-king. He was exposed under interrogation by the bishop of Constance and the abbot of St Gall.[15]

The problem was that there was no legitimate alternative to the government of Charles of Anjou. There were no Hohenstaufens left to champion – until John of Procida, a tireless campaigner for the Hohenstaufen cause, found in Manfred's son in law, Peter of Aragon, a willing alternative contender for the Crown of Sicily. After Peter took up the challenge, the need for pretenders diminished. Ironically, Peter was the great-grandson of Alphonso II, who had been threatened by the first pretender, the post-mortem Alphonso the Battler.

The demise of the house of Hohenstaufen gave rise to pretenders in Frederick II's northern lands as well; such pretences, however, took place later, in the 1280s, in opposition to Rudolph I of Germany. A friar called Henry, in the garb of a hermit, claimed to be the emperor in 1284.[16] More famously, Dietrich Holzschuh appeared at Cologne in 1285 claiming to be Frederick II: he was burnt at the stake by Rudolph. Two years after that, another friar appeared in Lubeck claiming to be Frederick – and was fêted and crowned by the crowd.[17] Even though more than thirty years had passed since Frederick's death, and even though a living Frederick would have been aged ninety, the Hohenstaufen name lived on as a political force. Finally, it is worth remarking that there were two impostors of the living Henry I of Mecklenburg (d. 1291) during his imprisonment, who Lecuppre suggests were inspired by the events at Lubeck in 1287.[18] One was drowned, the other burned at the stake. Even if a ruler was believed to be alive there was potential political value in feigning his freedom and assuming his power.

Prior to Frederick II's demise, no single death had led to multiple attempts to impersonate a dead king. What is striking is that most of these supposedly dead kings came back to claim their kingdoms in the guise of hermits. This is not surprising: some of the original rulers were old when they died, so their post-mortem selves had to be even older. It was important that contemporaries should perceive an ex-king's royal dignity as intact, regardless of his age. The strongest claim a pretender could offer was that, because he was the genuine, divinely chosen ruler, God would be displeased if the people were to reject their rightful king and continue to support the interloper. Therefore, returned 'kings' could not be presented as having been merchants (who would have been perceived as prioritizing the making of money over their responsibilities to their people). Nor could they be presented as lesser lords; if they remained secular they could only argue that they had been fighting the infidel in distant lands (like Baldwin of Flanders) – otherwise they would be perceived as having not given the good government of their people a high priority. But most were too old to pretend they could still don armour, and lacked the military equipment and supporters necessary to convince anyone that this had been their recent preoccupation. Obviously they could not have presented themselves as bishops or other ecclesiastical officials, whose appointments would have been documented. So they had no option but to don the religious habit, either of a hermit (if they were stationary) or a friar (if they were travelling about). Although it is tempting to see a connection between the aged Alphonso the Battler, the 'Franciscan' Baldwin of Flanders/Bertrand de Rais, and the friars and hermits who pretended to be various members of the Hohenstaufen dynasty, in reality there were no alternatives for a pseudo-king or a genuine ex-ruler. A religious life was the only option.

The next instance of a pretender in European history is, most unusually, that of a woman: the False Margaret, as she is known to historians. As noted in the previous chapter, Margaret of Norway was acknowledged heir to the throne of Scotland in 1284 and sought by Edward I as a bride for his son in 1290. She was despatched in a Norwegian royal ship but supposedly died at sea. The ship put in at Orkney and messengers were sent into England to relay the bad news to the king (although the only extant letter is unclear as to whether she had actually died or not).[19] It is reasonable to presume that the message was eventually conveyed to the king that the young queen had indeed died, for the marriage did not go ahead. The queen's body was supposedly returned to Norway, where it was buried in the chapel at Bergen alongside that of her late mother. However, a woman claiming to be Margaret of Norway came by a ship from Lubeck to Bergen in 1300 with her husband. She explained that a woman who had been attending her on the voyage in 1290, Fra Ingibiorg Erlingsdottir, had accepted a bribe to fake her death, and she had been taken to Germany where she had married a German. Found guilty of fraud the following year, no doubt after interrogation on the orders of the new king of Norway, Haakon V, she was burnt at the stake and her husband was hanged.

The post-mortem Margaret has always been dismissed as a fraud by historians. Referring to a letter written in 1320, Joseph Anderson wrote in 1872 that 'it leaves no doubt on my mind at least that the case of the false Margaret was an imposture of the daring political kind to which we have parallels in our own history in those of Simnel and Perkin Warbeck.'[20] Historians subsequently have followed this conclusion unwaveringly.[21] But Anderson's method was weak. The letter in question was written by Bishop Audfinn for the specific purpose of dissuading would-be pilgrims from going to Nordnes to visit the grave of the pretender 'Saint Maritte' (Margaret) in 1319 – nineteen years later. The evidence on which Anderson pinned his dismissal was self-evidently drawn up for the purposes of propaganda. The 'facts' in question may or may not have been true: they include the claimant being much older than the real Margaret would have been, and that King Erik had personally inspected her corpse on her return and deemed her to be his daughter. But these were things which, after the space of nineteen years, a bishop could easily state without fear of reprisal, especially when he had not only royal support but a royal mandate to proclaim them. Three things perhaps should restrain us from rushing to judgement and declaring the post-mortem Margaret an impostor. First, the letter of 7 October 1290 to Edward I containing the news of the death of the young queen contained a conflicting report that said she had recovered from her illness. The confusion is very strange; but if Margaret had been abducted (as the pretender claimed), that too would be a reason for the marriage not to go ahead. Second, Haakon V did not have local authorities interrogate the post-mortem Margaret and her German husband; he had her brought to Bergen and examined there the following year. Thus there seems to have been a specific political context to her claim. Third, 'Saint Maritte' was identified in an Icelandic source as relating at her trial how she had heard an Icelandic priest, Haflidi Steinsson, at Bergen before setting out for Scotland in 1290. After her death, the said priest confirmed that her words were correct.[22] One might add that the Scottish chronicler Wyntoun describes the Norwegians putting the genuine Margaret of Norway, granddaughter of Alexander III of Scotland, to death – a narrative that only emphasizes the confusion surrounding her case.[23] Although we may be confident that Edward I was eventually informed that the young queen had indeed died or disappeared (as the royal wedding did not go ahead), the circumstances are much more shadowy than historians have hitherto acknowledged. There were certainly those who would have benefited from her premature death – and those who would have wished to preserve her life at all costs, even at the loss of her royal identity.

For the purposes of the present narrative it does not matter whether the post-mortem Margaret was genuine or false. Had she genuinely wanted to make the most of her self-proclaimed identity, she should have gone to Scotland, not Norway, as the woman she claimed to be was the granddaughter of Alexander III and, as the sole survivor of his dynasty, entitled to the throne. Perhaps the plan was that she should establish herself first in Norway and, if successful in gaining Haakon's support, head to Scotland afterwards. Alternatively the plan may simply have been to create a rival to Haakon V. Although Margaret was lower in the Norwegian order of royal precedence than Haakon, the king had no sons. It has been suggested that the man who encouraged her to 'return' to Norway was Audun Hugleikson of Hegranes who had acted both as the attorney for the real Margaret and as a diplomat for her father in the 1290s.[24] The death of King Erik in 1299 and the accession of his brother, Haakon V (who executed Hugleikson in 1302), may well have been Hugleikson's motive in wanting a rival to return to Norway. Certainly he could have instructed Margaret as to what she should claim to remember about her departure from Bergen in 1290; he had been with the real Margaret there.

Over all this speculation, however, hovers the fact that 'Saint Maritte' had come from Lubeck. If she was as old as Bishop Audfinn later claimed, she would have seen first-hand the power of a pretender. If not, she would have heard about it from the citizens of Lubeck. The memory of the much-lauded post-mortem Frederick II in that city in 1287 may well have provided her and her German husband with sufficient incentive to take the risk and sail to Bergen. And if she had been led to *believe* that she was the genuine Margaret of Norway, and her husband believed it, then her townspeople's recollection of the post-mortem Frederick II may have inspired her to claim what she believed was her true identity. Thus there may well have been a direct connection between the false Hohenstaufens in Sicily in the 1260s, the false Frederick Hohenstaufen in 1284–87, and 'False Margaret' in 1300.

The final post-mortem royal claimant we have to consider before coming to Edward II is Andrew III of Hungary. In 1317 Robert, king of Naples, wrote to his brother-in-law, Sancho I of Majorca requesting that he send him the man pretending to be Andrew III, who was then at Montpelier. Sancho seems to have obliged.[25] This too seems to have been inspired by the Hohenstaufen pretenders. Andrew III had been the last male of the Arpad dynasty – very much as Conradin had been the last of the Hohenstaufens – and, as the Hohenstaufens had demonstrated, in the absence of genuine heirs, the supporters of a dynasty have to create artificial ones. In fact the comparison with the Hohenstaufens runs closer. The Arpad dynasty also had the problem of Rudolph of Germany to contend with: Rudolph saw Hungary as his domain and, five weeks after

Andrew III's coronation, he attempted to create his son, Albert of Austria, king of Hungary. Andrew III defeated this claimant but before he managed to conclude a peace settlement with him, he found himself having to face Maria of Hungary, the sister of his murdered predecessor, Ladislas IV, and the wife of Charles II of Naples. He also had to deal with the impostor Andrew of Hungary, supposedly a brother of Ladislas and Maria. Maria passed her claim to Charles Martel, her son, and he in turn passed it to his son, Charles, after his death in 1295. After Andrew III's death in 1301, Hungary passed to this last Charles, Maria's grandson, who was crowned Charles I of Hungary. In terms of cultural context, therefore, the Arpad case has much in common with the Hohenstaufen one.

A second reason for connecting the 1317 pretender with the Hohenstaufen–Anjou conflict lies in Maria of Hungary herself. Her husband, Charles II, was the son and heir of the Charles of Anjou who had forced the Hohenstaufen dynasty out of Italy and weathered all the pretenders thereafter. Charles of Anjou had transferred the capital of the kingdom of Sicily to Naples on his accession in 1266 and there it had remained until the division of the kingdom into the separate kingdoms of Sicily and Naples after the Sicilian Vespers in 1282. Although Peter III of Aragon took over completely in Sicily, the kingdom of Naples remained in Angevin hands; and it was here that Maria of Hungary resided until her death in 1323, first as queen and then, after her husband's death in 1309, as queen mother during the reign of her son, Robert, king of Naples, count of Provence and Forcalquier, senator of Rome and (from 1318 to 1334) lord of Genoa. It was therefore not just the post-Hohenstaufen dynastic context that provoked a post-mortem Andrew III: it was also an awareness of the power of the pretender in the geographical heartland of the Hohenstaufen–Angevin–Sicilian conflict.

POLITICAL IMPOSTURE IN ENGLAND BEFORE 1330

From the foregoing survey of post-mortem royal claimants prior to 1330, it is evident that there was a strong Continental awareness of the power of *le roi caché*. But England seems to have been wholly free of active post-mortem pretenders. There was only the case of John of Powderham: his claim to be a rightful son of Edward I (described in Chapter 6) is the earliest instance of a living English royal claimant of any sort. And his claim in itself was unusual, for he did not claim to be a supposedly dead king or prince or any specific member of the royal family but rather a child switched at birth with Edward II. One can say much the same for one 'Henriet' who tried to pass himself off as Thomas of Brotherton in Paris in 1320: he was soon exposed as a self-interested fraudster, on the lookout for royal gifts. The concept of a man claiming to be in reality a supposedly dead ex-king or heir was unprecedented in England.

Having said that, the concept of the pretender would clearly have been well known from the early thirteenth century. The stories of Harold and Henry V living out their days as hermits at Chester appear in chronicles that were circulating in England. The letter to the post-mortem Baldwin from Henry III allows us to say for certain that *le roi caché* was known to the English royal family by 1225. It may be considered doubtful that all of the Hohenstaufen pretenders of the 1260s came to the attention of the English but some of them must have done, as the pope's first candidate for the kingdom of Sicily was not Charles of Anjou but Henry III's brother, Richard, and his second choice was Henry III's younger son, Edmund Crouchback. Certainly the post-mortem Margaret of Norway came to Scottish attention, as shown in Wyntoun's description of her execution: however, it should be noted that he presumed she was the genuine Queen Margaret, not a post-mortem impostor. But all this was awareness of what happened *elsewhere*. Although suitable dynastic and political contexts for pretenders had developed in England over the period, not one had yet emerged except the misguided John of Powderham.

The significance of this has not previously been appreciated. So keen have historians been to distance themselves from pretenders' unsubstantiated claims that they have missed the significance of the *lack* of pretenders in England. Harold was not a pretender – his story is that of a 'once and future king' like Arthur: a post-mortem immortal hero. In this respect it is most significant that those whom one would have expected to give rise to pretenders on account of concealed circumstances at death and political gain thereafter did not emerge in England. No one claimed to be a royal survivor from the *White Ship*, which sank in 1120, or the 'true' living son of King Stephen. No one claimed to be the living Arthur of Brittany after his disappearance in 1203, despite the opprobrium in which King John was held and despite the mysterious circumstances of the boy's disappearance. Had the post-mortem archetype been widely known in England we might have expected a post-mortem Prince Arthur to have appeared long before the baronial showdown at the end of John's reign. The dead elder brothers of Richard and John were never resurrected as pretenders to counter either king; nor were the elder brothers of Edward II claimed to be alive, despite the opposition to the king's character throughout his reign. Every deceased member of the English royal family whose continued existence might have been considered politically useful failed to inspire a pretender. One would have thought that, in the reigns of Stephen, King John and Edward II especially, a royal rival would have gathered political support, as the opposition to each of these kings was so strong that their regnal legitimacy was in doubt as a result of their wayward government. This, indeed, was the strongest reason for believing John of Powderham's story: Edward II's kingship was so unkingly that he himself undermined his regnal legitimacy. But not even the opposition magnates supported him. No royal pretender appeared in England to challenge the king to the throne prior to the fifteenth century. Nor did a pretender appear in Wales to carry on the fight against Edward I after 1282. No pretenders appeared in Scotland either. The British simply did not do royal pretenders – until the fifteenth century.

The entry in Norwell's royal household account book for 1338 is thus significant for reasons quite beyond the question of Edward II himself and the diplomatic consequences of his survival. Edward II qua 'William le Galeys' stands outside the archetype of the 'public' royal pretender, being a private claimant with no aspirations to take the throne, whose claims were tacitly acknowledged (in his expenses being paid by his son). He was the first European claimant to a *dethroned* royal identity; thus he was the only claimant to a devalued royal status. Unlike every earlier royal claimant about whom we have information, he actually met his successor and was entertained at royal expense. And unlike the Hohenstaufen and Arpad pretenders, he did not claim to represent the last of his dynasty; the context for his emergence was not one of dynastic failure or the need for a royal leader of the opposition. His claim was simply for his identity to be recognized, not to gain royal power and responsibilities.

Having said this, Edward II was undoubtedly informed and aided by the archetype of the pretender. In considering why he took on the guise of a pilgrim, there seems little doubt that he knew one of the earlier stories and saw a pilgrim's disguise as the only suitable one for a king. In this respect he may have been following the story of Harold II or Baldwin of Flanders. Alternatively he may have been entering the church as a form of noble retirement – as many lords and lesser men did, and indeed as his aunt and grandmother had done. As to why he made his way to Avignon, as we have seen in Chapter 5, in this he was simply following in the footsteps of his half-brother – going to see the one man with authority to direct him in regard to the divine aspects of his royal self. But also he would have been aware from the foregoing stories of the danger of being a publicly recognizable ex-king: most were hanged, like the post-mortem Baldwin of Flanders and the impostor John of Powderham, or burnt at the stake, like Dietrich Holzschuh and 'Saint Maritte'. Furthermore, there were other personal literary models for Edward II. The 'Prophecy of the Six Kings', in its earliest form (written about 1312), declared that Edward would die in a foreign country.[26] Even more striking in this respect is the slightly earlier sequence, 'Adam Davy's Five Dreams': the second dream has Edward going to Rome as a pilgrim, wearing grey garb, to meet the pope.[27] As this was probably written for Edward himself by a friar and thus almost certainly known to him, it may well have been the inspiration for his journey to Avignon in the garb of a pilgrim.

EDWARD II, GIANNINO BAGLIONI
AND THE POSTNATAL SWITCH

Edward II's position in the development of the concept of the pretender depends very much on who knew his identity. This was secret information – we would expect many more sources to describe him if it was at all widely known. Nevertheless, we can be certain that his survival was known to members of Cardinal Luca Fieschi's household at Avignon (such as Jacobo de Sarzana and Manuele Fieschi) and Cardinal Luca Fieschi's nephews, including Antonio Fieschi and Bernabo Malaspina, whose responsibilities took them from Avignon to central and Northern Italy. This is particularly interesting because Cola di Rienzi, the architect of the next royal pretender, certainly had spent time among the cardinals at Avignon.

A notary by training, Cola entered the service of Rome. At the age of twenty-nine he had been sent as an ambassador to Pope Clement VI, arriving at Avignon in January 1343. By 9 August of that year he was sufficiently intimate with Clement to be described as a member of his *familia*.[28] In 1347 he was elected to the position of dictator of Rome and ruled the city until being ousted in late 1349. He then spent two years in remote Franciscan and Celestine hermitages in the Maiella Mountains before being imprisoned by Charles IV, the Holy Roman Emperor, in Bohemia. Having fallen out of favour with Clement VI, Cola was saved by the pope's death and the election of Innocent VI in 1352. Sent back to Rome by the new pope, he regained power on 1 August 1354, and almost immediately sent for Giovanni 'Giannino' Baglioni of Siena. On Giannino's arrival in Rome (2 October 1354), Cola revealed to the perplexed Sienese merchant that he was in fact none other than King John I of France, who had been supposed to have died shortly after his birth in 1316.[29] Just as John of Powderham claimed he had been switched with Edward II in the cradle, Cola claimed that Giannino was the real royal baby and the dead John I a false substitute. Cola was thus creating a pretender whose life story correlated with both stories of 'Edward II': (1) that he was switched in the cradle and (2) that after his supposed death he continued to represent a silent danger to his successor.

Giannino came to believe the Roman dictator and spent many years of his life and much money trying to assert that he was indeed the rightful king of France. We know this because, very unusually, he left a quasi-autobiography, the *Istoria del re Giannino di Francia*.[30] So remarkable is this document that scholars have long considered it a purely literary work. However, Tommaso di Carpegna Falconieri has recently shown that Giannino's existence and his story, including his claim to be king of France, are corroborated by documents in the Sienese archives and an enrolled papal letter in the Vatican (dated 27 October 1359 and 16 April 1361 respectively), as well as a comment in the writings of Benvenuto of Imola (c. 1375).[31] Whether his claim was genuine or not is not the issue here; rather it is the form of the claim and what it tells us about the development of the concept of the pretender that is significant.

Various individuals whom Giannino met already knew the story of the switched babies. Giannino himself had heard the story before – from a French knight who had travelled through Siena in 1350. Cola di Rienzi showed Giannino a letter from a friar which purported to contain the confession of Marie de Cressay, the mother of the baby that had died and been buried as John I of France; but, as he himself said, he had heard the story before that, at Avignon.[32] A Dominican friar, Bartolomeo Mini, from whom Giannino sought advice after speaking to Cola di Rienzi, told him he had heard the story of the switched babies twenty years earlier, while he had been a student in Paris. This would date the circulation in Paris of the story to 1334 – six years after the death of Charles IV of France, the last male of the line of Philip the Fair. The 'survival' of John I as a representative of the supporters of a deceased dynasty was thus comparable to the Hohenstaufen and the Arpad pretenders as representatives of the hopes of those dynasties. John of Powderham's story of Edward II being switched at birth with him, which was widely circulated in England in 1318, being recorded in a wide variety of chronicles, and no doubt repeated in Isabella's native kingdom, was relatively recent. There is a strong possibility that this story of shifted royal identities in England gave rise to the John I story in Paris, when supporters of Charles IV faced the prospect of their throne being claimed by Philip de Valois or Edward III. The same story, circulated at Avignon and around the rest of Europe, seems to have inspired Cola di Rienzi.

The essence of the John of Powderham story, recycled the French political whisperers, probably also inspired someone to tell the same story about John of Gaunt. He was later rumoured to have been switched in infancy, in Ghent, with the baby of a Flemish woman, due to the death of a royal baby and the queen's desire to avoid the king's anger. Although in John of Gaunt's case the rumours are known from much later English sources, Edward III and his wife may have heard the story from the archbishop of Canterbury within months of the baby's birth. On 18 November 1340 Edward III wrote to the pope stating that the archbishop had 'spoken to me separately of my wife, and to my wife of me, in order that, if he were listened to, he might provoke us to such anger as to divide us forever.'[33] Even if this extraordinary but mysterious statement is not to be associated with rumours of John of Gaunt being switched in the cradle, it seems probable that the John I story came to be associated with him at a later date; for not only are the circumstances of the supposed switch very similar, the means by which it became known are almost the same. In the case of the post-mortem John I, Marie de Cressay is supposed to have confessed to a Spanish friar on her deathbed that the dead John I was really her own child and the royal baby, the last of the Capetians, lived; and that his true nature should be revealed to him.[34] In 1376 the switch of John of Gaunt and a Flemish boy was said to have become known because Queen Philippa confessed on her deathbed to Bishop Wykeham; and she wanted him to know this in case there was ever any chance of John becoming king.[35] In this way it seems the story of John of Powderham led to the circulation of a variation on the political impostor theme – one which was very powerful because it could not actually be disproved. In such cases there was no dead person who could be produced to prove the falsehood of the claim. One dead baby would have looked much like another.

The important aspect about these stories is that, by example, the power of the post-mortem pretender and the switched baby were demonstrated widely around Europe. Knowledge of these political devices was disseminated as the king of France, the pope, the king of Naples, the king of Hungary and a great many nobles tried to get Giannino simply to go away. Giannino did not go away, however. Eventually he raised a mercenary army and may even have taken control of a French town, Pont-Saint-Esprit, in late December 1360.[36] Soon afterwards he was captured and thrown into prison by Joan, queen of Naples. He was still in that prison in October 1362 and dead by 1369, when his widow made her will.

The foregoing suggests that the axis of imposture shifted over the period 1260–1360 from the Hohenstaufen lands, especially the kingdom of Sicily, to France. In reality, the idea had simply spread across the whole of Europe. When Giannino Baglioni arrived at Buda, hoping to see the king of Hungary in December 1357, he found that the king was dealing with another impostor, King Andrew.[37] By the later fourteenth century the concept of post-mortem political imposture was widespread, and that of postnatal royal switch had become a political tool in England and France.

RICHARD II AND EDWARD II

Edward II's survival, while clearly not made generally known, cannot have been forgotten. Isabella did not die until 1358. Thomas Berkeley did not die until 1361; John Maltravers lived until 1364. And of course Edward III himself lived another thirteen years beyond that. Even if the principle participants in the events of 1327–30 never spoke a word to their families in the years after, there were still others who knew some of the details. That the knowledge of Edward II's survival remained a story re-circulated privately in England is potentially significant, for if a few important men knew or believed that an ex-king had genuinely survived his supposed murder, then the potential to believe it could happen a second time was that much greater.

That Edward II's survival remained a secret long after his death is implicit in the fact we have no chronicles describing it, even at a much later date. Edward III seems to have wanted all mention of his father's survival suppressed, understandably. In 1352 he summoned Ranulph Higden to bring all his chronicles from Chester to show him: the sodomitical torture contained in that chronicle no doubt displeased Edward III but at least he was protected from rumours of his father's survival. Nevertheless, there are indicators that lessons were learnt. As noted in Chapter 3, the custom of displaying the face of a deceased royal person started after 1327 – a practice known to have been stipulated in their wills by Henry, duke of Lancaster, in 1361, and John of Gaunt, duke of Lancaster in 1399; and to have been carried out for Edward III himself in 1377 and Richard II, at the direction of Henry IV, in 1400. This at least indicates a continued awareness of the dangers of letting a body be buried incognito as that of a royal personage.

The most important line of enquiry is what the earl of Kent's fellow plotters revealed to their families about Edward II after 1330. Of these, the most significant questions concern the family of the earl of Kent himself. What were his children told about their father's execution? That he was a traitor? Their mother, Margaret – who had herself written the letter to Edward II at Corfe Castle, which was produced at Kent's trial – not only secured his pardon and the return of his title and estates for the benefit of her children, she lived until 1349. Her eldest son died young but her second son John lived to 1352 and her daughter, Joan, the 'Fair Maid of Kent', to 1385. It is inconceivable that Margaret maintained to her children that their father had been anything other than a man who died trying to right a wrong and to free his unlawfully imprisoned half-brother. This is especially the case considering that she repeated in her petition to Edward III in 1330 that Roger Mortimer had confessed on the gallows that her husband had died 'wrongfully'. Margaret had been an accessory to the plot herself. She never remarried. But her daughter, Joan, married three times, having children by both Thomas Holland and Prince Edward. If Margaret passed on to her daughter Joan a burning sense of injustice at the treatment suffered by her husband, Joan's father – and there is every reason to suppose she would have done – we can see Joan's children would have inherited that sense of injustice. The most popular chronicles of the time repeated that the earl of Kent had given his life for his brother: every time one of Kent's grandchildren heard the relevant passages in the *Brut* read aloud, they must have been reminded. These grandchildren included Richard II and his half-siblings, Thomas, John and Maud Holland, so we can see why the stories of their grandfather's unjust death continued to have currency at court. This would only have added to the personal sense with which Richard II reflected back on his great-grandfather, Edward II: he was descended from both of the victims of the events of 1327–30, Edward II and the earl of Kent.

It is nothing new to point out that Richard II was fascinated by his great-grandfather, Edward II. As noted in Chapter 7, he made repeated attempts to have Edward recognized as a saint. In so doing he may have been motivated by a cynical desire to vindicate the rule of a man who, like Richard himself, did not conform to the image of a great king, with popularity, military prestige and respect as a law maker. Equally, and less cynically, he may have had a genuine sympathy with a man whose character was not suited to military kingship, who did not have a positive relationship with a powerful militaristic father, and who took to task those magnates who tried to inhibit his freedom to rule through ordinances and councils. But in addition, he may have been moved by the extraordinary story of his ancestors, and how Kent had sought to free the ex-king from his wrongful custody, had been put to death by Roger Mortimer for his pains, and how the ex-king had lived thereafter as a hermit in Italy. Perhaps he believed in the miracles alleged to have taken place at the tomb in Gloucester Abbey. Certainly he paid off the debt to the Bardi (as noted in Chapter 7) and, at the same time, petitioned the pope to recognize Edward II as a saint. He did not let the matter lie.

RICHARD II AND THE POST-MORTEM DUKE OF GLOUCESTER

Richard II's mindfulness of his great-grandfather's survival has an important context in understanding his reaction to Thomas Mowbray's failure to murder the duke of Gloucester in 1397. As James Tait demonstrated in a landmark essay on the subject, published in 1902, we may be sure that Richard murdered his uncle on account of the fact that he announced the duke's death in late August, some weeks before the duke's confession was made in Calais (8 September) and certainly long before the date of 15 September given in the duke's inquisitions post mortem.[38] Despite an attempt by A. E. Stamp in 1923 to argue that there is no good evidence that the death was announced in August 1397, this objection was destroyed in 1932 by H. G. Wright, who pointed out that the Fine Rolls include Richard's order to inquire into the value of the *late* duke's estates dated 7 September.[39] One would have thought that that would have sealed the case for

Richard II as a murderer. However, two scholars have subsequently suggested the duke died of natural causes.[40] Such suggestions ignore the information basis underpinning Tait's and Wright's arguments, which is a matter of certainty. So it is worth briefly repeating its essence.

Richard II's announcement of the duke's death before it happened – regardless of the cause – is proof that either he made a mistake or was aware of the impending event. Had it been a mistake we would not expect to find two independent information streams, both based on first-hand accounts, attesting to Richard's orders to have his uncle murdered. These are:

1. William Bagot's bill of 6 October 1399. This contains Thomas Mowbray's statement to Bagot, made in October 1397, that he (Mowbray) had been ordered by Richard II to kill the duke of Gloucester and had failed to do so, and 'had saved his life for more than three weeks', resulting in Richard despatching a man to Calais for the express purpose of killing him.[41]

2. The confession of John Hall (one of Mowbray's servants), that he saw John Lovetoft deliver the duke to the Prince's Inn in Calais and stood guard while William Serle (a valet of Richard's chamber) and a man named Francis (a valet of Rutland's chamber) smothered him under a mattress in a back room.[42]

Mowbray's testimony and Hall's confession amount to proof that the report of the duke's death before it took place was not an accident. That it was indeed announced before it took place is proved by the duke's confession, made at Calais on 8 September, and the report in the Fine Rolls entry, made at Westminster, on the 7th. In addition there are several testimonies that men had heard the death announced before they last saw him. Mowbray's statement above is one. John Hall similarly claimed to have been surprised to hear that the duke was still alive. William Rickhill testified in a petition to parliament, dated 18 November 1399, that he had heard the duke was dead before he saw him alive and recorded his confession in Calais.[43] Finally, Rickhill's petition also supports the accuracy of Hall's confession in describing John Lovetoft's presence as a keeper of the duke in Calais. Lovetoft was also one of the witnesses of the duke's confession, made on 8 September in the castle of Calais.[44] There can be no doubt that, whether or not the duke was ill, it was Richard's second order to kill him that proved fatal.

For the present purposes the most significant element of this whole episode is that Thomas Mowbray did not kill the royal duke straight away but kept him alive for three weeks. Richard simply presumed his orders to murder the duke, probably issued on or about 17 August, had been carried out.[45] As an intimate companion of the king's for many years, Mowbray would have known that Thomas Berkeley had not murdered Edward II in 1327 but had announced his death and kept the man secretly alive. It is more than ironic that this second royal 'murder' also did not involve the victim being killed – at least, not immediately.

The potency of a secretly alive duke of Gloucester, from Richard II's point of view, was too much. For Mowbray to place the duke of Gloucester, whom Richard despised, in the same role as Edward II, whom Richard thought worthy of sainthood, was shocking to the king. That Mowbray could disobey such important orders was probably less significant than the worry that the earl of Kent's plot – to free a supposedly dead man from his wrongful secret imprisonment – would be re-enacted, successfully this time, and Richard revealed not as a saintly great-grandson of Edward II but as a latter-day Roger Mortimer figure. Worse still, if the duke escaped he would have acquired the status and power of a wronged man – and a royal one at that. Small wonder, then, that Richard sent Mowbray back to Calais with William Serle to ensure that the killing was carried out quickly.

THE EARL OF KENT'S PLOT AND THE EPIPHANY RISING, 1400

The legacy of Edward II's survival seems to have continued to influence the grandsons of the doomed earl of Kent even after the duke of Gloucester's killing. The evidence for this lies in the circumstances of the Epiphany Rising. After Richard's fall and deposition and enforced abdication, he and his half-brothers were treated extraordinarily leniently by Henry IV. Indeed, the only accusation levelled against Henry throughout his first parliament was that he had been too lenient on Richard II's intimates. All that they lost were the ducal titles and estates they had been granted since 1397. They retained all their other titles and estates, many of which had been given to them by Richard. Despite this extraordinarily generous treatment, they rebelled against the new king in an attempt to rescue Richard II. Why?

Previous explanations have tended to stress the closeness of the rebel dukes to Richard II. And that is undoubtedly a correct view of the relationships. But it is not the whole explanation of their plot to kill Henry IV and his sons on the feast of the Epiphany, Richard II's birthday. It is likely that the key plotters were inspired by Kent's example in 1330, for there are a number of points of comparison between the Epiphany Rising and Kent's plot. First, Richard was now an ex-king, like Edward II. Second, he was imprisoned secretly, as Edward II was in 1328–30. Third, the ex-king in 1330 had a half-brother who tried to procure the said ex-king's liberty: the same circumstances applied in 1400. Fourth, the half-brother in question, John Holland, earl of Huntingdon, had much to lose: we cannot understand why he took such an enormous risk except in the same way we can understand Edmund, earl of Kent, taking the same risk in 1330: out of a deep sense of loyalty to the imprisoned ex-king. Richard II and his two Holland half-brothers (one of whom had died in 1397) must have reflected long before 1400 on Edward II and his two half-brothers in 1330. There was a question of loyalty hanging over all of them: if Richard II was in a similar plight to Edward II, in prison, would one of his half-brothers come to the rescue as their grandfather, Edmund, earl of Kent had in 1330? As things turned out in 1400, only one of them was able to try to live up to that expectation. He was joined in his efforts by his nephew, Thomas Holland, the son and heir of Thomas Holland. Both of these men bore the title of earl of Kent, like the faithful Edmund. The sense of duty which they must have felt in the wake of the sentence of perpetual imprisonment on Richard II, while they were at liberty, must have been overwhelming. Hence the Holland family risked all to rescue the ex-king.

Henry IV would no doubt have understood – and been fearful of – the motives which led to the Epiphany Rising. He would have realized that he would never be secure on his throne while Richard lived and the tradition of the earl of Kent rescuing his dethroned half-brother remained strong. Hence the order to kill the ex-king, almost certainly by starving him to death – a process complete on 14 February 1400. That Richard was murdered and that Henry IV was responsible is not in doubt in either respect: it is possible to build an information-based argument that leads to certainty in the matter (published in *Fears*).[46] But what docs need explanation is how the story of Edward II's survival, filtered through Richard II's death, resulted in the first post-mortem pretender in England.

'KING RICHARD IS ALIVE!'

The rumoured survival of Richard II is the first instance in England of an active post-mortem king. And as post-mortem careers go, it was dramatic. It had two dimensions. First there was the popular movement, which Simon Walker has called the 'infrapolitics', wherein 'King Richard is alive!' was more of a battle cry or a loyalty badge than a statement of actual belief.[47] Second there was the pretender as a political figurehead. These two dimensions cannot be treated separately. The popular movement was so widespread that it encouraged dissident lords and religious leaders; and the lords and religious leaders in turn fuelled the popular support. As a result, the post-mortem Richard II saw the relatively simple concept of *le roi caché* surpassed as a political force, for over the course of 1401–15 it managed to combine popular sentiment with an opposition leadership, complete with pseudo-royal figurehead, a royal sanctuary and a means of official communication. The pretender thus acquired longevity, and his supporters became indistinguishable from the supporters of a genuine claimant to the throne, the earl of March. This led to a powerful combination: a double-headed hydra which was unprecedented in European history and which could not be dealt with by the traditional means of the exposure, humiliation and execution of the pretender – not without concentrating all the support on the genuine claimant.

The popular movement supporting the post-mortem Richard II has been covered in some depth by Peter McNiven, Philip Morgan, Paul Strohm and Simon Walker.[48] Therefore it is not intended here to describe all the aspects of the 'infrapolitics'. Instead it is intended to maintain a focus on the development of the post-mortem Richard II as a consciously created political instrument, and the consequences of linking that instrument with the Mortimer claim, to examine the phenomenon that followed as the culmination of the development of the pretender.

Henry IV knew as well as Richard II the potency of a supposedly dead king. If Richard II had heard stories of Edward II's survival and of his grandfather's attempt to rescue him from Corfe, then so had Henry (who had been in Richard's household as a boy). Similarly, if Richard understood Edward III's predicament in knowing Edward II was alive and being kept somewhere in Italy in the 1330s, then so did Henry. Henry certainly knew from Bagot (and possibly other sources) that the duke of Gloucester had briefly been in a similar situation: kept alive after his death had been announced. Henry's councillors in 1400 also knew this. When they received preliminary news of Richard II's death – reported to them indirectly between 3 and 8 February 1400 by French envoys, in advance of his actual death – they recommended that Henry continue to keep him safely if he be alive and, if he be dead, 'let him be shown openly to the people that they might have knowledge of it'.[49] Accordingly Henry made every effort to let everyone know the ex-king was dead. Three contemporary chroniclers note the exposure of the face on the long journey to London, including Walsingham, who was writing at St Alban's, where the king's body lay for one night on its journey.[50] In London it was exposed in Cheapside, in St Paul's Cathedral and in Westminster Abbey. It was then taken away for an unobtrusive burial at King's Langley. As McNiven has pointed out, 'Henry IV steered a remarkably astute course between proving that Richard II was dead and avoiding public opportunities for demonstrations of hostility towards the new regime'.[51]

The comprehensiveness with which Henry IV destroyed his cousin's vitality – not just his life – partly explains why such a long period passed before any claims that he survived were recorded. It took nearly two years for the conclusiveness of the dead king's face to diminish in the popular memory. However, over the course of those months, England plunged into an abysmal period of harvest failure, social unrest, the breakdown of order and opposition to the government. This can be charted from a high in January 1400 – when several towns rose up spontaneously to quash the leaders of the Epiphany Rising – to the low of the Percy rebellion in July 1403. Already by May 1401 there was a widespread sense of despair, famously documented in the highly critical letter to the king, dated 4 May 1401, by his confessor, Philip Repingdon. Moreover, this sense of despair could be personally linked with Henry. The legality of his succession was a secondary factor in most people's minds – as stated in the previous chapter, the technicalities of male entailments allowing the principle of representation in respect of males but not females would have gone way over most people's heads. What had interested most people in 1399 was that Henry promised to rule better than Richard and had the credentials to do so. He still enjoyed that trust in January 1400. But within two years it had greatly diminished. By the end of 1401, Henry had failed to make any inroads in Scotland, had failed to pay his debts to several important magnates, had plunged the Exchequer into debt, seen royal officials murdered, had met with the beginning of the Welsh rebellion under Glendower, faced significant opposition in parliament, and burnt the first heretic priest (William Sawtre). People must have wondered whether their political masters had done the right thing in removing the legitimate monarch from the throne. Probably the harvest failures of 1400–1 were seen as signs of God's displeasure.[52] The people of England were not aware of the fact but the situation was ripe for stories to start circulating that Richard was not in fact dead but might be returned to the throne.

The chronology of the pseudo-Richard begins with the reference in the *Eulogium* to the arrest of a Franciscan friar in Norfolk for preaching a sermon that Richard II was still alive: he was handed over to the prior of his order for correction.[53] This reference appears under the heading 1401 in the chronicle but, due to the problem of the many interpolations, it is difficult to be certain of the dating of events in the *Eulogium*; it may have been early in 1402. Either way a rumour that Richard II was alive in Scotland spread rapidly. By April 1402, the news had reached the king of France in Paris, where Jean Creton penned a letter to Richard hoping that he was indeed safe.[54] Other Franciscans, from Leicester, Nottingham and Northampton, were spreading the news the same month: they were sent to the Tower on 1 June.[55] On 9 May 1402 the authorities in Cumberland and Westmorland were ordered to arrest anyone who maintained the truth of the story. On 11 May the king wrote to the prior of the Dominicans at Oxford warning him to keep his preachers under control. By 19 May the recently dismissed prior of Launde and eight Franciscan friars had been arrested and executed.[56] On 27 May the head of the Dominicans at Winchelsea and the rector of Horsmonden (Kent) were ordered to be sent to the Tower, along with four other Franciscan friars. A group of Franciscan friars from Leicestershire were arrested near Oxford.[57] John Norwich, prior of the Dominicans in Cambridge, was arrested along with one of his brethren, John Lakenhythe and sent to the Tower on 3 June. A Franciscan friar from Aylesbury was arrested and personally interviewed by the king. Nor was it just friars who were arrested: laymen were also tried for sedition, including the late king's illegitimate half-brother, Sir Roger of Clarendon. On 5 June the sheriffs throughout England were ordered to suppress all rumours of Richard II's survival. By 18 June a writ informed sheriffs that the danger had passed, and that people need not fear arrest as only the leaders would be punished.

It seems that history was repeating itself: the order to the sheriffs of 5 June was not so very different from that issued to the sheriffs on 13 April 1330 to prevent widespread belief that the ex-king was alive. News about the ex-king's supposed survival was distributed by friars, as it was in 1328–30. Nevertheless it is important to note that there were significant differences. Most of the men involved in the earl of Kent's plot had close connections with the king during his reign: they were acting out of loyalty. Several of them were secular lords and prelates of the first rank. The same is not true of the rebels in 1402. The most significant layman involved was Sir Roger of Clarendon – and Richard had never shown him much favour. Most were humble men or friars with no close connection to the king. It was a widespread protest more than a concentrated plot, and the role played by the friars was not as a series of go-betweens between magnates and prelates but as preachers to the people.

The autumn of 1402 saw the pseudo-Richard campaign take a radically different turn. Up until that point its philosophy was best expressed by the Leicester friar, Roger Frisby: if Richard II was alive then he was the true king of England and, if not, then he was dead at Henry's hands and Henry had thereby forfeited all right to the throne.[58] But in June 1402 Owen Glendower had captured Sir Edmund Mortimer, uncle of the earl of March, at the battle of Bryn Glas. Plans were made to ransom Mortimer; however, Mortimer joined his captor and married Glendower's daughter on or about 30 November 1402. He wrote to his tenants in Radnor and Presteigne on 13 December that 'he had joined Glendower in his efforts either to restore the Crown to King Richard, should the king prove still to be alive, or, should Richard be dead, to confer the throne on his honoured nephew Edmund Mortimer, who is the right heir to the said Crown'.

In the context of the development of the 'pretender' phenomenon, this shift is far more significant than the 'infrapolitics' in the name of a pseudo-Richard, or Frisby's simple philosophy of regnal legitimacy. The popular protest had no focus except the government which it opposed; so the protesters were essentially unorganized, divided among themselves, and relatively weak. As the figurehead of such a protest, the pseudo-Richard in Scotland was no more potent than a legend. However, the position adopted by Sir Edmund Mortimer in December 1402 was to elevate the pseudo-Richard from a legend to a full-blown political pretender. Technical legal arguments about the succession had little effect on public opinion, so most people took the view that the Crown was rightly subject to the law with which they were familiar – the common law – and by that reckoning the earl of March had a rightful claim to the throne. By using this as a fall-back position if the pseudo-Richard proved to be an impostor, Mortimer and Glendower elevated the dead king (as represented by the pseudo-Richard) above a genuine member of the royal family. To take up arms in the name of Richard II was therefore not an empty threat. Until proven false, in the eyes of the protesters the pseudo-Richard *was* the rightful king, and the earl of March his heir.

The irony was that the pseudo-Richard was obviously false. Many people had seen the dead king's body. Many more had heard of the exposure of the corpse. When Richard II did not arrive in England as promised in the summer of 1402, many would have known that he was never going to appear. But this obvious falseness gave the pretender an even greater authority among the political classes. Normally supporters of the real Richard II would not have supported an impostor; however, knowledge that the real Richard was dead meant that they could be confident that the pseudo-Richard was merely a figurehead, a stand-in for him. Men and women in positions of power did not have to worry about the pseudo-Richard actually becoming king: he would be exposed as soon as the political situation arose and the earl of March enthroned as his heir. The pseudo-Richard's allegedly simple or foolish character may even have helped in this, being a reassurance that no one could mistake him for the genuine Richard II. The pseudo-king could be held up as rightful in name because there was a safety net when (not if) he turned out to be false: a legitimate royal fall-back position, the earl of March. No post-mortem figure had acquired this level of political prestige. Thus the pseudo-Richard II remained a politically potent force for more than a decade. A pretender had finally become useful to a series of people with power, influence and a similar cause. The concept had reached its full development.

FIGHTING THE PRETENDER

How does one fight a figure who is merely notional and yet enormously dangerous on account of his potential to incite followers? How does one combat a man whose reputed foolishness actually *encourages* people to fight in his name? The pseudo-Richard, with his 'allies' Glendower and Mortimer, safely in exile in Scotland, was a force to be reckoned with – especially after he started despatching letters directly to specific lords. More magnates came to accept the pseudo-Richard as emblematic of the real Richard's authority. Welsh captains in the army of Mortimer's brother-in-law, Henry Percy, may have alluded to the pseudo-Richard in gathering the men of Cheshire prior to the battle of Shrewsbury: Welsh volunteers for his cause came wearing Ricardian badges.[59] Although Percy's defeat was a set-back for his family's cause, the pseudo-Richard did not lose his potency. Like Edward II in Italy, who did not need to lift a finger to be a major problem to Edward III, the pseudo-Richard did not need to do anything to be a great concern to Henry IV. All he had to do was to remain uppermost in people's minds, and he could rely on the real Richard's supporters to arrange that. From December 1403 to February 1404, one William Blyth, having visited the pseudo-Richard in Scotland, spread the word of Richard II's survival all around East Anglia.[60] On 22 December 1403 he met John Staunton, servant of the countess of Oxford, at her house at Great Bentley. The countess ordered Staunton to ride with Blyth to Ipswich to survey the land and to make preparations for 'Richard II' to meet them at Northampton. Sermons announcing the imminent return of the ex-king were preached at Colchester and in the Colne Valley. The countess's servants later confessed to hearing that Richard would return with the earl of Northumberland and his son, Henry Percy; and, according to John Russell, a servant of William Ayleway of Wixoe Hall in Suffolk, the date set was 28 June 1403. Blyth visited the abbot of Beeleigh in February 1404, claiming to have come from the earl of Northumberland. That same month Blyth met John Prittlewell of Barrow Hall (Essex) and explained to him how Richard had escaped from Pontefract, and had travelled to Scotland by way of one of the Isles. He may have delivered letters from the pseudo-Richard to Henry Despenser, bishop of Norwich (who paid them no attention). All these informants spread the word further: Walsingham even states that the countess herself issued letters announcing that Richard II was alive and would reward his followers.[61] It was only a matter of time before the king heard and had to take action. On 17 April 1404 Henry sent two men to arrest John Staunton, as well as a canon of St Osyth and a goldsmith.[62] The countess herself was arrested.[63] Yet prelates and magnates still continued to campaign in Richard's name. In June 1404 the abbot of the Cistercian abbey of Revesby (Lincolnshire) declared that there were ten thousand men in England who believed that Richard II was alive; and, in the sense that ten thousand men believed that Richard II was still a cause worth fighting for, he was probably not exaggerating.

In combating this threat, Henry IV acted as past rulers had done and identified and exposed the culprit, thereby attempting to reduce his royal status. Towards the end of the parliament of January–March 1404 he granted a general pardon to all, 'provided always, however, that William Serle, Thomas Warde of Trumpington, who affects and pretends to be King Richard, and Amy Donet, do not have or enjoy any benefit from this grace and pardon, but that they should be expressly exempted from the aforesaid pardon and grace.'[64] This pardon was issued as a letter close in April. But was the pseudo-Richard really Thomas Warde of Trumpington? We could be sceptical and say Henry could have named anyone; but there was much greater value in using the real name. It is probable that Henry had his spies working at the courts of Scotland and France, trying to find out the true nature of the pseudo-Richard from the moment he heard of the pretence. Jean Creton, who wrote so enthusiastically to the pseudo-Richard in April 1402, was sent to Scotland by Charles VI to enquire whether the man really was Richard. The following year the French royal family were firmly of the opinion that Richard was dead (as shown by the marriage of Richard's widow to Charles of Orléans. Thus, if Henry's Scottish informers could not identify the pseudo-Richard, he may have sought information from his French ones. By January 1404 Henry was sufficiently confident that he knew the man's identity to make it one of only three exceptions from the general pardon.

Henry IV's other line of attack was to seek out the man whom he saw as the primary agent behind the whole scheme. This was William Serle, one of the two murderers of the duke of Gloucester. He was an intimate companion of Richard II from at least 1391, described in the records as a yeoman of the wardrobe or yeoman of the robes (although John Hall described him as valet of the king's chamber). In 1399, having been richly rewarded with lands following the duke's murder in 1397, he held the manors of Whitchurch-on-Thames (Oxfordshire), East and West Tilbury (Essex), 'Lowe' and Farlow (both Shropshire), Alton (Hampshire) and Berkswell (Warwickshire), as well as lands in other counties (Herefordshire, Cornwall and Middlesex) and London.[65] He was named as an executor in the king's will in April 1399 and went with Richard to Ireland that year. On Richard's fall, he lost everything and went into exile. As a greatly trusted servant, Serle may have understood Richard's fascination with Edward II. The crucial point is that, as the case of the duke of Gloucester shows, he was conversant with the idea of a supposedly deceased royal personage who was not in fact dead.

The earliest direct evidence that William Serle was involved in spreading the news that Richard II was alive is the testimony of John Bernard, given at his trial on 2 June 1402.[66] Bernard claimed that he had been ploughing near his home in Offley (Hertfordshire) at about Ascension that year (4 May) when William Balsshalf of Lancashire told him that Richard was alive and well and living in Scotland, and that, with William Serle's help, he would return and meet his supporters at Atherstone, near Merevale Abbey in Warwickshire on 24 June. This is near-contemporary evidence that Serle was associated with a pseudo-Richard in Scotland in the minds of agent provocateurs like Balsshalf as early as the start of May 1402. Atherstone is about 14 miles north of Serle's manor of Berkswell but, being on the main road from London to Chester (Watling Street), it would have been known to anyone travelling long-distance. Travelling from Lancashire along this same road, Balsshalf would have passed Atherstone on his way to Offley. He would also have passed close to Leicester and Northampton. Friars in these towns were sent to the Tower on 1 June, along with those from Nottingham. Moreover, in order to get to Offley from Watling Street, Balsshalf would have turned off at Dunstable on the Cambridge road, which leads on to Norwich. Presumably he did not linger in Offley but left Bernard to gather his men and head to Atherstone while he himself headed to Cambridge. Thus we may postulate that he arrived in Cambridge a couple of days later (on or about 6 May), spreading news of Richard II being 'in full life' in Scotland. By 3 June the head of the Cambridge Dominicans and one of his brethren was under arrest for preaching that Richard II was alive, as noted above. It is quite possible – probable, even – that Balsshalf informed the people he met on his way south, especially the friars, about Richard II being in full life and with William Serle in Scotland in April and early May. Finally, evidence that his seeking out John Bernard of Offley and telling him to assemble men at Atherstone was not a mere idle comment as he passed through but carefully planned is to be found in a 1393 grant made by Richard II, which gave a messuage in the manor of Atherstone to one John Bernard, chaplain. It may well be that the pro-Richard chaplain recommended Balsshalf to seek out his kinsman in Offley on his way to Cambridge. This explains why a Hertfordshire yeoman believed a man from Lancashire that the dead king was alive in Scotland, and persuaded two men to go to fight for him. As others have observed, such messages were spread and believed in spite of their apparent extraordinariness not just because of the desire for the information to be true but also on account of where the message came from, and who bore it.[67]

The evidence of John Bernard suggests Balsshalf came down Watling Street, visiting certain friaries and telling the brethren about the supposed ex-king in Scotland and William Serle, and then travelled into East Anglia. In order to convince the heads of friaries, he no doubt had to have some credentials – probably a letter of credence from pseudo-Richard. The friars themselves then spread the word further. But even so, Balsshalf can hardly have been acting alone. In order for so many people to start preaching that 'Richard II is alive' at almost the same time, and for the same news to have reached Paris by April 1402, a greater system of information dissemination must have been employed. The *Eulogium* continuation notes that letters from the pseudo-Richard were sent to friends of Richard II in 1402.[68] The same source states that letters about the arrival of the pseudo-Richard in Scotland was sent to the king of France by the king of Scotland himself; and that, in the parliament of January–March 1404, letters purporting to be from Richard II were received by various men.[69] Henry IV summoned Richard II's erstwhile keeper, Robert Waterton, and asked him publically to explain the letters. Waterton responded by offering to fight a duel with anyone who claimed Richard II was still alive. But clearly the letters had authority, and that would have required Richard's seal. So it is worth taking seriously Walsingham's report that, after his arrest by William Clifford, William Serle confessed that he had taken Richard II's privy seal before he was captured in 1399 and used it to send comforting letters from the pseudo-Richard to many of Richard II's supporters.[70] Serle thus seems to have been the author of the letters to those attending the parliament in 1404 as well as an ally of the agent provocateur of 1402, Balsshalf. If the letters carried by the agent provocateur of 1404, William Blyth, truly emanated from Scotland, as seems likely, then he was acting with him too. Regarding the widespread nature of the protests in 1402 that Richard was alive, it is perhaps significant that Serle's own estates were spread across Southern England and the Midlands, so he may be confidently said to have had an extensive series of contacts. Needless to say, there were no more reports of letters after Serle's death. Finally, Serle's execution itself supports the belief that he was the main agent behind the creation of the pseudo-Richard. Henry IV had Serle hanged and cut down, barely alive, at most of the towns between Pontefract and London. Rather than take him swiftly to London a long detour was made, at the king's request, to hang him in Norwich and Colchester. Colchester was the focus of the most recent widespread protest that Richard II was alive. Norfolk was where the first of all the friars to maintain that Richard was still alive came from; but more recently Blyth had confessed to communicating with the bishop of Norwich about Richard II's survival. Hanging Serle in Norwich and Colchester connects him with the results of Blyth's agitation in both areas, including the countess of Oxford's household, thereby confirming his association with the second and third of the known agents provocateurs promoting the pseudo-Richard.

Serle's demise, his confession and multiple hanging, ending with a final hanging and quartering at Tyburn, was the equivalent of the exposure and bloody execution that normally put paid to most pretenders' careers. In this case, he was merely the agent and the instigator, not the pretender himself. Nevertheless, although the pseudo-Richard continued to be maintained by the Scots, his aura waned. His legitimacy had been tainted by the disclosure of the deception carried out in his name. Furthermore, opposition to Henry IV shifted its attention to the progress of his disease, seeing it as the consequence of God's judgement.[71] Although there were those who still fought in the name of Richard II, such as the earl of Northumberland, they were unable to advance on Serle's work promoting the pseudo-Richard in 1402–4. Gradually all the opposition to Henry IV died, was defeated, or lost impetus through old age. The pseudo-Richard acquired a status like the reclusive Glendower in his last days: a phantasm in whose name other men acted against Henry IV. As Henry lay dying John Whitlock took up the old cry 'King Richard is alive!' in the sanctuary at Westminster, repeating the same cry at the time of the coronation of Henry V.[72] In 1415 Richard, earl of Cambridge (Richard II's godson), revived the Mortimer-Glendower idea of 1402, of allying support for the pseudo-Richard with that of the earl of March. His plan was to obtain the pseudo-Richard, expose him and proclaim March king. Recruiting the support of his brother-in-law, the earl of March himself, was his undoing: March showed no loyalty to the man who would make him king, and betrayed him and his fellow conspirator, Sir Thomas Gray, and several other men. But had he not done so it is unlikely that many people would have joined the revolt. The greatest damage to the pretender had been done in the accession of Henry V, which had renewed the legitimacy of the dynasty.

The pseudo-Richard, whether or not he was Thomas Warde of Trumpington, probably died in 1419. There has been some confusion over this. In his book

Henry V and the Southampton Plot, T. B. Pugh confidently asserted that Warde died in 1414. However, this seems to be based solely on his interpretation of the lines in the earl of Cambridge's confession that he (Cambridge) would have taken the earl of March 'into the land of Wales without your [the king's] licence, taking upon him the sovereignty of this land, if yonder man's person, which they call King Richard had not been alive, as I know well that he is not alive . . .'[73] The *Rotuli computorum Scotiae* includes references to financial payments for '*Richardum Regem Angliae*' in Scotland for 1408, 1414, 1415 and 1417 and records his death in 1419.[74] Hence it seems that Pugh was mistaken that Cambridge was referring to Warde.[75] The final gasps in the name of the pseudo-Richard were made not after his death but in the last years of his life. In 1416 two men – a London innkeeper and a Lincoln gentleman – wrote to the Holy Roman Emperor Sigismund, who was then in England, asking him to help the pseudo-Richard in Scotland. The following year Master Thomas Lucas conducted a handbill campaign in London and Canterbury trying to persuade people that Richard II was still alive. Finally, at the trial of Sir John Oldcastle in 1417, the defendant declared that his liege lord was living then in the kingdom of Scotland.[76]

CONCLUSION

The power of the pretender changed: it waxed and waned, and it grew strong or withered according to the political season and the country of its seeding. But as a concept it developed and grew. From stories and legends of post-mortem kings, it came to have real political significance all across Europe. In the early days, pretenders were short-term experiments: most were caught, exposed and killed in a bloody and public fashion. They fall into two sorts. One, the 'charismatic' pretender, was a man who had been successful and popular in life, and whose memory meant that a post-mortem reappearance was hugely popular and potentially influential (as in Alphonso the Battler and Baldwin of Flanders). Such pretenders tended to be short-lived – not just because they threatened the new ruler but equally because they were unable to live up to expectations due to their lack of the dead man's charisma and, often, their old age. The other sort was the 'dynastic' pretender: a man who was championed in order to maintain the longevity of an extinct dynasty and to create a cover of legitimacy for what otherwise would have been ungodly treason by 'his' subjects. The Hohenstaufen and Arpad pretenders were good examples. They tended to be equally short-lived because the extinct dynasties ultimately needed more than a titular king: they needed a genuine leader, preferably one able to unite a kingdom and inspire an army. A pretender could only ever be an interim measure – and a vulnerable one at that.

Although the British Isles were late in producing any pretenders, it was the English political experience of the fourteenth century that broke the pattern. First, the story of John of Powderham seems to have led to or reminded people of the changeling motif. Quickly this was adopted within the armament of the dynastic pretender. The important development in this respect is that the pretender did not just *pretend* to be the deceased king, he believed he actually was the deceased king, either because he could not remember his infancy or because he was able to recall elements in early youth which seemed to accord with the story told to him. Both of these are probably true with regard to Giannino's faith in his royal identity. Rapidly, in Paris and Avignon, the story spread of the royal baby changed at birth. Although it was rarely used in creating pretenders, it seems to have been adopted instead to discredit genuine royalty (as in the case of John of Gaunt), thereby having implications for the legitimate succession of dynasties which were nowhere near dying out. A second English innovation was the later life of Edward II, which promoted awareness of the potency of a secretly alive ex-ruler. This precedent provided an example of loyalty to an ex-king that resulted in the Epiphany Rising. It also enabled dissidents from Richard II's court to re-create a symbolic ex-king in exile. The complex model of a legitimate king, deposed and incarcerated, who lived out his days at a foreign court under the protection of a foreign ruler had its basis in reality.

The third English innovation was perhaps the most important. It combined the motif of the wrongfully dethroned ex-king in exile, at an enemy court, with a genuinely royal heir. By giving the pretender a physical reality, Sir Edmund Mortimer and Glendower unwittingly created a sort of super-pretender: one who had greater regnal legitimacy than the king (albeit in a notional form) and a physical royal presence, in his heir apparent, who could answer on behalf of the notional legitimacy represented by the pretender. To kill the heir would have been unjust and would only have added to the power of the symbolic ex-king, the pretender. To kill the pretender would have increased the authority of the heir. The only way to attack the combination was to destroy the agency that linked the two, breaking the lines of communication and exposing the pseudo-king. Even then, this could not be wholly successful, for people could still dream of the living king in Scotland.

Out of all this grew the pretenders of the fifteenth century – the supposedly false royal births, murdered princes, alleged heirs and impostors. This is not to say they were all false – far from it. This book shows that, among all the pretenders and culture of doubt, a genuine member of a royal family might find himself alive yet supposedly dead – and powerless. In Edward II's case he went to the pope; in the duke of Gloucester's case he was kept in custody until he was killed. There may have been other genuine cases. Equally the assumption that all pretenders were self-interested tricksters who deserved their horrifying fates is equally erroneous. Giannino Baglioni clearly believed he was of royal blood – a conviction that ruined his life. False Margaret is an even more tragic case. Whoever instructed her with the appropriate memories she needed to persuade the Norwegian people that she was the real Margaret had managed to convince her of her royal identity – enough to take her German husband with her and to present her own case in Norway. Alternatively she may have been following her husband's direction: it is very unlikely the heiress to the kingdom of Scotland would sail to Norway with her husband and claim, without any protector to guide her, that she was Margaret unless she was convinced that she really was the daughter of the deceased king.

The final point that arises from this subject is a methodological one: what it reveals about the bias of the modern scholar. Historians tend to be hugely biased in favour of authority in matters of regnal legitimacy. This is not surprising, for they depend on the legitimacy of bureaucracies for the evidence on which they base their work. But the result is a failure to question things that should be questioned, and a tendency to accept things that should not be accepted. False Margaret is a classic case. In 1990, on the 700th anniversary of the fateful journey to Britain of 'the Maid of Norway' (as historians tenderly refer to her), a commemorative series of essays was published in the *Scottish Historical Review*. Five scholars contributed articles: all use the word 'tragic' to describe the death of the girl or the deaths of other members of the Scottish royal family. That is fair: the young girl's death so far from home was indeed tragic (presuming it happened). But none of the three scholars who mention False Margaret has a similar word of sympathy for the woman who was burnt alive for returning to the land which she believed (rightly or wrongly) to be her true homeland.[77]

Questions of true identity, secret intrigue and political subversion may be among the most difficult for empirically trained scholars to study, but we should not let the difficulties or our instinctive prejudices blinker us to the fact that there are 'more things in heaven and earth' than we can dream of, nor to lose our sympathy for humankind.

Notes

1 Cheeseman and Williams, *Rebels, Pretenders and Impostors*, 85–6.
2 Evans, *Death of Kings*, 148.
3 Evans, *Death of Kings*, 154–5.
4 Lecuppre, 343–4.
5 Evans, *Death of Kings*, 156–7.
6 *Perfect King*, 91–2.
7 Lecuppre, 19.
8 Lecuppre, 88–9, n. 1.
9 Wolff, 289.
10 Wolff, 290. One source claims that Ioannitsa had beheaded him and had had his skull turned into a jewelled drinking vessel; but this was probably a story based on the fate of a previous Byzantine emperor, Nicephorus I, in 811.
11 *Foedera* (1704), i, 277; Hardy (ed.), *Syllabus*, i, 28.
12 The account given here comes from Wolff, 294–9.
13 Lecuppre, 28 n. 1, 63, 139, 359; Runciman, *Sicilian Vespers* (1958), 56.
14 Baird *et al.* (eds), *Sallimbene*, 482.
15 Lecuppre, 359.
16 Lecuppre, 29–30.
17 Lecuppre, 29 n. 1, 107.
18 Lecuppre, 108.
19 Anderson, 'Icelandic sagas', 408–9.
20 Anderson, 'Icelandic sagas', 419.
21 See the comments by Knut Helle and Barbara E. Crawford in their respective essays in the special edition of *Scottish Historical Review* published in 1990 to commemorate the anniversary of the Maid of Norway's death (pp. 155, 175 respectively).
22 Anderson, 'Icelandic sagas', 416.
23 Anderson, 'Icelandic sagas', 404–5.
24 Anderson, 'Icelandic sagas', 414.
25 Lecuppre, 38.
26 Taylor, *Political Prophecy*, 162, quoting BL Harley 746. For clarification of the date, see Smallwood, 'Prophecy of the Six Kings'.

27 Coote, *Prophecy and Public Affairs*, 87.

28 Musto, *Apocalypse in Rome*, 75.

29 Falconieri, 3–6.

30 For its value as an autobiography, see Falconieri, 124–30.

31 Falconieri, 121–3.

32 Falconieri, 11.

33 *Perfect King*, 182, quoting *CEPR*, ii, 585.

34 Falconieri, 36.

35 *Perfect King*, 184–5.

36 Falconieri, 116–17.

37 Falconieri, 53–4.

38 Tait, 'Did Richard II murder the Duke of Gloucester?'.

39 Stamp, 'Richard II' (1923); Atkinson, 'Richard II'; Wright, 'Richard II' ; Stamp, 'Richard II' (1932). The 7 September entry on the Fine Rolls is an order and strict injunction – by the king – to Clement Spice, escheator in Essex and Hertford, to seize the goods of Thomas, the late duke of Gloucester. See *CFR 1391–9*, 224.

40 Goodman, *Gaunt*, 161; Tuck, *Richard II*, 189.

41 *PROME*, 1399 October, appendix, item 1.

42 *PROME*, 1399 October, item 11.

43 According to Rickhill, he received his instructions to sail with Mowbray at midnight on Wednesday 5 September at Easingham in Kent. The messenger, John Mulsho, insisted that he take himself to Dover to sail with Thomas Mowbray the next evening. He sailed in a separate ship with John Mulsho between 8 p.m. and 9 p.m. that evening and arrived the next day between ten and eleven o'clock. That evening at vespers he received his commission to take the duke's confession – and was surprised because he had already heard news that the man was dead. See *PROME*, 1399 October, item 92.

44 *PROME*, 1399 October, item 92. The other witness was John Lancaster, an esquire in Mowbray's household.

45 17 August is when Rickhill's first commission to go to Calais was dated. His second commission, handed to him in Calais on his arrival, was dated the same day: this being to take the duke's confession. The period of three weeks between these commissions and the confession may be what Mowbray was referring to in his statement to Bagot that he kept him alive for upwards of three weeks. See *PROME*, 1399 October, item 92 and appendix, item 1.

46 *Fears*, 211–17.

47 Walker, 'Rumour, sedition', 33.

48 McNiven, 'Rebellion, sedition'; Morgan, 'Henry IV and the shadow of Richard II'; 'Trouble' (republished as chapter four in Strohm's *England's Empty Throne*); Walker, 'Rumour, sedition'.

49 Wylie, *Henry the Fourth*, i, 115; *Fears*, 213, 420–1, ns 18–20; Strohm, 'Trouble', 90.

50 For Walsingham and Otterbourne, see Chapter 3 of this text, n. 43. For Adam Usk, see McNiven, 'Rebellion, sedition', 94. The suggestion in Creton, that the body displayed was that of Richard Maudelyn, Richard's look-alike, was written some months after he had returned to France. He did not see the body. Also, it is illogical, as Maudelyn had been killed during the Epiphany Rising. Thus, if the body displayed was Maudelyn's as Creton originally believed, it would follow that Richard had been killed in London in January impersonating a man whose role was to impersonate *him* until he could be released from Pontefract. Creton was in no doubt in later years that Richard was dead. See Creton, 221.

51 McNiven, 'Rebellion, sedition', 95.

52 Dyer, *Standards*, 263.

53 *Eulogium*, iii, 389.

54 P. W. Dillon, 'Remarks'; Walker, 'Rumour, sedition', 37.

55 *CPR 1399–1402*, 528. The other orders to send men to the Tower are all from the same volume.

56 *Eulogium*, iii, 389.

57 McNiven, 'Rebellion, sedition', 95–6; *Fears*, 248–51.

58 *Fears*, 250–1.

59 'Trouble', 96.

60 Morgan, 'Henry IV and the shadow of Richard II', 19–22.

61 *Historia Anglicana*, ii, 262.

62 *Fears*, 283–4.

63 *CP*, x, 227. She was pardoned in November, after the execution of Serle.

64 *PROME*, 1404 January, item no. 89.

65 For grants to William Serle, see *CPR 1389–92*, 420, 509; *CPR 1391–6*, 615; *CPR 1396–9*, 284, 323, 418, 463, 493, 499. For his lands in London and Middlesex see *CCR 1399–1402*, 542.

66 *CPR 1401–5*, 99–100. Henry IV ordered Serle's wife to be released from Newgate on 14 December 1401 where she had been 'long imprisoned . . . for alleged adherence to the evil design of her husband' (*CCR 1399–1402*, 450). Given the long duration of her imprisonment, this suggests the 'evil design' was that of 1397, for which she was probably arrested in 1399, and nothing to do with the pseudo-Richard.

67 'Trouble', 95, quotes Edgar Morin's *Rumour in Orléans*: 'The rumour's remarkable powers of self-perpetuation derive from the fact that what people trusted was not so much the information *per se* but rather *the person* who passed it on, because he was known (a good friend of acquaintance on whose "word of honour" one automatically relied).'

68 *Eulogium*, iii, 389.

69 *Eulogium*, iii, 394, 400–1.

70 *Historia Anglicana*, ii, 263.

71 *Fears*, 300.

72 'Trouble', 101.

73 Pugh, *Southampton Plot*, 100, 172.

74 'Trouble', 94; Strohm, *England's Empty Throne*, 245, n. 32.

75 Thus those who have accepted Pugh's reading have been misled. This includes me. See Mortimer, *1415*, 246–8.

76 'Trouble', 106 (Sigismund) 107–8 (Lucas, Oldcastle).

77 *Scottish Historical Review*, 69 (1990). Four authors describe the death of Margaret in a sympathetic way: 'the sad anniversary of Margaret's death' (p. 117); 'the tragic death of the Maid in Orkney' (p. 156); 'the tragic death of the Maid in Norway' (p. 157) and 'such a tragic event' (p. 175). The fifth used the word 'tragic' to describe the death of Alexander III himself (p. 126).

11

Concluding remarks

This book began by posing a question about certainty, and the challenge of making historical statements that will stand the test of time. In practical terms, it has mostly dealt with elusive questions – those which most people consider highly doubtful. Obviously if this book had been concerned entirely with matters of undisputed certainty – for example, the existence of Edward III, or the date of the Battle of Crécy – it would have been a pointless exercise. We already trust historians to agree on such facts, and most of us trust that such widely agreed facts are rooted in past reality. If such rootedness is at all in doubt, the philosophical basis for maintaining undisputed certainties may be inferred from the methodological introduction to this book. While postmodernists and critical theorists are correct to observe that historians study evidence, not the past per se, they are wrong to assert that 'no amount of epistemological effort can bridge' the gap between the two. The information linkages between the past and the evidence that describes that past can sometimes be reconstructed. Where they can, and where we have a large number of them that tally in respect of non-relatively defined acts or states of being, we may *show* the evidence to be rooted in past reality. Consequently, historians can start to say things with certainty about the past. And when multiple information streams underpin the evidence that historians use, permitting some things to be said for certain, these impose limitations on the degree to which we can re-describe the past. It is thus possible for historians to make some pronouncements and observations that will stand the test of time, albeit not as many as we would perhaps like.

It is not undisputed certainty that is the prime subject of this book – rather, it is the limits of certainty, or the fringes of what is factual, that are of concern, both in theory and practice. The key factor is that the greater the political importance of an intrigue, the less evidence is likely to have been created, let alone to have survived, and so the less we can rely on traditional historical methods. The information-based argument for the fake death of Edward II, based on four information streams from England and further confirmed by two more implicit in the Fieschi Letter, countered only by one self-denied information stream from the man who issued the news, allows no room for doubt that the man did not die in 1327. However, Edward III's deliberate destruction of evidence relating to his father's survival, combined with his policy of not writing down communications concerning the man's survival, means that in order to investigate the later life of Edward II we have to use methodologies far beyond normal historical practice as taught in higher education. Likewise the rules for the succession require us to go far beyond the evidence, or, rather, the lack of evidence, and to reconfigure legal issues and understandings in documents that have been systematically destroyed. Similarly, the study of the pretender may require us to adopt positions contrary to the traditional academic bias towards the evidence-creating authority – something that historians have traditionally found very difficult to do.

Narratives of political intrigue or secrecy in all ages, by definition, tend to leave little or no evidence. The nation's greatest secrets do not find their way on to paper, let alone a document placed in the National Archives for lowly archivists to guard. This lack of evidence is even more a factor in unofficial plots. So any narrative involving secret intrigue based exclusively on extant evidence is bound to be partial and prone to the distortions of propaganda. If we want to test what the limits of a political intrigue or a king's 'secret business' may have been, we have to move away from the assumption that direct evidence relating to the intrigue must still exist. We have to employ speculation in a positive sense – like an economist uses speculation, for the purposes of profit. Indeed, we may have to shift, cautiously, to a position in which certainty is impossible – as with the financial exploitation of Edward III – circumstantial details being the only means to reconstruct a possible narrative. It is necessary to go beyond the evidence itself, to reconstruct the information streams underpinning the evidence. Sometimes this will strengthen the evidence on which we rely. Sometimes it will reveal its fragility. Even then, it may be impossible to know the limits of an intrigue. As observed at the end of Chapter 4, it is likely that 'a sincere and ardent quest for certainty is more likely to reveal provable falsehoods than undisputed facts'.

This philosophy of history potentially creates a fork in the road of historical methodology. It goes without saying that there will be those who maintain traditional interpretations are best. There will undoubtedly be those who insist that old-fashioned selective scissors-and-paste history still has its place. There will always be those who prefer traditional source criticism. But for the dedicated students of political narrative, especially those dealing with covert events, these methodologies will not be sufficient. A far more rigorous interrogation of the evidence is necessary if we want to avoid the criticisms of those who select evidence, or quote from it selectively and ignore contradictory evidence, or insist on the need for evidence of intrigues to survive. Information-based approaches will, in all probability, alienate their exponents from the traditional mainstream. The dedicated student who employs such an approach is likely to tread a difficult path which the traditional source-critic cannot always follow, and sometimes will resist. Members of the public are likely to find it difficult to understand such revisionism, and will similarly reject it on principle. There is likely to be tension. But if we wish to maintain our ability to test understandings of past events for certainty, and thereby to maintain the social relevance of political history as an intellectual discipline in the wake of postmodernism, information-based methods are powerful tools that we ignore at our cost.

Full titles of works cited in the notes

AEC: see Bell, Brooks and Moore (eds), *Accounts of the English Crown*.

'Afterlife': see Haines, 'Edwardus Redivivus: the "Afterlife" of Edward of Carnarvon'.

R. Allen Brown, H. M. Colvin and A. J. Taylor, *The History of the King's Works: The Middle Ages* (London, 1963).

Joseph Anderson, 'Notes on some entries in the Iceland Annals regarding the death of the Princess Margaret', *Proceedings of the Society of Antiquaries of Scotland*, 10 (1875), 404–19.

Anonimalle: see Childs and Taylor (eds), *Anonimalle Chronicle*.

Joyce Appleby, Lynn Hunt and Margaret Jacob, *Telling the Truth about History* (New York, 1984).

C. A. J. Armstrong, 'Some examples of the distribution and speed of news in England at the time of the Wars of the Roses', *Medieval History*, 1 (1991), 64–85.

R. L. Atkinson, 'Richard II and the death of the Duke of Gloucester', *EHR*, 38 (1923), 563–4.

C. J. Aungier, *The French Chronicle of London*, Camden Society OS, 28 (1844).

Sir Joseph Ayloffe, 'An account of the body of King Edward the First as it appeared on opening his tomb in the year 1774', *Archaeologia*, 3 (1774), 380–1.

Joseph L. Baird, Giuseppe Baglivi and John Robert Kane (eds), *The Chronicle of Sallimbene de Adam*, Medieval and Renaissance Texts and Studies 40 (Binghampton, New York, 1986).

Joshua Barnes, *The History of that Most Victorious Monarch Edward III* (Cambridge, 1688).

G. W. S. Barrow, *Robert Bruce and the Community of the Realm of Scotland* (3rd edn, Edinburgh, 1988).

—'A kingdom in crisis: Scotland and the Maid of Norway', *Scottish Historical Review*, 69 (1990), 120–41.

David Bates, Julia Crick and Sarah Hamilton (eds), *Writing Medieval Biography 750–1250* (Woodbridge, 2006).

Natale Battilana, *Genealogie delle famiglie nobili de Genova* (Genoa, 1825; repr. Bologna, 1971).

Derek Beales, *History and Biography* (Cambridge, 1981).

Adrian R. Bell, Chris Brooks and Tony K. Moore (eds), *Accounts of the English Crown with Italian Merchants Societies, 1272–1345*, List and Index Society 331 (2009).

Michael Bennett, 'Edward III's entail and the succession to the Crown, 1376–1471', *EHR*, 113 (1998), 580–609.

—'Henry IV, the royal succession and the crisis of 1406' in Gwilym Dodd and Douglas Biggs (eds), *The Reign of Henry IV: Rebellion and Survival, 1403–1413* (Woodbridge, 2008), 9–27.

Joseph Biancalana, *The Fee Tail and the Common Recovery in Medieval England, 1176–1502* (Cambridge, 2001).

Douglas Biggs, 'Royal charter witness lists for the reign of Henry IV, 1399–1413', *EHR*, 119 (2004), 407–23.

F. D. Blackley, 'Isabella of France, Queen of England 1308–1358, and the late medieval cult of the dead', *Canadian Journal of History*, 15 (1980), 23–47.

T. C. W. Blanning and David Cannadine (eds), *History and Biography: Essays in Honour of Derek Beales* (Cambridge, 2002).

W. H. Bliss and C. Johnson (eds), *Calendar of Entries in the Papal Registers relating to Great Britain and Ireland*, vols 1–3 (1893–97).

Edward A. Bond (ed.), *Chronicon Monasterii de Melsa* (3 vols, 1867).

J. S. Bothwell, *The Age of Edward III* (Woodbridge, 2001).

F. W. D. Brie (ed.), *The Brut or the Chronicles of England*, Early English Text Society, OS 131 and 136 (2 vols, 1906–8).

Reginald Brocklesby (ed.), *The Register of William Melton, Archbishop of York 1317–1340*, vol. 4 (Woodbridge, 1997).

Brut: see Brie (ed.), *The Brut*.

Joel Burden, 'Re-writing a Rite of Passage: the Peculiar Funeral of Edward II' in W. M. Ormrod and Nicola F. McDonald (eds), *Rites of Passage: Cultures of Transition in the Fourteenth Century* (Woodbridge, 2004), pp. 13-29.

Umberto Burla, *Malaspina di Lunigiana* (La Spezia, 2001).

Calendar of Chancery Warrants Preserved in the Public Record Office, 1244–1326 (1927).

Calendar of Memoranda Rolls (Exchequer) Preserved in the Public Record Office, Michaelmas 1326–Michaelmas 1327 (1968).

Calendar of the Charter Rolls Preserved in the Public Record Office, 1226–1516 (6 vols, 1903–27).

Calendar of the Close Rolls Preserved in the Public Record Office, Henry III, Edward I, Edward II, Edward III, Richard II, Henry IV and Henry V (51 vols, 1892–1938).

Calendar of the Fine Rolls Preserved in the Public Record Office, Edward I, Edward II and Edward III 1327–1347 (5 vols, 1911–15).

Calendar of the Patent Rolls Preserved in the Public Record Office, Henry III, Edward I, Edward II, Edward III, Richard II, Henry IV and Henry V (43 vols, 1893–1916).

'Captivity': see Tout, 'Captivity and Death'.

David Carpenter, 'What happened to Edward II?', *London Review of Books* (7 June 2007), 32-4.

E. H. Carr, *What is History?* (London, 1961; Pelican Books edn, 1964).

J. R. Castro, *Archivo General de Navarra: Catálogo de la Sección de Comptos. Documentos . . .*, vol. 19 (1957).

CEPR: see Bliss and Johnson (eds), *Calendar of Entries in the Papal Registers*.

Justin Champion, 'What are historians for?', *Historical Research*, 81 (2008), 167–88.

Pierre Chaplais, *Piers Gaveston: Edward II's Adoptive Brother* (Oxford, 1994).

Clive Cheeseman and Jonathan Williams, *Rebels, Pretenders and Impostors* (London, 2000).

C. R. Cheney (ed.), *A Handbook of Dates* (2nd edn, London, 1991).

W. R. Childs and J. Taylor (eds), *The Anonimalle Chronicle*, Yorkshire Archaeological Society Rec. Series 147 (1991).

Chronicles: see Stubbs (ed.), *Chronicles*.

Adam Clarke, J. Caley, J. Bayley, F. Holbrooke and J. W. Clarke (eds), *Foedera, conventiones, litterae, etc., or Rymer's Foedera 1066–1383* (6 vols, 1816–30).

CMR: see *Calendar of Memoranda Rolls*.

G. E. Cokayne, revised by V. Gibbs, H. A. Doubleday, D. Warrand, Lord Howard de Walden and Peter Hammond (eds), *The Complete Peerage of England, Scotland, Ireland, Great Britain and the United Kingdom Extant, Extinct or Dormant* (14 vols, 1910–98).

Lesley A. Coote, *Prophecy and Public Affairs in Later Medieval England* (Woodbridge, 2001).

CP: see Cokayne, *Complete Peerage*.

CPMR: see Thomas (ed.), *Calendar of Plea and Memoranda Rolls*.

CPR: see *Calendar of the Patent Rolls*.

Barbara E. Crawford, 'North Sea kingdoms, North Sea bureaucrat: a royal official who transcended national boundaries', *Scottish Historical Review*, 69 (1990), 174–84.

Creton: see Webb (ed.), 'Metrical history'.

C. G. Crump, 'The arrest of Roger Mortimer and Queen Isabella', *EHR*, 26 (1911), 331–2.

G. P. Cuttino and T. W. Lyman, 'Where is Edward II?', *Speculum*, 53 (1978), 522–43.

J. S. Davies (ed.), *An English Chronicle of the Reigns of Richard II, Henry IV . . .*, Camden Society, OS 64 (1856).

DBI: see *Dizonario biografico degli Italiani*.

'DEII': see Mortimer, 'Death of Edward II'.

Frederick Devon (ed.), *Issues of the Exchequer* (London, 1837).

P. W. Dillon, 'Remarks on the manner of the death of King Richard the Second', *Archaeologia*, 28 (1840), 87–95.

Dizonario biografico degli Italiani (72 vols, 1960–).

Dizonario di Toponomastica Storia e Significando dei Nomi Geografici Italiani (Turin, 1990).

'Documents': see Moore, 'Documents'.

Paul Doherty, 'Isabella, Queen of England, 1296–1330' (DPhil thesis, University of Oxford, 1978).

—*Isabella and the Strange Death of Edward II* (2003).

Mark Duffy, *Royal Tombs of Medieval England* (Stroud, 2003).

Christopher Dyer, *Standards of Living in the Later Middle Ages* (Cambridge, 1989, revised edn, 1998).

'Entail': see Michael Bennett, 'Edward III's entail'.

Steven A. Epstein, *Genoa and the Genoese, 958–1528* (1996).

C. Eubel, *Hierarchia Catholica Medii Aevi*, vol. 1 (1913).

Eulogium: see Haydon (ed.), *Eulogium Historiarum*.

Michael Evans, *The Death of Kings* (London, 2003).

Richard J. Evans, *In Defence of History* (1997, extended edn, 2000).

Tommaso di Carpegna Falconieri, *The Man Who Believed He Was King of France: A True Medieval Tale* (Chicago, 2008).

Arnold Fayen (ed.), *Lettres de Jean XXII* (2 vols, Rome, 1908–12).

Fears: see Mortimer, *The Fears of Henry IV*.

Foedera (Rec. Comm.): see Clarke *et al.* (eds), *Foedera*.

Foedera (Rymer): see Rymer (ed.), *Foedera*.

'Foundations': see Wilson, 'Foundations'.

French Chronicle: see Aungier, *French Chronicle*.

Natalie Fryde, *The Tyranny and Fall of Edward II* (Cambridge, 1979).

V. H. Galbraith, 'Extracts from the Historia Aurea and a French Brut', *EHR*, 43 (1928), 203–7.

J. L. Gillespie, 'Thomas Mortimer and Thomas Molyneux: Radcot Bridge and the appeal of 1397', *Albion*, 7 (1975), 163–73.

Chris Given-Wilson, 'Royal charter witness lists 1327–1399', *Medieval Prosopography*, 12 (1991), 35–93.

—'Richard II, Edward II and the Lancastrian inheritance', *EHR*, 109 (1994), 553–71.

—'Legitimation, designation and the succession to the throne' in Isabel Alfonso, Hugh Kennedy and Julio Escalona (eds), *Building Legitimacy: Political Discourses and Forms of Legitimation in Medieval Societies* (Leiden, 2004), 89–106.

Chris Given-Wilson (ed.), *Chronicles of the Revolution* (Manchester, 1993).

—*The Chronicle of Adam Usk* (Oxford, 1997).

—*The Parliamentary Rolls of Medieval England* (CD edn, 2004).

Anthony Goodman, *The Loyal Conspiracy* (1972).

—*John of Gaunt: The Exercise of Princely Power in Fourteenth-Century Europe* (1992).

Grandison: see Hingeston-Randolph (ed.), *Register of Bishop Grandison*.

Antonia Gransden, *Historical Writing in England II: c. 1307 to the Early Sixteenth Century* (1982).

Greatest Traitor: see Mortimer, *Greatest Traitor*.

Stephen Haber, 'Anything goes: Mexico's "new" cultural history', *The Hispanic American Historical Review*, 79 (1999), 309–30.

R. M. Haines, *The Church and Politics in Fourteenth-century England: The Career of Adam Orleton, c. 1275–1345* (Cambridge, 1978).

—*Calendar of the Register of Adam de Orleton, Bishop of Worcester, 1327–1333*, Worcestershire Historical Society, NS 10; Historical Manuscripts Commission, Joint Publications 27 (1979).

—*Archbishop John Stratford: Political Revolutionary and Champion of the Liberties of the English Church, c.1275/80–1348* (Toronto, 1986).

—*Ecclesia Anglicana: Studies in the English Church of the Later Middle Ages* (Toronto, 1989).

—*Calendar of the Register of Simon de Montacute, Bishop of Worcester, 1334–1337*, Worcestershire Historical Society, NS 15 (1996).

—'Edwardus Redivivus: the "afterlife" of Edward of Carnarvon', *TBGAS*, 114 (1996), 65–86.

—'An innocent abroad: the career of Simon Mepham, Archbishop of Canterbury, 1328–33', *EHR*, 112 (1997), 555–96.

—'Looking back in anger: a politically inspired appeal against John XXII's translation of Bishop Adam Orleton to Winchester (1334)', *EHR*, 116 (2001), 389–404.

—*Death of a King: An Account of the Supposed Escape and Afterlife of Edward of Caernarvon, Formerly Edward II, King of England, Lord of Ireland, Duke of Aquitaine* (Scotforth, 2002).

—*King Edward II: His Life, His Reign and its Aftermath, 1284–1330* (Montreal, 2003).

—'Sir Thomas Gurney of Englishcombe in the county of Somerset, regicide?', *Somerset Archaeology and Natural History*, 147 (2004), 45–65.

—'The episcopate during the reign of Edward II and the regency of Mortimer and Isabella', *Journal of Ecclesiastical History*, 56 (2005), 657–709.

—'The Stamford Council of April 1327', *EHR*, 122 (2007), 141–48.

—'Roger Mortimer's scam', *TBGAS*, 126 (2008), 139–56.

—'Sumptuous apparel for a royal prisoner: Archbishop Melton's Letter, 14 February 1330', *EHR*, 124 (2009), 885–94.

Elizabeth Hallam, 'Royal burial and cult of kingship in France and England 1060–1330', *JMH*, 8 (1982), 201–14.

J. S. Hamilton, *Piers Gaveston, Earl of Cornwall, 1307–1312* (Detroit, 1988).

—'Edward II and the murage of Dublin' in J. S. Hamilton and P. J. Bradley (eds), *Documenting the Past* (Woodbridge, 1989).

—'Piers Gaveston and the royal treasure', *Albion*, 23, 2 (1991), 201–7.

—'Apocalypse not: Edward II and the suppression of the Templars', *Medieval Perspectives*, 12 (1997), 90–100.

—'Charter witness lists for the reign of Edward II' in N. Saul (ed.), *Fourteenth Century England I* (Woodbridge, 2000), 1–20.

—*The Charter Witness Lists for the Reign of Edward II* (List and Index Society, 2001).

—'The character of Edward II: the letters of Caernarfon reconsidered' in G. Dodd and A. Musson (eds), *The Reign of Edward II: New Perspectives* (Woodbridge, 2006), 5–21.

—'The uncertain death of Edward II?', *History Compass*, 6, 5, (2008), 1264–78.

D. A. Harding, 'The regime of Isabella and Mortimer, 1326–1330' (MPhil thesis, University of Durham, 1985).

T. D. Hardy, *Syllabus of Rymer's Foedera* (3 vols, 1869–85).

G. L. Harriss, *Cardinal Beaufort: A Study of Lancastrian Ascendancy and Decline* (Oxford, 1988).

Gerald Harriss, *Shaping the Nation: England 1360–1461* (Oxford, 2005).

John Harvey, *English Cathedrals* (Batsford, revised edn, 1961).

Stephen Hawking, *A Brief History of Time* (Bantam edn, 1989).

F. S. Haydon (ed.), *Eulogium Historiarum sive Temporis* (3 vols, 1858–63).

L. C. Hector and Barbara Harvey, *The Westminster Chronicle 1381–1394* (Oxford, 1982).

Knut Helle, 'Norwegian foreign policy and the Maid of Norway', *Scottish Historical Review*, 69 (1990), 142–56.

Hemingburgh: see Hamilton (ed.), *Chronicon Domini Walteri de Hemingburgh*.

Rosalind M. T. Hill (ed.), *The Register of William Melton, Archbishop of York 1317–1340*, vol. 3 (1988).

F. C. Hingeston-Randolph (ed.), *The Register of Bishop Grandison, Bishop of Exeter* (3 vols, 1894–99).

Historia Anglicana: see Riley (ed.), *Thomae Walsingham Historia Anglicana*.

HKW: see Allen Brown *et al.*, *History of the King's Works*.

Zdeňka Hledíková (ed.), *Raccolta Praghese di Scritti di Luca Fieschi* (Prague, 1985).

Joyce M. Horn, *Fasti Ecclesiae Anglicanae, 1300–1541, vol. 3: Salisbury Diocese* (1962).

Edwin Hunt, *Medieval Super-companies* (Cambridge, 1994).

Joseph Hunter, 'Measures taken for the apprehension of Sir Thomas de Gurney, one of the murderers of Edward II', *Archaeologia*, 27 (1838), 274–97.

Issues: see Devon (ed.), *Issues*.

Keith Jenkins, *A Postmodern History Reader* (London, 1997).

—*Re-thinking History* (London, new edn, 2003).

T. Johnes (ed.), *Froissart's Chronicles* (2 vols, 1848).

Hilda Johnstone, *Letters of Edward, Prince of Wales 1304–5* (Cambridge, 1931).

B. Jones, *Fasti Ecclesiae Anglicanae, vol. 4: Monastic Cathedrals* (1963).

John Kenyon, *The History Men* (London, 2nd edn, 1993).

H. P. F. King, *Fasti Ecclesiae Anglicanae, 1300–1541, vol. 1: Lincoln Diocese* (1962).

Knighton: see Lumby (ed.), *Chronicon Henrici Knighton*.

David Knowles and R. Neville Hadcock, *Medieval Religious Houses, England and*

Wales (1953), 328.

Thomas Kuhn, *The Structure of Scientific Revolutions* (Chicago, 3rd edn, 1996).

Lanercost: see Maxwell, *Chronicle of Lanercost*.

Le Baker: see Thompson (ed.), *Chronicon Galfridi le Baker*.

Gilles Lecuppre, *L'imposture politique au Moyen Âge: la seconde vie des rois* (Paris, 2005).

John Le Patourel, 'The Norman Succession, 996–1135', *EHR*, 86 (1971), 225–50.

Philip Lindley, 'Ritual, regicide and representation: the murder of Edward II and the origin of the royal funeral effigy in England' in his *Gothic to Renaissance: Essays on Sculpture in England* (Stamford, 1995), 97–112.

J. R. Lumby (ed.), *Polychronicon Ranulphi Higden monachi Cestrensis*, vol. 8 (1882).

—*Chronicon Henrici Knighton* (2 vols, 1889–95).

William E. Lunt, *Financial Relations of the Papacy 1327–1534* (Cambridge, Massachusetts, 1962).

Mary Lyon, Bryce Lyon and Henry S. Lucas (eds), *The Wardrobe Book of William Norwell* (Brussels, 1983).

G. H. Martin (ed.), *Knighton's Chronicle 1337–1396* (Oxford, 1995).

Herbert Maxwell, *The Chronicle of Lanercost* (Glasgow, 1913).

Sir Herbert Maxwell (ed.), *The Scalachronica: The Reigns of Edward I, Edward II and Edward III as Recorded by Sir Thomas Gray* (Glasgow, 1907, repr. 2000).

K. B. McFarlane, *Lancastrian Kings and Lollard Knights* (Oxford, 1972).

—*The Nobility of Later Medieval England* (Oxford, 1973).

A. K. McHardy, 'Some reflections on Edward III's use of propaganda' in J. S. Bothwell (ed.), *The Age of Edward III* (Woodbridge, 2001), 171–92.

Peter McNiven, 'Legitimacy and consent: Henry IV and the Lancastrian title, 1399–1406', *Medieval Studies*, 44 (1982), 470–88.

—'Rebellion, sedition and the legend of Richard II's survival in the reigns of Henry IV and Henry V', *BJRL*, 76 (1994), 93–117.

Melsa: see Bond, *Chronica Monasterii de Melsa*.

G. Mollat (ed.), *Lettres Communes de Jean XXII* (2 vols, Paris, 1904).

S. A. Moore (ed.), 'Documents relating to the death and burial of King Edward II', *Archaeologia*, 50 (1887), 215–26.

Philip Morgan, 'Henry IV and the shadow of Richard II' in R. E. Archer (ed.), *Crown, Government and People in the Fifteenth Century* (Stroud, 1995), 1–31.

Ian Mortimer, *The Greatest Traitor: The Life of Sir Roger Mortimer, 1st Earl of March, Ruler of England 1327–1330* (London, 2003).

—'Revisionism revisited', *History Today*, 54 (2004), 38–9.

—'The death of Edward II in Berkeley Castle', *EHR*, 120 (2005), 1175–1214.

—*The Perfect King: The Life of Edward III: Father of the English Nation* (2006).

—'Henry IV's date of birth and the royal Maundy', *Historical Research*, 80, 210 (2007), 567–76.

—*The Fears of Henry IV: The Life of England's Self-Made King* (London, 2007).

—'What isn't history? The nature and enjoyment of history in the twenty-first century', *History*, 93, 4 (October 2008), 454–74.

—*1415: Henry V's Year of Glory* (London, 2009).

—*The Dying and the Doctors: The Medical Revolution in Seventeenth-Century England* (Royal Historical Society, 2009).

Murimuth: see Thompson (ed.), *Adae Murimuth*.

Ronald G. Musto, *Apocalypse in Rome: Cola di Rienzo and the Politics of the New Age* (Berkeley, 2003).

J. Nichols, *A Collection of All the Wills Now Known to be Extant of the Kings and Queens of England* (London, 1780).

Northern Registers: see Raine (ed.), *Historical Papers and Letters from the Northern Registers*.

Norwell: see Lyon *et al.* (eds), *Wardrobe Book of William Norwell*.

Michael Oakeshott, *On History and Other Essays* (Oxford, 1983).

Augustino Oldoini, *Atheneum Ligusticum seu Syllabus Scriptorum Ligurum* (Perugia, 1680).

W. M. Ormrod, 'The sexualities of Edward II' in Gwilym Dodd and Anthony Musson (eds), *The Reign of Edward II: New Perspectives* (Woodbridge, 2006), 22–47.

—'Edward III', *History Today*, 52 (2002), 20–6.

—'The personal religion of Edward III', *Speculum*, 64 (1989), 849–911.

—*The Reign of Edward III* (revised edn, Stroud, 2000).

The Oxford Dictionary of National Biography (online edn, Oxford, 2004–).

S. J. Payling, 'Social mobility, demographic change, and landed society in late medieval England', *The Economic History Review*, NS 45 (1992), 51–73.

Perfect King: see Mortimer, *Perfect King*.

E. Perroy (ed.), *Diplomatic Correspondence of Richard II*, Camden Society, 3rd series 48 (1933).

J. R. S. Phillips, 'Edward II in Italy: English and Welsh political exiles and fugitives in continental Europe, 1322–1365' in Prestwich, Britnell and Frame (eds), *Thirteenth Century England X* (Woodbridge, 2005), 209–26.

— *Edward II* (2010).

Polychronicon: see Lumby (ed.), *Polychronicon*.

F. M. Powicke, *The Thirteenth Century* (Oxford, 1953).

Michael Prestwich, Richard Britnell and Robin Frame (eds), *Thirteenth Century England X: Proceedings of the Durham Conference 2003* (Woodbridge, 2005).

PROME: see Given-Wilson (ed.), *Parliamentary Rolls of Medieval England*.

T. B. Pugh, *Henry V and the Southampton Plot* (1988).

Raccolta Praghese: see Hledíková (ed.), *Raccolta Praghese*.

J. Raine (ed.), *Historical Papers and Letters from the Northern Registers* (1873).

V. B. Redstone, 'Some mercenaries of Henry of Lancaster', *TRHS*, 3rd series 7 (1913), 151–66.

Re-thinking History: see Jenkins, *Re-thinking History*.

H. T. Riley (ed.), *Johannis de Trokelowe et Henrici de Blaneforde . . . chronica et annals* (London, 1866).

— *Thomae Walsingham Historia Anglicana* (2 vols, 1863–4).

Clifford J. Rogers, *War Cruel and Sharp: English Strategy Under Edward III 1327– 1360* (Woodbridge, 2000).

Royal Wills: see Nichols, *Collection of All the Wills*.

RP: see Strachey *et al.* (eds), *Rotuli Parliamentorum*.

Steven Runciman, *The Sicilian Vespers* (Cambridge, 1958).

Ephraim Russell, 'The societies of the Bardi and Peruzzi and their dealings with Edward III' in George Unwin (ed.), *Finance and Trade under Edward III* (1918, rep. 1962), 93–135.

Thomas Rymer (ed.), *Foedera, conventiones, literae, et cujuscunque generis acta publica* (20 vols, 1704–35).

St Albans: see Taylor, Childs and Watkiss (eds), *St Albans Chronicle*.

Armando Sapori, *I Libri dei Comercio dei Peruzzi* (Milan, 1934).

Nigel Saul, *Richard II* (1997).

— *The Three Richards* (2005).

J. E. Sayer, *Original Papal Documents in England and Wales* (Oxford, 1999).

G. O. Sayles (ed.), *Select Cases in the Court of King's Bench under Edward III*, Selden Soc., 74 (1958).

Scalachronica: see Maxwell (ed.), *Scalachronica*.

'Scam': see Haines, 'Roger Mortimer's scam'.

Caroline Shenton, 'Edward III and the coup of 1330' in J. S. Bothwell (ed.), *The Age of Edward III* (York, 2001), 24–6.

Alessandra Sisto, *Genova nel Duecento: il Capitolo di San Lorenzo*, Collana Storica di Fonti e Studi 28 (Genoa, 1979).

T. M. Smallwood, 'Prophecy of the Six Kings', *Speculum*, 60 (1985), 571–92.

John Smyth, *Lives of the Berkeleys*, vol. 1 (Gloucester, 1883).

Pauline Stafford, 'Writing the biography of eleventh century queens' in Bates, Crick and Hamilton (eds), *Writing Medieval Biography 750–1250* (Woodbridge, 2006), 99–110.

A. E. Stamp, 'Richard II and the death of the Duke of Gloucester', *EHR*, 38, 150 (1923), 249–51.

— 'Richard II and the death of the Duke of Gloucester', *EHR*, 47, 187 (1932), 453.

A. B. Steel, *Richard II* (Cambridge, 1941).

W. H. St John Hope, 'On the funeral effigies of the kings and queens of England', *Archaeologia*, 60 (1907), 517–70.

J. Strachey *et al.* (eds), *Rotuli Parliamentorum* (6 vols, 1767–77).

Paul Strohm, *Hochon's Arrow: The Social Imagination of Fourteenth Century Texts* (Princeton NJ, 1992).

—*England's Empty Throne* (New Haven, 1998).

—'The trouble with Richard: the reburial of Richard II and Lancastrian symbolic strategy', *Speculum*, 71 (1996), 87–111.

William Stubbs, *Chronicles of the Reigns of Edward I and Edward II* (2 vols, 1882–83).

—*A Constitutional History of England* (3rd edn, Oxford, 3 vols, 1884).

Jonathan Sumption, *The Hundred Years War: Trial by Battle* (1990).

—'Plotting the past', *Guardian* (5 April 2003)

—'A glorious road to ruin', *The Spectator* (25 February 2006)

'Sumptuous apparel': see Haines, 'Sumptuous apparel'.

Super-companies: see Hunt, *Medieval Super-companies*.

Syllabus: see Hardy, *Syllabus*.

J. Tait, 'Did Richard II murder the Duke of Gloucester?' in J. Tait and T. F. Tout (eds), *Historical Essays by Members of the Owens College Manchester* (London, 1902), 193–216.

J. Tait (ed.), *Cronica Johannis de Reading* (Manchester, 1913).

F. J. Tanqueray, 'The conspiracy of Thomas Dunheved, 1327', *EHR*, 31 (1916), 119–24.

Craig Taylor, 'Edward III and the Plantagenet claim to the French Throne' in J. S. Bothwell, *The Age of Edward III* (Woodbridge, 2001), 155–70.

John Taylor, *English Historical Literature in the Fourteenth Century* (Oxford, 1987).

John Taylor, Wendy R. Childs and Leslie Watkiss (eds), *The St Albans Chronicle: The Chronica Maiora of Thomas Walsingham. Volume 1: 1376–1394* (Oxford, 2003).

Rupert Taylor, *The Political Prophecy in England* (New York, 1911, repr. 1967).

A. H. Thomas (ed.), *Calendar of Plea and Memoranda Rolls 1323–1364* (Cambridge, 1926).

E. M. Thompson (ed.), *Adae Murimuth Continuatio Chronicarum* (London, 1889).

—*Chronicon Galfridi le Baker de Swynebroke* (Oxford, 1889).

E. P. Thompson, *The Poverty of Theory and Other Essays* (London, 1978).

T. C. B. Timmins (ed.), *The Register of William Melton, Archbishop of York 1317–1340*, vol. 5 (Oxford, 2002).

Alexander Hamilton Thompson, *The English Clergy and Their Organisation in the Later Middle Ages* (Oxford, 1947).

John Tosh, *The Pursuit of History* (London, 2nd edn, 1991).

T. F. Tout, 'The captivity and death of Edward of Carnarvon', *BJRL*, 6 (1921), 69–113.

—*Chapters in Medieval Administrative History* (6 vols, Manchester, 1923–35).

'Trouble': see Strohm, 'Trouble with Richard'.

Anthony Tuck, *Richard II and the English Nobility* (1973).

'Uncertain death': see Hamilton, 'Uncertain death'.

George Unwin, 'The estate of merchants, 1336-1365' in George Unwin (ed.), *Finance and Trade under Edward III* (1918, rep. 1962), 179–255.

G. A. Usher, 'The career of a political bishop: Adam de Orleton (c.1279–1345)', *TRHS*, 5th series 22 (1972), 33–47.

Usk: see Given-Wilson (ed.), *Chronicle of Adam Usk.*

Claire Valente, 'The deposition and abdication of Edward II', *EHR*, 113 (1998), 852–81.

J. M. Vidal (ed.), *Benoit XII: Lettres Communes*, vol. 2 (Paris, 1910).

Simon Walker, 'Richard II's views on kingship' in Rowena E. Archer and Simon
    Walker (eds), *Rulers and Ruled in Late Medieval England* (London, 1995), 49–64.

—'Rumour, sedition and popular protest in the reign of Henry IV', *Past and Present*,
    166 (2000), 31–65.

W. H. Walsh, *An Introduction to Philosophy of History* (London, 1951, 6th imp.,
    1961).

W. L. Warren, *King John* (London, 1961, repr. 1964).

D. E. R. Watt, 'The minority of Alexander III of Scotland', *TRHS*, 5th series 21 (1971),
    1–23.

J. Webb (ed.), 'Metrical history', *Archaeologia*, 20 (1824), 13–239.

David Welander, *The History, Art and Architecture of Gloucester Cathedral*
    (Gloucester, 1991).

Westminster: see Hector and Harvey, *Westminster Chronicle.*

'Where is Edward II?': see Cuttino and Lyman, 'Where is Edward II?'.

Hayden V. White, 'The burden of history', *History and Theory*, 5 (1966), 111–34.

—*Metahistory: the Historical Imagination in Nineteenth Century Europe* (Baltimore
    MD, 1973).

—*Figural Realism* (Baltimore MD, new edn, 2000).

—'The public relevance of historical studies: a reply to Dirk Moses', *History and
    Theory*, 44 (2005), 333–8.

Adrian Wilson, 'Foundations of an integrated historiography' in Wilson (ed.),
    Rethinking Social History (Manchester, 1993), 293–335.

—'Collingwood's forgotten historiographic revolution', *Collingwood Studies*, 8 (2001),
    6–72.

Adrian Wilson and T. G. Ashplant, 'Whig history and present-centred history', *The
    Historical Journal*, 31 (1988), 1–16.

Christopher Wilson, 'Excellent, new and uniforme: perpendicular architecture
    c.1400–1547' in Richard Marks and Paul Williamson (eds), *Gothic: Art for England
    1400–1547* (London, 2003), 98–119.

Robert Lee Wolff, 'Baldwin of Flanders and Hainaut. First Latin Emperor of
    Constantinople: his life, death and resurrection, 1172–1225', *Speculum*, 27 (1952),
    281–322.

H. G. Wright, 'Richard II and the death of the Duke of Gloucester', *EHR*, 47, 186
    (1932), 276–80.

Writing: see Bates, Crick and Hamilton (eds), *Writing Medieval Biography.*

James Hamilton Wylie, *A History of England under Henry the Fourth* (4 vols, London,
    1884–98).

Index